Sustaining Democracy?

Journalism and the Politics of Objectivity

To the Woodsworth-Irvine Fellowship
with thanks and best
wishes,
Bob Hackett
March / 98

The Culture and Communication in Canada Series explores culture and communication in the Canadian context, examining a wide range of contemporary cultural experience. The editor seeks out works that cross disciplinary boundaries, offering fresh perspectives and stimulating debate. In this way, the series will act as a foundation for future research in the area in Canada and abroad.

Series editor: Richard S. Gruneau, School of Communication, Simon Fraser University

OUT OF THE GARDEN: TV and Children's Culture in the Age of Marketing
Stephen Kline

HOCKEY NIGHT IN CANADA: Sport, Identities, and Cultural Politics
Richard Gruneau and David Whitson

SUSTAINING DEMOCRACY? Journalism and the Politics of Objectivity
Robert Hackett and Yuezhi Zhao

Sustaining Democracy?

Journalism and the Politics of Objectivity

Robert A. Hackett and Yuezhi Zhao

Garamond Press, Toronto

Printed and bound in Canada

Garamond Press Ltd.
67 Mowat Ave., Ste. 144,
Toronto, Ontario,
M6K 3E3

Editor: Robert Clarke
Typesetting and Design: Robin Brass Studio
Cover Montage: Richard Slye

Canadian Cataloguing in Publication Data

Hackett, Robert A.
    Sustaining democracy? : journalism and the politics of
objectivity

(Culture and communication in Canada)
Includes bibliographical references and index.
ISBN 1-55193-013-7

1. Journalism – Objectivity. 2. Press and politics.
3. Journalism – Political aspects. I. Zhao, Yuezhi. II. Title.
III. Series.

PN4784.024H32 1997   302.23   C97-931017-2

The publishers gratefully acknowledge the financial support of the Canadian
Studies Bureau, Heritage Canada, in the publication of this book.

Contents

Acknowledgements vii

Introduction: In Search of a Metaphor 1

1

Democratic Discourse and the Origins of News Objectivity
(with Satu Repo) 15

2

From Positivism to Negative News: The Evolution
of Objectivity 36

3

Institutional Logics: Why It Still Pays to Be Objective 60

4

The God Who Won't Die: News Objectivity as a Regime 82

5

Epistemologies in Contention: Journalistic Objectivity as
(Un)workable Philosophy *(with Nick Dyer-Witheford)* 107

6

The Politics of Objective Journalism 136

7

Regimes in Crisis: Liberal Democracy and
Objective Journalism in Question 162

8

Straws in the Wind: Alternatives to the Regime? 189

9

Conclusion: Towards Public Communication
for Sustainable Democracy 223

Notes 239
Index 271

Acknowledgements

So many hands have helped this book along its lengthy journey that we are unable to thank them all. We apologize in advance to those whom we have inadvertently omitted.

We owe much to our students and colleagues at Simon Fraser University and elsewhere. The students in our undergraduate political communication course, which both of us have recently taught, provided a receptive (if captive!) forum for our ideas. In Hackett's fall 1996 graduate seminar in news analysis, Rob Ablenas, Gina Bailey, Albert Banerjee, James Compton, Kathy Cross, Tamil Kendall, Michael Jones, Michael Karlberg, and Hans Samuelson made very valuable comments and suggestions. As our endnotes indicate, some of their ideas and writings have directly influenced this text. Many SFU undergraduate students have helped us with library research over the years; they include Eve Lazarus, Christine O'Fallon, Dave Tanchak, and Tracey Wells.

We have tried to build upon the previous work of Canadian, British, and U.S. media scholars, many of whom have given us insightful responses to portions of earlier drafts – notably Stuart Allan, James Curran, Gail Faurschou, George Gerbner, Dan Hallin, Barry Hoffmaster, Elihu Katz and his "crisis of factual reporting" seminar at the Annenberg School of Communication, John Keane, Martin Laba, Christopher Norris, Nick Russell, Dan Schiller, Michael Schudson, Colin Sparks, Janet Wasko and her colleagues at the University of Oregon, Doug Williams, Jim Winter, and Michael Yeo. Dozens of thoughtful journalists have offered us their views and observations; those who have helpfully responded to portions of our written work include Brian Brennan, Frances Bula, Russ Francis, Frank Howard, Pierre Mignault, and Stephen Ward. Some of the ideas in this book have appeared in earlier publications, including *Critical Studies in Mass Communication, Peace Review,* the *Canadian Journal of Sociology*, and the book edited by Valerie Alia et al., *Deadlines and Diversity*.

For editorial assistance, we thank Lynne Hissey for input at an early stage of the project, and Mark Coté and Nick Dyer-Witheford for helping to bring it to completion. Nick also helped extricate us from the quagmire of epistemological debates by contributing to chapter 5 as a co-author. While she was not involved in the actual writing and is thus not responsible for the use we have made of her arguments, we are grateful to Satu Repo for permission to incorporate in chapter 1 material from her doctoral dissertation, "Journalistic Objectivity, the Discourse on Democracy, and the Birth of the Popular Press" (University of Toronto, 1986). As a friend and colleague, as well as editor of Garamond's Culture and Communication in Canada series, Rick Gruneau has offered editorial guidance, comments on several drafts, and ongoing understanding and encouragement beyond the call of duty these past several years. Similar thanks are due to Peter Saunders at Garamond Press for his support and patience, which we have much extended. We also want to express our deep appreciation of Robert Clarke's informed, incisive, and painstaking copy editing and indexing.

Modest but very important financial assistance came from SFU's University Publications Fund, federal and provincial student employment and work-study programs, and an SFU-administered research grant from the Social Sciences and Humanities Research Council of Canada. Lucie Menkveld and the SFU School of Communication's office staff provided irreplaceably efficient administrative support. Thanks for contingency funding are due to Brian Lewis, Director of the School of Communication, Ron Marteniuk, Dean of Applied Sciences, and John Stubbs, President, SFU.

Several colleagues provided the private space needed to complete this public document. For opening their homes or offices to his migrating laptop computer, Hackett thanks Pat Howard and Roger Howard, Donald Gutstein, Catherine Murray, and especially Jery Zaslove, Trish Graham, and Alan Whitehorn in SFU's Institute for the Humanities.

* * *

Many of the above-mentioned helping hands will undoubtedly take issue with our argument; certainly none of them are responsible for any errors or shortcomings in it. For those, the co-authors are prepared to take the heat jointly. While Hackett as senior author took more responsibility for the overall shape of the book and for the last "hands-on" editing of most chapters, it is a mutually collaborative project to an unusual extent.

Both authors had worked on the topic before launching this co-venture. Its genesis can be traced mainly to Hackett's 1984 article on the limitations of using objectivity and bias as evaluative standards for journalism and to Zhao's 1989 M.A. thesis on the discourse and politics of objectivity in North American journalism. Both of us were involved in the book's conceptualization from the start. Over the years we engaged in discussions on its general direction and specific arguments, exchanged and drew upon each other's research notes and previous publications, and revised almost all of each other's draft chapters. Still, for the record, we can roughly specify a division of labour. Hackett had primary responsibility for the Introduction and chapters 7, 8, and 9, and Zhao for chapters 1 and 6. Drawing from previous work by both of us, especially her M.A. thesis, Zhao produced the first drafts of chapters 2, 3, and 4, which Hackett then updated and revised. Drawing in part from Zhao's previous work, Hackett drafted chapter 5, which Nick Dyer-Witheford then revised. All of this rewriting was remarkably harmonious; we almost invariably felt that each other's revisions were an improvement.

None of this would have been possible without our forbearing spouses, Angelika Hackett and Jianxing Qian. We are deeply grateful for their love and support, even when it was expressed through urgent pleas to finish the thing. At the least, we are gratified that they did not divorce us during a project that sometimes imposed unreasonable burdens on them. To our spouses and to our children, Karina and Melanie Hackett and Linda Qian, we dedicate this book.

ROBERT HACKETT, *Simon Fraser University*
YUEZHI ZHAO, *University of California, San Diego*

Introduction

In Search
of a Metaphor

Journalism is arguably the most important form of public knowledge in contemporary society. The mass media – of which journalism is one, key, news-spreading part – have become the leading institutions of the public sphere – "that realm of social life where the exchange of information and views on questions of common concern can take place so that public opinion can be formed."[1]

In North America, for much of the twentieth century, the contours of journalistic practice have been shaped by what we call a *regime of objectivity* – an ensemble of ideals, assumptions, practices, and institutions – which has become a fixture of public philosophy and a supposed form of self-regulation. Interest groups and social movements as well as politicians use the criteria of objectivity to negotiate the terms of public discourse, journalists use it to enhance their claims to professional status, advertisers and media corporations find it a useful vehicle for maximizing market reach and credibility. It has become a cultural form with a life of its own.

This regime of objectivity is in turn indelibly tied to larger questions of democracy and public responsibility, public life, and public good. As Canada's 1980-81 Royal Commission on Newspapers put it, "The great majority [of Canadians] believe that newspapers, and the mass media in general, have responsibilities to the public different from those of other businesses."[2] In other words, Canadians widely believe that news media should seek more than their own profitability in the economic marketplace. Accordingly, as institutions central to democratic life, they are widely expected to function in the public interest.

In Canada journalism's mode of functioning has had a long and close connection with the dominant liberal-democratic mode of governing; and in general North American liberal-democratic capitalism, including its giant media corporations, is inseparably joined to the social practices and cultural understandings of journalism. The profession of journalism and the institutions of the mass media, then, bear a heavy weight in the support they provide for a particular brand of "democracy."

Democracy, though, is a concept much contested. Unlike other political ideas such as capitalism, socialism, federalism, or separatism, democracy has *connotations* that are widely shared. It is a nearly universal "hooray" word, to be contrasted with such "hiss-boo" words as dictatorship, fascism, or communism. But what is contested is its *denotation*, its exact meaning.

Political theorists identify a number of political models or systems with some claim to being considered democratic. In his acclaimed 1965 radio lectures for the Canadian Broadcasting Corporation (CBC), C.B. Macpherson sketched communist, underdeveloped, and liberal versions of democracy in the postwar world.[3] Within the liberal-democratic tradition, he later identified several different and sometimes antagonistic rationales for democracy: the *protection* of citizens from each other and from state tyranny, the *development* of the human personality and the citizenry, the maintenance of political *equilibrium* in a pluralist society, and the promotion of widespread direct political *participation* both as an end in itself and as a means to building a more humane and equitable society.[4] Journalism's objectivity regime correlates especially well with the equilibrium model (also known as competitive elitism) of liberal democracy – to the relative exclusion of other models that emphasize citizen participation and social equality as preconditions of sustainable democracy.[5]

As central institutions in political life, the news media are expected to function according to certain criteria. For instance:

• **Freedom of the press.** This concept historically first meant freedom from government censorship, but it can also be taken to mean freedom from undue influence by hidden interests or by excessive concentrations of private power.

• **Equality and justice.** There should be equitable opportunities for society's diverse voices to communicate their own interests and perspectives to broader publics through the media system.

• **Social order and solidarity.** Even the most pluralistic democracy needs some degree of consensus and shared values, and public communication is essential to building and maintaining them. Journalism has a distinct role in promoting "civil" discourse in both senses of the word: as an arena for discussing matters of common concern, and for debate based on mutual respect, with the aim of reaching mutual accommodation if not consensus.[6]

Although these values are widely shared, their relative importance and the appropriate trade-off between them are subject to dispute. Consider, for instance, the debate over pornography, involving social conservatives who see pornography as a threat to social order and morality, feminists who regard porn as a threat to gender equality and justice, and libertarians who see government censorship as the biggest threat of all. How these values should be interpreted and put into practice is similarly open to debate. Some might argue, for instance, that the concept of equality implies that every political party deserves equal media time, and others that a party's access should be proportional to its current political support.

There is particular contention over the extent to which these values can best be realized by the private sector or by public policy. Most news media in most Western countries are privately owned, but many Western countries have established publicly owned broadcasting corporations to pursue cultural and other objectives that commercial broadcasting was unlikely to achieve. Given that Canada has long faced cultural inundation by the United States, the goal of maintaining a public sphere co-extensive with the national territory became a major rationale for the creation of the CBC. Given their political, economic, and cultural importance, even the most market-oriented society, the United States, has regulated broadcasting media in the public interest, on the basis of the scarcity of broadcasting frequencies. In light of its public functions, many countries have also given favoured treatment to the privately owned press, through such policies as press subsidies in Sweden, certain tax exemptions in Canada, and the exemption from U.S. antitrust law to allow competing newspapers to share resources. For several decades following World War II, such policies underwrote an apparent equilibrium between private profit and public interest, between the values of freedom, equality, and order in the political and media systems.

That apparent equilibrium has always had its critics. For at least thirty years, conservatives have been accusing the media of systematic "left-liberal bias," while progressives often analyse the media as part of the corporate and political establishment.[7] Recent developments have heightened controversies over press independence and diversity and the appropriate balance between public policy and private media in pursuing these values. Most notably, the years 1995 and 1996 saw unprecedented multibillion-dollar mergers in the North American media. In the United States the feeding frenzy included Walt Disney Company ingesting Capital Cities/ABC, Westinghouse swallowing CBS, and Time Warner's takeover of Ted Turner's CNN empire. The four largest television news organizations in the United States are now part of vast corporate empires with holdings extending from cable, publishing, films, and multimedia entertainment to finance, transportation, nuclear power, and military production. Ben Bagdikian's earlier prediction that by the 1990s six large corporations would own all the most powerful media outlets in the United States seems on target.[8]

Canada's media corporations have followed suit. Rogers Cable has absorbed the Maclean-Hunter publishing stable, and press baron Conrad Black's Hollinger has been buying newspaper properties at such a pace that his papers could now line 2.4 million Canadian bird cages every publishing day. Hollinger now accounts for forty-three of every one hundred copies of dailies sold across Canada, a degree of press concentration almost certainly unparalleled among major Western countries.

Corporate concentration is not confined to national borders and markets. A worldwide market with high barriers to entry, dominated by a handful of global, vertically integrated multimedia companies, is now crystallizing.[9] International media monopoly is one aspect of global political, economic, and technological transformations, including the liberalization of international capital flows through arrangements like the North American Free Trade Agreement (NAFTA), digital revolution and technological convergence in communications media, and the crisis of public finance. Sometimes called globalization, this firestorm of change presents both journalism and democracy with an unresolved crisis.

The consolidation of media power has been abetted by a general government retreat from even nominal efforts to regulate the media behemoths in the public interest. The Telecommunications Act, passed by the U.S. Congress in 1996, turned the retreat in that country into a rout. Although it was one of the most significant federal laws in a generation, the bill was passed with minimal public awareness, let alone debate. It sharply raised the allowable ceiling on the size of national TV networks and virtually removed restrictions on the ownership of different types of media in the same market.

In Canada the recent reform of telecommunications legislation has also smoothed the path towards further international media conglomeration. Meanwhile the CBC has faced sharp funding cutbacks by the federal government, resulting in the loss of over a third of its workforce in a decade.

Perhaps even more striking is the absence of effective press policy. The federal Liberal government greeted Hollinger's 1996 takeover of Southam, the country's largest newspaper chain, with a yawn. Indeed, its competition-law watchdog preapproved the takeover – a far cry from 1980, when smaller scale corporate manoeuvres sparked a federal enquiry and a prosecution, albeit unsuccessful, of two newspaper companies under federal anti-combines law.

These dramatic shifts in media industries and public policy have been accompanied by a rhetoric of consumer choice, audience empowerment, and the need for bigness to compete in the global "information highway." These claims have been shouted from the rooftops far more loudly than other potential and more likely consequences: a decline in public accountability, escalating contradictions between independent journalism and corporate interests, and more mergers, increased concentration, and "downsizing."[10] Long-standing questions about the representativeness, accountability, and diversity of news media, and their ability to constitute an independent public sphere, have fresh urgency. In the past corporate journalism's time-honoured standards of objectivity, impartiality, and balance worked to legitimize corporate ownership, or at least deflect attention away from the structure of media organizations to the performance of journalists. Now more than before, perhaps, the great potential private power over the public agenda, hidden behind a mask of objectivity, is imperilling political democracy.

The recent shifts in media ownership and policy might be seen as the equivalent of a non-violent coup d'état, a metaphor evoking the inherent link between media power and state power – between the colonization of the popular imagination and the allocation of social resources through public policy and market relations. Communications scholar Herbert Schiller suggests that what is at stake is "packaged consciousness": the intensified appropriation of the national symbolic environment by "a few corporate juggernauts in the consciousness business."[11]

But the metaphor of a coup is limited and misleading. Politicians may fear to tread on the toes of the media giants, but no formal transfer of state power has taken place, and our political leaders could potentially be pushed in a different policy direction. Nor, crucially, is media power over the public agenda simply imposed from above. The social practice of news and politics, the production of cultural meanings and public policies, is constrained by, but cannot be reduced to, the intentions or manipulations of a handful of media moguls or political powerbrokers. Their influence would be slight without the consent or at least acquiescence of audiences and voters.

Moreover, journalism's sense of crisis is fuelled not only by media centralization, but also by other straws in the wind. Opinion polls show declining public esteem for news media, especially in the United States. Marketing surveys reveal a growing disconnection between media and their audiences, and younger people in particular are simply shunning the conventional news media en masse. Contemporary media culture, particularly with the dominance of television and its entertainment imperative, seems to be eroding boundaries that were once (however illusorily) considered sacrosanct – boundaries between media images and social reality, news and entertainment, fact and opinion, the newsroom and the bottom-line bean counters. In politics we see the fragmentation of public spheres and a growing cynicism and declining participation in official politics. For some the very survival of democratic public life in North America is in question. These developments have as much to do with politics and culture as with economics and business.

The metaphor of "regime" that we use in this book has a long but mixed pedigree. In everyday language, as well as (not coincidentally) in the news, "regime" usually refers to a specific and repressive government, such as "the regime of Saddam Hussein" in Iraq. Political scientists may use the term more neutrally and generally to refer to types of government. But the term also has usages in cultural studies and political economy. The late French social theorist Michel Foucault, during the 1970s, wrote of "discursive regimes" – of how power is imbricated with knowledge, not by directly imposing censorship or coercion from outside, but indirectly and internally, through the criteria and practices that "govern" the production of statements.[12] Within a particular institutional setting, whether it is science, medicine, psychiatry, law, or journalism, the governing criteria determine what kinds of accounts come to be regarded as valid, acceptable, or true.

A related pertinent usage is Scott Lash's notion of "regimes of signification."[13] For Lash, a regime of signification has two components: a "cultural economy," comprising relations and institutions by which cultural objects are produced and consumed; and a specific "mode of signification," a typical way by which cultural objects become meaningful to those who use them. (Lash and other theorists make distinctions, for example, between discursive and figural, modernist and postmodernist, and cognitive and aesthetic ways of seeing and knowing.)

Our own use of the "regime" metaphor owes something to each of these usages.[14] In using the term we want to imply an unavoidable connection between journalism and relations of social and political power. Power may indeed be imposed on journalism from "outside." Direct, indirect, or anticipated pressure from owners, advertisers, or governments can result in stories being spiked or journalists censoring themselves. That is one of the main reasons why a globally concentrated, conglomerate ownership of the media is so dangerous to democracy. At the same time, power relations are not always obvious; they are not always expressed through deliberate manipulation or even conscious intentions. They may be expressed through professional codes and institutional practices, including those by which "objective" news accounts are produced. As a way of producing that-which-can-be-regarded-as-valid accounts of the world, journalism's objectivity regime is entrenched in news workers' occupational routines and norms, the economic and other organizational imperatives of news media, and in broader cultural understandings and relations of social power.

In treating journalism objectivity as a knowledge-producing discursive regime, we are not taking the seductive and fashionable position, sometimes associated with Foucault, that collapses all truth-claims into power, self-interest, and/or the internal validity rules of particular discourses. We need to question both the naive positivism that claims that facts speak for themselves, and the opposite position of relativism, which sees truth or reality as simply products of language games. We are critics of journalism's claims to objectivity, but we do not entirely discard the very idea of objectivity.

Thinking of journalism as a discursive regime, however, does imply that it has a certain degree of autonomy from external influences. News is a shared cultural form that media owners or other elites cannot simply manipulate at will and with impunity. Media genres and professional codes impose their own disciplines; audiences, with their expectations of media fare, are also part of the media system. At the same time, journalism objectivity is not a free-floating or entirely self-generating discourse. It does have material conditions of existence, in the institutions and political economy of North American media, which we need to explore. A different kind of social or political order would generate a different kind of journalism.

In calling attention to connections between journalism and power, we are not claiming that this is always and everywhere a bad thing. We accept Foucault's idea that power is not simply repressive and exclusionary, but can also be productive and enabling. As a cultural and institutional complex, the regime of objectivity not only facilitates but also regulates, constrains, and disciplines the production of public knowledge. But power is not immanent, dispersed, and diffused throughout society. Power is impersonal in that it derives more from social relations and institutionalized techniques than from personal characteristics; for that very reason, some people have much more of it than others. While he is frequently demonized by his critics, Conrad Black is, to put it crudely, the product of a system. The concentrated and hierarchical distribution of power, even in representative democracies, remains key to how news media and public policy operate.

Its historical dimension is another advantage of the regime metaphor. A regime is not a timeless, historically transcendent manifestation of a natural order of things; nor is it simply an ephemeral, short-term phenomenon. It entails the articulation, the joining together, of a range of beliefs, practices, and institutions. It implies a set of relationships that is relatively stable for months, years, or decades, but is open to contestation, change, and perhaps eventual overthrow or replacement. The regime of objectivity was not born yesterday, but neither will it last into the indefinite future.

Finally, the regime metaphor is precisely that – a metaphor. It is not an actually existing thing-in-itself. Rather, it is a way of highlighting the relationships between a range of practices and institutional arrangements associated with the ethos of objectivity.

Even if we accept the metaphor, why should we call it a regime of *objectivity*? For some academics and journalists, after all, objectivity is a dull and antiquated word, one to be discarded along with much of the other modernist cultural baggage of the fading century. Journalists prefer to stress fairness or balance or credibility. "Objectivity" may seem as musty and quaint as the city editor's whiskey bottle or the battered Remington typewriter in the stereotypical early twentieth-century newsroom.

Nevertheless, as we have argued elsewhere, reports of the death of objectivity are greatly exaggerated.[15] The concept has for decades provided North American journalism's governing ethos, integral to its self-understanding. Journalism manuals and textbooks, debates in reviews and conferences, and academic research on news production all attest that it is "a god that won't die."[16] It still obliges reporters to follow its routines and, in public at least, to speak its language. Even if it is often regarded with a sense of irony or cynicism, nothing has arisen to take its place: it is still a benchmark against which alternative approaches to journalism are measured. It remains a part of journalists' sense of professionalism and occupational identity, an expectation of media audiences, and, partly for that reason, a legitimizing rationale for media owners.

Moreover, even if it is fraying at the edges in North America, the regime of objectivity is acquiring new global relevance and resonance, especially in the post-communist societies of China and the former Soviet bloc. For would-be reformers of China's authoritarian, corrupt, and semi-commercialized media system, the apparent political impartiality, legal independence, and commercial profitability of North America's press seem to constitute the Holy Grail. In Russia, Western-style objectivity now provides the benchmark for evaluating political news. To be sure, Russian journalists consciously abandoned objectivity in order to promote Boris Yeltsin over his Communist rival in the 1996 presidential election. The press largely ignored Yeltsin's health problems and his more unpopular policies, as well as the hecklers at his rallies. CBC correspondent Céline Galipeau observed that Russian media covered Yeltsin's every move "in the best possible light."[17] Significantly, the one-sided coverage provoked debate within Russia precisely *on the grounds of objectivity*, and Russian journalists felt compelled to defend their partisanship in the very terms of Western-style liberal-democracy: as a temporary aberration to protect freedom of the press from the perceived Communist threat.

So, a regime of objectivity exists in journalism, we would argue. But why a book on that subject, and why now?

Writing this book, we confess, has involved more than the usual aggravation inflicted upon the authors' forbearing families. History moves faster than books can be written. Since the genesis of this particular work, the ossified, hierarchical Soviet system has collapsed, the supposedly distributed power of the Internet has arisen, and the public journalism movement in the United States has started to shift the very terms of debate about the news. Moreover, we are aware that this book, along with much other media scholarship, may be dismissed in some quarters as a misguided critique from outsiders who lack salty first-hand anecdotes or the we-were-there credentials of years in a newsroom or a foreign bureau. To counter this complaint, we would suggest that reporters themselves spend their working lives observing and writing about other institutions and occupations from the outside. Turnabout is not only fair play, but is also crucial: the news media are too multifaceted, and too important to democratic life, to leave their analysis only to those who work inside the belly of the beast. Good journalists can undoubtedly convey detail, personality, the specific, the idiosyncratic, far better than we can. But what we can do is emphasize the general and the routine, denaturalize what in journalism is taken for granted, and stand outside the accepted paradigm and hold it up to a different light. In that task, our understanding of the media has been enriched by interviews with dozens of astute and thoughtful journalists over the years.

Ultimately then, there are several rationales for this book. First, while a number of other scholars have written on news objectivity – and we owe them a considerable debt – none have conceptualized it as we do, as a regime. This conceptualization suggests new questions and new ways of entering debates about an appropriate democratic public philosophy for journalism. In particular, we hope that identifying the elements of the regime will provide an aid both to comparative historical analysis and to political strategies for democratizing the news system.

We suggest a second reason for a book on the regime of objectivity: the whole configuration provides journalism and popular culture with many of the categories and concepts, such as bias, balance, and objectivity, that we conventionally use to evaluate and critique the news. While these elements are widely shared, the meaning of the terms is very much negotiated and contested, and a good deal is at stake in how they are defined. We need to do far more than ask simply *whether* the news media are biased or objective; such a question avoids the issue of whether *unbiased* communication is even possible. It is far more important to analyse *how* these terms are understood and deployed in struggles over the public agenda.

There is a third and decisive rationale for this book. Ours is a time of profound economic and ecological crisis, a time that calls for the critical re-examination of dominant institutions and belief systems. We need to consider whether that re-examination is facilitated or hampered by a news media system driven largely by commercial imperatives. Despite its continued efforts to legitimize itself through its claims of objectivity, the news system itself is at a crossroads. Like Leninism before the Soviet Union's implosion, the ideology of objectivity is beginning to resemble a walking corpse, kept in motion only by the interests vested in it and the absence of a stronger alternative. More and more, thoughtful journalists themselves are raising fundamental questions about the public philosophy and the future of their craft. More and more, they are using the word "crisis" to describe its current state. Some fundamental reflection is indeed in order, given the media's still increasing power, combined with their vulnerability to new technologies and economic retrenchment, as well as the malaise of public life in 1990s North America.

This book is an attempt to contribute to debate on journalism's public philosophy. We are often critical of the current practices and institutions of Canadian and U.S. news media. But it would be a grave mistake to read this book as an attack on working journalists – and not only because so many of them have been our students, friends, and colleagues that we can't possibly share Conrad Black's contemptuous dismissal of them as "ignorant, lazy, opinionated, intellectually dishonest and inadequately supervised."[18] This book is motivated throughout by a commitment to the potential of journalism as a crucial form of democratic public communication and by a desire to contribute to debates that dedicated and concerned journalists are themselves sparking.

Finally, the two co-authors were encouraged to pursue this book by the fact that we arrived at a similar perspective on democracy and journalism from different sides of the globe, and from vastly different cultural backgrounds. One of us – Robert Hackett – has been fascinated with newspapers since at least age eight, and had early stints with student and youth papers in Richmond, British Columbia. His academic interest in journalism derives from graduate work in political science. At Queen's University his studies of ideology and political change pointed to the news as an arbiter of political reality. One catalyst for this book was his 1984 article on the limitations of using objectivity and bias as evaluative standards for journalism.[19] His work with Project Censored Canada (now called Newswatch Canada), which researches blind spots in the news, has further highlighted the seemingly paradoxical co-existence of the practices of objectivity with systemic bias in the news agenda.

The other – Yuezhi Zhao – was raised in a peasant family in rural China and experienced first-hand the plight of China's voiceless peasants. Zhao was attracted to the mystique of journalism, especially its proclaimed ideals of telling truth, seeking justice, and giving voice to the people. While receiving her journalism education in China in the early 1980s, a period of relative political openness, Zhao began to question journalism theories and practices in China. She became interested in Western models of journalism and their applicability to her home country. This led to graduate studies at Simon Fraser University and a fascination with the peculiar and contradictory Western concept of news objectivity. She has seen first-hand the frustrations and dangers of a party-dominated authoritarian media system – but also the limitations of the heavily commercialized North American media system. She has also learned first-hand the risks of binary thinking, all too characteristic of the dominant political cultures of both East and

West. Her book *Media and Democracy in China* tries to transcend such either/or thinking in analysing the contradictions of China's media system.[20] This book, too, is in part a challenge to prevalent but questionable dichotomies and equations: the reduction of freedom of the press to unaccountable corporate control of the media, the conflation of democracy with the market, and the positing of objectivity as the opposite of ideology, among others.

In making an argument about the regime of objectivity, we have primarily emphasized the news media of English-speaking Canada. The analysis has geographically broader relevance, however, so long as we do not lose sight of national differences in media and political contexts. Even within Canada, journalism has followed a somewhat different trajectory in Quebec's distinct society; traditions of advocacy and participant journalism have much stronger historical roots there. Nevertheless, Armande Saint-Jean, a twenty-five-year veteran of Québécois broadcast journalism, argues that apart from "a few cultural particularities" Quebec's journalism scene, including the evolution of professional ethics, "follows the same patterns and trends as in the rest of Canada and, for that matter, North America."[21]

An even stronger case can be made for the relevance of our analysis to U.S. journalism; indeed, we draw from many U.S. writers and examples. The United States, after all, is the historical and global bastion of the objectivity regime. Perhaps not coincidentally, it is also a society in which market forces and the doctrine of market-liberalism are even more ascendant than in Canada. Partly for that reason, the malaise of the United States' political and media systems is more advanced; but so too are its alternative media, debates about journalism, and emergent movements to democratize the media. The United States' movements for media reform and Canada's tradition of public broadcasting can inspire citizens on both sides of the border in the search for effective ways to democratize a corporate-dominated media system.

This book is neither an anecdote-filled narrative nor a detailed blueprint for political strategy or media reform. Rather, it is meant as an analytical essay and an exercise in normative reasoning, an inquiry into public philosophy. Some long-standing as well as recent critiques of news objectivity, we find, conceal the actual social and political forces informing the media's construction of news, disguising the values necessarily embedded in news judgement and thereby short-circuiting debate about what purposes journalism should serve. In the end journalism does not or cannot achieve its goal of accurately representing the world, and its generally conservative consequences are naturalized as the outcome of "balanced" and "objective" news practices.

Add to these critiques the challenges of participation, performance, and legitimacy facing North American liberal democracy, and it becomes an open question as to whether the regime of objectivity still offers a useful model for democratic journalism. Quite apart from its limitations as an ideal, the regime in historical practice is buckling and perhaps disintegrating. This is not, however, cause for unmitigated celebration. If objectivity once held journalism in a straitjacket, it seems to have spawned its opposite: a celebration of self-conscious subjectivism and an abandonment of the very ethos of public service.

Compared to the staid objectivity of traditional "serious" journalism, tabloid journalism and TV talk shows appear to be less concerned with procedures of factual verification, and less inhibited about openly taking sides, especially against perceived moral deviance, or in favour of the populist "little guy." Serious news media are step by step embracing entertainment values, to the extent that they followed the lead of the tabloid *National Enquirer* in covering the murder trial of ex-football player O.J. Simpson. Spectacle, sleaze, and sensationalism come to substitute for substantive investigation. Celebrity profiles and superficial sound bites eclipse the discussion of fundamental political choices. The lines between fact and fiction (never as secure as defenders of objectivity would claim) blur in docudramas, reality-based crime shows, and other species of infotainment. A seductive but corrosive cultural relativism encourages us to view all truth-claims with equal cynicism. The crisis of democratic journalism arises as much from this self-indulgent subjectivism (itself not unrelated to commercial imperatives) as from any continued allegiance to objectivity.[22]

These "postmodernist" turns in popular media are, in part, the flip side of the current crisis of objectivity, a reaction against the very elitism of both traditional "objective" journalism and North America's political institutions. The objectivity regime is implicated in a dual crisis: its rigidities and its marginalization of alternatives – its functioning as a largely conservative ideology – have helped to provoke a crisis of journalism as a potentially democratic form of communication; and recent economic and technological developments have brought the ethos of objectivity itself into crisis, as a framework for doing the news. That crisis may open up possibilities for new ways of doing journalism. We do not celebrate the wanton abandonment of objective public affairs-oriented journalism in favour of sleaze, trivia, or relativism. We argue indeed that some of the principles of the regime should be retained, but that its radical reform – particularly its liberation from market imperatives – is crucial to developing critical public awareness, debate, and engagement at a time when the world is undergoing massive structural and cultural change.

In the nineteenth century a well-established labour press – based on an emancipatory democratic discourse springing from the Enlightenment – provoked a shift away from the imperatives of the elite-oriented partisan press of the time. Today we may need a similar shift if contemporary journalism is to contribute positively to a viable democracy in the twenty-first century. One first step, perhaps, towards a democratized media system is to demystify and open for critical analysis the practices and principles of newsmaking, especially those of objectivity. We hope that our book can contribute to such a project.

1

Democratic Discourse and the Origins of News Objectivity

(with Satu Repo)

In the dark days before freedom of the press, the government had strict control over the printing trade and therefore over the publication of the earliest journals and newspapers. If printer/editors criticized the authorities, they could lose their printing licences, face arrest, or suffer other forms of repression. Only in the eighteenth and nineteenth centuries did the press really become free from such government repression. In Canada a key event was a jury's acquittal of Nova Scotia editor/politician Joseph Howe in 1835. The verdict effectively struck down the law of seditious libel that had previously been used to punish any published criticism of the authorities.[1]

Open the pages of a conventional history of the press in Canada, the United States, or Britain, and you will probably find a narrative like this: a story of more or less continual progress towards a more or less free and responsible fourth estate. This standard story continues:

The newly freed press was partisan and sectarian, unashamedly promoting particular interests without regard to accuracy or honesty. A variety of mechanisms, from the personal ambitions of editors to financial sticks and carrots (such as subsidies from parties), kept most newspapers narrowly tied to political factions or other special interests. This partisan press was eventually overthrown by the independent penny papers – so called because of their price, which was a substantial reduction over the cost of the partisan papers.

The penny papers were made possible by developments that reduced obstacles to publishing. Some of these developments were technological, others

*involved the removal of legal and economic restrictions as the public clam-
oured for a freer press. The penny press ended "the dark ages of partisan journalism" and ushered in the golden age of the newspaper as it evolved into the
more or less independent, non-partisan, and socially responsible commercial
press of today – one whose freedom to indulge in the temptations of bias, sensationalism, cynicism, and excessive hostility to authority is tempered by such
professional ideals as the ethos of objectivity.*[2]

This narrative is not merely a fable. The struggle to free the press from
sometimes harsh repression was a very real and sometimes bitter part of
the broader democratic struggle to end authoritarian colonial and monarchical privileges. The dominant liberal narrative about the triumph of the
free and independent press, though, is misleading and incomplete. It omits
the broader political and intellectual context of the transformation from
the partisan to the commercial press and, in particular, the seminal role of
the labour movement and the radical labour press, each of which was influential in Britain, the United States, and Canada at different times in the
nineteenth century. Indeed, only by examining the broad ideological context of nineteenth-century journalism and the relations of the commercial
press with the radical working-class press can we understand the profoundly ambiguous, even paradoxical, nature of contemporary news media
and the ethos of news objectivity.

Democratic Discourse: The Enlightenment Legacy

Alongside political revolutions in France and America, a profound revolution in social thought emerged in the eighteenth century. At the heart of
this change was an emphasis on Science and Reason, which were seen as the
appropriate instruments for understanding the world. Enlightenment
thinkers such as Jean-Jacques Rousseau (1712-78) and Tom Paine (1737-
1809) declared the supremacy of reason for understanding, and indeed for
controlling, nature. Moreover, Enlightenment thinkers argued, if reason
can control the natural world, it can also be used to discover the "laws" governing the *social* world. They believed, then, that reason had an emancipatory character – that it could challenge the "irrational" religious and social
orthodoxies of the day and create rational and liberating modes of social
organization.

At the risk of oversimplifying, we can roughly understand the Enlightenment as a secular movement dedicated to freeing people from ignorance
and mystification through the application of reason and the construction

of new social forms. Enlightenment thinkers wanted to extend the use of the scientific method, which had been so successfully used to unlock the mysteries of the physical universe, to the understanding, reform, and reconstruction of human society.

Theorists increasingly saw the most reasonable form of social and political organization as a democracy, built on the principle of universal individual rights – universal, at least, for male citizens of the body politic. In other words, all *men* were created equal and had certain rights based on this equality; democratic government would ensure the protection of these "natural" rights; and the universal principle of reason would apply to all. But in the existing states (like Europe's monarchical regimes, dominated by landowning, aristocratic, and clerical elites), the men who held substantial property had confined the rights of citizenship to themselves. Therefore, a central Enlightenment project became the transformation of the state – and through the state, the civil society – so that it would operate according to the dictates of reason. First of all, the suffrage, the right to vote, should extend to "everybody" (all free men, that is, all adult males who were not slaves) so that all of them could participate in deciding the proper course of action for the state.

For this participation to work effectively, the non-privileged majority would have to be educated on how society works. After scientists discover the laws of society, teachers and journalists can communicate this learning to the general population. With universal (male) suffrage and proper knowledge, state intervention can correct the shortcomings of civil society – the sphere of human relations and associations outside the state – which means that the state can be called upon not only to safeguard natural rights from both greedy monopolists and criminal elements, but also to provide other services necessary for the public good. A harmonious civil society in which all live peacefully without infringing upon each other's natural rights is entirely possible, given a democratic state. While there will be employers and employees, there is no inherent conflict between these groups, provided employers are not driven by greed.

Such was the legacy of the Enlightenment and its democratic discourse, a discourse that *claimed* to take the perspective of all members of society, rather than a privileged group within it. But this assumption clearly had its problems. The body politic as it was defined excluded women. It tolerated slavery. Indeed, some eighteenth-century advocates of Enlightenment democracy (like Thomas Jefferson) were themselves slave-owners. And, crucially, the dominant line of thought did not recognize the possibility of fundamental differences of interest within society, such as those between different social classes. It saw conflict as the result of greed, short-sightedness, or misunderstanding, rather than of the social structure itself.

Nevertheless, the nineteenth-century labour press adopted fragments and strands of this democratic discourse, which was in turn, later in the century, appropriated by the emerging popular commercial dailies. From this democratic discourse, the popular commercial dailies developed the *first version of journalistic objectivity*: an independent, universalizing stance that looked at the world and the body politic from the viewpoint of the ideal citizen: a prudent, rational, fair-minded individual, committed to individual rights, political democracy, a market economy, and progress through science and education.

Of course, no intellectual revolution, let alone one as profound as the Enlightenment, occurs in a vacuum. The eighteenth century was a period of changing class structures. Entrepreneurs, artisans, and intellectuals alike were critical of the dying feudal world's relations of privilege, rank, and status based on birth. The clarion call to rational social institutions was at once a cause and a consequence of the increasing attacks on the institution of the aristocracy. In a sense, the Enlightenment was the cultural revolution of the capitalist class. The core ideas of the liberal-democratic discourse, such as science, reason, natural rights, and public good, became political weapons in the power struggle of this class against the landowners.

The Enlightenment notions sketched here not only helped to destroy the old (the aristocratic society they critiqued), but also potentially threatened the fabric of the new (the industrial, capitalist social order that they helped to establish in Western Europe and North America). Enlightenment ideas became the core components of a popular, universalizing political language, and in the nineteenth century the political struggles between dominant and subordinate groups became couched and fought out within this language system. The principal conflict by then, however, was no longer between the aristocracy and an emerging merchant class, but between the established capitalist industrialists and the emerging urban working class.

The Partisan Press: Marginalizing the Democratic Discourse

By the nineteenth century, established society, including industrialists, had rejected much of the emerging democratic discourse and particularly its philosophical grounding in natural rights and reason. While the idea of government by majority consent slowly made inroads, even pro-democratic reformers avoided the heady eighteenth-century language of the natural rights of individuals. Instead, they offered the less stirring doctrine of utilitarianism, which advocated as a goal the greatest good of the greatest number. For the members of the ruling order, including its middle-class reformers, the old democratic discourse seemed dangerous and inflammatory. By endowing human beings with inalienable rights superior to those of positive law – that is, law established or recognized by governmental authority – it was a standing invitation to insurrection and anarchy. In contrast to the quest for democracy, conservative elements articulated their fear of mob rule.

The concept of nature – the ground of Enlightenment thought – became gradually more ambiguous and contradictory as the nineteenth century evolved. In the works of British economist Thomas Malthus and evolutionist Charles Darwin, nature was no longer God's creation: rational, benign, and inherently harmonious, as it had been in the writings of Rousseau. Instead, scarcity and ruthless competition for limited resources were seen to rule the natural world. When Herbert Spencer in the late nineteenth century added the "social" to Darwinism, an important antidemocratic philosophy was born. Foreshadowing the "globalization" rhetoric of today, social Darwinism appealed to nature "red in tooth and claw" in order to justify a bruisingly competitive and exploitive laissez-faire market economy, characterized by widespread poverty and inequality. Laissez-faire capitalism and its cultural heroes, the supposedly self-made men who became the captains of industry, were the chief instruments of progress.

Such political conservatism had a direct influence on pre-Confederation Canada. The dominant political ideology was "imperial, Tory, conservative" and worked to bolster the authority of the colonial regime and Canada's merchant, clerical, military, and administrative elite.[3] In opposition were democratic elements inspired by the British Chartist movement and the American and French Revolutions. The democratic reformers, including sections of the growing middle class of merchants, artisans, professionals, and farmers, as well as skilled and semi-skilled workers, wanted small and cheap government, universal suffrage, abolition of non-elected ruling bodies, control over finances by the elected representatives, disestablishment of the Church, public education, free trade, local government, good roads, and an end to hereditary titles, land monopolies, and absentee landholding. This Reform movement was the first political force in Canada to adopt the Enlightenment democratic discourse as its own political language.[4]

The political struggle between Tories and Reformers led to the emergence of a common political culture in the 1850s. All major political parties, despite their surface antagonisms, came to agree on such fundamental issues as the role of government in nation-building and capital formation. Although both liberal and conservative traditions were considerably amended, the new synthesis was basically a modified Tory culture. It absorbed some of the liberal ideas of the Reformers, but still rejected democracy and emphasized rule by elites.[5]

The Canadian partisan press, which flourished in the mid-nineteenth century, reflected this degeneration of the Enlightenment democratic discourse. Often owned by a group of wealthy partisans, these papers had the explicit purpose of representing a political party. Overall, they tended to serve the ruling political and business elites. As Doug Fetherling notes, "Behind every successful politician was a newspaper doing his dirty work; behind every proprietor or editor, a politician, or group of politicians, offering support."[6] Newspapers often counted on financial support from government patronage or direct party subsidies.[7] Shaped by party affiliations, the journalism of the time was replete not only with special pleading for the politicians who financially supported each paper, but also with vicious personal attacks on political foes. Indeed, one of the reasons for the rapid growth of newspapers in the mid-nineteenth century was the "perceived need for both a Tory publication and a Reform one in every important population centre so that each could check the outrages of the others."[8]

Despite their biases, the partisan newspapers were operating within the conservative political culture of the 1850s. Both Conservative and Reform-cum-Liberal papers took a cautious approach to popular representation. Democracy was still a suspect word. Comparing the leading Conservative and Liberal organs in Toronto, a renowned Canadian historian stresses the ideological consensus of the partisan press in the 1850-67 period:

> Both the *Leader* and the *Globe* in their views of democracy expressed the central position of mid-Victorian liberalism. Both declared for a wide, popular electorate but still wanted a qualified franchise to recognize property and intelligence, and to prevent the rule of ignorance and mere numbers.... There was in this mid-century Canadian press little of the spirit of American Jeffersonian or Jacksonian democracy with their faith in the natural worth of the common man.[9]

The Labour Press: Speaking for "the People"

The Enlightenment's radical-democratic discourse survived among the political leaders of the disenfranchised majority. In particular it was used as an ideological weapon by the radical and labour movement to challenge established society and the dominant partisan press and to agitate for extended popular rights, both political and economic. The political and ideological weapons forged by the merchant class in its struggle against the aristocracy were now taken over by the emerging industrial working class in its own struggle. The social landscape had changed considerably from the Enlightenment era; the dominant conflict was now between the emerging working class and the capitalists. As typically described by the U.S. labour press of the 1820s and 1830s, this conflict pitted the rich, who seemed to hold a monopoly on property, power, knowledge, and a corrupt legal system, against the artisans, mechanics, and tradespeople, whose natural rights to justice, equality, and property were impeded.

Between 1850 and 1900 Canada experienced its own industrial revolution, and along with it an emergent working class that slowly established its own institutions – most notably, the trade union movement, spearheaded by artisans struggling to maintain their craft autonomy and their standard of living against the dissolving and deskilling impact of capital. Craft unions were established in some Canadian cities as early as the 1820s and 1830s, grew steadily in the next few decades, and reached a peak in the 1870s. In the 1880s the U.S.-founded Knights of Labor swept across Canada, aiming to organize all workers, not just skilled craftsmen, and regardless of race or gender. By the early 1880s Hamilton, Toronto, and Montreal had become centres for its organizing activities.

The ideological perspective of Canada's nineteenth-century labour movement was not yet unified. It was an amalgam of emerging and competing traditions and perspectives. Earlier craft unions stressed *trade* rather than *class* consciousness. A producer ideology arguing for a reciprocity of interests between workers and owners was popular among workers. Emphasizing the unity of interests between employers and employees, the craft unions aimed simply to maintain their members' share of the pie vis-à-vis owner-proprietors. The craft unions did not necessarily challenge Tory paternalism, which rationalized inequality by providing a social model of a hierarchical organic order. But this ideological stance lost its appeal as mercantilism gave way to industrial capitalism late in the century. Gradually radical-democratic ideas came to dominate the labour movement.[10]

As trade unions emerged, so too did a labour press claiming to represent workers' aspirations. In English Canada, *The Ontario Workman* (founded 1872) was followed by the *Trades Union Advocate*, the *Labour Record*, the *Canadian Labour Reformer*, the *Labour Union*, the *Palladium of Labor*, and the *Trades Journal*. These papers were put out on behalf of workers and unions, and their publishers counted on unions for financial backing and subscription, but unlike today's union house organs they were often independently owned and operated.[11]

In this emergent press of the 1870s and 1880s, as in the labour movement as a whole, the democratic perspective – somewhat strained by the difficulty of applying it to the increasing polarization between capital and labour – gained ascendancy. Labour journals challenged both the Tory/Reform ideological synthesis of Confederation-era Canada and the party orientation of the established elite press. They offered the democratic perspective as an alternative, stressing its universal rather than particularistic point of view. The labour journalists emphasized the reformation of society through knowledge and popular education. The *Ontario Workman* (April 18, 1872) expressed something of this Enlightenment spirit: "Co-operation is a principle that has shone upon the world through the progress of intelligence, and that it will gradually grow with the intelligence of the masses we have no doubt. It, or some like system, will gradually supersede the present system, as the present system has superseded the serf system of the past."

While they were concerned with the immediate aims of labour, such as the nine-hour movement, the labour papers did not restrict themselves to trade union issues. Rather, they developed analyses of industrial capitalism and provided a general social critique in the name of reason, public good, and natural rights – the very language of the Enlightenment. Based on this universal democratic perspective, the Canadian labour press, like its British and U.S. counterparts that had flourished decades earlier, criticized existing social inequalities and attacked capital as a form of social privilege contrary to justice and rights.[12] Encouraged as we are today to regard trade unions as just another special interest group, such a point might now be difficult to appreciate. But precisely because private interest was seen as the chief villain, workers were able to voice their *own cause* as a *universal* cause or right.[13]

Moreover, as Dan Schiller puts it, "Because the interests of journeymen could thus be universalized, the notion of public good could also be revitalized."[14] This concept of public good can be traced back to Paine's conception of the citizenry as "a homogeneous body with a definable common interest."[15] The labour journals, like Paine before them, were critical of political parties, seeing them as expressions of factions and classes. They attacked the party system and saw existing political parties as the parties of the privileged class. They urged their readers to stay aloof from partisan politics, criticizing the existing party press for being biased in favour of privilege and against labour. The *Ontario Workman*, for instance, complained that every effort "to secure to labour it[s] just reward is howled down by the 'press.'"[16]

Denouncing the partisan orientations of the established newspapers, the labour press proclaimed its own non-partisan, non-sectarian character. The *Palladium of Labor*, considered the finest labour paper of its era, stated that its cause was "the cause of the People." Its mission was to "Spread the Light; to expose the inequalities of distribution by which the few are enriched at the expense of the many."[17] The *Wage-Worker*, the Knights' first paper in Canada, announced that it "will be fearless and independent ... and will not truckle to any party."[18] For the labour press there was no contradiction between a stance of political independence, on the one hand, and the advocacy of the interests of artisans and mechanics, on the other – for their interests were *universal interests*, the interests of all citizens.

The labour press thus distinguished itself from the partisan and sectarian papers of religious, ethnic, and political factions by its adoption of the democratic discourse of the Enlightenment and its universalizing language. *This universalizing perspective can be seen as a precursor, indeed, an early version, of objectivity in journalism.* In their critique of the established press, labour journalists held up the ideal of *disinterested* – in other words, *objective* – knowledge as the only solid foundation for social reform. In this way the labour press subscribed to "the universal radical belief that political change would only come about through enlightenment, when the people would no longer tolerate the exclusive power of wealth and privilege."[19]

According to the labour journals, the newspaper was potentially a mighty power of Reason, but it was being perverted by private interests. "The newspaper is just as necessary to fit a man for his true position in life as food or raiment," opined the *Ontario Workman*, but a corrupt newspaper "poisons all who come in contact with it."[20] The labour papers set out to rectify this problem and promised their readers that they would fill the moral vacuum created by the established partisan press. They charged themselves with the duty of public enlightenment and producing information for the public good only. The *Canadian Labour Reformer*, for example, wrote: "We believe the object of a Labour journal should be to *report things as they really are*, unmask iniquities, uproot prejudices, expose falsehoods, advocate genuine reform, and assist the toiling masses to attain a higher degree of intellectual, moral and social development than they have yet enjoyed."[21] More than half a century earlier, the *New York Mechanic* had similarly promised to "*view dispassionately* the events passing around us, and in our capacity of public journalists submit calmly and *unprejudiced* our opinions."[22]

Such promises indicate an embryonic form of journalistic objectivity – promises to deliver reports of the world as it is, undistorted by private or sectional interest, for the purpose of the public good and the benefit of the worker-cum-universal citizen. Clearly, the labour press saw no contradiction between disinterested accounts of social reality and a crusading moral concern with justice. The paradigm is thus not yet twentieth-century objective journalism, with its conscious attempts to separate facts from values. Before the twentieth century, as media sociologist Michael Schudson notes, "It was uncommon for journalists to see a sharp divide between facts and values."[23] Nevertheless the labour press left an important legacy for the commercial dailies that came to dominate Canadian journalism by the turn of the century.

At the same time, though, we must take care not to mythologize Canada's labour press of the 1870s and 1880s. It had its ideological limitations, apparent in an ambiguous attitude towards women workers and particularly in its racism towards Chinese immigrant labourers. The labour press too often hurled abuse at Chinese workers rather than adopting a broader political perspective that would recognize them as fellow victims of industrial capitalism.[24] Moreover, like the mainstream of the labour movement and the Enlightenment discourse itself, the labour press also lacked a class analysis of capitalism. It did not see social class, with its attendant inequalities and conflict, as inherent to capitalism, but as something imposed by special interests. Rather than offering a structural analysis of capitalism, it provided an ethical critique of economic concentration or monopoly, which it blamed for the breakdown of the "natural" economic order. Monopoly, in its view, was an ethical problem, caused by greed on the part of some masters. Reforms of and through the state were still seen as the path for rectifying injustices in civil society and for achieving a thoroughly democratic society in which each individual could exercise "natural rights." Labour journalists were more interested in social improvement and reform than in radical social change or political revolution. It was precisely the absence of class analysis, the denial of structural antagonism within the society, that made it possible for the labour press to fuse the advocacy of labour's interests, the universalizing radical-democratic discourse, and a stance of impartiality or objectivity.

In addition to its ideological ambiguities, the labour press led a fragile existence. Financed either by independent subscriptions or by trade unions and supported mainly by artisans and mechanics, the labour press had limited circulation and reflected the financial vulnerability of its supporters. With too little advertising, too few paying readers, and an unstable trade union movement, few labour papers survived more than a year or two.[25] Their frailty paved the way for a new kind of popular press that would return the democratic discourse to centre stage – mass-based urban commercial newspapers.

The Popular Commercial Press: Appropriating the Democratic Discourse

By the late nineteenth century, Canada's increasingly industrialized and urbanized market economy had created a demand for advertising outlets on the part of merchants and retailers. Technology – the telegraph, the steam-powered cylinder press, paper-making from wood pulp – made it possible for newspapers to become the modern era's first mass medium. Shrewdly taking advantage of these new opportunities, independent commercial dailies soon established themselves as a popular forum of public discourse. Conscious of the working-class audience that had been cultivated by the labour press, the commercial dailies tried to steal its thunder. They discovered in the democratic discourse the universal perspective that enabled them to address, with a schoolmaster's judiciousness, "capitalists and mechanics" alike. The popular commercial dailies took Canadian journalism one step closer to the twentieth-century ethos of objectivity.

The popular commercial dailies proved to be strikingly successful. They pioneered new ways to produce, distribute, and consume news. In contrast to both the partisan and the labour newspapers, the independent dailies reached their readers mainly through street sales (rather than subscriptions), sold copies very cheaply, and depended on advertising (rather than subsidies from parties or unions) as their major financial support. For the first time newspapers became business enterprises, operating primarily to make profits through the dual transaction of selling news to readers and readers' attention to advertisers.

In the United States entrepreneurs had launched the business of popular daily newspapers in the 1830s. Still handicapped by the Stamp Duty, a government tax on newspaper sales, their British counterparts were experimenting with popular commercial journalism in the form of Sunday papers during the 1830s and 1840s. Canadian imitators of the New York penny papers emerged in the 1830s, but the popular commercial dailies did not take full bloom until the 1870s, starting in the larger cities.[26] In 1870 Hugh Graham, the business manager of the one-cent evening daily Montreal *Star*, took control of the paper and decided unabashedly to target the "low-brow" public, the masses. In this way Graham gave birth to "people's journalism," a new approach that "flouted the conventions of newspaperdom."[27] Other influential people's journals were the *Telegram* (founded 1876), *World* (1880), and *News* (1881) in Toronto, the *Journal* (1885) in Ottawa, and the *Herald* (1889) in Hamilton.

The independent commercial press did not, however, evolve "naturally" or as the manifestation of an abstract principle such as press freedom; nor did the labour press decline simply as a matter of course. Such a point is particularly relevant in the case of Britain, where class tension was more intense than in North America. The radical labour press that flourished in the earlier nineteenth century was considered dangerous to established society, and opponents made various political attempts to destroy it. An important factor for the decline of the radical press and the success of the commercial press was the purposeful liberalization of newspaper publishing through the relaxation of legal and economic restraints previously imposed by the state. Historically these restraints were formidable obstacles for newspaper publishing, and they served important political objectives. Until 1853 the Stamp Duty, for instance, actively discouraged publication: its purpose was to prevent dangerous ideas from seeing the light of day. If that restriction was not successful, the sweeping powers of the seditious libel laws could be used to punish any criticism, whether true or not, of the governing authorities or institutions.

The conventional history credits a libertarian outcry for freedom of expression for removing these obstacles to printing. But as James Curran has persuasively argued, at least with respect to the British Stamp Duty, the principal motive was "to destroy radical working class journalism."[28] The British parliamentary debate over the press and the Stamp Duty revolved around pragmatic concerns – how best to deal with a revived underground radical press that was bypassing the tax. Traditionalists wanted the government to crack down on unstamped and seditious papers and to keep newspapers under "the control of men of wealth and character" by raising publishing costs and restricting circulation levels through tax-inflated retail prices.

More perceptive reformers argued that only the free market would put an end to the radical press and promote "responsible" popular journalism.

Rather than suppressing the radical press, the stamp tax had given rise to a contraband underground press filled with "the most pernicious doctrines," with papers selling at less than half the price of their taxed and respectable rivals. By ending or reducing press taxation, reformers argued, the government would increase the flow of advertising to "the best papers" and encourage men of capital to invest in exploiting an expanding market.[29]

The British reformers won the day, and the Stamp Duty was repealed. Along with technological developments, this calculated liberalization gradually marginalized and contained Britain's radical press by increasing the costs of publishing a competitive, popular-oriented newspaper.

In the United States, by contrast, there was no comparable state strategy to destroy the labour press. With fewer legal restrictions on market relations, a popular commercial press emerged more readily. The U.S. commercial newspaper, according to Dan Schiller, "was left relatively free to develop alongside the working class itself."

Indeed, while the English working class found the newspapers a vital contributor to an unfolding class consciousness over two crucial decades (1815-1836 ...), the U.S. working class had barely begun to employ the press as an agency of class identity when the commercial penny papers began to enlist the interest and identification of laboring men.... Only in the United States was mass communication left free to develop as a private business *before* class relations hardened the terms of perception that it employed.[30]

Canada's experience more closely parallels the U.S. pattern than the British. Canada's labour press had hardly established itself when it faced competition from the emerging commercial dailies, especially the people's journals modelled after the U.S. penny dailies. Seeing themselves as "purveyors of objective news," the people's journals "struck out against the stodgy style and partisan politics of the party press."[31] They invaded the working-class market by touting their journalism for the ordinary citizen, along with often sensational, sometimes probing, coverage of social issues. Some popular daily papers such as the Toronto *News* even became supporters of labour's cause and reflected labour's views.

The labour press saw a double-edged sword in the new people's journals. On the one hand, with their explicitly democratic creed and their news stories exposing violations of the public good, they appeared to be allies in educating the public. On the other hand, as one labour journalist warned his readers, the commercial papers had no interest in the cause of working people beyond "its market value."[32] Labour journalists' sense of betrayal and failure intensified as the commercial press increasingly siphoned away their working-class readership. Forced to close his paper in 1891 after losing most of his readers to the commercial dailies, T.P. Thompson, Canada's most prominent labour journalist, left with a bitter parting shot that has been echoed many times since: "It is much to be regretted that the wage-earners are so stupidly blind to their own interests that they cannot see the advantage of having a live outspoken journal to plead their cause."[33]

To be sure, the labour press contributed to its own demise by often using strident rhetoric that went over working people's heads.[34] But most crucially, the labour press had to compete with the commercial dailies not only for readership but also for advertising – with little success. The advertisers whose dollars sustained the ascending daily press wanted to sell either brand-name mass products to a mass readership, or luxury items to affluent consumers. In neither case did the working-class readership of labour papers fit the bill. The labour papers, therefore, were unable to attract the capital investment and advertising revenue needed to keep pace with growing mass circulation and technological changes in the newspaper industry – for indeed it had become an industry. As Ron Verzuh concludes, "New technologies and journalistic conventions gave the commercial press an indisputable edge over the financially strapped labour press in attracting and influencing workers and their families."[35]

As the cheap dailies eclipsed the radical press, they adopted the latter's language, appropriating and softening its anger into "a blustery rhetoric of equal rights, enlightenment, and political independence."[36] The critical democratic discourse of the labour press was absorbed into, and neutralized by, the very forces – business and capitalism – it had once opposed, however equivocally. The people's journals were so intent on absorbing the working-class readership that they openly attacked monopoly and privilege and even "championed the cause of the masses" in their reporting. The formula of a "slangy style, sensation and crusades, much amusing or entertaining matter, and a surfeit of trivia" proved popular.[37] It "was so appealing to readers that the labour press often reprinted the material alongside sharp criticisms of the 'monopoly' or 'capitalistic' press."[38] The U.S. penny dailies and the people's journals of Toronto and Montreal were, according to Paul Rutherford, first and foremost "business enterprises, which their proprietors expected would produce a large advertising revenue.... Consequently the papers were designed to appeal not only to professionals and businessmen but also to clerks, workingmen, women and the young."[39] The Montreal *Star* (1869), for example, stated its aspiration "to be the organ of the people particularly the portion known as the working class."[40]

The people's journals became omnibus papers trying to offer something for every type of reader irrespective of class, gender, politics, or religion. They crusaded for workers' rights and "universal" male suffrage, denounced the domination of big business, mounted campaigns for reforming society through state intervention, and exploited the social tensions in the late nineteenth century by voicing the resentments of the masses towards social snobbery or economic privilege. In this way the popular dailies presented themselves as fearless champions of the people and guardians of the public good. The paradigmatic news story was an exposé of specific infractions to the public good, particularly the abuse of state power and the infringement of the natural rights of citizens by criminal elements and big business.

In this way the popular commercial dailies foreshadowed modern journalism's regime of objectivity by creating a new creed for professional journalism. The press had to appear independent of cliques and factions; its task was to be both a popular educator and a people's tribune.[41] For Schiller this pre-emptive claim to the defence of natural rights and the public good was nothing less than the "enduring foundation upon which the structure of news objectivity was built."[42]

The new commercial dailies' concern for objectivity was expressed in their claim to offer independent and impartial information that allowed citizens to form their own opinion about important local, national, and international issues. The importance of the editorial page declined in the typical newspaper.[43] Newspapers started to emphasize *news*, rather than *views*. The Toronto *News*, for example, wrote on December 8, 1883: "When it comes to the struggle in this paper between news and editorial matter, the news will have preference every time, for every reader who has news before him in intelligible shape can skirmish around for opinion for himself." Independent journalism was tying the news revolution in the public mind with independence from party, with the cool, deliberative politics of education.[44]

This nineteenth-century version of journalistic objectivity was different from what would emerge later, in the twentieth century. The distinction between news and views was not yet rigid. In any case an *ideological* perspective was still explicit in both the news stories and editorial writing. The journalists of the late nineteenth century had not yet acquired the twentieth-century narrative art of burying the writer's assumptions. When the popular commercial papers trumpeted their impartiality and lack of party ties, they were not suggesting that the facts offered were without a moral lesson. In fact, advocacy was part of the appeal of these popular commercial dailies. What they were saying was that instead of a particular class bias they were taking a universal perspective – the perspective of reason itself. Sharing the "naive empiricism" of the time, journalists of the late nineteenth century were not yet bothered by how their own values shaped their perceptions of the facts. Moreover, as Schudson said, they "understood facts to provide moral direction of themselves and prided themselves that their own moral precepts grew naturally out of their association with the real world." Their moral declarations seemed to them "as irrefutable as the facts they uncovered."[45] Consequently they saw no inconsistency between advocacy and objectivity.

Similarly, nineteenth-century journalism's detachment did not mean standing entirely on the political sidelines. Traditions of partisanship lingered in many Canadian newsrooms, co-existing with an increasingly professed but inconsistently practised commitment to objectivity as the hallmark of journalistic professionalism.[46] Despite their original attacks on party journalism, many of the popular dailies, such as the *Montreal Star*, the *Toronto Telegram*, and *The Toronto Star*, remained known well into the 1950s for their pronounced editorial preferences towards one of the two major political parties, the Liberals and Conservatives. Even as newspapers became concerned with producing profits more than propaganda, they began to acquire political loyalties of a new type – not to a particular party, but to the policies and ideology of free enterprise. Rarely did the political independence of Canadian newspapers extend to editorial endorsements of the democratic-socialist Co-operative Commonwealth Federation or even its more "pragmatic" successor, the New Democratic Party.

The mass readership-oriented newspapers permanently transformed the relationship between political parties and daily newspapers. Following their model, all newspapers gradually became first and foremost commercial enterprises, without any direct financial or institutional ties with political parties. Such independence enabled them to develop a critical distance from even the party of their preference, and to switch political allegiance over any given issue. Through either economic demise or editorial revamping, the pure party organ was permanently replaced in the late nineteenth century by the newspaper as a commercial enterprise.

The Ambiguities of Objectivity

The nineteenth-century version of objectivity was more progressive, holistic, and far-reaching than the "strategic ritual" that is sometimes taken to comprise journalism objectivity today. The concern for news rather than views flowed directly out of the Enlightenment notion of the educated man in politics: newspapers had to provide the factual information that people needed to make informed, independent judgements about public life.[47]

In the commercial press the democratic perspective provided not only the foundation for the emerging concept of journalistic objectivity, but also the ideological framework for telling news stories. It functioned as an organizing principle, a narrative framework purporting to take the universal rather than a particularistic perspective. The typical democratic storyline of nineteenth-century commercial papers imposed meaning on social events through a belief in four principles: individual natural rights, a benign market economy, a state able to represent the popular will and reform the shortcomings of civil society, and a concept of progress through the expansion of popular knowledge. In the twentieth century these principles became incorporated as key legitimations of liberal-democratic capitalism.

This particular kind of democratic discourse enabled the popular commercial dailies to address, in the same breath, business people, civil servants, and the new working-class readers responsive to the rhetoric of the labour press, as well as their own advertisers. They offered themselves as experts on public affairs, taking the perspective of Reason. Trumpeting their concern for the public good, they saw themselves in the double role of being spokesmen *for* the people when criticizing civil society and the state, and of being the educators *of* the people. In reporting social conflicts, for example, the commercial press, as the voice of reason, stood above the disputing parties, acting sometimes as an impartial observer and sometimes as a kind of Greek chorus on behalf of democracy.[48] In this way the press successfully appealed to what the Italian social theorist Antonio Gramsci called "the popular will": it helped to foster intellectual and moral cohesion among the various groups that constituted its readership.

The independent commercial papers of the nineteenth century did have a progressive face. They helped to expand the right to vote and break down the elitist and authoritarian Toryism that had dominated Canadian politics in earlier decades. Together with the labour press, the independent commercial press helped to modify the terms of public discourse. By 1890 the idea of democracy had become one of the accepted public beliefs acknowledged by the editors of both partisan and independent papers alike.

"Democracy is upon us," argued the Victoria *Times* on June 19, 1890. "We cannot get out of it if we would. We must therefore make the best of it." An approximation of universal (male) suffrage was instituted both federally and throughout the provinces. As one media historian points out, "The era of the common man was 'dawning' in society ... requiring that publicists (and especially editors in search of popularity) pay lip-service to dreams of equality."[49] In short, the late nineteenth-century commercial press helped to popularize democratic liberalism and turn it into common sense.

In some ways the commercial dailies also democratized the press itself as a political institution. No longer the mouthpieces of particular political parties, newspapers now became widely accessible through the lowering of prices. At the same time the popular commercial dailies greatly expanded newspaper content. They expressed their concern for the local and the mundane through reports from the police, the courts, the streets, and even private households. In that sense, the newspaper "reflected not just commerce or politics but social life."[50]

Indeed, the popular newspapers promised to make information about the world democratically accessible to everybody and to "record facts on every public and proper subject, stripped of verbiage and coloring." The ideal of objectivity, with its universalistic intent and its concern for public rationality based on equal access to the facts, harboured a profound democratic promise.[51]

The people's journals helped to create new occupational groups that could see themselves as the bearers of that promise. In previous eras the first proto-newspapers had been published irregularly by printers as a sideline to their business, and then by editors with political affiliations that shaped their material. But the late nineteenth century witnessed a veritable revolution in Canada's press. The advent of the telegraph (and the earlier development of shorthand techniques) made possible, and created a demand for, speedy and accurate reports of the day's intelligence.[52] A new breed of journalist emerged whose economic livelihood rested upon producing such reports, helping to culturally entrench the concept of news as a set of factually accurate and non-partisan accounts of events. The people's journals emphasized not opinion, but news, especially sensationalist news.[53] They increasingly distinguished news from commentary, and within the staffs of the dailies, growing in circulation size and capital investment, a division of labour emerged between reporters, editors, and columnists. The drive towards objective news was reinforced by journalists who came to regard the ethic of objectivity as integral to their emerging conceptions of professionalism.

The rise of the market-oriented, liberal-democratic commercial papers had its darker side. For one thing (among others that we will explore later) their spectacular success helped to extinguish, marginalize, or transform the radical working-class journals. The consequences of this victorious displacement were both ideological and structural.

Ideologically, the commercial papers turned labour's (admittedly ambiguous) calls for significant if not revolutionary social change into a popular discourse less hostile to existing social institutions. Despite their crusades for social reform and their expressed sympathy with the workers' causes, the emerging popular dailies were increasingly commercial ventures, seen as sources of profit rather than centres of radical feeling. Their origin was in no sense a simple reflection of working-class consciousness, but rather a shrewd assessment of the possibilities of an expanding mass market. The papers' commercial synthesis between democratic rhetoric and sensationalism resulted in the manipulation of the old tradition of radical journalism so that the structural causes of distress were effectively ignored. Writing about the ideological significance of the popular Sunday papers in Britain, Virginia Berridge explains that "the commercial dictates of mass circulation" helped to sustain "a radical analysis that was little more than surface rhetoric." Radicalism itself became "a commodity marketed to provide an easy appeal" – a commodity presumably to be dropped once it was no longer helping to attract a profitable readership.[54]

The commercial press, governed not by the goal of social emancipation but by the logic of profit-making, thus took up the democratic discourse and used it for its own purposes. In the radical and labour papers, the discourse of Rousseau and Paine had been stretched and teased into a framework for interpreting and challenging the class injustices of industrial capitalism. But in the commercial press that discourse often turned into hollow rhetoric and empty gestures. The Enlightenment's universal perspective of Man was used by these papers to construct a new public: low-born citizens, indignant at injustice, resentful of privilege, yet taking a prurient interest in the private lives of both aristocrats and criminals; big-hearted, but short in memory and understanding and, above all, easily distracted with amusement of any kind. In these papers, while the radical discourse still reverberated, the common man gradually became a caricature that increasingly resembled the disdainful image that the dominant class had of him – perhaps not surprisingly, when one recalls that this class, after all, had come to own and operate the commercial press.

Perhaps it would be too cynical to say that the democratic discourse, which for the labour papers had been a rallying cry for social action, became for the commercial press *simply* a rhetorical device to increase circulation and profits. After all, a sincere acceptance of liberal-democratic principles and a definition of the public good consistent with those principles have become too well-embedded in the culture of Canadian journalism over the past century to be reduced to a marketing strategy. However, notwithstanding the exposés of individual monopolists, the commercial press accepted market relations and property rights much more unequivocally than did the growing trade union movement, which was turning towards socialism by the early twentieth century. The commercial papers' democratic discourse, therefore, was blind or accepting towards the structural inequalities of social class, even though it provided a universalistic ideological framework (natural rights, reason, state reform) to express class tensions. In this respect and others, Canadian journalism partakes of the blind spots as well as the achievements of liberal democracy.

It may be objected that when the commercial dailies emerged in the 1870s, their ideological distance from the nascent labour movement was not in fact great. Certainly we would not want to exaggerate labour's radicalism. Indeed, some labour journalists initially greeted the new people's journals as allies in the task of educating the public. It soon became apparent, though, that the commercial logic of the new papers, including their efforts to appeal to advertisers and business people as well as workers, constrained the kind of journalism they could offer. They appropriated the democratic discourse, but could be counted on to actively promote democratic social change only when it was profitable and convenient to do so. The newly commercialized press system did permit diversity, perhaps best epitomized by the bitter rivalry for over half a century between the conservative *Telegram* and the reformist *Star* in Toronto. But even the most liberal dailies were not hospitable to radical egalitarian critiques of the economic system; none followed the labour movement's eventual turn towards democratic socialism.

The ascendance of the commercial press also meant that alternative voices from below could no longer enjoy direct access to the public forum. Henceforth trade unions and other movements for social change would be dependent upon commercial mass media with priorities quite different than the crusading labour press. The labour press was economically and thus politically marginalized just as it was beginning to articulate explicitly socialist critiques of industrial capitalism.

Moreover, the popular commercial dailies paved the way for the eventual centralization of the means of political communication in the hands of large multimedia corporations. At the same time as the popular dailies claimed to bring information to the people as a whole, they excluded ordinary people from participating in generating information and campaigning for their own causes. To be sure, the press claimed to provide the facts, and occasionally it crusaded *on behalf of* the people. However, it was not the people themselves, but a privileged group, namely, the major media and their sources, that came to define the terms of public discourse and be (in Schiller's phrase) the "lord of the facts."[55]

Along the way the news was transformed into a readily saleable consumer commodity and the public into consumers of apparently "balanced" commentary and "objective" information. In the context of such a system, objectivity was to acquire quite different uses and consequences than it had in the democratic discourse of the labour press.

2

From Positivism to Negative News: The Evolution of Objectivity

"**N**ow what I want is, Facts.... Facts alone are wanted in life. Plant nothing else and root out everything else. You can only form the minds of reasoning animals upon Facts: nothing else will ever be of any service to them.... Stick to the Facts, sir!"

These words from Thomas Gradgrind, a particularly anal-retentive character in Charles Dickens' 1854 novel *Hard Times*, capture something of the spirit of late nineteenth-century intellectual culture in North America. The period was a high-tide mark for realism in art and literature, for empirical enquiry in social science, for the status of science in popular culture, and for the pursuit of factuality in journalism.[1]

By the turn of the century the holistic notion of objectivity as speaking from a universalizing perspective had been set firmly in place. The promise of the penny paper publisher/editor James Gordon Bennett in the 1830s, that his *New York Herald* would record facts without verbiage and colouring, had became a journalistic doctrine rigidly enforced through the hierarchical structure of the newsroom, with an elaborated division of labour. Facticity, the pursuit and indeed veneration of facts considered to be unvarnished statements about the world, drew upon the rationalist and democratic premises of the Enlightenment: facts were potentially knowable to all, and the press's job was to gather and make them available without fear or favour, so that rational citizens could make up their own minds.[2]

Facticity in the Age of Naive Realism

For journalists themselves, facticity could be a harsh discipline, often at odds with their own desire to develop a distinctive narrative style. U.S. reporters of the 1890s would recall caustically how they had learned the rules of the newsroom. Reminiscing in his memoirs, one wrote: "Facts; facts, nothing but facts. So many peas at so much a peck; so much molasses at so much a quart. The index of forbidden words was very lengthy, and misuse of them, when they escaped the keen eye of a copyreader and got into print, was punishable by suspension without pay for a week, or immediate discharge. It was a rigid system, rigidly enforced."[3]

Another journalist gave a similar account: "Reporters were to report the news as it happened, like machines, without prejudice, color, and without style; all alike. Humor or any sign of personality in our reports was caught, rebuked, and in time, suppressed."[4]

The obsession with unvarnished facts as the basis of sound judgement and the emblem of detachment from narrow sectarian interest was reinforced by the introduction of new technologies in the newspaper industry – the telegraph, the wire services, photography, and photo-engraving. But perhaps the most important development was a newly invented form of newswriting – the "inverted pyramid" report.

Previously dominant genres of newswriting could not well express the "reverence for facts," as a leading news historian explains. The essay was too heavily weighted with point of view, the first-person narrative with subjective experience, and the straight transcript (of parliamentary proceedings, for instance) with details that overwhelmed essential facts. But once journalists began to transmit news copy over expensive and/or unreliable telegraph lines, they learned to compress "the most crucial facts into short, paragraph-long dispatches."[5] No longer was the news report governed by chronology, the development of an argument, or the unfolding of a narrative. Rather, the reader was presented with facts, in descending order of perceived newsworthiness. So was born a remarkably artificial kind of newswriting, far removed from everyday speech – the inverted pyramid. A century later it remains the daily newspaper's dominant form.

To be sure, even in its heyday, the pursuit of facts – the information function of news – never completely overrode the desire for pleasure and the drive for persuasion. In news reports journalism never altogether abandoned the use of colourful narrative, imaginative embellishment, or even the insinuation of opinion. Moreover, in post-World War I journalism in the United States, the naively empiricist belief in facts as a way to photograph the world verbally was already crumbling.

But the form of facticity, if not always underwritten by faith in the purity of facts, lingered on in news presentation. Indeed, in Canadian political journalism, with its permanent time lag behind its U.S. counterpart, the emphasis on facts devoid of commentary or interpretation did not reach its zenith until World War II – paradoxically at precisely the historical moment that called for the greatest commitment to clearly defined values, the greatest mobilization of public opinion and sacrifice of blood against an outside enemy, ever undertaken by liberal democracies. Perhaps not so paradoxical: public-service broadcasters in Britain set an international standard for apparently impartial, authoritative, and accurate reporting, and the global credibility that the British Broadcasting Corporation thereby earned arguably enabled it to function all the more effectively as a weapon in the Allies' political arsenal. Certainly on the home front, the BBC's wartime performance, including "its ability to remain clear of political affiliation or involvement," solidified its status as a national cultural institution.[6]

Canada's own public-service broadcaster, the CBC, followed suit. Under the leadership of former Toronto newspaper reporter Dan McArthur, CBC Radio's fledgling news service inaugurated a national news bulletin on New Year's Day, 1941.[7] Hungry for accurate, up-to-the-minute reports from the battlefronts, Canadians welcomed it, and CBC Radio newsreader Lorne Greene soon became "the best known voice in the country," the embodiment of credibility and the forerunner of television news anchormen like Walter Cronkite and Lloyd Robertson.[8] Known then as the Voice of Doom, Greene later also became a star for the television generation in his role as Pa Cartwright on the western series *Bonanza*.

In contrast to the heads of other CBC programs (including features sponsored by government departments) that consciously promoted the war effort, and contrary to some Ottawa officials who wanted news to be a vehicle for government-authorized information and announcements, McArthur insisted on integrity and objectivity as the cornerstones for the News Service. However, remarkably consistent with the U.S. newspaper journalism of a half-century earlier, McArthur adopted a narrow concept of objectivity as "accuracy and a rigid adherence to facts, a commitment to unbiased reporting, and the exclusion of any form of interpretation, analysis and editorial comment from the *National News Bulletin*."[9] As Robert Albota puts it, "McArthur believed that the News Service would be more vulnerable to ... accusations that it was biased if the editor writing the bulletin deviated from the straight, factual content of a news story" or "if the CBC's newscasts attempted to analyze or explain political or controversial issues." According to Albota, in McArthur's view, "It was more important to deal with facts and let the listeners draw their own conclusions about where the truth lay."[10]

McArthur evidently thought that objectivity would be guaranteed by sticking to the straight, factual prose offered by Canadian Press or British United Press.[11] The naivety of this view is perhaps clearer in hindsight. Moreover, it was a view that inhibited, and could not long survive, the eventual expansion of CBC's news services into newsgathering, as distinct from simply selecting and editing the copy of external news agencies.[12] Before the end of the war, the CBC's overseas correspondents, such as Matthew Halton (father of CBC-TV reporter David Halton), were acquiring an avid following for their own reports.

Perhaps more than the practitioners of any other news medium, public-service broadcasters, concerned to establish their own institutional credibility and independence from the party in power, were obsessive about maintaining factuality and objectivity in news. They wanted to confine commentary to attributed statements balanced carefully within the news or to programs specifically designated as commentary or current affairs and safely outside the boundaries of news broadcasts. Indeed, a French-language CBC (Radio-Canada) journalist who later served in Pierre Trudeau's cabinet complained that as late as 1960, CBC reporting was "objective to the point of being virginal."[13]

But for at least a brief period, Canadian newspapers too adopted the ethic of "just the facts ma'am." Writing from his own long experience in print journalism, George Bain likewise sees World War II and its aftermath as the era of "Objectivity, with a capital O." By then the explicitly partisan paper run by an editor or publisher full of his own opinions had been superseded by a new ethos:

> A "church and state" separation came into being between the editorialists and the newsroom. Although the built-in slant in reporting never vanished altogether, now, at least, "slant" had become a bad word. A paper's views on politics were to be confined to the editorial page; reporters' opinions belonged nowhere; reporters recorded the news, they did not make it, and they intruded very little upon it. Newspapers and the rapidly sprouting television were to serve as pipelines, taking in information at one end and delivering it unadulterated at the other.[14]

Similarly, media scholar David Taras argues that the "culture of objective journalism" entrenched itself in Canada after World War I, and even more so after World War II when journalism schools were established, leading to the elimination of all but vestiges of the party press.[15]

Accommodating Subjectivity: Objectivity as Strategic Ritual

The meanings and practical applications of objectivity, though firmly established, were not carved in stone; they were flexible, adaptable, and subject to negotiation. Moreover, the dominance of this ethos over news discourse was never entirely unchallenged.

As the twentieth century marched bloodily on, increasingly in North American journalism the faith in the ability of straight factual reporting to provide adequate and unblemished accounts of the world was collapsing. Facts were no longer self-evident, they no longer spoke for themselves, and they no longer automatically provided moral direction. In his provocative social history of the U.S. press, Michael Schudson traces the irruption of scepticism and relativism to pessimism about the viability of "democratic market society" in the immediate post-World War I period.[16]

The carnage of World War I, the apparently powerful impact of wartime propaganda, Freudian psychology, new and historically unprecedented totalitarian fascist and Stalinist regimes in Europe, and the Great Depression of the 1930s all contributed to a culture's loss of confidence in the reliability of facts, the rationality of citizens, and the superiority, inevitability, or even viability of democratic capitalism. Speculatively, we suggest that the new media of radio and film, including newsreels, seemed to offer new opportunities to represent the world in a realistic mode. In that respect these media would seem to have lent new life to the positivist ideal of unmediated, purely factual representation. Still, there was anxiety that the new media could be harnessed to propaganda, all the more effective for its apparent realism. In their consolidation of power, for instance, the Nazis made brilliant use of both radio and film. Leni Riefenstahl's 1935 documentary *Triumph of the Will*, celebrating the Nazi regime, is still regarded as a classic propaganda film.

Along with the broader culture, journalism's self-understanding was also in transition after World War I. For the first time social science offered systematic evidence of journalists' own subjectivity. In 1920 Walter Lippmann and Charles Merz removed the veil of objectivity from the United States' most prestigious paper, *The New York Times*. Its coverage of the Russian Revolution, they concluded, was "a case of seeing not what was, but what men wished to see."[17]

Journalism also had to adjust to the appearance of the public relations industry, which arose from elites' needs to manage public opinion in the era of the mass franchise and mass media, particularly during a time of potential socialist revolution or at least of much greater government regulation of the marketplace. With a now well-established influence over public opinion and separation of function from politicians, journalists found themselves courted by the PR industry. Selectively peddling convenient facts, this new occupation earned the scorn and dislike of reporters; but they could not escape their own substantial dependence on PR handouts.[18]

Consequently, the nineteenth-century version of journalistic objectivity was significantly transformed after World War I. The positivistic version of objectivity-through-factuality and the impartiality of journalists themselves could no longer be easily assumed.[19] Journalism's authority to speak from the perspective of generalized reason became problematic. And yet the commercial logic of non-partisanship and the perceived need for objective rather than malevolently propagandistic accounts of the world were still very much in play.

In this new context, journalistic objectivity came to be expressed in the form of a range of "organizational mechanisms" or "strategic rituals," through which journalists could establish the truth-value of stated facts, protect themselves from such hazards as editors' reprimands and libel suits, and distance themselves from responsibility for the values or consequences implicit in news reports. According to Schudson, it was "the assertion of a method designed for a world in which even facts could not be trusted."[20]

These conventions came to include the use of quotation marks to designate unconventional concepts, the attribution of opinion to sources, the construction of information in an appropriate sequence and format (the news story), the presentation of both or all major sides or viewpoints on public issues, and adherence to prevailing standards of decency and good taste.[21] Through this set of methods, objectivity became a *cultural form*, with distinct technical codes and practical rules. The news industry established codes of ethics and formally enshrined the requirement of objectivity. In 1935, for example, the American Newspaper Guild's code of ethics officially endorsed the ethos of objectivity by stating, "The newspapermen's first duty is to give the public accurate and unbiased news reports."[22]

As objectivity became more technically defined as a method rather than a universalizing discourse, it also became narrower. Since journalists could no longer believe that facts contained a moral lesson on their own, advocacy became the antithesis of objectivity, which gradually came to be defined as straight, factual reporting and was indeed further reduced to the reporting of factual descriptions and statements produced by accredited sources.

Interpretive Reporting: Beyond the Facts?

Apart from the ritualization and codification of objectivity, other twentieth-century adjustments have been made to the recognition of subjectivity in journalism. Perhaps the most important was the expansion of the rubric of objectivity to include interpretive as well as "straight" reporting.[23] As a genre of journalism, interpretive reporting emerged as a response to both increasing news management by sources and dissatisfaction with news that simply "let facts speak for themselves." In the throes of the Great Depression of the 1930s, social relations in advanced capitalist societies were perhaps less transparent and less comprehensible than ever before to those who had been schooled in the American Dream and the Protestant work ethic. Dark and threatening forces were brewing in Europe; and even in the remaining liberal democracies, state power was becoming more centralized and remote from ordinary people, despite the spread of the franchise to nearly all adult citizens. The world was not only complex, but was becoming visibly and problematically complex.[24] To adopt journalism's own catchwords, audiences wanted to know why, not simply who, what, when, and where.

To its proponents, interpretive reporting means placing news into an appropriate context and furnishing additional relevant background. It means explaining, amplifying, and clarifying situations for readers.[25] As the influential 1947 Hutchins Commission report on the U.S. press put it, reporters should not only report the facts truthfully, but report the truth about the facts.[26] Promoted by archaeological metaphors, interpretive reporting implies a distinction between outward or surface appearances and an underlying reality that must be excavated to be revealed. Interpretive reporting rejects the positivist assumption that facts speak for themselves, but accepts the realist position that, ultimately, there is a truth to the matter.

One manifestation of the departure from straight news was the "invention of the syndicated political columnist" in the U.S. press of the 1920s.[27] In Canada many newspapers, wire services, and private radio stations began, by the early 1940s, to adhere to a broader concept of objectivity based on interpretive reporting. Still, the CBC budged little from its early definition of objectivity as straight, factual reporting until the 1960s.[28] As in the United States, Canada's foreign correspondents were particularly keen to be released from the straitjackets of facticity. The late David Levy, for example, testified that had Dan McArthur's concept of objectivity not been considerably broadened by the time he took a posting at CBC's new Moscow bureau in the mid-1960s, he simply could not have functioned as a reporter. Presumably he meant that the older notion of objectivity would have required him not only to act as a transmission belt for Soviet officialdom, but also to avoid interpreting an unfamiliar Soviet politics and culture to his Canadian audience. Even in the 1960s Levy's appointment was apparently resisted by an old-guard editor who distrusted Levy's background as a commentator and an academic as well as his lack of schooling in the rigours of "objective" writing.[29]

The provocative and controversial 1967 documentary *Air of Death* was a landmark for CBC in pushing the limits of television journalism. The program suggested that a fertilizer plant in Ontario's Niagara peninsula was causing an air pollution problem. Doubtless the program's location within the public affairs rather than news genres contributed to its relative boldness, but the program nevertheless led to charges of journalistic bias from the plant owners and an inquiry by the Canadian Radio-television and Telecommunications Commission (CRTC). In its 1970 report the CRTC concluded that broadcast journalists dealing with controversial material may well display "honest bias" so long as that bias is not "malicious, distorting, or taken to the point of propaganda."[30]

The key point, though, is that interpretive reporting has been *subordinated to*, and *disciplined by*, the ethos of objectivity. This is so both in its conceptual exposition and in the practice of news work.

First, the term "objectivity" was reconceptualized in such a way that it did not exclude interpretation. The practice of objectivity as straight reporting was labelled as old-fashioned, simplistic, naive, shallow, and misguided; interpretive reporting would enable a fuller, deeper form of objectivity. An article in a 1950 issue of the professionally oriented *Nieman Reports*, significantly entitled "Reporting Background: You Can Interpret and Still Retain Objectivity," argued: "This isn't a condemnation of objectivity as such. But if the newspaper is to do the job it should do in a democracy, where things are eventually decided by the people, the reader is entitled to his objectivity served up in a form that he can understand."[31]

Other examples from journalism teachers and practitioners abound. In a 1951 front-page series on interpretive reporting, the prestigious *Christian Science Monitor* told its readers that interpretation requires "integrity and knowledge and understanding and balance and detachment," which can only be secured by "steadfast news objectivity." Speaking to his staff in 1943,

Associated Press general manager Kent Cooper called for "direct, factual and wholly *objective* news reporting that *digs below the surface* and *tells the true story*."[32]

The CBC's adoption of a broader concept of objectivity was predicated on conceding the unavoidability of some degree of bias or subjective judgement in news. Nevertheless, the rule of thumb, according to Robert Albota, was that "a reporter or correspondent, as an impartial and disinterested observer, would take on an assignment and follow it through to wherever it might lead, regardless of the outcome. Journalists would consider their reporting to be 'objective' if they undertook a process of enquiry that led to the discovery of truth." Following this rationale, Albota says, "The CBC's journalists could state their interpretations, assumptions and opinions and still be considered 'objective' if their reporting was accurate, fair and balanced."[33]

Such policies and admonitions allow an active role for the responsible journalist under the rubric of objectivity. But they clearly pose a problem of how to reconcile the (supposedly) neutral and mirror-like presentation of facts with the journalist's active interpretation of those facts. Conceptually, the advocates of this approach were forced to distinguish honest or legitimate interpretation, on the one hand, from distortion, subjective editorializing, or "corrupt interpretation," which "vents the writer's [own] prejudices and slants," on the other.[34] For instance, Canada's 1980-81 Royal Commission on Newspapers argued that beyond the older obligation "to be accurate and fair and balanced in their reporting," newspapers should also "go below the facts to their significance, to give the truth by *interpreting without distorting*."[35] Journalism professor and former Washington newsman Bernard Roshco argues that since interpretation and objectivity are not incompatible in the natural and social sciences, they are logically reconcilable in journalism too, so long as reporters avoid "subjective editorializing."[36]

But the line between "objective interpretation" and "subjective editorializing" often proves difficult to define. Certainly, given this conceptualization, it becomes difficult to distinguish objective interpretations from those coloured by journalism's shared cultural biases or values.

In practice, without necessarily dwelling upon these conceptual problems, news workers have developed their own ways to integrate interpretive reporting into objective journalism. One such strategy is *attributed* interpretation. Reporters include opinions or evaluations of an event in their reports in the form of quotes attributed to an acceptably relevant source. For this reason, a growing number of "experts" in different spheres of social life have joined government and institutional spokespeople as authoritative interpreters and definers of public reality.

Frequently the objectivity of such interpretations is accomplished through the conventional method of balancing two (or very occasionally more) contrasting interpretations of an event from experts, or advocates, without taking a position in favour of one or the other. This procedure of counterbalancing attributed statements in news reports precludes other ways of establishing knowledge, such as using documentary evidence. Richard Ericson and his colleagues recount an example of a Toronto television news reporter covering a local controversy in the early 1980s. Citing an internal police memo as evidence, Rastafarians held a news conference to accuse the authorities of planning to prevent delegates to an international conference of Rastafarians from entering Canada. The reporter counterbalanced this claim by interviewing the local deputy chief of police, who offered a less sinister interpretation of the memo. The news worker reported these two conflicting claims without consulting the actual memo, even though it appeared to be readily available. Obtaining the document would have forced the reporter, the authors concluded, "to make judgments that might well have led him to violate journalistic standards of balance, neutrality, and objectivity," by forcing him to favour one side over the other.[37] Even today, it seems that the conventions of objectivity encourage reporters to attribute interpretation to sources rather than to offer interpretations themselves.

While interpretive reporting has conceptually and practically refreshed the older ethos of objectivity, several considerations caution us not to exaggerate the extent to which it has changed old reporting conventions. Interpretive reporting has been advocated as a philosophy, but its problems and methods have not been well developed.[38] In practice, explicit evaluation by reporters tends to be confined to the more senior and experienced journalists; and it is often consigned to a specifically designated genre – the backgrounder, the analysis column, the television "magazine" program – carefully segregated from both opinion (letters, columns, editorials) and straight news reports.

Moreover, the lip service given to interpretation has not always allowed journalists to escape functioning as stenographers for the powerful, one of the chief pitfalls of straight reporting. In the 1950s Senator Joe McCarthy sustained his tawdry political crusade against largely non-existent Communists in U.S. public life by exploiting the conventions of objectivity, which, it seemed, forced journalists to disseminate McCarthy's accusations while knowing them to be false. In January 1969 national media gathered on a beach in Santa Barbara to report, matter of factly, President Nixon's claim that the beach had been cleaned up after a huge oil spill. All concerned dutifully ignored the very real oil slick and debris lying just a hundred yards away.[39] In the 1980s, many critics argue, President Reagan was able to exploit the conventions of straight reporting, particularly on television, to avoid public exposure of the gap between his preferred image and his actual policies.[40]

The emergence of interpretive reporting and its incorporation into the tradition of journalistic objectivity, then, suggest a modest reform within the tradition rather than a fundamental deviation from it. Interpretive reporting had challenged old-style straight reporting and opened the way for more contextualization. Given the power of tradition, as well as the largely unchanged structure of news production (including the commercial imperative of minimizing production costs and maximizing audiences), the potential of interpretive reporting was very much limited.

Critical Journalism: An Adversarial Culture?

Underground newspapers full of four-letter words, drug-inspired comic strips, free love advice columns, anarchist politics; newspaper headlines of war casualties, racial violence, and government deception; visual images of a Southeast Asian girl, screaming in terror, running in pain from a sheet of burning napalm; an anguished student kneeling over the body of her classmate, slain by a National Guard bullet; police truncheons flaying into a crowd of protesters; a Vietnamese general firing a pistol into the head of a bound prisoner: these are some of the media images that linger from the 1960s, the decade that refuses to lie down and die.[41]

Perhaps with good reason: on the surface at least, the 1960s ushered in a new era in journalism. For the first time television, with its vast audiences and its occasionally evocative and riveting images, surpassed newspapers as the primary source of news for a majority of Americans and Canadians. In the eyes of some commentators, especially older conservative-minded journalists, news media have strayed from or even abandoned the ethos of objectivity in favour of a critical or adversarial approach. This observation is usually also an accusation: adversarial journalism is held responsible for undermining political leadership, trivializing public issues by transforming them into soap operas and emotional dramas, rendering effective government more difficult, discouraging good people from entering politics, and, in Canada, displacing the role of parliamentary opposition parties.[42]

Some observers point to television as a catalyst for "critical" rather than "objective" journalism. They suggest that the medium's predominant entertainment orientation – its "infotainment agenda"[43] – impels television journalism towards telling stories with strong, dramatic, visually compelling, and personalized themes rather than explaining ideas or emphasizing factual details. Similarly, it is said that due to television's logic of "flow" – its need to hold the attention of broad audiences over a period of time – TV news stories are tightly organized around "short and simple but continuous" narratives, far more so than the newspaper's inverted pyramid report.[44]

There is something to these arguments, but the relationship of television to facticity and objectivity is more complicated. In some ways television news has reinforced objectivity. With its regulated mandate for balance and impartiality in political coverage, television has been credited with helping to undermine the vestiges of old-style partisanship in the print media. Moreover, the "reality effect" of the television camera connotes transparency, the unmediated observation of events-out-there. Such an impression is, of course, an illusion, a "naturalistic fallacy."[45] Even the simplest camera shot can be used to create different impressions depending on choice of location, angle, and filter. TV news stories are very much a constructed product, shaped by technical and ideological codes. Yet with its constant talk of "eyewitness news" and "taking you to the scene," television news works hard to naturalize, to render invisible, its conventions.[46] During the emergence of TV news in the 1950s and beyond, television's supposed "reality effect" probably breathed new life into the public expectation that news media could be neutral and objective windows on the world.

Quite apart from the respective technological biases of television and print media, other factors acted on the emergence of supposedly "critical" journalism. Journalism could not fail to respond to its political, cultural, and social environment. The Vietnam War created a "credibility gap" between government and media, as the U.S. leadership delivered continually inflated estimates of its military successes and tried to cover up its failures and atrocities. That credibility gap was reinforced by the Watergate scandal, when the White House ordered a break-in of the Democratic Party's headquarters and then tried to cover up incriminating evidence. Like their fellow citizens, U.S. journalists had to confront the demythologizing possibility that their president was not only a liar but also a crook.

In addition to the enormous influence of U.S. politics and media on Canada, Canadian observers have also found specifically domestic catalysts for critical journalism. One factor was the growing social distance between politicians and a rapidly expanding Ottawa Press Gallery after the 1950s, eclipsing the previous chumminess and clubbiness of their relationship. Another landmark was CBC Television's controversial current affairs program *This Hour Has Seven Days*. Although the program attracted huge audiences with its confrontational interviews and sensational exposés, CBC management (predictably, some critics would say) cancelled it in 1966. In Quebec, where the objectivity ethos had never enjoyed the same hold as in anglo-Canada, journalists were active political participants in the province's so-called Quiet Revolution of modernization.[47] The politicization of Quebec journalism escalated along with bitter disputes between news workers and their employers, general labour militancy, and the growing independence movement. The October Crisis of 1970, when the Trudeau government imposed the War Measures Act in response to political kidnappings, was a moment of truth, revealing stark fractures between the political and media cultures of Quebec and anglo-Canada.[48]

Some observers reach further back for the origins of antigovernment political journalism in Canada, to Parliament's great 1956 pipeline debate. David Taras summarizes that watershed event:

> After introducing a controversial bill that would offer government financial support for the building of the Trans-Canada pipeline, the St. Laurent government invoked closure to prevent debate at every stage of the bill's passage; in fact, closure was moved immediately upon the bill's introduction by C.D. Howe. Emotions were at a fever pitch on all sides of the House, and journalists were caught in the swirl of controversy and partisanship. The Press Gallery felt itself in a peculiar moral dilemma. Since the opposition's voice was being stifled, many in the press now felt that it was their obligation to do the work of the opposition and criticize government policy.[49]

Speaking from his own involvement as both a columnist and a reporter in Ottawa at the time, George Bain sees the pipeline debate as having direct implications for journalists' self-concept: "The doctrine of the time said reporters were observers; they saw, they heard, they made notes and they wrote. But this was an important and exciting game and there was a pleasurable sense of not just observing but being part of it. In addition, it was not always easy, writing a new lead at midnight with the House in an uproar, to keep the two jobs, news and comment, surgically separated."[50]

Disregarding the philosophical problem of whether reports can *ever* be devoid of judgement, Bain concludes that the debate helped to legitimate "the intrusion of the reporter's judgement into accounts of events," an intrusion that grew during the television era "to the point that news became virtually indistinguishable from commentary."[51]

All these developments have undoubtedly influenced journalism since the 1960s. Critical advocacy journalism, the reporting of events from an explicit and oppositional viewpoint, gained a new lease on life in the 1960s, most evident in the blooming of the "underground" papers of the youthful "counterculture," as well as in new alternative magazines such as *Canadian Dimension* and *This Magazine*. In the United States a movement known as New Journalism began to emphasize fictional techniques and first-person experiences to offer subjective interpretations of social issues and political events.[52] The New Journalist rejected the goal of objectivity and instead became "a living and breathing part of the story," searching for "the hidden truths that lie in human consciousness and memory."[53]

In the mainstream press the Watergate scandal and the subsequent resignation of Nixon in 1974 inaugurated a wave of scandal-hunting investigative journalism in the following years. Political journalism seemed to adopt a generally cynical tone towards politicians and their motives, reducing their actions to the pursuit of electoral advantage – or worse, raw power, sex, or money. In covering government policies, the press would often emphasize hostile reactions while barely sketching the actual policy. A recent case in point is *The Vancouver Sun*'s front-page treatment of the release of the B.C. NDP government's budget of March 29, 1995, a release marred by a mysterious advance leak of budget highlights to the Victoria *Times Colonist*. The headline preceding budget day read, "'SMOKE AND MIRRORS' FORECAST IN B.C. BUDGET" and led with sceptical statements from Liberal opposition leader Gordon Campbell. On budget day the *Sun* greeted readers with "LEAKY BUDGET 'WON'T HOLD WATER'" over two stories, one on the leak and the other on business reaction to the budget: "'REAL BUT SKINNY' SURPLUS DRAWS LUKEWARM REVIEWS." Readers had to scour the inside pages for (rather skimpy) details of the budget itself.

There is some validity, then, to perceptions of the adversarial media, but it is important to recognize that critical journalism in the mainstream media has not been entirely hostile to authority; and in any case the practices considered to constitute critical journalism are not typical of the news media's daily performance. Many of these practices are either in decline or have been confined to the margins. Investigative journalism that aims to uncover wrongdoing by individual powerholders has ebbed since the late

1970s. The political climate became more conservative, and exposés of culturally legitimated and even mythologized institutions such as the Royal Canadian Mounted Police were disconcerting to audiences. Media owners themselves were reluctant to invest in legally risky and time-consuming investigations with uncertain payoffs.[54] In his relatively sympathetic history of *The Globe and Mail,* business writer David Hayes notes the rapid displacement of investigative reporting by something rather less critical: "The enthusiasm for mounting costly, speculative muckraking projects had declined in the post-Watergate era.... Instead, at a time when television was robbing North American papers of their timeliness and their younger readers, many of them, including the *Globe,* increased their coverage of social trends and leisure pursuits – sometimes lumped together under the title 'lifestyle.'"[55]

As well, those practices of critical journalism that have found a place in the major media can be conceptualized not as *departures from* the ethos of objectivity, but rather as *developments of* particular aspects of it. The negative tone and the superficially hostile treatment of politicians can be traced to the universalizing impulses of the nineteenth-century rebels against the partisan press. Today's adversarial political journalism, after all, can claim (however dubiously) to be non-partisan in its negativity and to speak on behalf of all of us, the general public, a universal or commonsensical perspective above and beyond political parties and special interests.

Likewise, the investigative journalism of the 1970s can trace its roots to the U.S. muckraking journalism of the turn-of-the-century Progressive era and to the democratic storyline of the earlier commercial popular press. Although it is critical in intention and controversial in character, the approach remains "objective in manner."[56] It is still expected to respect such requirements as factuality, balance, and neutral presentation. According to one Vancouver newspaper reporter, investigative stories tend in practice to be scrutinized extremely carefully to ensure that the conventions of objectivity are followed, and that "they appear to be completely objective."[57]

Those aspects of critical journalism that really are departures from the ethos of objectivity, however broadly defined, have been pushed to the margins. Politically progressive advocacy is almost entirely confined to alternative periodicals and to books, especially by dedicated smaller publishers. It takes a talent as prodigious as Linda McQuaig's to break into the realm of the larger mass publishers, but even her incisive critiques of economic policy barely penetrate the daily press, with the exception perhaps of the book review sections and a publicly declared preference by media mogul Conrad Black that she be horsewhipped.[58]

By contrast the voices of market-liberalism have enjoyed much greater media access. Their affinity with elite interests makes it easier to attract sponsors and advertisers, and they have captured (and worked mightily to promote) a rightward shift in the popular imagination. Nevertheless, even in a press swarming with right-wing columnists, explicit advocacy is still supposed to be kept off the news pages. However much they are converging, explicitly and self-consciously conservative periodicals are still distinguishable from mainstream "objective" news media. For instance, the Western Canadian newsmagazine *B.C. Report*, which weaves its Christian fundamentalist and conservative economic ideology into news reports, does not even attempt to present itself as objective.

In addition to critical or adversary journalism, other movements have arisen to try to adjust or correct perceived flaws in North American journalism. A veteran U.S. journalist and scholar, J. Herbert Altschull, identifies nine such movements in recent decades. A brief review of these movements shows that, to date, none have dethroned the objectivity ethos. *Interpretive* journalism has been incorporated within the ethos, and *investigative* journalism and *adversary/critical* journalism are aspects of it, along with their close cousin, *enterprise* journalism. The enterprise journalist digs behind the "facts" supplied by sources to discover the context or truth behind the facts – but she or he remains an objective reporter "by concealing his or her own opinions."[59]

Precision journalism is a pragmatic relative of interpretive and enterprise journalism, one entirely concerned with method and technique. Inspired by the empirical social sciences, the precision journalist conducts her own research, using public and official documents, census data, surveys, and computer-aided analysis, rather than simply random interviews. The precision journalist intensifies rather than challenges the prevailing ethos: "His values are scientific detachment and he adopts the yardstick of objectivity."[60]

Celebrity journalism is not a philosophy, but rather a development associated with the predominance of commercial television in North American news media. Network news anchormen, celebrities for decades, have been joined more recently from the fringes of journalism by the hosts of "tabloid" TV talk shows. It could be argued that they depart from, and even threaten, the ethos: "The celebrity journalist is not an objective observer but rather teacher or guide. He interprets, but he also expresses his own opinions; he stands aloof, perhaps even above those of whom he writes or speaks."[61]

But surely "standing aloof" is one of the hallmarks of objectivity. Newscasters may be celebrities, but they are marketed in terms of their credibility and trustworthiness, qualities they are assumed to earn precisely due to their alleged ability to speak wisely, on behalf of all of us, and to "stand aloof" from any narrow or partisan biases. Otherwise, why should Canadian viewers be asked to believe Lloyd Robertson when he rhythmically closes the CTV *National News* with "That's the kind of day it's been," a claim of near-omniscience only slightly more modest than Walter Cronkite's own ritual truth-assurance for an earlier generation of TV viewers: "That's the way it is."

Only three of the nine movements that Altschull identifies have unambiguously challenged the objectivity ethos. All of them have been confined or marginalized. *Advocacy* journalism, which frankly supports a cause, is still demarcated from professional reporting in the mainstream media. Many of the *underground papers* of the 1960s counterculture died or moved "aboveground" into more conventional journalism. Vibrant alternative media still exist throughout North America, some of them survivors of the 1960s, others emerging with a later generation, but their conscious rejection of objectivity or other factors keeps them clearly distinct from the dominant corporate media.

As for the subjectivity of *New Journalism*, while it has influenced the weekend supplements, it too has found expression mainly outside the daily news media – for example, in magazines such as *Rolling Stone* or books by Tom Wolfe, Norman Mailer, and others.[62] Although some of the practitioners of these forms of journalism eventually won prestige, their reputations were not earned within mainstream journalism. Rather, they were renowned as "New Journalists," although one of their number, Jack Newfield, questioned the very label, equating his approach with the much older tradition of advocacy journalism: "To begin with, there is not that much new about new journalism. Advocacy preceded the who-what-when-where-why of the AP by a couple of centuries. Tom Paine and Voltaire were New Journalists, so was John Milton when he wrote his Areopagitica against government censorship in the seventeenth century."[63]

Thus, while advocacy journalism, which had a historic tradition, was labelled as "new" and extreme, "objective" journalism, which is also historically specific, tends to be seen as the natural, proper, and undisputably legitimate form of journalism.

A Love-Hate Relationship

It seems fair to conclude, with Schudson, that while there is "simmering disaffection with objective reporting," no new ideal in North American journalism has successfully challenged it.[64] Apart from institutional imperatives, journalists themselves also have important stakes in the ethos of objectivity. To be sure, the rules of objectivity constrain and discipline journalists, suppressing their creativity and initiative at work. The approach can induce a sense of helplessness or frustration with the processes and consequences of news work.

For instance, apart from sadistically malicious gossips, most people normally would not relish disseminating statements they know to be lies. Yet the practices of "straight" reporting, and conventional criteria of newsworthiness, seemed to require journalists to do just that, when powerful politicians made false accusations. Their guilt and frustration with this practice came to the surface in the 1950s, in the McCarthy era.[65] The rules of objectivity offer would-be news manipulators openings for access, particularly for established sources, and constrain journalists from being openly adversarial: they must instead seek out opposing voices (preferably governmental or other respectable, institutional authorities) willing to go on the record.[66]

Playing the old-fashioned objectivity game strictly, journalists are denied the powers of informed observation, encouraged to depend on established authority for definitions of reality, and discouraged from developing the habits and skills of challenging the self-interested view of official sources. They are constrained to believe that to "accept contradictions is to be objective, to question them is to be subjective."[67] To demonstrate their objectivity, journalists sometimes bend over backwards to produce reports that contradict their own personal views. Sometimes, as if in desperation, journalists have found ways to incorporate their own interpretations and analysis by selecting and quoting like-minded sources. This seemingly strange ritual is one response to the straitjacket of objectivity.

The requirements of objectivity even impinge on journalists' own basic political rights as individual citizens. Canadian newspaper editors generally believe "that a newspaper's reputation for objectivity or impartiality would be harmed if its journalist employees were observed to be engaged in political activity."[68] Some major media employers explicitly and contractually prohibit journalists from publicly expressing political views or engaging in political activities, even on their own time.[69] (Interestingly, media management has no such squeamishness about the extensive and interlocking political and economic connections of media owners.) One political reporter from a Toronto newsroom suggested that although he had a strong personal loyalty to a particular political party, he would be "finished" in his job if his political leanings become known publicly.[70] Sometimes journalists are forced to choose between their jobs and their political activities.

Objectivity, in short, situates the journalist as an "outsider," as a spectator of political reality. Journalists are not supposed to make claims, engage in arguments, or make judgements between contending positions. Carried to extremes, the rituals of objectivity deny journalists the opportunity to exercise the intellectual faculty of independent judgement and their citizenship right to be engaged in political activities. Objectivity expresses the alienation of journalists' intellectual labour under commercial relations of news production.

Still, journalists as an occupational group also have important stakes in the ethos of objectivity. A range of evidence, including academic research based on participant observation, interviews, and surveys of journalists, demonstrates their continuing commitment to objectivity. In the United States a 1974 survey found that 98 per cent of reporters and editors polled "virtually defined journalism as adherence to the norm of objectivity," to such an extent that they adopt "habits of mind, attitudes, and personal characteristics which depend on and are structured around, the ideal of objective reporting." From her own and other studies, the author concluded that "the norm of objectivity forms the core of the defining logic and mission of news creation."[71] Similarly, a 1982 survey of 153 U.S. journalists found that most of them all but equated ethics with "objective" news coverage.[72] More recently, a journalism professor and former reporter described objectivity as "the fuel that fires journalism's engine, an ideal and an ideology."

> It is the way a reporter approaches his sources, his material, and his public; it is the hidden frame of reference around which the U.S. press organizes its existence; it is an unwritten guide book that is passed on, unquestioningly, from one generation of journalists to another. To some it is a god and to others a devil. Some journalists embrace it and others damn it.[73]

Journalism schools, ethics textbooks, and written ethics codes continue to privilege the ideal of objectivity. In the United States the code of ethics of the Society of Professional Journalists, Sigma Delta Chi, highlights objectivity as "the mark of an experienced professional," a "standard of performance toward which we strive." The code stresses accuracy, the separation of news from opinion and advocacy, non-partisanship, and the use of qualified sources – all components of the ethic of objectivity.[74]

Journalists are attracted to the ethos of objectivity because, at one level, it expresses a sense of professional responsibility and awareness about the impact of news stories. As the most significant scholarly study of news production ever undertaken in Canada suggests:

> Appreciating that their craft is a creative enterprise, journalists recognize the need to be sensitive to the possible impact of their work. If one is telling stories about real people, then the consequences for those people must be taken into account. This consideration is especially salient because news mostly deals with imputations of deviance and efforts at control, and itself can have social-control effects. Journalism has attempted to manage this aspect in terms of notions of objectivity, balance, and fairness.... Since journalists are interpreters of other people's lives and organizational arrangements, they must strive to be fair with these people and offer an objective and balanced view of their affairs.[75]

Although such professional ethics are undoubtedly important and sincere, objectivity provides a means by which journalists can negotiate their social status and enhance their public legitimacy. It underpins their claims to autonomy and status. In common with people in other white-collar occupations, including professors, doctors, scientists, and lawyers, journalists have sometimes claimed professional status by virtue of possessing specialized skills that are exercised ethically and objectively. As Graham Knight suggests, the cultivation of objectivity and professionalism in journalism was closely linked to the emergence of a new middle class of salaried intellectuals employed in bureaucratic institutions. By contrast with the old middle class of self-employed commodity producers, the work orientation and career commitment of this new middle class are based on ideals of objectivity and ethical neutrality.[76] As Walter Lippmann once claimed, reporting could not be considered a profession until "modern objective journalism was successfully created, and with it, the need of men who would consider themselves devoted, as all the professions ideally are, to the service of truth alone."[77]

The modern commercial media are both commercial and political institutions. Journalists thus serve two lords: profits, and the truth. The pursuit of professionalism and objectivity enables journalists to dramatize the cultural and political meanings of their work (as the fourth estate, defenders of the public good), while downplaying their function as employees of profit-driven corporations. It likewise provides some degree of psychological comfort, social legitimation, and practical insulation vis-à-vis the compromises that the editorial side of the daily newspaper must make with its business side.[78]

Objectivity, therefore, reinforces an occupational self-image of independent truth-seeking and serves social and psychological needs for journalists. That observation in no way calls into question their integrity and sincerity, and we cheerfully concede that the same point applies to the cherished concepts of academic freedom and scholarly rigour in universities.

Nor do we want to imply that occupational psychology *explains* the longevity of the objectivity ethos. That ethos, we repeat, is fostered within an organizational environment. Large media corporations with complicated structures of ownership and control have replaced the family-owned outlets of yesteryear; and until recently, patterns of concentrated ownership and monopoly markets have been relatively stable. That stability, the infrequency of dramatic property transactions, and the infrequency of direct (as distinct from potential) ownership intervention in daily editorial decisions all reinforce journalists' feeling of insulation from their corporate employers. That sense of insulation almost makes it possible to believe in the disinterested pursuit of truth. When they do occur, newspaper closures and other heavy-handed ownership machinations tend to make news workers more cynical about journalism – just as top-down university administrators may have a disillusioning impact upon academics.[79]

It is not surprising, then, that the interventionist style of a new breed of owners, including Rupert Murdoch and Conrad Black, has ruffled many a newsroom feather.[80] These owners' headlong media acquisitions, their blunt exercise of ownership power, their intrusive newsroom behaviour, their hand-rubbing interest in the economic performance of their properties, and their apparent disrespect for cherished journalism ideals sharply expose the economic forces and power relations underlying the fourth estate.

Roy Megarry's 1989 transformation of *The Globe and Mail*, for example, generated considerable protest and criticism among the journalistic community at the time.[81] Apparently undertaken in response to competition from the new daily *Financial Post*, critics perceived the changes as "Thomsonizing" the paper. The strengthening of *The Report on Business*, the abandonment of the labour beat in favour of a more management-oriented approach, and the appointment of business-oriented senior editors "completely beholden to Megarry" were seen as measures to woo the business community at the expense of the *Globe*'s objectivity and its status as Canada's national newspaper of record. David Hayes, writing relatively favourably of Megarry's management achievements, nevertheless noted the reaction of those who saw the *Globe* as a cultural institution following Megarry's decision to reduce costly circulation in low-return rural areas:

> Was this part of Megarry's noble vision, tailoring the *Globe* to a wealthy urban elite at the expense of intelligent readers who fell outside the ad community's ideal consumer? In the April issue of *Editor and Publisher* ... he was quoted as saying: "By 1990, publishers of mass circulation daily newspapers will finally stop kidding themselves that they are in the newspaper business and admit that they are primarily in the business of carrying advertising messages."[82]

To journalists' ears such an admission may well sound like fingernails on a blackboard. "*The Globe* is going to become Canada's *Wall Street Journal*," lamented Walter Stewart, "a slick and single-minded publication designed for and devoted to the interests of a small, ad-buying portion of the community."[83] This lament implies, debatably, that left in the hands of autonomous journalists and claiming to serve the entire public, the *Globe* had previously presented a genuinely universal and objective perspective.

Objectivity Is Dead! Long Live Objectivity!

We cannot agree, then, with those journalists and scholars who regard objectivity as simply hackneyed and obsolete. One of Canadian journalism's most respected practitioners and educators suggested a few years ago that journalism had experienced a rupture in its entire cosmology. It had "undergone a revolutionary process in recent decades that parallels ... the effect of relativity on physics," wrote Peter Desbarats. "As scientists abandoned the idea of absolute time, journalists lost faith in the value of objectivity, until then one of the constants of the craft."[84]

This sweeping claim is both less persuasive and more modest than it might first appear. To start, Desbarats defines objectivity narrowly – as the journalistic stance of being a neutral "camera," a "who-what-where-when-why" machine, a stenographer recording the statements of newsworthy people without any injection of subjective bias.[85] Desbarats quite rightly doubts that such practices can generate truth, but his assertion that the old model had been replaced (by what is unclear) is not convincing. Desbarats's quote may indeed reflect journalists' widespread distrust of the possibility of objective reporting, but a crucial distinction must be made between news workers' personal doubts and beliefs, and the institutional processes and imperatives that hugely influence the practices and products of the job. Journalists may deny the possibility of achieving objectivity or even avoid the term altogether in their language, but they cannot simply discard it as a regulatory principle for journalism. The introduction to the 1992 version of the Montreal *Gazette*'s stylebook is illustrative:

> If you want to display your creative power or your sophistication or the scope of your intellect – or for that matter, if your purpose is to lead mankind to global peace, universal love and an end to leghold trapping – you're not in the right place.... Be reserved and dispassionate. Avoid over-familiarity.... Avoid words that suggest how you feel about something. Just tell them what you know. Let them decide how to feel. They have a right to draw their own conclusions. Your job is to decide what the point is – and get to it.[86]

Moreover, some of Desbarats's own statements indicate that in newsrooms, even if objectivity is a walking zombie, it still commands fear and obedience. Desbarats does concede, "If journalists have become more adept at identifying their own biases, this process must still remain private; in public, neutrality must be maintained." But if objectivity is indeed dead, why then must bias be treated like masturbation – something to be kept hidden, acknowledged in general but rarely admitted in specifics? Desbarats also concedes that "average newspaper readers or television viewers ... continue to expect objective truth (or at least some effort to approach it)."[87] That too is a significant admission, because if they are to attract audiences profitably, commercial news media must attempt to satisfy (or at least avoid violating) audience expectations.

Objectivity may well be on its death bed in the social sciences and other fields, and in poor health even in journalism.[88] Most likely, many journalists, especially younger ones, regard objectivity with a sense of detached irony: it is not an ideal to be personally embraced, but a set of institutional rules and routines to be followed. But that is precisely the point. We have tried to suggest why an eminent media sociologist has called news institutions "the strongest remaining bastion of logical positivism in America," and why one of Desbarats's reviewers called objectivity, because it still obliges reporters to follow its routines, "a god that won't die."[89]

We must address one last premature obituary for the ethos of objectivity. This is the claim that journalists have found objectivity an ideal too broad, pretentious, and unachievable. Instead, they prefer to pursue the more modest goals of fairness, balance, and (more recently) credibility. The proclamation of veteran journalist and author Walter Stewart in 1980, "Fairness, yes, balance, yes, but objectivity, no," has become virtually an occupational mantra. Knowlton Nash, CBC's avuncular and horn-rimmed icon of national TV news, follows suit: "Objectivity is impossible because every human being has personal views and biases, but we do try to be fair and balanced." And the Kent Commission wrote that "the notion of fairness has replaced objectivity," which was discredited by the McCarthyist experience and by 1960s protest groups who saw objectivity as "a hypocritical neutrality that camouflaged complicity with those in power."[90]

To some extent, "fairness" does imply a subtle shift in news practice towards a greater recognition of subjectivity in news judgement, because somebody has to decide what constitutes fair treatment, and who deserves it. As its premise, this approach assumes "that journalists were biased sources of information who had to work to identify those biases and take them into account as they strove for accuracy and fairness."[91] Indeed, interpretive, investigative, and pseudo-adversarial journalism have shifted news work away from the uncritical reporting of official statements, prevalent during the 1950s, a practice that some commentators rather narrowly equate with "objective journalism." But on the whole, as a U.S. political communication scholar argues persuasively, "fairness" constitutes old wine in new rhetorical bottles.[92] Fundamentally, it has neither transformed the practice of news work nor resolved the problems that critics have perceived with objectivity. Fairness still implies the same old claim – that news is basically impartial, and independent of particular interests. Frequently defined in practice as a matter of reducing complex issues to two sides and giving them approximately equal time, fairness can be conceptualized as a component of the more abstract ideal of objectivity, rather than as a substitute for it. Much the same could be said of the latest buzzword, "credibility." To be accepted as credible by media audiences, news reports must surely embody those same perceived characteristics of accuracy, fairness, and impartiality.

Still, the restlessness within journalism's culture vis-à-vis the ethos of objectivity suggests that journalists' endorsement cannot alone account for its persistence. In the next chapter, we consider the social relations and structural "logics" that make objectivity not simply an occupational ethos, but an institutionalized regime.

3

Institutional Logics:
Why It Still Pays
to Be Objective

By 1900 the daily newspaper had emerged as the world's first mass medium. The press had become an industry, and news had become a commodity produced within a media system dominated by commercial logic. The triumph of that logic was almost inevitable once the Victorian-era people's journals began enlarging their circulations to attract advertisers, evolving into large-scale integrated organizations geared to growth. "Consumer journalism" oriented towards capturing as much as possible of the mass market became the norm during the early part of the century,[1] just as technological developments and larger circulation sizes made newspaper publishing more capital-intensive and costly.

Especially in times of recession, with pinched advertising revenues and advertisers gravitating towards papers with larger circulation – even if just slightly larger – some papers could not meet these increased costs. The papers that got more advertisers thus gained more money to spend in attracting still more readers and advertisers. Competition and independent ownership in the industry began to fade, as smaller fish died or were eaten by the bigger fish – and as newspapers faced new competition, first from radio and then from television.

After the 1920s the technologies and institutions of broadcasting transformed the North American mediascape, including the practices of journalism. As a mass medium, radio came into its own in the 1920s and 1930s. Initially dominated by private and U.S. stations, radio's development in Canada was spearheaded from 1932 by the publicly owned Canadian Radio Broadcasting Commission, which was replaced by the CBC in 1936. As a medium for journalism, radio initially laboured in the shadow of the press, but by World War II the immediacy of its reports was attracting mass audiences. Today CBC Radio remains an important national news medium, but radio news in the private stations has on the whole been in decline since the 1970s.[2] Moreover, the national radio networks (again with the exception of CBC) were largely displaced by television, which became a mass medium in the 1950s and the leading source of news for North American audiences in the late 1960s and 1970s.

With their immediacy and apparent veracity, radio and television have strongly influenced the expectations of audiences and the occupational culture of journalism. At the same time, given their national cultural importance and the limited number of broadcasting frequencies, radio and television have engendered a greater degree of state regulation and policy – including public financing and ownership of the CBC, which operates with a legally mandated independence from the government of the day. Notwithstanding the CBC and the relatively smaller U.S. Public Broadcasting Service (PBS), however, North American broadcasting is dominated by a commercial logic similar to that of newspapers. The goal is to attract audiences whose attention can be sold to advertisers.

Canada's Corporate Press Today

While audiences regard television as their primary source of news, the "elite" dailies and the print-oriented news services such as Canadian Press still tend to set the agenda for the news system as a whole, especially at the national level.

During the past century Canada's daily newspaper industry has developed distinct structural characteristics, which include its far greater dependence on revenues from advertisers than on readers and its tendency towards monopoly within local markets: few cities have competing dailies. Ownership is concentrated: the industry is dominated by a handful of "chains," companies that own a string of papers in different cities. Moreover, papers are increasingly owned by conglomerates, corporate empires with a range of holdings in different industries. These characteristics are not the result of some malevolent conspiracy. They are by-products of the commercial logic of the press, operating within an industrial capitalist economic system, and a legal framework that in effect defines freedom of the press as freedom from government intervention.

Newspaper chains began to emerge in Canada at the start of the century. As early as 1912 the Southam group already controlled important dailies in

Hamilton, Ottawa, Calgary, and Edmonton. Since then the shift towards concentrated press ownership has never stopped; indeed, it accelerated in the mid-1990s. For many years, two major chains, Southam and Thomson, dominated the Canadian newspaper industry. By summer 1996, the politically archconservative Conrad Black, after buying a dozen Thomson papers and a regional chain in Saskatchewan, had swallowed Canada's largest chain, Southam, which was itself still digesting a southern Ontario chain it bought in February 1996. By the end of the year Black's company Hollinger, with 58 of Canada's 104 daily newspapers as well as titles in the United States, Britain, Israel, and Australia, comprised the third largest newspaper empire in the world.

Between them Canada's top three chains control 72 per cent of national daily circulation.[3] "Independent" dailies (published by a company owning no other dailies) are few and far between. English-Canada's most important independent daily, *The Toronto Star*, is also the largest, but its parent, Torstar Corporation, is itself a multimedia conglomerate owning twenty-seven Toronto-area community papers and other ventures.

Concentration is magnified within Canada's regions. With the notable exception of *Le Devoir*, all the dailies in Quebec are part of three chains owned by Paul Desmarais, Conrad Black, and Pierre Peladeau respectively. The Irving family, owners of a huge conglomerate with more than three hundred businesses, controls all four English-language daily newspapers in New Brunswick, while Black owns all ten dailies in the provinces of Newfoundland, Prince Edward Island, and Saskatchewan.

Chains arose for several reasons. Compared to independents, chains had more access to the capital funds and administrative expertise required by the modern paper. Chains also enjoy economies of scale, finding it easier to attract national advertising contracts, or to buy newsprint in bulk. Their deep pockets have enabled them to renovate and upgrade money-losing papers, to keep papers alive during prolonged work stoppages, and to outlast and undercut competing independent papers.[4]

Just as newspaper chains began to emerge nationally, competition in newspaper markets began to shrink locally. The golden age of the popular press, when a city of 200,000 people might have had five or six competing dailies, soon went the way of silent movies and the Model-T Ford. The number of dailies in Canada peaked at 138 in 1913. Between 1914 and 1922, forty of them were swallowed up by rivals pursuing a larger market share. By the 1920s the metropolitan newspaper had come to be regarded as a kind of franchise, a "privately owned utility, free of any government control or regulation and enormously lucrative if managed correctly."[5]

Today most Canadian cities sustain only a single daily. In the several markets that still support two or more dailies, one is typically a Southam broadsheet, an "omnibus" paper trying to reach the broadest possible market, while the other is a tabloid (typically in the *Toronto Sun* chain) oriented towards working-class readers and a generation of television-oriented media consumers. At the other end of the market spectrum, *The Globe and Mail*'s national edition with its strong international and business news reaches "upscale" readers. While newspapers do compete with other media for advertising dollars, there is much less direct competition *within* the industry for readers or editorial content by comparison with the early part of the century.

Once a newspaper has killed off a competitor and acquired a monopoly, it is difficult to dislodge. Typically, it is quite profitable due to economies of scale. Taking over its former competitor's readership, the surviving paper can reach many more readers and charge much more for advertising space, without greatly increasing its production or distribution costs. Furthermore, a monopoly paper is protected from new competition by increasingly high start-up costs and the difficulty of luring readers and advertisers away from an established paper.

Typically high profits earned in monopoly markets have fuelled the growth of chains. From the viewpoint of economic rationality, the best way for a company to redeploy such monopoly profits is not to invest in better journalism, but to start buying up other newspapers, thus extending and maximizing the skills, resources, and economies of scale it already enjoys.[6] High profits also attract investment from conglomerates looking for "cash cows" to feed corporate growth.

Conversely, chain ownership has sometimes directly hastened the process of monopoly, as competing newspaper groups agree to exchange their shares of different markets. Canadian journalism's "Black Tuesday" provided a dramatic example of such a trade-off. On August 27, 1980, Southam closed its *Tribune* to grant the Thomson-owned *Free Press* a monopoly in Winnipeg, while on the same day Thomson closed the Ottawa *Journal*, leaving the Southam-owned *Citizen* alone to reap profits in the national capital.

Unfettered commercial logic, therefore, has led to a newspaper structure characterized by concentrated ownership and monopoly markets; and the broadcasting media don't necessarily provide an alternative to the logic of monopoly and commercialism in the press. Many of the newspaper industry's characteristics – the profit orientation, the commercial need to attract audiences whose attention is sold to advertisers – prevail in broadcasting too. Light-handed regulation by the Canadian Radio-television and Telecommunications Commission and the presence of the publicly owned CBC only slightly modify the system's logic of commercialism. Privately owned radio and television stations have the lion's share of resources and audiences; they are even more dependent than the print media are on advertising revenue (97 per cent in the case of English-Canadian commercial radio stations, for example).

Moreover, notwithstanding its mandate to provide non-commercial programming, which it does particularly well in its radio networks, the CBC has to fit into a pattern of mass communication established by North America's commercial media. The CBC must also compete for mass audiences to win political support for its annual parliamentary subsidy. Its television networks depend in part on advertising revenue and, to reach part of their audiences, on privately owned affiliate stations. The commercializing pressures on CBC are likely to intensify; the latest retrenchment plan, in autumn 1996, introduced advertising to CBC's national TV newscasts. As a series of funding cuts jeopardizes its revenues and even its very existence, CBC is increasingly challenged to provide an effective counterweight to commercial broadcasting.

The emergence of pay-TV services represents another potential modification to the logic of commercialism. According to its promoters, pay-TV gives more direct power to consumers over media programming – especially in a pay-per-view scenario, in which viewers select individual programs rather than simply subscribe to an optional cable channel. But such services do not entirely escape the biases of commercialism. Affluent consumers have far more power than the less affluent, and even their dollars are not able to override the conformism of television programming, a homogeneity imposed by high production costs that must be recouped over a broad market. The Atlanta-based Cable News Network (CNN) is available to Canadian cable subscribers; but like the conventional TV networks, CNN's journalism takes a broad-common-denominator approach.

Thus, despite the continuing importance of public broadcasting, the dominant institutional forms of journalism in Canada are private and corporate-owned, advertising-based, profit-oriented, and generally profitable media organizations. Although owners such as Conrad Black and (in Britain and the United States) Rupert Murdoch may be partially returning the press to an age of explicit partisanship, most media organizations are owned by conglomerates or shareholders more interested in balance sheets than in either journalism or politics – except as these impinge on their commercial or business interests. In other words, news media as corporations still have political interests, but these do not necessarily influence the news as directly as in the days of the partisan press. Market structures and commercial logic, rather than partisanship as such, have become the primary context of journalism.

Commercial Logic, Editorial Consequences

At both the macrolevel of audience production in media markets and the microlevel of news production in the newsroom, the political economy of the news media has important links with the ethos of objectivity. A number of analytically distinct but interacting forces of the dominant commercial logic – cost-optimization, homogenization, non-partisanship, depoliticization, consumerism, marginalization of progressive alternatives, specialization, and legitimation – help to constitute journalism's regime of objectivity.

From the viewpoint of the corporations that dominate the production of news, journalism is a means of earning a profit in a market, rather than a form of cultural and political expression valued in its own right. In its favour, the logic of the system is to distribute news cheaply and efficiently to consumers – but only as a by-product of attracting consumers in order to sell their attention to advertisers. From a strictly business viewpoint, a newspaper's incentive is to devote as much space as possible to paid advertising. By contrast, while journalism is needed to attract readers to the advertising, it is a *cost to be met as economically as possible*, rather than a direct means of generating revenue. The industry term "news-hole," the space not filled by advertising, is a prime indication of this attitude.[7]

Monopoly papers are particularly given to trimming editorial spending, even though they are generally quite profitable, because there is little economic incentive to do otherwise. Why spend extra money on more reporters or better-researched stories if you are already reaching the whole market, and if there is virtually no chance of a competitor moving in to fill the void?

Owners who spend more than the optimal amount for attracting audiences are vulnerable to takeover bids by less generous and more profit-oriented rivals. Family-owned firms proud of their journalistic standards have all but given way to shareholder-driven companies seeking maximum short-term profits. Canada's once formidable Southam chain had been praised by the 1980 Royal Commission on Newspapers for its generous editorial spending. In the hands of the far more cost-conscious Conrad Black the chain seemed set to take a different tact. Black and his associate David Radler have become legendary in the industry for "demanning" newsrooms and wringing high profits from their papers. Symptomatically, their first act after taking over the Saskatoon and Regina dailies in 1996 was to fire 182 employees.[8]

Such cutbacks have obvious significance for the general *quality* of journalism. Under the guiding principle of cost optimization, the *approach* to journalism becomes based even more strongly on a narrowly defined form of objectivity: straight, factual reporting. Straight reporting is typically reactive, consisting of reports of statements from legitimized sources. Such "straight" news is financially cheaper and legally safer to produce than (for example) investigative journalism, which consumes more time and other newsroom resources and carries a greater risk of lawsuits.

In their defence, chains do sometimes contribute to the quality and diversity of journalism. With their resources, they have sometimes transformed weeklies into dailies, upgraded technologically out-of-date papers, or originated news services (Southam News, for example) that independent papers could not afford on their own. But chains can also threaten journalistic diversity with the drift to *homogenization*, which is as much a matter of style as story content or editorial position. The imposition of a common editorial policy by chain owners remains an ongoing but infrequently attempted possibility. More significantly, chains often rationalize their economic resources by replacing local writers with the chain's own syndicated columnists. Even before the era of newspaper chains, the Canadian Press news agency was helping to standardize news copy and establish facticity as the norm.

Advertising provides an even more subtle but important homogenizing influence. As they compete for the same mass audiences, dailies seek to maximize audience size by tailoring editorial content (including news) to the broadest common denominator and thus conquering the core of that market. The commercial press is less interested in a loyal but limited special-interest readership than in the support, however lukewarm, of a broader readership. Thus, as one scholar notes:

> Insofar as newspapers are viewed primarily as a business with little emphasis on the "something else" which they are supposed to encompass, the tendency will be to find a middle ground position of its audience. Since the advent of the mass press, there has been an inherent tendency toward homogenization in newspaper content, just as there is an inexo-

rable tendency for political parties to move to the middle of the ideological spectrum so as to maximize their potential voter support. Thus the economics of efficiency tends to supersede the politics of diversity.[9]

If anything, the economic incentive to homogenize content for a broad audience is even stronger in commercial radio and network television. This is because of the high production costs of TV programs, TV's historical effectiveness at reaching mass rather than elite or segmented audiences, and the broadcasting logic of "flow," which places relentless pressure on every program to attract the largest demographically profitable audience at any given time. Newspapers, by contrast, can at least develop specialized sections for different segments of the readership market.

Related to homogenization, economic pressures also encourage *nonpartisanship* and *depoliticization* in the press. In the first place, as we have seen (chapter 1) the decline of overt political bias in newspapers was closely linked to the transformation of newspapers into politically independent commercial enterprises. The nineteenth-century ideal of objectivity was at once a political stance *and* a commercial imperative. The need to maximize audiences made it difficult for newspapers to continue functioning primarily as party organs. To avoid offending significant portions of the intended audience, news had to be perceived as impartial.[10]

At the same time, the commercially minded newspaper owners realized that a newspaper should contain something suited to every palate; fractious politics alone would hardly do. Following the lead of the penny press, dominant newspapers de-emphasized politics in favour of crime, high society, and human interest stories. This is not to say that the press was suddenly devoid of political values; topics like crime are often inherently political. Rather, the political values expressed in the commercial media tended increasingly to be implicit and hegemonic (dominant and consensual), rather than explicit, abrasive, and partisan.

This relative depoliticization was accompanied by an increasing emphasis on the reporting of "facts," an emphasis connected with the empiricist mood of the time. When *The New York Times* claimed that it simply presented "facts, in such a form and temper as to lend men of all parties to rely upon its statements," it was not only expressing a commitment to the democratic ideal of providing universally accessible facts for public enlightenment.[11] It was also articulating a shrewd business approach – that of selling a particular product called "news" to a general audience. In this context facts became equated to the news. Like other commodities in a capitalist economy, they were stripped of their origins and the particularities of production. As such, they came to be seen as having an equal, universal appeal to everyone in the marketplace, something people of all political persuasions could buy. They were naturalized, turned into something seemingly beyond artifice or question.

The flip side of such depoliticization is *consumerism*. Dallas Smythe argues that entertainment and information, which we are accustomed to regarding as media content, are little more than a "free lunch" designed to entice an audience to the most important content: the advertisements.[12] Not only must the free lunch attract an audience of appropriate size and demographics, but it must also cultivate a frame of mind appropriately receptive to the advertising messages.

The implications of this commercial imperative for news can be subtle but profound. For stories to be told intelligibly, the storyteller must make assumptions about the audience – what its members know and value, and what they do not. The same is true of news or any other discourse. The commercial press no longer assumed that readers were the followers of a particular party or faction, or even that they were active participants in political life. Instead, they increasingly addressed or positioned readers as citizens of the whole nation, as spectators of politics, and perhaps above all as consumers. This consumerist mode of address or narrative orientation is most evident in the fusion of "news" and advertising in the fashion, living, home, travel, sports, and leisure sections of Canadian dailies. Arguably, even the hard-news reports subtly complement the ads. In their selection and construction of stories, middle-market commercial news media appear to take the standpoint of the assumed average consumer. Coverage of labour-management disputes, for example, tends to focus on inconvenience and disruption to consumers. The labour press covering the same story would be more likely to emphasize the implications for working people, while the explicitly business press would have its own class vantage point, perhaps highlighting the impact of the disputes on investment opportunities and the labour market.

Thus, the non-partisanship and depoliticization of the mass-market press should not be confused (as they too often are) with absolute political neutrality or the absence of politically loaded values. In fact, a related implication of commercial logic is the *marginalization of progressive alternatives* in the news. The nineteenth-century transformation of the press into an advertising-based commercial enterprise in effect created a new form of press control within which advertisers became "a *de facto* licensing authority."[13]

Dependence on advertising revenue helped to marginalize the radical press and bolster a more conservative version of objectivity, pushing content away from the radical implications of the Enlightenment democratic discourse and towards a blander, less politicized non-partisanship. For one thing, large advertisers "disliked liberal and radical-left views that might raise questions about the role of big business."[14] By toning down liberal or radical political views in their editorials, news selection, and investigative initiatives, newspapers were more likely to attract conservative-minded advertisers. When, for instance, Montreal's *Daily Advertiser* expressed liberal sentiments in the polarized climate of 1838, advertisers withdrew and the paper folded.[15]

But quite apart from their own political interests, advertisers favoured newspapers that were most efficient at reaching potential customers. Advertisers of brand-name household products, for example, wanted to tap the mass market of middle-class as well as working-class consumers, whose relative lack of purchasing power as individuals was compensated by their large numbers. Newspapers that softened their political edges and emphasized human interest stories could more easily attract mass audiences.

Other advertisers sought not the mass markets of "popular papers" but the relatively small, affluent, and elite markets reached by "quality" papers with more politically conservative and well-educated readers. The content of these "quality" papers tends to reflect the conservative dispositions of their business and professional readers, but that does not mean that these dailies thereby abandon the ethos of objectivity. To the contrary: for political and cultural as well as economic reasons, they embrace it. Indeed, objectivity remains an essential factor in their appeal, and these papers are often seen as setting journalism's standards of objectivity and excellence. Although papers like *The Globe and Mail* and *The New York Times* are skewed towards affluent audiences with the greatest stake in the existing social system, the news may still seem to be objective in avoiding consistent favouritism towards a particular party or interest group, in covering "both sides" of issues, and in claiming to represent a general public interest. An elite paper's reputation for objectivity enhances its prestige. Given this approach, it is not surprising that the nineteenth-century radical labour papers were systematically driven to the margins of the market. As the Kent Commission on Newspapers admitted, "It was left-wing viewpoints that tended to be under-represented as commercialism increased its hold."[16]

The sheer size and *specialization* of newsroom staffs, driven by the logic of industrialization, further undermined old-style partisanship in news reporting. In complex news organizations, news is no longer a one-person product. The division of labour between owners, managers, editors, reporters, and columnists meant that "enforcing a standard political line became a more difficult proposition."[17] Moreover, occupational norms, such as criteria of objectivity and newsworthiness, provide journalism with a cushion against owners' potential partisanship. To be sure, commercial newspapers are hierarchical organizations; working journalists have no legally or professionally enforced guarantees of their autonomy, nor can autonomy be taken for granted in any clashes with ambitious and interventionist owners. Still, shared criteria have endured partly because they facilitate the efficient functioning of news organizations themselves. The constant pressure of deadlines does not permit news workers to frequently debate or clarify first principles.

In addition to economic imperatives, the twentieth-century development of concentration and monopoly in the newspaper industry has made objectivity a means of political *legitimation*. Concentration and monopoly mean that more and more people have become dependent upon fewer and fewer newspaper companies for detailed daily information. This reality has rendered obsolete the old liberal ideal of a competitive marketplace of ideas operating through a richly varied smorgasbord of partisan newspapers.

Accordingly, press owners have sometimes feared that governments might intervene to restore competition or to regulate newspapers, as governments tend to do with other monopolies. In Canada, that threat came closest to reality after journalism's "Black Tuesday" in 1980 and the subsequent Royal Commission report. While the politicians ultimately chose not to act on the Commission's report, the findings did succeed in briefly focusing public attention on press monopoly and concentration – which in turn highlighted the potential conflict of interest inherent in operations that act both as important providers of public information in a political democracy and privately owned businesses pursuing profit. The ethos of objectivity helps the commercial news media escape this dilemma and establish their own legitimacy as important if unofficial political institutions: the media can argue that the news is produced by autonomous professionals who put aside their personal biases. If their news is perceived to be objective, spoken from the perspective of everybody in general and nobody in particular, the private and commercial character of corporate media needs not be a source of public concern. It should not even be questioned; at least, so media owners hope.

The claim that they are offering objective news, then, helps media owners justify their oligopolistic domination of the public sphere and thereby pre-empt government regulation, meaningful public accountability, and effective competition from radically "alternative" media. Still, the primacy of this ethos of news objectivity is not just a matter of political and economic self-interest. There is not necessarily a rigid correlation between a capitalist economic context and a particular mode of journalism. For instance, the commitment to journalistic objectivity is more pronounced in North America than in other capitalist liberal democracies. The structure of Western European newspaper markets, combined with distinct national histories and press policies, permits a greater degree of open press partisanship.

As well, the political economy of media organizations can in itself produce shifts in news discourse and significant variations between media, leading to different articulations of the objectivity ethos. For instance, journalism has long been characterized by competition and tension between "news as information" and "news as entertainment." While "quality" papers and public broadcasting have historically set the idealized standards for journalism, and while Canada did not follow the British and U.S. trend towards "popular" tabloids earlier in the twentieth century, "news as entertainment" has always found a niche. Since the 1970s, testosterone-loaded tabloids such as *The Toronto Sun* have gained ground at the expense of the long-established middle-market broadsheets in the Canadian newspaper market. These papers appeal to their audiences not through dispassionate information, factuality, and balance, but through a style that purports to speak *for* the common people and *from* the universalizing perspective of "common sense." In the tabloids, objectivity assumes a different form, foreshadowed by the nineteenth-century popular press.

In addition to the economic and political self-interest of the commercial press, technological developments and the state's broadcasting and press policies have also helped to entrench the ethos of objectivity. Objectivity expresses more than the interests of media corporations; it has become part of technological, regulatory, and legal reality.

Technology and Objectivity

The adoption of the telegraph as a means of transmitting news, and the subsequent emergence of news agencies based on the telegraph, contributed significantly to the ethos of objectivity in journalism. The telegraph began to spread throughout Canada's budding press system during the 1850s. The cost and occasional unreliability of telegraph transmission encouraged journalists to organize their reports into brief factual dispatches, devoid of descriptive embellishment and commentary. And, as we've seen (chapter 2), the telegraph was midwife to a new form of newswriting, the inverted pyramid.

With the laying of the Atlantic cable in 1866, the telegraph became intercontinental. The new rapidity of news transmission triggered the rise of national and international news agencies or wire services, which distributed news to a variety of clients. More than most other news organizations, wire services are often taken as the standard-bearers of straight, factual reporting in North American journalism, and for good reason. From their inception the news agencies turned news into a wholesale commodity available to a range of subscribers – newspapers with different partisan orientations. To serve them all, the wire services had to provide middle-of-the-road, factual reportage, to which individual newspapers could add their own "spin" as they saw fit. In short, a non-partisan straight-facts style suits the political economy of news agencies.

Some media scholars attribute the very emergence of objective journalism to the telegraph and the wire services.[18] But such a reading of history attributes too much power to telegraph technology alone. Without doubt, the wire services further eroded partisanship in the press and facilitated the full-fledged development of the commercial dailies. But those who argue that the telegraph produced objectivity overlook the historical reality that telegraphy came into use *after* the U.S. penny press had articulated its non-partisan stand.[19] The penny papers were the first to exploit the telegraph, and they did this in a way that reinforced their own journalistic orientations. The wire service was a technological configuration "superimposed on a news-gathering system that already placed a premium on apparent factual accuracy."[20] As it increased the speed, efficiency, and economy of news-gathering, the wire service was a logical outgrowth of the political economy of the commercial news media.

The introduction of another technology, broadcasting, also had important implications for the ethos of objectivity. The authenticity and realism of radio sound were underscored in 1938 by Orson Welles's legendary dramatization of H.G. Wells's *War of the Worlds* – a broadcast that convinced thousands of Americans that a Martian invasion was actually happening. Television in particular brought new dimensions to the notion of objectivity. To be sure, television journalism seeks to establish its objectivity in ways quite different from the print media. In television news, factual accounts of the world are furnished with the sensual appeal of visual footage and the celebrity appeal of the news anchor and reporters. The conventional objectivity strategy of "balance" is personified and visualized by opposing interviewees on the screen or opposing groups in dramatic conflict-settings: government and opposition politicians trading abuse in Parliament, police arresting demonstrators. In print news the narrator's subjectivity was rendered as transparent as possible in an attempt to portray the world "out there" accurately and without bias.[21] In television journalism the transparency effect of reflecting the real is achieved not through suppressing the narrator's role, but rather through the illusions of television technology, which seems to enable the audience to see the world "out there" without human mediation.

Television journalism, again, has *reinforced* the ethos of non-partisanship. Its apparent visual truthfulness, no matter how illusory, has given it credibility with audiences and intensified the pressure on other media to avoid the appearance of bias. It is much better suited to conveying personalities and images than complex ideas or institutions. Within a commercialized media culture it has helped to transform political campaigns into contests that market political leaders' images rather than mobilize pre-existing partisan loyalties. Finally, TV news is consumed within a flow of programming consisting primarily of entertainment, and it often attracts viewers far hungrier for diversion than for information. In the last two decades, TV entertainment has increasingly adopted a stance of ironical but ultimately vacuous knowingness: nudge-nudge wink-wink to everything. Perhaps best epitomized by late-night talk-show host David Letterman, this "attitude" devalues and corrodes political commitment of any kind, let alone strong party preferences.

For all these reasons, some observers even see a direct link between the dominance of television as a news medium and a decline in the effectiveness of parties as political institutions.[22] Whether or not that conclusion is warranted, television has hastened the decline of partisanship in the press. It has tended to "put staunch partisans on the defensive" and to "legitimate attitudes of wariness and scepticism towards the political parties" among the broader public.[23]

Fairness and Balance in Broadcasting Regulation

Beyond broadcasting's own techno-logic, the state regulation of broadcasting has further entrenched journalism's ethos of objectivity. Most obviously, objectivity, often in its limited form of balance, has become an explicit *regulatory* requirement for news operations in broadcasting media. Unlike newspapers, which obtained their formal independence from government before they became a mass media industry, radio and television were regulated almost from birth. Based on the assumption of its scarcity, the radio spectrum is legally considered to be a public property, and broadcasting operations are regulated, and sometimes partly or wholly owned, by governments throughout the world. In Western countries, such regulation is typically conducted by a state agency operating with a public interest mandate at arm's length from the government of the day, which does not want the political headaches of directly awarding broadcasting licences to competing applicants.

Even in the United States, where free enterprise is virtually a national religion, radio licences have been awarded "as public convenience, interest, or necessity requires" since 1927 by a body now known as the Federal Communications Commission (FCC).[24] The commercial news media's proclaimed commitment to objectivity and the public interest became a criterion by which broadcasting resources were allocated. In the early 1930s the regulatory agency had already officially endorsed the commercial broadcasters' claim to objectivity, equating their perspective with the "neutral," "universal" perspective. Commercial broadcasters were seen as "general public service" broadcasters. Those stations that did not operate for profit and did not derive their revenues from the sale of advertising were regarded as "propaganda" stations, more interested in spreading their particular viewpoint than in providing impartial information. For the FCC, this assumption became the rationale behind allocating airwaves in favour of commercial broadcasters.[25] After the private commercial broadcasting system was firmly established, the ethos of objectivity became embodied in court rulings and FCC regulations surrounding the 1949 "Fairness Doctrine." Each broadcaster was required to maintain standards of fairness and balance by affording "reasonable opportunity for discussion of conflicting views on issues of public importance."[26]

The Fairness Doctrine did not open the airwaves equally to all perspectives: broadcasters had much leeway in deciding how to apply the doctrine, and the FCC itself disavowed any intention to mandate airtime for Communists or "the Communist viewpoints."[27] Even with these safeguards for the status quo, the Reagan administration repealed the Fairness Doctrine in 1987 in a frenzy of deregulation. Nevertheless, this specific action did not produce a fundamental questioning of the ethos of objectivity in regulatory thinking. Indeed, through osmosis and competition over time, the requirements of fairness, balance, and non-partisanship, originally mandated for broadcast journalism, have influenced the press as well.

Similarly, the concept of balance has served as an important regulatory principle in Canadian broadcasting too, with a lasting impact.[28] The 1968 Broadcasting Act, for instance, called upon broadcasters to "provide reasonable, balanced opportunity for the expression of differing views on matters of public concern."[29] The 1991 Broadcasting Act maintained this mandate and, indeed, specifically added clauses on equal rights for women and men, Canada's multicultural and multiracial nature, and the special place of Aboriginal peoples as criteria for broadcasting programming and employment.[30] In principle, the CRTC reviews the performance of broadcasters in meeting these mandates.

Since 1968 various CRTC statements, seminars, and inquiries have endorsed balance and objectivity as standards of journalism, implying a role for professional journalists as "the exclusive representatives of public debate."[31] Such semi-official endorsements further reinforce and legitimate the ethos of objectivity as well as the state-owned and private corporate media with which this ethos has come to be identified in broadcasting. To be sure, the CRTC does sometimes impose constraints upon the media; but at the same time it serves to legitimize and protect the power of media corporations that have economic and other incentives to maintain the appearance of objectivity and social responsibility. In practice, regulation has been light-handed since the 1970s. Stations may occasionally have their wrists slapped over perceived violations of the balance mandate, but rarely if ever has a station had its licence yanked for failure to comply with the Broadcasting Act's mandate. Indeed, some observers argue that notwithstanding its legal status as a public resource, the broadcasting spectrum has come to be treated in regulatory practice as virtually a form of private property.[32]

If anything, the ethos of balance and fairness was stronger in Canadian than U.S. broadcasting policy, even before the FCC repealed the Fairness Doctrine. In the first place, the CRTC has been inclined to apply the "balanced viewpoint" criterion to each and every broadcaster, rather than pursuing balance simply at the level of the system as a whole. In the United States, sectarian religious groups, for example, have been able to obtain licences for their own single-minded soapboxes of the air, especially on cable channels.[33] In rejecting this approach, the CRTC has made Canadian religious broadcasting (notably the specialty network Vision TV) more ecumenical.

Moreover, Canada has a much stronger tradition of public service broadcasting. However much it is threatened by current cutbacks to its budget, the state-owned CBC is far less marginalized than are PBS and National Public

Radio in the U.S. profit-driven system. During radio's early years, Canadian political and cultural elites feared that a system as heavily commercialized as that of the United States would have detrimental effects – too much advertising and entertainment at the expense of educational programming, too much programming originating outside Canada, too little program exchange between Canada's regions, too many stations crowding the profitable urban markets and too little service elsewhere, and the likelihood that, left to themselves, private commercial stations would affiliate with U.S. networks.[34] As a result of this thinking the Conservative government of R.B. Bennett created a publicly owned broadcasting service in 1932. Today the CBC has an explicit mandate to offer distinctively Canadian programming in both official languages throughout the country and to contribute to both interregional communication and "shared national consciousness."[35]

The CBC is not immune to the commercial logic that has contributed to the homogenization and relative depoliticization of content, but it has an additional reason why, in the words of its 1983 *Journalistic Policy* handbook, "objectivity and balance ... must characterize its information programming."[36] For the CBC, non-partisanship and a demonstrable independence from government serve the political imperative of establishing its own long-term institutional credibility and legitimacy. As a former CBC correspondent, Peter Stursberg, once wrote, the CBC as a Crown corporation "could not take political sides; it could not seem to be pro-Liberal or pro-Conservative or its very existence would be endangered."[37]

In short, then, broadcasters are obliged, according to Jay Blumler and Michael Gurevitch, "to adhere to such non-partisan – perhaps even anti-partisan – standards as fairness, impartiality, neutrality and objectivity, at the expense of such alternative values as commitment, consistent loyalty and readiness to take sides."[38]

Objective Journalism and the State

Although Canada has no explicit press policy for the print media that would parallel the Broadcasting Act, a range of laws do influence the operation of newspapers. In principle, some of these laws bolster the ability of the media to gather news, determine their own content, and publish that content without legal interference. Examples include the Charter of Rights' guarantee of freedom of expression and the media as well as the various provincial and federal access to information laws. By contrast, other laws potentially restrict newsgathering and dissemination on a range of grounds: the prohibition of hate literature and incitement to commit crimes, official secrecy, censorship during times of war or civil emergency, contempt of court and the reporting of judicial proceedings, copyright, protection of personal privacy and property, parliamentary privilege, and, above all, the laws of defamation, which enable an individual to sue the media for publishing untrue statements that call his or her reputation into question.[39] Still other laws affect the operations of news media as businesses. Some of these laws, including Canadian ownership and content rules in broadcasting and anticombines measures, potentially limit the power and profits of media owners. Other laws, such as income tax rules that encourage mergers or inhibit foreign competition, can be seen as de facto subsidies for Canadian media owners.

Whether they support or restrict press freedom, such laws have a clear rationale in liberal theory. In principle they are intended to balance the media's freedom of expression and the right of media owners to run their businesses as they see fit with other individual rights and institutional interests considered vital to the functioning of a liberal-democratic society. Such vital societal interests include the right of courts to operate without hindrance, the protection of fair competition in the marketplace from monopolistic practices, and the right of the state to withhold or suppress information on grounds of national security. Taken as a whole, these laws, combined with the informal publicity practices by which governments seek to manage the news, constitute an implicit news or press policy that places limits and pressures on the media and articulates the ethos of objectivity.

The approach as a whole provides for the formal and *legal independence of journalism from the state*. Such (perceived) independence is a keystone of the ethos of objectivity and of the social legitimacy of the press. Conventional wisdom draws a fundamental contrast between the free press of liberal-democratic societies, and authoritarian or totalitarian systems elsewhere. Such freedom has been fought and paid for dearly.

At the same time, though, the ethos of objectivity informally pulls the media in the direction of the state, in part by helping to *define and manage the symbiotic relationship between news media and politicians*. Politicians and officials need access to the media's mass audiences; and news organizations need a stable legal, political, and economic environment, as well as efficient access to senior officials and politicians, who provide the very stuff of what is defined as news. In return for following the rules of objectivity, news media gain this stability and access without sacrificing their self-image and public image of political independence and neutrality.[40]

The routines of objective journalism benefit politicians as well, normally guaranteeing them a high degree of media access, and an opportunity, by no means always perfectly realized, to shape the public definition of political issues. Journalism's criteria of newsworthiness and factuality, and its routines of newsgathering anchored in bureaucratic institutions with designated spokespeople and prescheduled routines, are mutually constitutive.[41] Taken together they tend to ensure routine and privileged access for bureaucrats and agency officials, who provide the hard "facts," credible claims, and background information for objective reporting. (Non-bureaucratic accounts, by contrast, are seen as soft data, unconfirmed reports, or speculation that cannot be published as hard-news without further investigation.)[42] Because the practices of objectivity tend to preclude reporters from introducing their own inferences in hard news stories, it often follows that reporters transmit what newsmakers (who are often government officials) want to have transmitted. The more "objective" the news becomes, the more it risks becoming a pure information outlet for established authority. Journalists routinely present political accusations, image-enhancing statements, and political "trial balloons" as news "objectively," that is, without adding their own inferences. Thus officials often have their views and definitions published as objective news, while journalists are ensured of a continuous supply of "facts" and opinions well-tailored to their storylines and news formats. When that happens, as W. Lance Bennett suggests, objectivity and political authority "become one and the same."[43]

This type of relationship does not always run smoothly. Objective journalism does not absolutely guarantee a privileged position to political authority, especially on divisive issues or breaches of liberal-democratic norms. Journalists may question politicians' motives or place their actions in a negative context. Taking for granted and overlooking their mutual dependence, journalists and politicians often describe their relations as adversarial. It is important, then, that the objectivity ethos provides politicians with flexible but distinct criteria to identify and denounce perceived journalistic excesses. Ironically, since the decline of the partisan press, politicians' accusations of media bias have become almost routine in North American public life. Such attacks perpetuate the popular myth of an independent adversarial press. If they are successful, they also set boundaries to media coverage; and if journalists go beyond those boundaries they risk losing their access to key sources. Objectivity, therefore, tends to allow the authorities to get their messages across credibly; and when this does not work, they can publicly appeal to the idea of objectivity in an effort to pressure journalists into compliance.

The state has a different kind of relationship with dissident (non-"objective") media outside the political and cultural mainstream. In the twentieth century, legal repression of the media has been infrequent in Canada, but when used, it is disproportionately against media that stand outside the accepted borders of objectivity. Occasionally the far right has faced criminal charges. The anti-Semitic activist Ernst Zundel, for instance, was prosecuted in the 1980s (ultimately unsuccessfully) for publishing pamphlets denying the historical reality of the Nazis' mass extermination of Jews. More typically, though, state action has been aimed at left-wing media.[44] The Communist Party of Canada and its publications have been banned at various times. Under authoritarian premier Maurice Duplessis, the Quebec government used its Padlock Act of 1937 to shut down what it considered to be "bolshevik or communistic" publications. The Supreme Court overturned the Act in 1957. During the 1970s the Royal Canadian Mounted Police placed left-wing groups and periodicals under surveillance. The "underground" papers of the 1960s counterculture were often legally harassed, especially on grounds of obscenity. Commercial success and a changing political climate have greatly mellowed the alternative urban weeklies from the days when one of them ran a cartoon of Jesus Christ masturbating. As recently as 1990, however, on the basis of its classified sex ads, police charged the Toronto weekly *NOW* with communicating for the purpose of prostitution. Similar ads in the major dailies (and the Toronto phone directory) did not result in similar charges. Some observers saw a vendetta by Toronto police against a paper that had been editorially critical of them, and the charges were dropped.[45] But police harassment of this sort can have a chilling effect on the alternative press.

Canada's 1970 October Crisis offers an especially dramatic example of state repression against the dissident press. In response to the kidnapping of a British diplomat and a Quebec politician by a small band of violent separatists known as the FLQ, the government of Pierre Trudeau gave itself the power, by invoking the War Measures Act, to suspend civil liberties and censor the media throughout the country. In practice, Québécois activists, journalists, and writers with real or suspected separatist sympathies bore the brunt of the Act's enforcement. Some 450 of them, most neither terrorists nor supporters of terrorism, were arrested and held without hearing in Quebec jails for a week or more.[46] Most were eventually released without ever being charged. Alleged intimidation of the media extended outside Quebec to campus papers that contemplated publishing the FLQ manifesto.

Mainstream news outlets that accept the dominant cultural and political norms are more likely to claim to be objective, and to be perceived as being objective. Not coincidentally they are less likely to be subject to legal harassment. Media and governments frequently spar legally over such issues as restrictions on the reporting of court proceedings, but rarely do the mainstream media cross the recognized boundaries that would spur the state to prosecute a news outlet.

Another dimension of the state-journalism relationship concerns how *the state validates the dominant media*. Through its legal framework and practice, the state has both accepted the media's claim to objectivity and defined "freedom of the press" as a property right of media owners. Since 1982 Canada's Charter of Rights and Freedoms has enshrined "freedom of thought, belief, opinion and expression, including freedom of the press and other media of communication," subject to "such reasonable limits prescribed by law as can be demonstrably justified in a free and democratic society." Only a few years after the Charter was adopted, legal scholar Harry Glasbeek predicted that the existing "economically and politically dominant, mature press" rather than "the special needs of brave experiments in alternative presses" would provide "the parameters of the context in which legal balances must be struck." Glasbeek predicted that the Charter's freedom of expression clause would be used "to defend individuals generally and the media in particular from state controls, but not individuals or their defender, the state, from private interests," thus helping the private press "to retain *its* sovereignty as a purveyor of information and opinion."[47] In effect, free speech is interpreted as a property right of corporate entities, not as a human right of individual citizens.

Subsequent court rulings seem to bear out this prediction. Because freedom of the press includes the freedom to be biased, the print media (by contrast with broadcasting) are not legally required to be objective or balanced. Nevertheless, these concepts are often viewed as professional journalistic criteria to be respected and relied upon in court decisions protecting media owners' property rights. Canadian or U.S. citizens have sometimes sought court-ordered access for their opinions or rebuttals in the pages of newspapers or magazines. The courts have consistently refused such a right of reply or access, citing the integrity and responsibility of journalists in producing "balanced" and "objective" reports.[48] Thus, even without an explicit state mandate, the objectivity criterion has legal relevance to the print media.

While the state implicitly endorses the objectivity claim of news organizations, it does not recognize or protect journalists' objectivity or independence vis-à-vis media owners. Apart from some clauses in collective agreements, notably in Quebec, few legal supports protect the job security or editorial independence of working journalists from their corporate employers. Canadian laws do not define journalism as a profession; journalists do not enjoy anything like the individual autonomy or collective self-governance of doctors or lawyers.

Legal discourse, embodied and operationalized both in Canada's explicit broadcasting and implicit press policy, has recognized objectivity as an economic and political imperative of news media organizations. Courts and government agencies that regulate the distribution of communication resources have explicitly or implicitly based rulings, decisions, and guidelines on the concepts of balance and objectivity. Originating in the democratic discourse of the labour press, objectivity in both the United States and anglo-Canada has become a discursive regime, deeply entrenched in the mainstream corporate media system, its technological structure, and its regulatory, political, and legal environment.[49]

4

The God Who Won't Die: News Objectivity as a Regime

In contemporary Western societies, faith in the possibility of objective truth and in the detachment and separation of observer from the observed has been thrown into crisis in the social sciences and other fields.[1] Journalism, too, is less self-assured now than it was before the upheavals of the 1960s. There is now less naive realism, less acceptance of the self-evident nature of facts, a greater sense of scepticism and irony, more tolerance for a broader range of approaches to covering the news, and more scope for the voices of reporters themselves.

Journalism has become more explicitly interpretive, driven in part by commercial television's entertainment imperatives as well as by audience demand for easy and understandable answers – not just "balanced" presentations of "both sides" – as they try to overcome their sense of displacement and confusion in a complex world. Promotional slogans for CTV National News and Vancouver's BCTV News promise to "make sense" of your world for you. During Canada's 1988 free trade debate, CBC Television news received calls from viewers begging the network to provide not a wealth of information objectively presented, but a definitive verdict: "Is free trade a good thing or not?" Supporters of journalism orthodoxy are feeling the heat of criticism and discontent, as attested by a spate of recent articles entitled "In Defence of Objectivity."[2]

Objectivity, as we have already noted, is a very much contested concept, subject to a wide range of different and sometimes competing definitions. As a *regime* (in the sense described in the Introduction), it is multifaceted. One research team has identified four possible meanings: the negation of journalists' subjectivity, the fair representation of each side in a controversy, balanced scepticism towards all sides in a dispute, and the search for hard facts that can contextualize a dispute. Each of these definitions commands some support among journalists.[3] Like the proverbial blind men describing an elephant after each of them had explored one part of its body, critics and defenders of objectivity alike have a range of definitions for what news objectivity "really" or "essentially" is – a set of rules or rituals, an attitude or state of mind, a convenient ideology to ward off critics, or a desirable or contestable ideal.

It is, we suggest, all those things. First of all, it is a *normative ideal,* a set of desired goals that journalism should aim at, even if those goals can never be perfectly achieved. These ideals are expected to guide not only the stance or attitude and methods that journalists adopt in gathering and telling stories, but also the content of news stories themselves. The goals can be broken down into two broad clusters. The first concerns the *cognitive* dimension of news: its capacity to impart information about the world as it is. Here the objectivity ethos calls upon journalists to follow certain criteria, such as:

- factualness, in the sense of clearly distinguishing fact from opinion, interpretation, or comment, backing reports by reference to named sources, and avoiding vagueness and redundancy;
- accuracy, making the report adhere to reality, or to other reliable versions of reality, especially on matters of fact;
- completeness, or fullness of account, based on the assumption that a minimum amount of pertinent information is required for understanding.[4]

The journalist, then, should seek to tell the truth about whatever is relevant to the story. At the same time the objectivity ethos enjoins journalists to pursue a second cluster of normative goals related to the *evaluative* dimension of news: its capacity to convey value-laden meanings and interpretations of the world. In this regard journalists should take a stance of detachment, neutrality, impartiality, and independence, avoiding partisanship, personal biases, ulterior motives, or undue influence by outside interests. An objective news account is one that is fair, even-handed, and balanced in presenting different sides of a contentious issue.[5]

We can easily see the normative or evaluative character of these criteria by contrasting them with their opposites: who would strive to be inaccurate, unfair, biased, or imbalanced (or worse, unbalanced!)? But, in addition to the guidelines of objectivity, media performance is also evaluated in terms of other principles, including independence, access, diversity, solidarity, and cultural conditions. These criteria in turn can be considered aspects of modern Western society's "core values" – freedom, justice/equality, and order/solidarity – as they apply to the media.[6] Media objectivity draws upon all three of those core values. It is linked to the principle of freedom, insofar as media independence is "a necessary condition of detachment and truthfulness." Similarly, objectivity is linked to equality – a "fair and non-discriminatory attitude" to sources, objects of news reporting, and differing viewpoints when the facts are in dispute.[7] Journalists should treat all sources, objects, or viewpoints on equal, or at least equitable, terms. Objectivity can also be linked to social order, insofar as a media system that is perceived to be blatantly biased can provoke political unrest among those aggrieved or excluded.[8] Conversely, the dominant social order (including both cultural values and political forces) significantly influences what the media take to be objective, fair, and reasonable in the presentation of news; objectivity is not an absolute and unchanging standard, but is always relative to its cultural and political context.[9] In wartime, for example, journalists tend to be ambivalent, and governments and many audience members hostile, to news coverage that gives enemy states the benefit of the "normal" criteria of balance and objectivity.

The first dimension of the objectivity regime, its normative criteria, implies a second: an *epistemology*, a set of assumptions about knowledge and reality. The ideal of objectivity hovers between different and incompatible epistemological positions, roughly related to its injunction for factual accuracy, on the one hand, and balance and neutrality, on the other. If journalism objectivity is to be taken seriously as an attainable ideal, it follows that it must be possible to separate facts from values and the observer from the observed. It must be possible in principle to "reflect" or "mirror" the world, to offer "a complete and unrefracted capture of the world."[10] This dimension suggests that journalists can stand apart from events without influencing them and transfer the truth or meaning of events to the news audience by means of neutral language and competent reporting techniques. It also suggests that news can be presented from a universalistic perspective, from "everybody's" viewpoint.

The regime also entails a set of newsgathering and presentation *practices* or "uniform technical criteria," which give flesh to the spirit of objectivity.[11] These practices evolve and shift over time, and they differ between different media. The contemporary conventional practices include *reportorial* conventions that shape how journalists construct the news. In selecting individuals to provide information and comment for a story, for example, a journalist is expected to seek appropriate sources: those who have accredited knowledge, who are recognized representatives of the relevant institutions, and/or who are personally directly involved in the story. Objective journalists emphasize "cognitive, rather than emotional response" from sources and avoid sensationalism.[12] They observe prevailing standards of decency and good taste and deploy "documentary reporting practices" that allow them "to transmit to the public only what they can observe or support with physical evidence" and "only the facts that credible sources have confirmed."[13] Objective journalism takes care to separate such observable facts from the presentation of opinions or evaluations, which are confined to specialized genres such as columns, features, and documentaries. As Richard Ericson, Patricia Baranek, and Janet Chan put it, "Historical or explanatory frameworks which give an explicit interpretive basis (and bias) for construing truth" are bracketed out.[14]

Objective journalists also downplay their own roles as narrators of the news stories, which is the standard format for packaging the news.[15] Print journalism accomplishes this impersonal and conventional format by emphasizing the use of supposedly "transparent" and "neutral" language. According to Frances Bula, "Distinct turns of phrase, adjectives, adverbs, bits of extraneous description – anything that calls attention to the writer or appears to imply some kind of subjective assessment is generally removed in hard-news stories."[16]

These *reportorial* practices can be distinguished from *editorial* practices, which include the differentiation of genres in journalism, especially the sharp separation of "facts" from "opinions" through the segregation of the latter into the Op/Ed pages and the use of bylines. Uniting what we have called reportorial and editorial objectivity is a third, more general stance or *methodological imperative* involving the method of "neutrality," signalled in part by the use of the passive voice. By this means journalists and editors take themselves out of the picture and adopt the stance of an impartial and politically neutral observer, critically examining all sides of an issue and separate from the struggles and events being reported. As well, and this is a crucial point, objectivity requires that both reporters and editors adopt a stance of representing the universal public interest, a position not contaminated by partisanship. This stance implies the political independence of news workers, including freedom from pressures that might be generated by the news organization itself as an institution with political and economic interests.

So far we have seen objectivity as, first, a goal or ethic, second, an epistemology, and, third, sets of practices or methods. It is also important to recognize a fourth dimension – the way in which the regime is *institutionalized* in concrete social structures (as discussed in chapter 3). We are not arguing that objectivity is itself an institution, but rather, that it operates within a particular institutional framework – a framework that it has actively helped to construct, rather than simply reflect. That framework consists of complex, specialized news organizations, with compartmentalized roles and departments (the marketing and advertising departments over there, the newsroom pristinely over here), staffed by professionals with appropriate skills and ethical commitments, and enjoying autonomy from the state – which, in classical libertarian press theory, is the main potential threat to freedom of the press. That posited autonomy is reinforced by legal guarantees of freedom of the press, while the provision of revenue from advertisers and media audiences supposedly makes the commercial media both more responsive to consumers and less vulnerable to pressure from the state. (As a Crown corporation the CBC is heavily dependent on state revenue, but it has a legal mandate to operate at arm's length from the government.)

Finally, objectivity is very much an active *ingredient in public discourse* about news. It is part of "commonsense" audience expectations of the news and thus, as Denis McQuail puts it, "plays an important part in assessments of performance by the media public."[17] Typically, when audience members criticize individual journalists or news reports for being biased rather than objective, they are actually reinforcing objectivity as the benchmark against which news should be evaluated.

The idea-complex – and set of practices – of journalistic objectivity, then, provide *a general model for conceiving, defining, arranging, and evaluating news texts, news practices, and news institutions.* The diversity of the model is especially evident through national comparisons. A survey of journalists in Italy, Germany, Britain, and the United States found that "for almost all journalists objectivity is an important and indispensable professional value." But journalists in different countries differed in their understanding of the term. North American English-language journalists stressed the media's common-carrier function of fairly representing the position of each side in a political dispute, while continental journalists emphasized the more active role of digging beneath the rhetoric of the contending sides to uncover the "hard facts" of political disputes.[18]

The regime of objectivity is thus polysemic, carrying multiple meanings. It has different articulations across media and a certain degree of flexibility, enabling it to accommodate and contain alternative practices. Moreover, its coherence as the dominant regime of journalism comes about partly through the compartmentalization of different genres within mainstream journalism. "Hard-news" reporters achieve objectivity through dispassionate factuality and the balanced presentation of contrasting views and/or conflicting accounts of an event. Feature writers can loosen the rules of dispassionate factuality, although the profession is quick to condemn those who engage in practices such as creating composite characters and reconstructing scenes that they never witnessed.[19] The industry pays a minority of journalists to express their values, vent their spleen, offer their interpretations, or simply stage a debate. Examples are the newspaper's opinion column, television's point-of-view documentary, radio talk shows, or television talkfests like CBC's *Face Off* and PBS's *McLaughlin Group*, with their parade of media-based pundits-cum-celebrities.

Even in relation to these genres, the medium as a whole can still claim objectivity by arguing that it offers a "balance" of different opinions, stands above partisan politics, and speaks for the public interest. Nevertheless, the objectivity regime creates a hierarchy of journalistic genres, with the hard-news story at the pinnacle, dominating front pages and leading nightly newscasts. It is a truly rare event when a paper or TV newscast displays a passionate feature story, an editorial, or a letter in these privileged positions. In a recent case of such genre discrimination, private broadcasters successfully pressured the CRTC into forcing CBC Newsworld to drop its programming of *This Hour Has Twenty-two Minutes* and *The Royal Canadian Air Farce*. Although these popular programs satirize public figures and news events, the CRTC deemed them simply "entertainment" and therefore beyond Newsworld's licensed mandate.[20]

Still, above all else objectivity is an ideology. It co-exists with and indeed contributes to how news excludes and marginalizes subject-matter, and how it constructs hierarchies and blind spots. Feminist scholarship has tellingly critiqued the basic tenets of objectivity, in journalism as well as science. Objectivity disguises and denies how the culturally conditioned gaze of the observer helps to construct that which is observed. With regard to gender, it has been argued that objectivity is "primarily a male construct."[21] It privileges the male as the gender that is more capable of "objective" observation. Similarly, the interpretations embedded in seemingly objective news reflect and reinforce patriarchal metanarratives of women as passive subjects to be acted upon, ones defined by their bodies, appearance, or relations with men. Patriarchal categories are deeply embedded in news discourse: consider the distinction between "hard" and "soft" news, for instance. Historically, women first entered mainstream North American journalism as human-interest feature writers rather than hard-news reporters or political correspondents.

Empirical indicators reveal that objective news continues to be "what affluent white men define it to be." Gina Bailey points out:

> Stories and narratives are constructed around groups and institutions with which, in general, men are familiar – politicians, diplomats, business executives, doctors and lawyers ... in other words, the elite which relatively few women have joined in rank. Social issues and the way the majority of people live, work, organize and find meaning are relegated to the back sections of the news media, often as 'human interest.' These become the sections in which women predominantly appear. When women are covered in first page/top story features, it is often because they are somehow extraordinary.... It is no coincidence that stories of child abuse did not begin appearing until working mothers infiltrated the newsroom or that it was a woman who broke the first 'A' section story on birth control.[22]

Society's hierarchies of gender, class, and race are evident even in the CBC, whose journalistic policy manual identifies accuracy, integrity, fairness, and thoroughness as cornerstones of "the optimum objectivity and balance which must characterize CBC's information programs."[23] A study of CBC national television news found that 84 per cent of the sources used were male and 70 per cent worked in "elite" occupations, while 8 per cent were visible minorities. Women were disproportionately likely to appear in social issues or soft news stories.[24]

Still, while news discourse is structured in dominance, it is not entirely predetermined. The meanings and applications of objectivity are a site of constant struggle and negotiation; and the objectivity regime persists precisely because it does offer openings, however unequally, to different social and cultural groups.

A Public Clucking of Tongues:
Objectivity as a Resource for Negotiating News Content

In addition to regulating news production, objectivity also regulates the relationship between news and its public. It is a widely available (although unevenly distributed) cultural and political resource, providing a common language through which the meanings and content of news can be negotiated, contested, and evaluated. Interest groups seeking to influence media content or structure are unlikely to gain a hearing unless they declare an acceptance (however spurious) of the principles of objective journalism.

Groups that explicitly reject the language of objectivity (say, fundamentalist Christians who denounce the "secular humanist" media for violating God's law, or vanguard leftist groups who want media to promote their version of political change) find it difficult to gain public credibility for their critiques of media.

But objectivity and its components such as fairness and balance are vague concepts, and contending social groups negotiate and contest their meanings and application. The components of the regime are sites of struggle over meaning and representational power. Groups seeking media access or positive coverage are likely to declare their adherence to freedom of the press and news objectivity and then go on to define these terms in ways that serve their own purposes. As one official said of the Pentagon's Gulf War media strategy, its aim was to obtain "favourable objectivity."[25]

In joining in this task, interest groups can creatively exploit the polysemic character of objectivity. The elements that constitute objectivity in the reporting of specific events are open to negotiation. What journalistic practices are ethical? What news reports are fair and balanced, rather than biased and distorted? Who are "responsible" sources with a legitimate claim to speak publicly through the media? Given broadcasting regulation, what constitutes an appropriate balance in coverage of social issues? What issues are of public importance and thus deserving of balanced treatment?

The audience undoubtedly has an active role in framing the answers to these contested questions. Some writers have argued that bias, often considered the absence of objectivity, is a psychological and cognitive state of the audience rather than an evaluation of the relationship between news accounts and the world. Noting that both supporters and opponents of the failed Meech Lake constitutional agreement accused the CBC of bias, one journalist, Randy Boswell, put it more simply: "Bias is in the eye of the beholder." Boswell argued that while bias is conventionally understood as a tendentious distortion of reality at the expense of objectivity, fairness, and balance (F&B), and professional standards, "It might be more accurate to say biased reporting by a journalist occurs at the expense of other (including journalists') political agendas. With truth unattainable and F&B as nebulous as a cloud, charges of bias dissipate into differences of opinion on the subject covered."[26]

This position suits journalists and media executives just fine. They can point to criticism of the same story from advocates on "both sides" of a controversial issue as proof that the media are "playing it down the middle" or "getting it about right." Considered critically, such a defence is not completely logical. Accusations of media bias from opposing interest groups do not necessarily cancel each other out: as a recent survey of Canadian interest groups suggests, such accusations are not necessarily contradictory, and both sides can well have validity.[27] For instance, when right-wing critics see media coverage of social and moral issues, such as abortion, as being "liberal," they are not necessarily contradicting left-wing critics of perceived conservatism in business and economic coverage. Nor do such accusations or "bias calls" from both right and left imply that the media are ideologically neutral or value-free.[28] It may well be that one side has a much better case than the other.

Still, there is much to the claim that interest groups' bias calls are selective. The regime of objectivity becomes the political smokescreen under which concrete struggles over media content are fought out. Interest groups often use the notion of balance to try to "shift the goalposts," so that their positions become defined as centrist and their opponents' as extremist. The rhetoric of balance and objectivity, with its tone of universalism, altruism, and high-minded abstraction, can therefore be harnessed to concrete, partial, and self-serving interests. Moreover, because these concepts have long been cultivated by the mainstream news media and state regulatory agencies, those who can effectively invoke them in the struggle for media access will typically have the upper hand, no matter how sectarian or narrow their ends may be. In politics, as Murray Edelman points out:

> The term "balance" has no objective meaning ... for there is manifestly no scale or reference mark that assures people with opposing interests that an equilibrium has been reached in the way that a butcher's scale satisfies both the seller and the buyer that a quantity of meat weighs a pound. In politics, references to a "balance" are common because they help win general acceptance for the values of those who use the term. This is an appeal for support, not a term of measurement, though its users are likely to deceive themselves as well as others into believing that they are being objective. The use of the term "balance" in political and legal rhetoric ... makes an effective appeal because it presents itself as descriptive rather than polemical.[29]

However strategic and self-interested the rhetoric of balance frequently is, news media must often respond to hostile bias calls. A number of mechanisms and forums allow media organizations to deal with these while holding on to their audiences and their credibility. In the non-regulated print media, such forums include letters to the editors, ombudsmen, and press councils in many of Canada's provinces. In the regulated broadcasting industry, the CRTC until recently had many of the same functions of handling complaints. Each of these mechanisms permits the airing of specific grievances against perceived news bias, and sometimes they may even be resolved to the satisfaction of complainants. But they all have important limits.

The "letters to the editor" column is perhaps the most commonly used forum through which newspaper readers can address a perceived imbalance in the reporting of particular issues. Newspapers publish these, in part, because they help foster the paper's image of providing an open and representative forum for its readers. The letters can sometimes challenge the dominant terms of debate and are often seen as the least mediated, most democratic component of a newspaper.

But letters can rarely initiate discussion of issues outside the mainstream news agenda. Newspaper editors do not normally consider attempts to do so as sufficiently newsworthy. And although it has the character of an ongoing conversation, it is a conversation that is very much structured in dominance. Editors have the overriding power to select and reject, to alter, delete, juxtapose, and to affix headlines and photographs, so that the writers of letters are always either being silenced or granted permission to speak.[30] This practice – so structured as being "open" to comment – is done in private, out of public view: readers as a matter of course never know what is being left out in the selection and altering process. Moreover, the selection tends to parallel inequalities of class, gender, and social status. Ericson, Baranek, and Chan's study of *The Globe and Mail*'s editing practices revealed that a writer's social and political status as well as organizational affiliation plays an important role in the editor's selection of letters; and, as in the news columns, the authorized knower is given preference over ordinary citizens in the letters section.[31] As it turns out, the letters column as a forum for negotiating news content is subject to many of the same hierarchical rules that apply elsewhere in the newspaper.

As another forum of content negotiation, press councils accept and adjudicate complaints about specific instances of news reporting. Many of these grievances are bias calls. For instance, more than half of the Ontario Press Council's cases during its first eight years concerned the honesty and objectivity of reporting.[32]

By arbitrating bias calls, press councils have amplified and seek to protect the dominant ideal of objectivity. Partly for that very reason, they have important limitations. Their mandate generally confines them to complaints about specific cases of reporting, rather than omissions or generalized bias. Membership in most provincial press councils is voluntary, and most of them do not deal with grievances against non-member news media. Winning a case typically yields at best a publication of the council's decision in the offending news medium, a prize that many potential complainants may not consider worth the effort. Peter Desbarats argues that Canadian press councils have had "relatively successful histories," apparently because they have built a useful body of rulings over the years and promoted understanding between newspapers and their readers. But he also notes that the councils "have been criticized for being primarily reactive, for failing to advertise and promote themselves sufficiently, and for failing to initiate research and other activities that could strengthen their role in improving standards."[33]

An even more fundamental limitation is that press councils are usually creatures of the industry itself. Their membership may include working journalists and members of the public, but they are financed by the member media organizations whose political and economic needs they were, in large part, formed to meet. Their history suggests that they were created to ward off the threat of legislation that would deal with concentrated media ownership. Canada's first press councils appeared in the early 1970s in the wake of Keith Davey's Senate Committee report on the mass media, and a second wave followed Tom Kent's 1980/81 Royal Commission on Newspapers. Their establishment also had a commercial impetus. The 1960s and 1970s saw an increasing challenge to the credibility of the press and a growing tendency towards the fragmentation of newspaper markets, threatening dailies that rely on mass markets. As a research report for the Kent Commission pointed out:

> It is those newspapers with a large advertising market to protect and with a readership representing all social classes of society that have taken the initiative of setting up existing press councils.... The various press councils established in Canada until now are seeking to perpetuate the social consensus which has ensured the success of the so-called omnibus newspapers ... whose formula is specially designed towards advertising-led consumer patterns and whose basic unit is the traditional family.[34]

Much the same could be said of the ombudsmen appointed at several Canadian dailies, including *The Toronto Star* and *Calgary Herald*, as well as the CBC. While they are undoubtedly individuals of integrity, they have an ambivalent role: they are expected both to explain the newspaper's editorial decisions to readers and to represent readers' interests at the paper. When they criticize their own paper too vigorously, they can be removed at management's pleasure.

Such was the apparent fate of the ombudsman for the once prestigious *Winnipeg Free Press*. Barry Mullin's column of May 1, 1992, criticized his own paper for its coverage of the Los Angeles riots the day before. The continent's major news story, he charged, had been buried on the early morning edition's back page, while the front page ran soft, happy news about a pair of local heroes and biodegradable golf tees. The publisher, appointed by the Thomson chain two months previously, reportedly immediately summoned Mullin to meet with him and the managing editor. Laying down conditions that effectively undermined the credibility and independence of the ombudsman position, he allegedly forced Mullin, who had eight years' previous experience as the city editor, to leave the paper. The subsequent chill in the *Free Press* newsroom, argued media critic Stan Persky, made a mockery of the paper's name.[35] Its role-ambiguity may help explain why the institution of ombudsman is in apparent decline, at least in Canadian dailies.[36]

In the broadcasting media the CRTC appears at first sight to be a different kettle of fish. It is a creature not of industry but of government, a public body created in part to ensure that the industry would meet certain programming standards, including "balance." As such, the CRTC is equipped with more investigative and punitive powers than the press councils, including the power to revoke or fail to renew the licence of a particular broadcaster. However, the CRTC has not used these formal powers vigorously in supervising news content, especially in recent years. Rarely has it imposed conditions in a Promise of Performance, withheld or changed the terms of a broadcasting licence, or ordered a licensee to undertake specific actions to fulfil the balance obligation. Rather, the CRTC relies greatly on broadcasters' goodwill and general declarations about broadcasters' responsibility to achieve balance through their own editorial judgements. Under the prevailing ideology of self-regulation and deregulation in the 1980s, the CRTC moved to shift its grievance-handling function to an industry body similar to press councils.[37]

All of the above forums for negotiating the content and meanings of objectivity and balance are confined within the regime of objectivity. Rather than being designed to deal with fundamental criticisms of the accepted standards of journalism, they confine their attention to perceived failures to meet those standards. Even more restrictively, they deal with complaints concerning specific content in the news media rather than with challenges to media practices and the particular structural arrangements behind those practices. The Ontario Press Council, one of the most effective in Canada, for example, stated clearly in its policy that it would not handle grievances concerning systematic media bias. Rather, like other press councils, it investigates only complaints that address specific stories. David Waters, CBC-TV executive producer and once a charter member of the more ambitious Québec Press Council, reflected upon its unfulfilled promise:

> Many of us wanted a strong and effective press council. We got a press council, which while it may still be one of the best in the world, still falls far short of what we sought. We wanted one which would not only look into individual cases of harmful journalism but which would be able to gather evidence and lobby forcefully against the systemic shortcomings of contemporary journalism. It was structured to be able to do so, but it has always lacked the funds to do much more than slap a limited but growing number of individual shortcomings with a public clucking of tongues.[38]

Indeed, by highlighting particular instances of perceived departures from the standards of objective journalism, press councils help implicitly to "naturalize" those standards, to render them the baseline against which transgressions are identified.

These forums of negotiation may be valuable in resolving individual disputes and perhaps in increasing the media's sense of accountability to audiences. But they do not fundamentally increase public access to the media or redress other inequalities in media representation. Powerful politicians' attacks on media bias may make headlines, but potentially more valid complaints from those who are less powerful may not. Moreover, because elites have more financial and staff resources, they can more effectively use existing forums of negotiation by launching large advertising campaigns, backroom lobbying, CRTC interventions, or large-scale media research. In arbitrating disputes over journalistic balance, the seemingly impartial CRTC is not immune to these kinds of pressures. As researchers Peter G. Cook and Myles A. Ruggles argue, the extent to which a complaint against a specific case of media bias is investigated "depends on the political power and authority of those who complain." From their analysis of the CRTC's record in handling complaints, they concluded "that the Commis-

sion has responded vigorously only when governments or powerful interests came under attack. This evidence suggests that balance performs an
ideological function in that it is more likely to be enforced when powerful
institutions are threatened. 'Balance' is thus really constrained to balancing
the opinions of elite groups."[39] In struggles over media content, "balance"
has often proved a key weapon.

Panic in Pigeon Park: The Imbalance of Balance

On the east side of downtown Vancouver, a neighbourhood that the affluent
call seedy and many of the city's less well-heeled residents call home, stands
a small square known locally as Pigeon Park. Poor economically but rich in
diversity, it is perhaps a fitting location for the aging building housing one
of Canada's most distinctive broadcasting stations, Vancouver Co-op Radio,
CFRO-FM. One of only two English-language community-access radio
stations in Canada, CFRO has a mandated responsibility to provide access,
reply, and programming opportunities to members of the community at
large.[40] With a shoestring budget financed largely by memberships, overall
policies made by a member-elected board, and programs produced by
collectives of volunteers using antique and makeshift equipment, Co-op
Radio has been broadcasting since 1975 with passion and commitment if
not always professional polish.

The station's member-owned, volunteer-operated, and non-commercial
nature means that programming production practices differ greatly from
commercial radio. The station's policy statement openly celebrates its partisanship, its efforts "to cover issues and events from the perspective of social movements concerned with and affected by those issues and events."[41]
The social movements identified include labour, women, gays and lesbians,
environmental and peace groups, and others. Such movements have a significant presence in British Columbia, with its relatively strong trade unions and a left-leaning social-democratic party (the NDP) usually contending for power, but the progressive side of the province's polarized political
spectrum has generally been significantly underrepresented in the commercial media.

Co-op Radio's approach to information programming reflects its mandate of "giving voice to the voiceless." Accordingly, the conventional rituals
of balance – the presentation of both sides of an issue in a given program –
are almost non-existent. Volunteers working on advocacy public affairs
programs take such an "imbalance" as their distinctive character. As one
researcher noted:

They are committed to an audience group, whether it be pro-labor, pro-Palestinian or pro-gay and express the sentiments of the audience as they interpret them. Within the station no one sees a problem with the Coming Out Show actively promoting gay rights and a gay perspective on issues. Certainly it would appear ludicrous to station members for the show to balance every pro-gay sentiment with an anti-gay one.[42]

Co-op activists regard the very effort to accord access to groups and viewpoints excluded from the mainstream media as itself a form of balance – a counter-weight to the perceived imbalance of the broadcasting system as a whole.

This particular interpretation of balance puts the station at odds with the CRTC's narrower emphasis on balancing viewpoints or program types within a single station. That tension burst into open conflict at Co-op Radio's 1988 licence renewal hearing, sparked by a bitter complaint levelled by the Canadian Jewish Congress against the weekly Co-op program *Voice of Palestine*. The CJC accused the station of using the publicly owned airwaves to broadcast very strongly worded pro-Arab views while completely barring the Jewish side in the Middle East conflict.[43]

In its defence Co-op reiterated its view that the system as a whole, not each station, should be responsible for providing the balance mandated in the Broadcasting Act, adding that Co-op's unique programming helped to balance the radio fare available in the Vancouver area market. "We find it hard to believe," the station's representatives told the CRTC, "that the interpretation of balance as it is related to community radio would require us to establish programs that give voices to sectors of society that already have voices in the media."[44]

Although CRTC policy officially recognizes the distinctiveness of community radio, the regulators accepted neither Co-op's broad definition of balance nor the special status of community radio in relation to its own narrower definition. Although the CJC's intervention was arguably a strategic effort to silence *Voice of Palestine*, the CRTC sharply rapped Co-op's knuckles.[45] The regulators reduced the station's licensing term from the normal five years to thirty-four months and required the station to submit a report within six months outlining how it intended to meet its balance obligations in the future. The Commission's decision was unusual not only in disciplining a licensee on grounds of balance, but also in suggesting specific mechanisms to achieve it: the station was to search out alternative points of view and, if necessary, use its own resources to produce or acquire counterbalancing programming.[46]

Ignoring the dynamics of community radio, the CRTC's proposals reflected the practices of commercial media, in which salaried reporters routinely obtain quotes from opposing views on controversial issues. "Were we to follow these suggestions, it would no longer be Co-op Radio," argued public affairs programmer and board member Peter Royce. He pointed out that volunteers would find it awkward and odd spending their scarce time and resources on interviewing their political opponents and working to present their views in a detached manner.[47] Ultimately such a practice would destroy the station or transform it into one more commercial medium. Some people on the station felt that they had been misunderstood by the CRTC. Others saw it as an attempt at intimidation.

Following the CRTC's ruling, Co-op Radio revised its procedures for dealing with complaints, ran more announcements about the station's access opportunities, and provided more on-air phone-in time during its public affairs programs. The *Voice of Palestine* programmers installed a segment called "Balancing the Act" in which "statements and quotes are read on air which express the sentiments of leading figures and others who directly and adamantly oppose any degree of Palestinian self-determination."[48]

Not surprisingly, these changes did not satisfy the CRTC, which rejected the station's initial report, including its defence, based on the principle of access, of its programming practices. Nor did the CRTC respond to the pointed questions being raised by Co-op directors and volunteers. Cook and Ruggles ask:

Against what abstract standard of "balance" was the range of views volunteered by the station's members and audiences to be measured? What selection of views constituted a "balanced" range? Which issues did, and which did not, trigger this obligation? How was the station to know when it had achieved "balance," and thus met its licence obligations? Was the Commission prescribing imitation of the public affairs coverage of ... mainstream commercial broadcasters, whose programming "balance" seemed to be acceptable to the Commission? If no volunteers came forward to present contrasting views, was the station obliged to change its internal policies and hire professional journalists to augment the volunteer programming (which it could not afford)? And what should the station do if ... the complainant's views verged on abusive comment?[49]

Some Co-op members were developing a critique of the very principle of balance as a regulatory criterion. In their retrospective analysis of the dispute, the two communication researchers involved with CFRO raised even more fundamental questions. Referring to the CJC as "a relatively powerful intervenor" to the CRTC, Cook and Ruggles add, "That the Commission took vigorous action in this case is thus consistent with earlier evidence the Commission is most responsive to complaints from more powerful institutions."[50] Given that "imbalance" surfaced to view only when complaints were made, should a lack of complaints against mainstream broadcasters be interpreted as evidence of balance, or does it mean, rather, that aggrieved or excluded groups lack the resources to mount effective complaints? Do commercial stations simply appear balanced because, in keeping with commercial priorities, they avoid controversial programming as far as possible? Does the Commission acknowledge the ideological elements of much mainstream broadcast journalism, including the limitation of debate to a range of elite perspectives and the exclusion of direct access for grassroots constituencies? Why is there no right of reply or balance in advertising, which consumes so much air time? Why does the CRTC act so stringently against CFRO as a station with elaborate access procedures, while commercial stations, with no rights of access or reply, escape regulatory sanctions?[51]

The two activists went even further, arguing that the CRTC's balance policy contained an inherent bias in favour of commercial broadcasters:

> The fact is that the commercial media are special interest groups in the precise sense that their structure determines their content.... The problem here is that whatever framework or system of selection and representation is employed by dominant firms, its implicit values are then the point across which other views must be balanced, and will – by tautology – turn out to define the median opinion. The tendency to imitation among the majority of licensees (the commercial sector of broadcasting) renders the commercially optimum range of views so ubiquitous and monolithic in the attention of the public that any departure from it appears "biased" and "unbalanced."[52]

These are excellent arguments, which raise fundamental questions about the meaning of democratic communication. The researchers concluded that the balance requirement, with its emphasis on citizens' right to hear but not to speak over the airwaves, was "the regulatory correlate of the elitist conception of democracy, in which most citizens are considered un-qualified for more than a passive role as observers of the political scene."[53]

Holding the regulatory whip hand against a station with little political or economic clout, though, the CRTC apparently felt no need to respond to such arguments. After further measures by CFRO to appease the CRTC and after a second report, and more strained correspondence between the two parties, the dispute was allowed to moulder. CFRO and *Voice of Palestine* ultimately stayed on the air, but the station was unable to win acceptance of its own definition of balance or clarification of the CRTC's definition.

This case suggests again that mechanisms of objectivity and balance, in this instance regulated by a state agency, can be used to discourage or in-timidate alternative media and their practices in favour of dominant me-dia. Although balance and objectivity can occasionally serve as political weapons in challenging the media's signification of particular events, they also serve to naturalize the media's dominant institutional arrangements. If commercial imperatives tend to homogenize the journalistic programming of mainstream broadcasters, institutions or content that departs from the commercial norm are more likely to appear as biased or unbalanced. While Co-op Radio had cause for relief that the CRTC finally dropped the case, it was a potent reminder that, while it is relatively easy to problematize the specific content of the news media, it is very difficult to challenge the defi-nitions and practices of journalistic objectivity and balance from outside the regime.

Balance and Religious Broadcasting

While the commercial news media are generally regarded in officialdom as representing the general public interest, alternative media that reject the regime of objectivity are seen as propagandistic representatives of special interests. Such has been the rationale for allocating broadcasting licences to commercial concerns at the expense of non-profit groups in the United States since the early years of radio.

Although the CRTC has licensed specialized FM radio stations and ca-ble television networks (sports, rock music) on the basis of market segmen-tation and consumer tastes, it has been far more cautious with respect to religion and politics. Would-be "special-interest" broadcasters have been denied licences on the grounds that they would be unlikely to fulfil the bal-ance requirement. Premised on the scarcity of broadcast frequencies, that requirement was derived from the principles of maintaining the airwaves as public property or a public trust. The idea is to represent the diversity of major viewpoints in matters of controversy or public concern and to prevent wealth or special position from being used as a basis for controlling the airwaves.

Sustained pressure by religious groups finally forced the CRTC to open a public hearing on religious broadcasting in 1982. Supporters of religious broadcasting made arguments strikingly similar to those of Co-op Radio. Arguing against the view of the commercial and state media as representing general interests, religious groups maintained that commercial media themselves constituted a "special-interest" group. In the words of one brief, from the Committee for Justice and Liberty Foundation:

> The commercial broadcaster is not a "neutral," "balanced" or "universal" broadcaster, it is rather a particular type of broadcaster who selects programs according to its own interest in and commitment to profit-making.... With slight exception, [private broadcasting] has led to a chase after ratings, a predominance, in TV, of American programs, to an overwhelming focus on resultant idiotic advertising, and to a numbing sameness of programs from station to station.[54]

Supporters of evangelical channels went further, describing the values of commercial broadcasting as typically humanistic, materialistic, hedonistic, and nihilistic. Like Co-op Radio, they argued that they were aiming to counterbalance a pervasive bias in the broadcasting system as a whole. But whereas Co-op had failed to persuade the CRTC as to its definition of balance, the CRTC accepted the religious groups' arguments, at least to the extent of granting the broadcasting licence that gave birth to the Vision TV network.

This decision, though key, did not constitute a shift towards a regime of access, in which different groups have their own media outlets that bypass the mediation of supposedly objective, professional communicators. No such licences have been awarded to feminist groups who perceive systemic media bias towards patriarchy, to labour unions who perceive a pro-business slant, or to environmentalists who see a pervasive consumerism. The CRTC has not abandoned its traditional concept of balance, and Vision TV supplies access to a range of denominations and viewpoints rather than coming under the control of any one of them.

While the Broadcasting Act was revised in 1991, it retains the criterion of balance. Indeed, for that very reason, the parliamentary committee charged with reviewing the new act rejected as unnecessary the explicit recognition of an "access" sector in broadcasting – ignoring very real differences: between access as a group's right to speak in its own voice through the media; and balance as the appropriated and mediated representation of one viewpoint among many others.[55] If Canada's broadcasting system does acquire channels dedicated to explicit and single-minded political or religious advocacy in the near future, it will most likely be on the coattails of narrowcasting technology, privatization, deregulation, and market logic – to the disproportionate benefit of affluent "market niches." If the rhetoric of balance, access, fairness, or other universalizing concepts that could potentially benefit underrepresented groups is deployed at all, it would increasingly be part of a market discourse of consumer choice.

But the case of religious broadcasting does suggest that the terms of discourse set by the regime of objectivity are not absolute, nor do they automatically determine particular policy outcomes. The interpretation and application of balance are subject to negotiation, and much may depend on the political, economic, and social resources of the groups using this rhetoric. Co-op Radio self-consciously represented the marginalized. By contrast, a coalition of Canada's major religious groups carried much greater cultural and political weight.

Balance Rhetoric in a Free-Market Crusade

A few blocks from Co-op Radio and Pigeon Park, but a world away in wealth and status, loom the steel-cold glass and concrete towers of Vancouver's financial district. Here, in its heart, nestles the office of the Fraser Institute, a corporate-funded think-tank with a self-declared mission to educate Canadians about "the use of competitive markets as the best mechanism for responding to change."[56] Founded in 1974 by a group of Vancouver businessmen annoyed by the left-leaning policies of British Columbia's New Democratic government, the Institute's consistent promotion of market approaches to all manner of public policy issues is tantamount to an ideological crusade. By the mid-1980s the Institute had an annual budget of over $1 million and a staff of eighteen, thanks to the backing of over four hundred corporations and prominent right-wing Canadian businessmen such as Peter Pocklington and Conrad Black.

One of the branches of the Fraser Institute is its National Media Archive (NMA), founded in 1987 with an annual budget of about $200,000. While the NMA does make research materials available to scholars, it is not so much a public archive as a research unit engaging actively in conducting and publicizing content analyses of the media. Through its monthly newsletter *On Balance*, the NMA claims to examine the "fidelity" of the public information function performed by national media, particularly the extent to which their coverage of public affairs is "balanced." Indeed, the newsletter says it puts the "objectivity, balance and fairness" of media coverage of public issues to "scientific scrutiny."[57] Its 1988 study of the CBC and *Globe and Mail* coverage of free trade, for example, counted apparent expressions of opinion by journalists and their interviewees in every free trade story that appeared on *The National* and *The Journal* and the front section of the *Globe* for twelve months in 1987/88, concluding that each medium's coverage weighed heavily against the trade deal. The CBC, argued the NMA, was especially unbalanced, because when CBC reporters aired their opinions they were twice as likely to be against free trade as for it.

Media scholars have criticized the *On Balance* research on a number of grounds, including the unreflective nature of the NMA's content analysis, how it makes claims for the straightforward objectivity of the technique while ignoring the degree of interpretation inherent in categorizing and coding media texts. Also evident in the early *On Balance* research are ambiguities and apparent empirical errors, as well as a tendency to oversimplify, or even to ignore, the context and the complexities of producing news and its meanings.[58] Most importantly for our purposes is the NMA's conception of balance, and the political uses to which it is put.

The NMA's assumptions about balance, its benchmark for evaluating media coverage, share some of the positivism and other conceptual limitations of other conventional research on news bias.[59] In particular the NMA seems to equate the "fidelity" of the media's public information function with the symmetrical treatment of two competing sides of public issues, and it considers the origins of those issues to be unproblematic. This approach assumes that all issues as a matter of course have two antagonistic and equally weighted sides and that "balance" comprises quantitatively equal treatment of these two sides. Yet, in identifying the relevant "two sides" of a given issue, the NMA often seems to rely upon its own implicit assumptions instead of analysing the origins and relevant perspectives on public issues. Moreover, in terms of political support and/or moral validity (in relation to generally accepted normative standards), not every issue has two sides. Some have only one, some have more than two, and all depend on who is looking at them. It is also neither possible nor necessarily desirable that *every* side receives equal treatment in the media. For instance, if news emphasizes the negative effects of sexual assault, few people expect counterbalancing portrayals of positive effects: this type of balance would not be a faithful representation of public discourse. The same could be said of other near-consensual positions in Canadian politics, such as the principle of publicly funded health care.

When the NMA tries to find replacements for balance as a benchmark for evaluating news coverage, further problems of arbitrariness arise. In one study of AIDS coverage, *On Balance* (July/August 1989) contrasted news mentions and official statistics on the means by which the HIV virus is spread, arguing that CBC was underreporting HIV transmission by gay and bisexual men. But what was the relevance of this finding if the NMA's purpose is to help readers to understand and evaluate news media? Was the NMA inviting the media to indulge in intensified homophobia? Should CBC have connected 85 per cent of its coverage of AIDS with homosexual transmission in order to achieve "fidelity" or "balance"? From a public health viewpoint, this approach would surely not be productive given that the fastest-growing groups of victims at the time were young people and heterosexual women.

The term "balance" is, then, not a rigorous concept that can be measured objectively and scientifically, as the NMA claims of its work. Rather, it is a rhetorical term, one inextricably linked to, and intended to win support for, its users' judgements about the legitimacy of contending political actors, positions, and issues. The NMA's own political use of the concept can be inferred from the Archive's association with the Fraser Institute, and from its origins in research conducted in the 1980s by University of Calgary political scientist Barry Cooper alleging left-wing bias in CBC Radio. More directly, the rhetorical use of balance is evident from the "spin" that the NMA frequently places on its research findings. Without using the word "bias" or making its own model of the news explicit, the *On Balance* newsletter's inferential structure consistently supports a "political-attitudinal theory" of news, one that "sees the personal political opinions of newspeople as regularly influencing decisions about what to cover and how to cover it."[60]

Newspaper columnist Andrew Coyne, himself a market-liberal ideologist, was on the mark in describing the *On Balance* research agenda: "Ostensibly, it's just disinterested empirical observation, like bird-watching, but the intention is clear: to gather proof of the leftist conspiracy conservatives are convinced is running the media."[61] In that respect the NMA's research parallels that of the Center for Media and Public Affairs in Washington, D.C., which does reputable research, but research systematically guided by a search for evidence of what it considers to be left-liberal bias in the news.

In June 1989 *On Balance* offered an example of such a research agenda. Reviewing its own previous findings, *On Balance* said that "reporters' opinions follow a consistent pattern" – against privatization and free trade, for public rather than user funding of health care, and for labour's position rather than management. (The same study also found a pro-life over pro-choice pattern in abortion coverage, but the NMA failed to comment on this apparent contradiction to its finding of ideological consistency in the news.) More recently, in an analysis of local television coverage of British Columbia's May 1996 election, the NMA's report stated that the centre-right opposition party, the Liberals, received more negative coverage, and more coverage overall, than did the other parties, including the governing social-democratic party, the NDP. Citing evidence that in the previous election in 1991 the governing centre-right Social Credit party had received the most negative and most overall media attention, the report implied that journalists' "underlying political allegiances" (presumably in favour of the NDP) accounted for negative coverage of the Liberals in 1996.[62]

The NMA arrived at such an interpretation only by selectively highlighting and contextualizing its own results. Its own numbers showed that the NDP received proportionately far more negative coverage than the Liberals did. The NMA's comparison with the 1991 campaign was selective. In terms of the relationship between media coverage and political incumbency, the 1986 provincial campaign more closely paralleled the 1996 one. In 1986 the newly elected leader of the governing Social Credit party tended to receive glowing coverage, especially on TV, while the NDP opposition's campaign got a generally bad press. The NMA study also overlooked the local media's concentration in 1996 on government debt – the NDP's weakest issue – far more than was warranted by polls of voters' issue priorities.[63] New Democrats could have made a case that the media were out to get them at least as much as the Liberals.

More plausibly, campaign coverage is most strongly influenced by factors unrelated to journalists' partisanship – factors such as the parties' standings in the polls, journalists' perceptions of the competence, openness, and newsworthiness of the leaders and their campaigns, the parties' own choices of campaign tactics and issues to emphasize, rivalry between major media to gain insider access, and the tendency of particular themes or storylines to dominate coverage in brief but intense bursts.

Other NMA studies, such as its research on labour coverage, could be similarly reinterpreted, particularly in light of other scholarly work that the NMA generally ignores except when it suits its own spin.

Notwithstanding its conceptual and methodological limitations and its potential subordination to the Fraser Institute's open and single-minded free-market philosophy (including hostility to public broadcasting), the NMA research has enjoyed some apparent media and political impact. Through the newsletter's wide distribution to Canadian political and business elites and its non-academic style, as well as such channels as press conferences and news releases, the NMA's conclusions are highly publicized. Its study on free trade coverage, for example, was released in the middle of the 1988 federal election campaign revolving around that issue, and made good press itself. Both the NMA and its director have enjoyed growing media access as authorities on the media. The NMA's studies have had a particular impact within the CBC, where they are often brandished as evidence of left-liberal bias by board members like Mulroney-appointee John Crispo – a man who had decried the CBC as a "propaganda agency" for "left-wing producers" and as acting like "Radio Baghdad" during the Gulf War. At a 1991 CRTC hearing, Crispo called the NMA study on free trade "definitive," and other columnists and organizations, from Doug Fisher of *The Toronto Sun* to the Business Council of British Columbia, have likewise uncritically accepted and amplified the NMA research.[64]

On balance, the NMA's research must be understood as a deliberate political intervention, an implicit campaign to pressure the media into providing greater access for its own spokespeople and viewpoints. The campaign has been relatively successful, for a number of reasons. First, the NMA has an annual budget comparable to the entire staff and programming budget of Co-op Radio, and it has access to the broader networks and public events of the parent Fraser Institute. The NMA thus has the resources to engage in what Oscar Gandy calls "information subsidy," the subsidized distribution of expensively produced, newsworthy, and potentially self-serving or self-promoting information.[65]

Second, a process of elective affinity was at work: that is, the NMA's critiques of the media, particularly CBC, coincided with pre-existing right-wing perceptions. The NMA has a receptive audience eager to believe its conclusions without worrying about methodological rigour. Third, the NMA's definition of balance, conceptually limited though it is, coincides with existing dominant practices in the media.

Unequal Negotiation

Behind the rhetoric of objectivity and balance is a social struggle over media access and influence and, beyond that, the very terms of public discourse in Canada. In this struggle, as Marc Raboy observes, the abstract and basically contested concept of objectivity and particularly its more restricted component, balance, often become reified. They are treated "as an actually existing *thing*, as something that can be grasped and squeezed, measured and assessed."[66] In that process, the role of power, the unequal ability of contending social groups to have their definitions of balance accepted as appropriate, can become obscured.

5

Epistemologies in Contention: Journalistic Objectivity as (Un)workable Philosophy

(with Nick Dyer-Witheford)

Are journalists also working philosophers? This question might well provoke howls of derision at the press club, because journalists do not usually think of themselves as heirs of René Descartes or Immanuel Kant. Yet it is not too much to suggest that the practices and claims (both explicit and implicit) of objective journalism imply certain views on issues such as the nature of truth and the possibilities of human knowledge about reality; and that journalists practise a form of workable – or perhaps unworkable – philosophy.

Here we want to suggest that both journalistic practices and criticisms of these practices are always informed – tacitly or overtly – by what philosophers would call an epistemology, that is, a theory about human knowledge. An epistemology usually has something to say about the nature of the real, the material world, the "furniture of the universe." That is, an epistemology may imply an ontology. It also comments upon the relationship between this real world and our actual or potential knowledge of it. Finally, it states or implies something about the degree of correspondence between the real world, our knowledge of it, and our ability to adequately express that knowledge through language.

In the world of journalism some of this philosophy is embedded in debates about the regime of objectivity. Indeed, most news journalism, and also many of its critics, are deeply dependent on concepts of truth, knowledge, and objectivity derived from nineteenth-century philosophic traditions known as positivism and empiricism. Despite this grounding, a radically different tradition – conventionalism – attacks the very possibility and/or desirability of objectivity. The most recent manifestation of this line of thought – postmodernism – has produced a body of controversial writings about media practice.

But neither objectivist journalism nor its postmodern critics have, we believe, provided an adequate standpoint from which to describe and evaluate the practices of news reporting. What makes more sense to us is a third, alternative position – critical realism – which, we tentatively suggest, might provide the philosophic underpinnings of a journalism for sustainable democracy.

Some critics would reject our argument about the "philosophic" content of media practice. They would say that journalism should instead be seen as a form of literature or symbolic expression, whose function is to provide "acquaintance with" rather than "knowledge of" socially significant and/or humanly interesting events.[1] There is a limited merit to this view. It reminds us that it is inappropriate to judge journalism negatively, as if it were a failed form of social science.[2] News, after all, does not follow the same procedures of systematic investigation and validation as do the sciences; nor does it seek to build generalizations and theories. We still talk of the "progress" or "accumulation" of scientific knowledge (although some would challenge this linear and empiricist notion of scientific development); but we cannot talk of "progress" in news in the same way.[3] Certainly, journalists do not consciously work from a well-developed, abstract theory of knowledge. The practices of objectivity, as we've seen, can be a sort of "strategic ritual" by which news workers protect themselves from occupational hazards such as missed deadlines, audience complaints, and bosses' reprimands. These concerns are eminently practical, not philosophical.

Still, news workers and news organizations do make claims for the truth-value of news. As media theorist Denis McQuail puts it, objective news implies an "unwritten contract" that leads the news consumer to expect that "news can be believed, trusted, taken at face value, readily understood, without the need to "read between the lines."[4] Sometimes the contract is quite explicit. Edward Jay Epstein describes the dominant " 'dialectical' model for reporting controversial issues": "The correspondent, after reporting the news happening, juxtaposes a contrasting viewpoint and concludes his synthesis by suggesting that the truth lies somewhere in between."[5]

Even when, as often happens, journalists report conflicting statements from sources without trying to assess the validity of those statements, they are implicitly claiming that at least they have presented the relevant possibilities. The layout of a newspaper also makes an implicit truth-claim insofar as it carefully differentiates between opinion/editorial pieces and news reports, implying that it has filtered subjective viewpoints and evaluations out of the news reports. Journalists' workaday language, their professional debates, and their organizations' handbooks of ethics and practices all imply or proclaim faith in the capacity of news, at least in principle, to provide objective and valid accounts of the world. For such reasons, we believe we are justified in unpacking some of the epistemological and ontological problems buried in today's controversies about news and objectivity.

The Epistemology of Objectivity: The Legacy of Positivism

Along with the objectivity regime's pedigree, stretching back to the early nineteenth century, comes some heavy philosophical baggage. When the commercial dailies of the nineteenth century championed the sanctity of facts against the flagrant biases of the partisan papers, they were adopting not only the democratic discourse articulated in radical and labour papers but were also expressing something of the spirit of the epistemological position now known as *positivism*.

A highly influential body of thought, positivism was firmly based in the Enlightenment confidence in scientific method, rationality, and progress. The founding fathers of positivist philosophy, such as the nineteenth-century thinker Auguste Comte, were enormously impressed by the achievements of the science and technology of their age. They concluded that all fields of knowledge – including the study of the social world – should follow the methods of natural sciences, such as physics and biology. This method entailed careful, "objective" observation and recording of events, perceivable through the senses. Such observation would reveal the regularities, patterns, or laws of both the natural and the social worlds. This approach, Comte believed, would yield solid, incontrovertible "positive" knowledge – as distinct from religious faith, superstitions, prejudices, and other unsubstantiated beliefs. This positivist knowledge of the laws of society and nature would then provide the basis for intervention – allowing human behaviour and institutions to be "engineered" just as effectively as the inanimate realm of rivers and mineral resources.

Underlying positivism is a firm belief that the real world exists independently of the consciousness of the observer. Positivism is an extreme instance of a broader philosophic current known as empiricism, which bases its ontological claims about the nature of the world on the evidence of the senses.[6] What sense experience yields, in the positivist/empiricist view, is facts – data about a substantial, solid reality. What cannot be sensed or observed, and thus verified as fact, does not exist. Mr. Gradgrind, the Dickens character who wanted facts, and nothing but facts, is a stunning caricature of nineteenth-century positivism, with its confidence that the accumulation of "facts" represented the ultimate goal of knowledge acquisition.

The fly in the ointment for positivist and empiricist epistemologies is the status of the observer – the nature of the consciousness that studies the world. For it can be objected that in understanding the world we never rely just on "facts." Rather we are constantly organizing sense data, according to some sort of pregiven schema or pattern. As Thomas McCoy notes, "Empiricism cannot account for the generation of meaning, the connection of a series of associations or facts. In other words, somewhere along the line one must account for the process by which the subject advances interrelationships and draws conclusions, structured by values over a course of time."[7] Indeed, the very designation of a "fact" – the selection and definition of a phenomenon significant and worthy of attention – depends on predecided priorities and premises. According to these critiques, theory, whether consciously or unconsciously, precedes and constitutes fact. The possibility that knowledge is not just a reflection of a world but is in some degree an active construction of the observing subject poses a massive problem for the positivist approach.

Indeed, ever since its nineteenth-century origins positivism has been subjected to a variety of attacks along these lines. In response thinkers broadly sympathetic to the positivists' confidence in what they understand as "scientific method" have revised the original position. Their qualifications add an enormous sophistication to the early positivist and empiricist thought, but only to the extent that they dilute their initial, and central, claim to direct, objective apprehension of the world and concede a more active role to the perceiving subject.

Although positivism has been seriously challenged at a philosophic level, it has entered deeply into the structure of contemporary "common sense" and continues to influence much of our everyday thought and action. While most of us, and most working journalists, do not care two hoots about Comte and his successors, we nevertheless tend to pay tribute to their influence every time we hope to find out "just the facts" about a certain problem or issue.

If we look at early objective journalism, we see a notion of knowledge with roughly the following contours. The world exists "as it is," independently of human knowledge about it. Nevertheless, through the application of particular techniques of observation and data gathering, we can discern the world as it really is. Further, we can transmit this knowledge to others without distortion by using particular methods of expression.

Accordingly, in this view, journalism's ethical obligation is to reflect the real world, with accuracy, fairness, and balance. Journalists can separate facts from opinion or value judgements. Journalists, as detached observers, can stand apart from the real-world events and transfer the truth or meaning of those events to the news audience by employing neutral language and professionally competent reporting techniques, such as the standardized story format. Truth or knowledge depends upon the observer's (journalist's) neutrality in relation to the object of study. The news medium, when "properly used," is neutral and value-free and can thus guarantee the truthfulness of the message. The news can therefore potentially transmit an unbiased, transparent, neutral translation of external reality. Objective news media offer a faithful compression of the day's most newsworthy events – those most pertinent and interesting to the audience. Unbiased media accord quantitatively and qualitatively balanced coverage to the contending, legitimate political perspectives.

Behind this widely accepted view of journalistic practice are the epistemological assumptions of positivism and empiricism. McCoy, writing of modern mass communication, suggests, "Objectivity is clearly a contemporary form of empiricism, and as such is susceptible to a ... critique of empiricism, behaviorism and positivism." He links this philosophic legacy to such "common characteristics and assumptions" of objective journalism as "the passive recording of facts which are patently neutral and self-evident; standardized presentation of these facts by attributing expert sources, and, most importantly, separation of fact from value."[8]

Although, baldly stated, an abiding belief in the media's capacity to report impartially on the world "as it is" sounds embarrassingly naive, when confronted with perceived accusations of bias or selectivity in reporting journalists will frequently counter that what they report is, simply, true. In this view, critics are wrongheadedly "shooting the messenger" for bearing bad news. Two of the more common clichés about TV news, for example, are that it holds up a "mirror to society" and provides a "window on the world," even if it is conceded (as in the title of a 1970 Canadian Senate report on the media) that the mirror is "uncertain."[9] The reflection metaphors and the truth-telling claims of the objectivity regime help to constitute journalists' sense of professionalism, and they continue to provide the terms of reference within which journalists usually debate and defend their craft – at the expense of questioning the underlying assumptions and framework of news production.[10]

In an age of increasingly generalized (though often superficial) irony and scepticism, it may seem dubious to claim that this objectivist epistemology continues to dominate journalism. After all, it might be said, in pubs and living rooms, at academic conferences and journalists' conventions, critics often attack news for *failing* to achieve objectivity, either in particular instances, or in general. But these criticisms do not necessarily challenge the epistemology of objectivity. Rather, they are critiques of *departures from* journalistic objectivity, critiques that endorse, however implicitly, the desirability and possibility of objective journalism as an undistorted representation of reality. The criticisms are levelled against the constraints, individual or collective, contingent or structural, on the achievement of this ideal. Adapting a distinction made in feminist epistemological and media theory, we call such attacks the critique of "bad objectivity" (using the word "bad" in the sense of badly done) – as distinct from the critique of "objectivity-as-such."[11]

Criticisms of bad objectivity – the argument that journalism in practice has not lived up to its claim to tell the whole truth about the world – are frequently manifested in charges of "bias," understood as departures from objectivity-as-usual. In this view the problem with news is that the practices and ethic of objectivity do not rule uncontested: personal views or other pressures have slanted or distorted particular news stories, rendering their truth-value questionable. One version of this critique, probably most common within newsrooms themselves, focuses on particular shortcomings – an individual editor's error of judgement, an incompetent reporter, a news owner or medium with an axe to grind. This kind of criticism affirms the possibility, desirability, and the general achievement of objectivity in journalism. Certain shortcomings are highlighted as departures from an ideal that, usually, more or less, is achieved in practice.[12]

While such criticisms of the news are diverse, most of them have several elements in common. They claim allegiance to the concepts of fairness, balance, and accuracy, and for the most part they profess that objectivity is desirable. They believe in the possibility of accurately representing the world as it exists: why else accuse particular news accounts of bias?

Nonetheless, some journalists will doubtless feel that we overstate the positivist heritage of their profession, and it is true that twentieth-century journalism has come to be increasingly sceptical of naked facts: their accumulation does not necessarily produce accurate, comprehensive, and meaningful accounts of the social world. If Mr. Gradgrind's "school of hard facts" was a caricature of nineteenth-century journalism, it is even less applicable now. Michael Schudson traces journalism's abandonment of naive positivism and its growing scepticism of facts to the emergence of wartime propaganda and the public relations industry in the early decades of the twentieth century.[13] While the emphasis on facts may have been a useful antidote to the wilful dogmatism and cavalier distortions of the nineteenth-century partisan press, it became evident that facts were also political weapons. They could be selectively amplified, decontextualized and recontextualized, and even fabricated by corporate, government, and political publicity machines.

This disillusionment with value-free "facts" helps to account for the emergence and incorporation into mainstream journalism of specialized and interpretive reporting, which aimed to uncover the larger meanings behind a surfeit of facts. It also confronted journalism with the besetting problem of positivism – that of the status of the observer. One increasingly oft-heard argument, popular among journalists themselves, denies the possibility of objectivity on the grounds that human beings, as knowing "subjects," can never be completely neutral. Every human is necessarily and inevitably subjective; thus, no individual can render a complete, value-free, and accurate account of the world, no matter how factual it may be. Each individual has a personal viewpoint and perspective, and any claims for absolute objectivity are therefore false.

Paradoxically, this recognition of fallible subjectivity led to the entrenchment of the rhetoric and a more specific and more narrowly defined concept, of objectivity – objectivity as the assertion of "a method designed for a world in which even facts could not be trusted."[14] One of those methods is the practice of "fairness." While objectivity is impossible, we can strive for fairness. According to McCoy, "Practitioners ... assume that the truth, no easy matter to get to, is fraught with pitfalls of bias and competing interests. One can, however, employ a method by which one can neutralize the various forces and in the process protect oneself."[15] But "fairness" has not so much displaced objectivist epistemology as introduced into it a serious inconsistency. Journalism textbooks, scholarly research, and news practices indicate an important tension between balance and accuracy, both of which are commonly regarded as aspects of objective journalism.

A consideration of the commonly posited opposite of objectivity, "bias," reveals some of this tension. Most definitions in everyday language regard news bias as the intrusion of subjective "opinion" by the reporter or news organization into what is purportedly a "factual" account. Thus Eleanor Maclean suggests, "When a story does not distinguish clearly between its author's interpretations and the facts being reported, it is a biased or slanted report."[16] Media sociologist McQuail suggests several possible manifestations of bias: explicit argument and compilation of evidence favouring one view; a tendentious use of facts and comments, without any explicit statement of preference; the use of language that colours an otherwise factual report and conveys an implicit but clear value-judgement; and the omission of points favouring one side, in an otherwise straight news report.[17]

These explanations seem solid enough, but a closer look suggests that the concept of news bias has two moments, two aspects, that are not entirely consistent. One is a lack of "balance" between competing viewpoints; the other is a tendentious, partisan "distortion" of "reality." A survey of journalism textbooks for synonyms and antonyms of reportorial bias shows that the texts suggest the moment of imbalance by using the synonyms preferential, one-sided, and partial, and the antonyms equal, equally forceful, neutral, and fair.[18] They suggest the moment of distortion by using the terms warped, distorted, indirect, and stereotyped, versus straightforward, factual, factually accurate, and truthful.

To avoid accusations of bias, then, journalism is expected to be *both* balanced and accurate. Yet the two goals can impose contradictory imperatives. For example, in the 1974 Canadian federal election campaign opposition leader Robert Stanfield made many more public appearances than the incumbent prime minister, Pierre Trudeau. With Trudeau nursing a healthy lead in the polls, his handlers decided to "low-bridge" the volatile prime minister: he had been known to make ill-advised remarks on issues and once even gave the middle finger to a group of voters. More importantly, the strategy restricted journalists' opportunities to corner him on difficult issues and relied on television newscasts to give him equal time with the opposition – as indeed they did.[19] Such news coverage was "balanced" – and yet it also "distorted" the strategies and actual events of the campaign.

At the level of epistemology, a tension (however implicit) also exists between the goals of balance and of accuracy or non-distortion. The notion of accuracy implies a positivistic affirmation of the ultimate knowability of "the straight facts," which can be discerned and expressed so long as the journalist keeps personal biases in check. By contrast, the notion that journalists can avoid bias by balancing between competing, incompatible perspectives draws on a more relativist epistemology. The concept of balance, deriving partly from Karl Mannheim's sociology of knowledge, seems to assume that different "worldviews" all have their own (limited and partial) validity, without any one of them being able to lay claim to final, objective truth.[20]

The issue of balance raises further troubling epistemological questions. If the partial perspective of the group that produces them limits the validity of different ideas, the familiar paradox of relativism comes into play: what, then, justifies the truth-claims of news organizations themselves? Moreover, the practice of balance implies that a plurality of viewpoints approximates truth. Is that really the case? What about the possibility of dubious but unexamined assumptions that are shared by the major contending viewpoints? During the U.S. intervention in Vietnam, for example, after an initial period of conformity a major debate emerged within the U.S. political elite (reflected in the mainstream media) between "hawks" and "doves." That debate centred on the costs and benefits of the war to the United States. The two sides shared certain assumptions (that U.S. intentions were good, that their Vietnamese enemies were Communists and therefore evil) and blind spots (the devastating costs of the war to Vietnam, or America's legal and moral right to intervene in the first place). By following the rules of balance, the news media reproduced not the truth in some abstract or absolute sense, but the definitions of social reality that had gained dominance in the political arena.

While many journalists would acknowledge that a positivist adherence to sheer facticity is an inadequate philosophical underpinning for their profession, it is far from clear that the news media have found a coherent alternative to that approach. Rather, the piecemeal, pragmatic attempts to revise and qualify a simple objectivist view of the world that have emerged over the course of the twentieth century have resulted in a serious epistemological incoherence being implanted at the heart of news reporting; elements of the old positivist faith have been uneasily cobbled together with implicit concessions to philosophic relativism. Although the recognition of individual subjectivity and the disillusionment with facts have taken hold within the realm of journalism, the regime of objectivity has not been displaced. The consequence is an uneasy amalgam of incompatible assumptions about truth-claims – a mixture whose very lack of consistency makes it easy for journalists to avoid carefully examining the premises of their everyday practice.

In practice these epistemological confusions do not trouble the producers of news. The news organization does not, after all, intend balance in the news to be a method for discovering truth, but a means of both attracting audiences and dealing with the realities of political power. The effectiveness of such strategies depends largely on journalists' claims to be presenting "the truth." Thus, although the philosophic premises underlying notions like balance and objectivity may remain, as it were, "unthought" by most journalists, they paradoxically have an enormous consequences for the contemporary position and power of the media and therefore deserve serious interrogation. And, indeed, some quite far-reaching critiques of the very epistemological foundations of objectivity have recently appeared. As quickly and gently as possible, we shall now tiptoe through the philosophical minefields of these critiques.

Conventionalist Epistemologies

A much more radical challenge to the epistemology of journalistic objectivity is one that we call the critique of "objectivity-as-such," which maintains that objective journalism *cannot* live up to its ideal. While the critique of bad objectivity laments a promise unfulfilled, the critique of objectivity-as-such argues that the promise itself is bogus. Its criticisms attack the very epistemological assumptions upon which objective journalism rests.

Critiques of objectivity-as-such generally arise from a philosophic tradition at an opposite pole from positivism – one that Terry Lovell terms "conventionalism."[21] Although conventionalism manifests itself in many different variants and registers, we can, at the risk of considerable over-generalization, summarize its main propositions. Whereas positivism claims that it is possible to have direct knowledge of the world through sense experience, conventionalism says that the subject is always separated from direct perception of the world by the mesh of categories, concepts, or conventions that grid and filter our perceptions of it. Although conventionalism does not necessarily deny that there is an existing, real world somewhere out there, its insistence that we are always encapsulated within the bubble of our own mental categories would indicate that, in effect, such a reality – if it exists – is inaccessible. The desire for direct, unmediated, objective knowledge is condemned to frustration. Nothing can be said about the "furniture of the universe" with certainty, because the attempt to know the world takes place through mental activity that creates, as it were, an impenetrable screen between reality and knowledge.

One famous recent example of conventionalist thought is the critique of scientific method made by Thomas Kuhn, who provided a frontal challenge to positivism's belief in the experimental methods of the natural sciences –

as methods that supposedly resulted in ever more accurate and refined understanding of the facts of the natural world and an inexorable, cumulative progress in the development of knowledge.[22] Kuhn suggested that science had not advanced by an incremental process of experimentation and observation. Rather, he said, scientific knowledge about the natural world altered only through shifts in "paradigm," and by paradigm he meant a whole framework of enquiry including methods, concepts, propositions, theories, and blind spots. Regular, workaday scientific practice – what Kuhn termed "normal science" – always assimilates observed facts within the established paradigm, ignoring or dismissing discrepancies and anomalies as insignificant aberrations. Thus, for example, for centuries Ptolemaic astronomers adjusted their calculations about planetary movements to conform to the belief that the Earth was the centre of the universe. Only when a major paradigm shift occurred – such as the change precipitated by the advent of Galilean astronomy or Einsteinian physics – could a new vision of how the world works emerge.

This argument implies that, rather than facts correcting theory, as positivists like to imagine, theory often determines what is counted as significant fact. From this point of view, the value/fact distinction breaks down. Taken to its limits, the argument sees competing paradigms, or theoretical and discursive optics, as creating exclusive and incommensurable frames of reference, each with its own criteria of what is to count as truth. Thus conventionalism arguments tend towards a philosophic relativism. Different cultures, epochs, or paradigms accept different standards for evaluating truth-claims, and there is no independent way, no theory-neutral observation language, to choose between these alternative sets of standards.[23]

Of particular importance to us is the significance that many conventionalist theories ascribe to language. Conventionalist thought tends to emphasize the power of language, understood broadly not only as verbal language but also as all systems of signs through which human beings endow the world with meaning to help us organize our perceptions of the world. In their view, language does not directly, neutrally, and transparently transmit the supposedly inherent meaning or truth of events; rather, language in some sense helps to construct the world.

Such arguments often draw on the linguistic anthropology of Edward Sapir and Benjamin Lee Whorf – who gave us what has come to be known as the Sapir-Whorf hypothesis. In this view, language acts as a guide to social reality. Rather than simply reflecting or labelling an external reality, language helps to construct our sense of that reality. Nature, the world, is not simply "out there," presenting itself to us for description. Instead, we constitute our maps of the world through how we talk about it. Different languages describe, and create mental maps of, different real worlds. If the Inuit people have sixteen different words for "snow," then, for them, there are sixteen different kinds of snow. In a sense, reality is relative: it varies according to how we talk about it.

With language, both verbal and visual, being the key tool of the journalist's trade, in recent years a wide variety of media critics, influenced in different ways and to different degrees by conventionalist epistemologies, have suggested that the value-laden and prestructured nature of language compromises journalism's claims to objectivity from the word go. In David Morley's words, neutral value-free language "in which the pure facts of the world could be recorded without prejudice" is impossible, because "evaluations are already implicit in the concepts, the language in terms of which one observes and records."[24] Thus, labels like "mugging" and "terrorism," which are attached to social actors and events in the news, imply evaluation and context. Journalists must often wrestle with how to label protagonists in the news: "terrorists" or "freedom-fighters," "strikebreakers" or "replacement workers," "environmentalists" or "anti-loggers." Are those picketers outside the abortion clinic "pro-life," "anti-choice," or "anti-abortion"? Is Belfast in Ulster or Northern Ireland? Should Canadian soldiers in the Persian Gulf be called "our" troops? Such labels "not only place and identify those events; they assign events to a context. Thereafter the use of the label is likely to mobilise this whole referential context, with all its associated meanings and connotations."[25]

Moreover, the structuring power of language extends beyond that of particular words or phrases: it also includes how those words or phrases are organized into stories or narratives. Journalists recognize that the mere necessity of selecting from millions of potential sources and events means that news cannot possibly give an exhaustive or complete account of the social and political world. But telling the news involves far more than mere selection, as if there were a pregiven menu of events, sources, and issues from which to choose. Journalism must also involve the much more active process of providing *frames of reference* if the news is to make sense to its readers. Usually implicit, such frames comprise "persistent patterns of cognition, interpretation, and presentation, of selection, emphasis, and exclusion, by which symbol-handlers routinely organize discourse."[26]

Frames, the theory goes, are unavoidable if you want to tell a complex story intelligibly. Like other storytellers, journalists need to be able to take certain things for granted about their audiences: they speak the same language; they have a shared repertoire of cultural concepts, notions of what exists, what is good and bad, what is important, and what is related to what.[27] And storytellers need to have a narrative to thread the story together, to determine what counts as a relevant and noticeable fact or event, and to hold the audience's attention. Not surprisingly, frames are especially robust and explicit in television news, given its technological complexity (and thus the need for a story angle to co-ordinate the tasks of different news workers) and its visual flow (and thus the need to capture the attention of viewers with an entertaining storyline). But while they may be more subtle in newspaper journalism, there too frames are evident in the wording of headlines, the juxtaposition of news stories under common themes, the news angles and themes emphasized, and the values and reality judgements taken for granted.

Frames also convey meanings that are not pregiven in the reported events themselves. For journalists as storytellers, events have to be *made* to mean by being placed in a context considered appropriate; the meanings of stories are far from inherent and self-evident. If Canada's banks report record high profits, is that a sign of prudent investment and sound management, as bank presidents tend to say, or an indication of corporate gluttony, excessive interest rates, and governmental indifference, as bank critics say? Undoubtedly an "objective" news report would quote "both" sides, yet through the juxtaposition of stories and in other ways, news accounts can actively work to privilege some interpretations and exclude or marginalize alternative ways of interpreting or contextualizing the seemingly same event. Framing devices are cues inviting but certainly not forcing readers to accept the "preferred readings" embedded in news accounts.

Most crucially, perhaps, frames co-exist with, and are not dispelled by, the practices of objective journalism. The news can cumulatively establish and amplify particular frames without abandoning the formal criteria of objectivity – factual accuracy, attribution of explicit opinion, counterbalancing quotations – in individual reports. Indeed, such objectivity markers can help to disguise or render unseen the dominant frame. The frame may be especially difficult to recognize when it is closely linked to the culture's master narratives, because unlike individual cases of perceived bias, it does not stand out as foreground against taken-for-granted assumptions. For example, news reports of female politicians and their politics can be both objective – in the sense of balancing her views with that of her opponents within the framework of parliamentary politics – and anchored within patriarchy and the dominant male-oriented patriarchal view of politics, with different narrative focuses and evaluative criteria in news reporting.[28] The typical narrative focus has long been on women politicians' dress, looks, and hairstyle: the media were obsessed, for instance, with the photo of a bare-shouldered Kim Campbell – Canada's first female prime minister. In recent Canadian politics the frames include the images of a passive, soft-spoken, and "lightweight" Audrey McLaughlin who won her leadership of the federal New Democratic Party in the late 1980s because of her gender and her feminist support, not her different approach to politics and her unconventional professional credentials; and to McLaughlin's contrary, a "tough," aggressive, outspoken Sheila Copps, the federal Liberals' deputy leader, who plays by the masculine rules of the political game.

The analysis of media frames suggests that reality judgements and normative values unavoidably intrude upon the selection of events, language, and interpretive context. Such an intrusion appears to threaten the possibility of achieving that which the objectivity creed implicitly claims, namely, "a complete and unrefracted capture of the world," one that clearly distinguishes "fact" from "opinion, interpretation or comment."[29]

At about the same time as the analysis of framing was becoming an important part of critical media analysis, another distinct but related line of thought challenged objectivist claims. This focused on how media participate in the making of the very world on which they report. The regime of objectivity implies that the media can stand separate from the events they observe. "We don't make the news, we just report it," goes a standard response to audience criticism. In academic media sociology, however, few themes are more common (and more open to misinterpretation) than the media's active participation in constructing social reality. David Altheide and R.P. Snow go so far as to argue that modern U.S. society is dominated by a "media logic." Media are "the dominant force to which other institutions conform," including "the entire political process," which is now "inextricably tied to the logic of media work and has been transformed by it into an extension of media production."[30]

One need not accept such sweeping media determinism to acknowledge the interventions of journalism in society and politics. One example is the widespread production of "pseudo-events," which are preplanned or incited and have the primary purpose of being reported or reproduced.[31] Any news conference, and most political speeches and demonstrations, are arranged for media propagation and would not occur in the absence of the media. Apart from the deliberate production of pseudo-events, news media may influence the very social or political trends that their reports supposedly reflect.[32] Thus television has been credited with undermining party identification and altering the qualities of successful party leaders.

These kinds of arguments seem to throw a double-whammy at the epistemology of objectivity. They suggest that news is a manufactured product subject to organizational biases, rather than the mirror-like reflection proclaimed by strong versions of objectivity; and because the process of creating news is also one of creating social reality itself, the media cannot be regarded as a separate observer. The media actively help to constitute reality, even if it is only by helping to make "real" the ways that dominant social institutions structure social and political processes. For example, could an election campaign today have any meaningful existence apart from the media that amplify it?

It is doubtful whether the social constructionist critique necessarily undermines the possibility of objectivity-as-such. Certainly in principle it applies no more to journalism than to the social sciences (if not the physical sciences, which have a greater claim to not affecting the phenomena they investigate – although even that claim is disputed).[33] But this critique does challenge claims that the media can be objective insofar as they constitute a distinct fourth estate. It implies the need for journalism to recognize and render explicit its own unavoidable involvement in the very social processes it reports.

Postmodernism and the Media: The Reality Gulf

In recent years writers associated with the "posts" of contemporary social theory – postmodernism and poststructuralism – have taken these arguments about the linguistic mediation and construction of reality to dizzying new heights. What are they on about, these "Posties," as philosopher Richard Rorty once ironically nicknamed them? It is not our intention to offer a comprehensive account of the many divergent themes clustered under the labels of postmodernism and poststructuralism, but we can give some sense of what thinkers associated with these terms characteristically reject.

The refusals include what the theorists see as the totalizing repressive certainties and universalizing values (justice, reason, progress, truth) of post-Enlightenment rationality, the coherent self-contained knowing subject of Cartesian philosophy, the search for epistemological certainty, the privileged status of "high" culture vis-à-vis popular culture and everyday life, and the cultural "metanarratives" of science, politics, and religion that no longer function effectively to endow the humans' world with meaning.

In their place, postmodernists emphasize and celebrate difference, otherness, marginality, disjuncture, fragmentation, simulation, contingency, and chaos. This position has been taken up most notably by media and cultural studies, but has also found recent expression in the sociology of knowledge, the philosophy of science, and other fields. Here, again at risk of oversimplifying, we want to extract some notions about the power of language that underscore the postmodernists' attack on objectivity.

One starting point is the theory of meaning known as semiotics, developed in the early twentieth century by the Swiss linguist Ferdinand de Saussure. Taken up by French structuralists, including Roland Barthes, in the 1960s, semiotics has heavily influenced the academic study of popular culture and media, including the news. Its essential insights begin with the notion of language as a system of signs, and meaning as a product of the structural relations that exist within that system. The position rejects the commonsense understanding that the intentions and choices of its individual author create the meaning of a text (such as a news report). Thus structuralism suggests that to understand news we do not get very far by knowing about the background and biases of journalists; we need (as we have attempted here) to analyse the codes and conventions of news as a socially structured discourse.[34]

Moreover, if the meanings generated by signs are produced by their relationship with each other within the sign-system, it is not enough to examine the linkage of linguistic signifiers (words) with extralinguistic referents (the actual thing to which the word refers). If we want to grasp the meanings generated by the signifier "black," we need to know how it plays off against and differs from other signifiers (white, grey, ebony, Oriental) within discourses of colour and race.[35] We cannot be content to understand it simply as a means of *referring* to very darkish objects and people. Language, in this view, is not simply a tool for naming a pre-existing world. With an intensity that would no doubt surprise even Sapir and Whorf, structuralism began to dethrone the referent and instead celebrate the intermingling of world and text.

Poststructuralism (along with its literary cousin, deconstruction) both challenges some of structuralism's concepts and takes them to further lengths. Structuralism had focused on differentiation within sign systems in the creation of meaning, significantly undermining the privileged position of the real-world referent without discarding it altogether. Poststructuralism extends the emphasis on difference to infinity and sees meaning as the "spin-off" of a potentially endless play of signifiers (words or images). Rather than being fixed to a particular signifier, meaning is now "scattered or dispersed along the whole chain of signifiers." Meaning cannot be easily grasped and is never fully present in any single sign alone.[36] In one version of deconstruction, the French literary analyst and philosopher Jacques Derrida emphasizes the instability of the sign. He aims to show how the apparently fixed binary oppositions (such as black/white) that structuralism uncovers in sign-systems undermine each other in the process of textual meaning. Language and the meanings it generates are simply more slippery than we had traditionally thought.

By conceiving the linguistic process as an endless play of signifiers without fixed meanings, poststructuralism poses a radical challenge not only to traditional theories of meaning but also to the very possibility, in journalism or any other field, of using language to represent an extralinguistic reality. Instead, reality itself is dependent upon language or, to use the favoured postmodern term, discourse – that is, relatively fixed ways of using language and generating meanings in particular social and institutional settings. In effect, there is no independent reality outside of our discourses that can be appealed to in the evaluation of truth-claims. Thus the very notion "that there could be an objective, true account of things is a fiction."[37] Taken to its limit position, there is nothing outside of language, and we end up (however provocatively tongue-in-cheek) with a definition of reality as nothing more than "the sense or product of discourse."[38]

Some poststructuralists simply want to bracket or sidestep questions of epistemology. Michel Foucault, for example, suspended questions of the truth or falsity of any given discourse in favour of looking at the perpetual interplay of power and knowledge, the processes and institutions whereby belief, knowledge, and truth are produced and deployed in particular regions of social management, such as the penal system, medicine, or sexuality. He was interested, in short, in the politics of the discursive regime – an approach to which we owe some debt in our own analysis of journalistic objectivity.

Others have more directly challenged the distinction between objects-in-themselves, and our talk or thought about them. For Jean Baudrillard, the voluminous multiplication of images – signs – has gone hand in hand with their progressive loss of meaning, or reference to the real. In an age of advanced information technologies he argues that signs, which once pointed to reality and later served to mystify it through advertising and propaganda, now entirely substitute for reality. We enter a world of simulacra, in which models come before originals. In this so-called hyperreality, according to Baudrillard, "The territory no longer precedes the map, nor survives it. Henceforth, it is the map that precedes the territory."[39] With reality itself constituted by wall-to-wall media images, the epistemological ground for the distinction between actuality and imaginary, truth and lies, and fabrication and authenticity evaporates.

Critics and journalists influenced by postmodernism have brought radical new perspectives to the issues of media and reporting. They have thrown into sharp relief the many submerged problems attending what Stuart Allan calls "the will to facticity" that is so deeply constitutive of news production. They have reinforced the recognition, already emergent in structuralism, of the constitutive nature of language and discourse. They have offered a well-deserved critique of any theory of knowledge that claims to escape the reflexivity of language.[40] They make it clear that truth and knowledge are not guaranteed by virtue of the observer's "neutrality" or by balancing between a plurality of competing (dominant) perspectives. Language and the media help to actively construct our perceptions of the world; they do not and cannot function as transparent reflections of reality. Values unavoidably intrude. Media help to construct the social world and cannot stand outside it as detached observers. Language itself cannot be used with any certainty to represent an extradiscursive reality. This kind of critique fundamentally challenges the epistemology of objectivity.[41]

Indeed, if it were logically coherent, postmodernist relativism would surely imply bracketing or even abandoning a truth-telling ethic for journalism. Truth-claims would be limited by and to their particular paradigm, culture, or historical period. Any objectivity that was possible would operate on the basis of consensual standards shared within, but not across, the boundaries of discourse-communities. If indeed we live in a "post-truth society,"[42] journalists should give up the pretence of pursuing objectivity and instead write in ways that are more self-critical and self-reflexive or that celebrate subjectivity (as the New Journalists did), playfulness, and fictional techniques – and that are more open to previously marginal voices and excluded Others. And postmodern media scholars would probably recommend that we abandon the modernist project of teasing out the underlying structure of news and that we cease evaluating the news in terms of its truthfulness, its accuracy, its representational adequacy. Instead, treat news as a form of fiction – as, indeed, one Australian colleague told us he tells his students – and focus attention on its characteristics as a genre of narrative, its structure of appeal to audiences, its "presentational aspects, its visuality and its discursive visualizations."[43]

Postmodern views of news and journalism have – for obvious reasons – proved highly contentious. Indeed, a series of articles written by Baudrillard on the Persian Gulf War highlighted many of the most problematic aspects of postmodern thought. Written at the time of the conflict, and published in the French newspaper *Libération*, the articles focused on the role of the media in a war in which "our strategic site is the television screen, from which we are daily bombarded."[44] Although Baudrillard made many provocative, and somewhat contradictory, suggestions in these articles, his basic claim is that the barrage of propaganda and disinformation from both sides in the conflict made it *impossible* to know what was actually going on in Kuwait or Baghdad. Epistemological certainty, including even the confidence that what was occurring constituted a "war" at all, had been swallowed up in a "reality gulf." While Baudrillard admitted that large numbers of people had undoubtedly been killed and cities bombed, he proposed that the "virtual" nature of the electronically mediated hostilities made any "practical knowledge of this war ... out of the question."[45] All that sceptical intelligence could do was "reject the probability of all information, of all images whatever their source." The aim of this exercise was not to "seek to reestablish the truth" – for which, Baudrillard insisted, "we do not have the means" – but rather to "avoid being dupes" by refusing to give credibility to any truth-claims about the conflict.[46]

Baudrillard's point was not simply that "the first casualty of war is truth" – that governments withhold and falsify information for propaganda purposes. That old-fashioned, modernist claim would simply imply that the task at hand was to sift truth from falsehood, to ferret out what was really happening. His argument was far more extreme: according to the postmodern *savant*, the clash of incommensurable discourses, facilitated by new electronic technologies, had gone so far that there was no longer any operative way to distinguish between truth and falsehood. We simply don't possess any yardstick, Baudrillard says – any grounds of comparison – that could enable even the most expert observer to achieve such a critical perspective.

Baudrillard's articles provoked a furious reaction. In particular, they incited a book-length response from the British philosopher and long-time opponent of postmodern thought Christopher Norris, who attacked Baudrillard's positions as the height of intellectual irresponsibility. Of course, Norris says, media coverage of the war was deluged with propaganda and misinformation. This is, however, no reason to go along with Baudrillard and take the view that truth and reality are nowadays wholly indistinguishable from the kinds of whole-sale simulation – or the forms of institutionalized pseudo-debate – that exert such a hold upon the currency of thought and belief. For it is still possible to perceive the various blind spots, gaps, contradictions, mani-fest non-sequiturs and downright lies that punctuate "official" discourse and which thus give a hold for constructing an alternative – more ad-equate and truthful – version of events.[47]

To support his case Norris cited the example of television footage – censored in the United States but shown on BBC television – showing a U.S. cruise missile strike on an allegedly civilian-occupied bunker in Iraq. The U.S. accounts of the episode showed certain discrepancies: U.S. sources alterna-tively claimed that the country's targeting system was so accurate that its bombs wouldn't hit civilians and that they didn't know about civilians being hit because of a breakdown in the technology. Although the footage is open to contradictory interpretation, Norris suggests that the discrepancies, and the U.S. government's evident motive for denying civilian deaths, create an overwhelming balance of evidence against the Pentagon's denials of civilian casualties. Not only is Baudrillard philosophically wrong about the "reality gulf," Norris suggests, but he is morally and politically dangerous. For to say that it is impossible to discriminate between "truer" and "falser" versions of reporting is in effect to surrender the discursive ground to whatever side has the stronger propaganda apparatus. In the case of the Gulf War, this would be to fail to challenge the well-orchestrated Allied media blitz. For Norris, writing from a strongly antiwar position, this failure was totally objection-able: Baudrillard and other postmodern writers who espouse a potentially nihilist relativism should be condemned as "uncritical intellectuals."[48]

In a broader context, a wide variety of critics have advanced similar ob-jections to the postmodern critique of objectivity. Postmodernists, these critics say, seriously exaggerate the status and power of discourse. They tend towards a linguistic determinism that overestimates the autonomy of signifying practices from other aspects of social relations. They collapse the world into the word, cavalierly dismissing the extent to which referents, real things out there, assert a regulatory influence on our use and expectations of language. The British Marxian scholar Perry Anderson, for example, acidly accuses poststructuralist thinkers of an "exorbitation of language" that has "strafed meaning, over-run truth, outflanked ethics and politics and wiped out meaning."[49]

Furthermore, other critics suggest that the characteristic postmodern emphasis on difference massively exaggerates the lack of common ground between even conflicting discourses or paradigms. As Judy Lichtenberg argues, although there are different worldviews, "We share a great deal even with those from very different cultures.... Our world-views are not hermetic: others can get in and we can get out."[50] The constructivist view of language confuses meaning with referent. An event, such as record bank profits, can carry different meanings, but all sides can often agree on at least a few basic facts. What is usually in dispute is the appropriate interpretation and context of those facts.

Perhaps the most important argument against postmodern relativism is its apparently self-refuting character – its tendency towards what Jurgen Habermas terms "performative contradiction," indicating that it is difficult for postmodernists to live up to their theories in practice.[51] In the real world of politics, they have found it necessary to appeal to truth-statements that lie above the mêlée of interest groups and language games. They deny the possibility of valid knowledge of the world, yet they make unequivocal claims about its nature. They reject any possible correspondence between language and the real, yet they use language in a way that itself expects to be taken seriously.

Most poststructuralists say they regard truth as "a kind of strategy within a language game," one that typically marks "a kind of conceptual domination, a claiming of hegemony, and effecting a curtailment of conflicting discursive moves ... [so that] as a criterion of justification the true is judged in terms of its strategic effects or the configuration of possibilities a claim makes possible, rather than by its correspondence to a non-linguistic realm."[52] But this position does not escape the problem of self-refutation: it still implies the possibility of making valid analytical connections between a discourse and a reality external to the discourse, namely, its political effectivity.

The position does, however, suggest a revealing way to evaluate postmodernist discourse itself. Critics such as David Harvey have suggested that the net effect of postmodernism has been to help paralyze and fragment opposition to the intensified ideological hegemony and increasingly globalized logic of market relations.[53] Indeed, a strong case can be made that postmodernism has, on the whole, encouraged the cultural left to engage in textual navel-gazing while Rome burns. Its abstruse style, obsessive complexity, and overprivileging of language have siphoned intellectual energy away from the difficult but mundane tasks of organizing for political change. Its practices have moved energy into the realm of the ultra-theoretical and purely discursive – helping to create a political vacuum that has been filled by the victim-bashing simplicities of the new right. Its radical epistemological scepticism undermines the grounds for ethical and political decision. For example, if eyewitness accounts of survivors of the Nazi death camps are just a language-game with similar status to the revisionist history of Holocaust deniers, on what basis can we invoke their testament to warn against the rise of neo-fascism?[54] When such relativism is taken together with the thoroughgoing rejection, common among postmodern thinkers, of such universalizing Enlightenment principles as equality, it becomes difficult to see how this alluringly fashionable intellectual tendency could coherently support a politics of constructive social change – or foster a journalism that facilitates democratic citizenship.

Towards a Third Position? Critical Realism

The extreme emphasis on the linguistic construction of reality offered by late-twentieth-century conventionalism is the polar opposite to the nineteenth-century objectivist view of news reporting as the compilation of hard facts. Neither seem to us to offer a satisfactory approach to issues of reporting and media practice. But it is possible to take up a philosophic stance that avoids both positivism's superficial faith in facts and the dead-end relativism of postmodernism. Much recent work on the epistemological underpinnings of social research has been devoted to resolving precisely this dilemma and has resulted in the presentation of a wide range of possible alternatives.[55] Our own position – the basis from which we criticize both objectivist and postmodern ideas about journalism – derives largely from a perspective known as *critical realism*.

Philosophically, realism is a concept with a long and enormously complex genealogy. The school specifically referred to as critical realism, although building on this heritage, has, however, been developed fairly recently as a philosophic perspective by thinkers such as Roy Bhaskar and William Outhwaite.[56] From its inception critical realism has been specifically intended to provide a philosophic basis for the practical struggles of movements concerned with issues of social change and emancipation. And as a general orientation to issues of knowledge it has been applied in a number of other fields closely related to journalism – for example, in Terry Lovell's discussions of literary theory, in Christopher Norris's writings on postmodernism in art and journalism, and in Hilary Wainwright's discussion of the politics of knowledge implicit in contemporary social movements.

Because critical realism has developed as a refutation of both positivism and conventionalism – as, indeed, a *critical* position – it can best be described by contrast with these schools of thought. Unlike conventionalism, critical realism strongly affirms the existence of a real world, a world independent of the observer and his/her categories and concepts. Indeed, it holds that such an ontological confidence in a world "out there" is the prerequisite for any attempt at knowledge-production. Moreover, critical realists maintain, the world is accessible and understandable. It is not a perpetually opaque and impenetrable "thing in itself" that always eludes language and thought. Rather, it can be meaningfully described and explained.

In opposition to positivism, critical realism acknowledges that such descriptions of the real unfold only through concepts that are themselves socially constructed. Indeed, as Lovell argues, critical realism "accepts much of the conventionalist critique of empiricism." It "concedes that knowledge is socially constructed and that language, even the language of experience, is theory impregnated." Yet it rejects the conventionalist notion that the world can be reduced to concept or discourse. The task of knowledge-production is to construct in words and thought accounts of that which is outside words and thought, and not – to cite Lovell again – simply to generate "elegant and internally consistent constructions which endlessly refer inward to themselves."[57]

Critical realism thus holds that knowledge emerges as a result of the interactive or dialectical to and fro between subject and object, concepts and reality. As Lovell says, "Experience may be a treacherous and misleading guide to the structures of the real when unassisted by theory. On the other hand theories are mere flights of fancy unless they retain their link to the world of experience."[58] In a recent study of the political economy of communication, Vincent Mosco enunciates an epistemology that is close to our position when he says: "A realist sees existence as mutually constituted by both sensory observation and explanatory practices. According to this view, reality is made up both by what we see and how we explain what we see.... There is no pure theory or pure fact – each presents itself as mutually contaminated."[59]

Conception constructs our knowledge of the world, but the world can challenge, interrupt, and alter concepts. We cannot, then, collapse knowledge into either fact – as in positivism – or concept – as in conventionalism. Rather, in producing knowledge we need to recognize that, as Mosco puts it, theory "extends beyond" facts, insofar as it organizes and constitutes what those facts are; yet at the same time fact extends beyond theory, insofar as the events of the world have the potential of "pressing one to justify a particular conception or to change it."[60]

Crucially, the critical realist perspective proposes that recognizing theories about reality as socially produced is *not* the same as adopting a totally relativist position. Although all knowledges are socially produced, some socially produced knowledges are better than others.[61] We can recognize that all knowledge is constructed and nevertheless affirm the possibility of distinguishing between "truer" and "falser" depictions of reality – in the sense of identifying more or less coherent and comprehensive accounts. On the one hand, Outhwaite says, "Even the best possible explanations ... are in no sense ultimate; there is no 'one true theory.'" But "This does not mean that any theory or explanation is as good as any other; only that there is no philosophical concept of Truth which can provide the ultimate seal for a particular account."[62]

What makes one theory better than another? For critical realism the discovery of adequate accounts of the real is not, as the positivists suggest, just a matter of assembling facts or immediately observable phenomena. Rather, it consists in digging to find what lies beneath the supposed facts, in going behind events to find causes, beneath surfaces to discover underlying structures – in discovering a reality that is deeper than appearances. As Lovell says, critical realism "does not identify the real with what can be experienced, but as a multi-layered structure, consisting of entities and processes lying at different levels."[63] Knowledge lies in establishing links and relations between these differentiated levels. The world is knowable – but not at first sight.

Lovell uses a well-known example from natural sciences: a stick that appears to be bent when placed in water. The theory of optics tells us why we see the stick this way. Wainwright suggests an analogy from the social arena: in our society women frequently appear as "objects of display." The reasons for this positioning lie in "deeper, not necessarily observable mechanisms of oppression," and an identification of "the mechanisms of domestic, cultural and economic subordination" reveals the forces behind it.[64] By establishing causal links between deep structures and surface appearances we produce the knowledge of the real, which makes its transformation possible.

While critical realism rejects conventionalism's scepticism about the existence and/or intelligibility of an external world, it also – against positivism – enjoins a self-reflexive attitude towards knowledge. Recognition that knowledge is a construction, rather than simply a mirroring or reflection of the world, entails an obligation to be aware of the provisional and historical nature of the categories we use to apprehend the world, to realize that, as Bhaskar puts it, "all beliefs are socially produced, so that all knowledge is transient, and neither truth-values nor criteria of rationality exist outside historical time."[65] Because critical realism does not – like positivism – minimize the importance of the concepts we use to order experience, or – like conventionalism – believe that we are completely englobed within these concepts, it includes within itself an injunction to work at understanding the origins of these concepts and categories and to be open to revision and change.

For conventionalists such an attempt should be logically impossible, because conventionalism cannot explain how we might "look around the edges" of our own worldviews. For positivists it is unnecessary, because correct method gives us direct perceptions of reality. But for critical realists, understanding only emerges through continuing criticisms of the concepts that mediate our perceptions of reality. According to Norris, critical realism demands not only "a constant testing of theories and hypotheses against empirical research" but also that "this enterprise can itself be subject to critical assessment in terms of both its specialized procedures and its wider (socio-political) accountability."[66]

Critical realists understand this construction and reconstruction of concepts and theories as a social process. Although individuals may make significant contributions to the advance of knowledge, they do so only as agents inserted within traditions, networks, and institutions of knowledge creation. As Wainwright says, critical realists look at the creation of knowledge as a form of "social production":

> Knowledge, like language, is not a physical or natural attribute of individuals. According to critical realism it must therefore be an attribute of individuals by reason of their social character, their participation, in relations with others within inherited structures.... This means that the content, distribution and structure of any particular area of knowledge pre-exist any individual. An individual is born into a heritage of knowledge. But how that knowledge and its organization are reproduced or transformed depends on the individuals who in any way participate in it, whether passively or actively.[67]

This emphasis on the *social* construction of knowledge is quite different from the admission that *individual* subjectivity can intrude on the production of news. As we have seen, editors and journalists are often quite willing to concede the latter point – and install formalized procedures to immunize reporting against such subjective contamination. But to recognize knowledge-production as a social process is to suggest that its advance requires the constant examination of the larger scale, collective structures on which we depend for our understanding of the world – including our language, our lexicon of categories and concepts, and the institutional apparatus to which we delegate the tasks of investigation and communication.

Critical realism, then, provides a sophisticated philosophic grounding for projects of social transformation. It suggests that knowledge of the world – including the social world – is a real possibility, and that improvements in such knowledge can be an important factor, although by no means the only one, in winning emancipatory changes in social institutions. It also insists that such knowledge must go beyond surface appearances to identify underlying structures and causes. But, further, because critical realism recognizes that knowledge-production is a social act, in which the generation of concepts and theories occurs within a network of organizations and institutions, it also affirms the possibility that our knowledge of the world can be altered and potentially improved by changes in the operations of these knowledge-making institutions.

Indeed, activists such as Wainwright have suggested that critical realism, by affirming both the emancipatory potential of knowledge and its provisional, socially produced nature, offers a way of maintaining the progressive aspirations of the Enlightenment without subscribing to the arrogance of positivist scientism. Looking at the practice of social movements such as the women's, peace, and green movements, Wainwright suggests that they have been characterized by a "politics of knowledge" that has broken away from a "confidence in scientific reason as providing the complete social map" without, however, foregoing emancipatory aspirations. Rather, she says, much of their practice "indicates a belief in the possibility, through social organization, of extending and combining fragmented knowledge to gain not a 'complete picture,' but rather a better understanding of the social mechanisms at work."[68] This practice is, she suggests, a sort of "street-level" analogue to the process of sceptical, self-reflexively aware investigation proposed in more abstract terms by the philosophic practitioners of critical realism.

Although it may be that Wainwright has not detailed this argument closely enough to be completely convincing, we are in broad agreement with her line of thought. Critical realism – which is very much an intellectual project still "under development" – does not yet resolve all the perennial problems of subject/object interaction that largely constitute the history of Western philosophy. In simultaneously insisting on the possibility of truth and demanding a constant self-critical interrogation of categories by which we attempt to realize that possibility, the theory walks what is, necessarily, an unstable tightrope. But then, at the end of the twentieth century, what philosophical position does not have the wobbles? Critical realism at least *initiates* an alternative both to objectivist theories of knowledge, with their unconscious alignment with the structures of established power, and to the nihilism of much postmodernist thought. It thus potentially provides a philosophic support for projects such as our own advocacy of "sustainable democracy."

In its confidence that the world can be known and explained, critical realism clearly rejects the extreme scepticism towards the notion of truth apparent in many postmodern discussions of news and journalism. In this sense it ratifies the unease surely – and, in our view, rightly – felt by many journalists and laypeople confronted with the postmodern claim that reporting is just another form of fiction, or that we live in a "post-truth" society in which claims to veracity are all *entirely* reducible to so many ploys of competing power groups. In adhering to the possibility of explaining the world, the theory upholds the journalist's vocation of truth-telling.

Social realism does this, however, in a way that rejects the superficiality of reporting that so often masquerades under the veneer of objectivity. If much of objective journalism echoes the positivist belief that knowledge is equivalent to the accumulation of facts, critical realism insists that this is an altogether inadequate approach. Rather, it says that truth only emerges by digging deeper, by looking beyond immediate appearances for underlying causes and structures – in precisely the way that so much allegedly objective reporting eschews. Critical realism upholds one, positive side of the journalistic regime of objectivity – the impulse towards sceptical, investigative, critical examination of contemporary events – but also exposes the other, negative side – the sacrifice of this investigative spirit to routine, safe, standardized, and therefore superficial practices, such as "balance."

A critical realist perspective suggests that the ideal of objectivity serves to excuse journalists from self-reflexive examination of the categories, concepts, narrative structures, and linguistic filters that they use to organize their own accounts of the world. The residue of positivism is evident in the assumption that established practices simply "mirror" or "reflect" the world. If we instead accept critical realism's understanding that all knowledge of the world is a construction, the door is opened to considering how news might be constructed or produced differently, using other categories, concepts, narratives, and languages. Although understanding that knowledge of the world is made, not given, does not amount to equating all knowledges as equally valid, it does invite exploration of new ways of building journalistic knowledge, which may amplify, deepen, or even replace current practices. To the extent that the regime of objectivity helps to conceal various news filters and to delegitimize alternative ways of seeing the world, it is indeed an undesirable deception.

Perhaps most importantly, a critical realist position provides a philosophic underpinning for institutional changes. By assuming that methods of objective reporting guarantee journalism's independence from social pressures or "bias," the objectivist epistemology is blind to and complacent about specific institutional constraints of news production. While many postmodern critiques have focused on how social institutions shape the production of knowledge, to the extent that they regard the imbrication of power and knowledge as an unavoidable, constant, and universal product of language, they produce no political critique, no program of reform, no project of emancipation. Critical realism's insistence that knowledge-construction is a fundamental social endeavour, constrained and enabled by structures of production and distribution, helps us to put into perspective political economy and sociological critiques of news production, and it invites us to understand how the concepts and categories currently prevailing in journalistic knowledge-production are generated, shaped, and circumscribed by their institutional matrix. It puts more clearly in focus than either objectivist or postmodern perspectives the possibility that the reform or transformation of media institutions might drastically change – for the better – the knowledge created by such institutions.

Beyond Both Objectivity and Relativism

In our critique of journalistic epistemologies we are, then, broadly in agreement with the position enunciated by Peter Dahlgren, who, although focusing on television reporting, reaches conclusions that could be applied to news discourse in general:

> Television is constructed, and understanding the constructed nature of television's representations of social reality is immensely important. The significant dose of relativism which follows from this is a healthy antidote to lingering objectivist notions of journalism's representations.

However, absolute relativism is not how this story ends. Our knowledge of the social world via television does not become entirely up for grabs, nor are we left without criteria for judging the validity of television's representations.[69]

It would clearly be catastrophic for democratic values to regard journalism as just another genre of fiction. It is often a good thing that journalists attempt to put aside or reserve personal judgements in an effort to produce honest reportage; and during a time of globalized concentration and conglomerization of media power it is more important than ever to identify and critique instances in which news reportage violates its own best professional standards.

But it would be equally disastrous to ignore how the very idea of objectivity, in various fields of social thought, has been rendered problematic, especially by feminist and postmodernist critiques. The stance of detachment, the claim of neutral observation, is no longer tenable. All news reports have their own socially produced standpoints; no knowledge is produced in an entirely disinterested and value-free fashion. The regime of objectivity's claim to authoritative and final factuality obscures the inadequacy of analysis and investigation that so often underlies its products.

Our rejection of objectivism does not come from a perspective that has abandoned the journalistic ideal of truth-telling, but rather from adherence to a more complex, ample, recursive, self-critical concept of that vocation. One aspect of such a critically realist journalism would, indeed, be to preserve the positive side of the objectivist regime – to affirm the need for better research, more investigation, and analysis into the deep causes underlying surface appearances, to reassert journalism's role in critically unearthing social reality and unwelcome truths. But the other side of the project would be to constantly bring under scrutiny and into question the concepts and categories through which media create and assert their knowledge of the real.

Critics and educators should repeatedly call attention to how the rhetoric of news constructs its authority at the expense of alternative possible accounts. For its part, journalism should be more self-reflexive, more aware of its own frames and master narratives, and more experimental and pluralistic in its usages of them. Ultimately the creation of such a socially critical and self-aware journalism depends on greater real independence from, and awareness of, the heretofore unacknowledged social institutions and interests that influence the production of news.

6

The Politics of
Objective Journalism

*Once upon a time, in the good old days – the 1950s, that is – politicians
and journalists were both held in high public esteem. This was a golden age
when, in the words of Alberta's Conservative premier Ralph Klein, Canadians
"looked to newspapers for their information, and ... to governments for answers."[1] The news simply reported on "reality," and political journalism treated
politicians and authority figures with enough respect that they could communicate with their publics without worrying about the distorting lenses of the
media.*

*But those good old days are long gone. Ever since the 1960s, with the rise of
adversarial – or attack or "gotcha" – journalism, the news has had a pervasive
"left-liberal" or anti-authority bias. The news media have become active and
disruptive players in the political process, sowing seeds of cynicism towards
elected officials and threatening the very legitimacy of government.*

In the 1990s this narrative – brought into our homes regularly by conservative think-tanks, business, and many politicians and media scholars – is
dangerously close to becoming unquestioned orthodoxy. Many people, it
seems, see mass media as drenched in sex and violence and therefore promoters of antisocial behaviour, or as mindlessly negative vehicles for the
knee-jerk hostility of left-liberal journalists towards business and government.

According to the popular narrative, several villains are to blame for this
destructive, critical brand of journalism. One is television, a medium
driven by visual and entertainment imperatives, which is responsible for
everything from losing the Vietnam War (by showing more bloodshed than
American publics could stand) to reducing political debate to the level of

eight-second sound bites. By covering staged photogenic and disruptive spectacles, or victim sob stories high in human interest, TV – according to the narrative – has been a boon for special-interest groups seeking to raise their own issues, embarrass authorities, derail the agendas of elected governments. With the emergence of "tabloid" TV programs and the blurring of the lines between fiction and fact in TV newscasts, television is further eroding the residues of serious and responsible journalism.

Another villain is "Watergate envy," a quality instilled as journalists schooled at the feet of Nixon-toppling reporters Bob Woodward and Carl Bernstein strove to uncover scandal in high places, bring down politicians, win journalism awards, and get invited to the best parties.[2] This kind of media scandal-mongering, they say, makes life difficult for elected officials in the United States; imported to Canada, it is even less appropriate because it usurps the role of opposition parties.

A third villain is the generation of journalists who emerged in the 1960s and 1970s. They were less interested in reporting on "the system" than in opposing it. These muckrakers and nihilists are at least in part the products of the counterculture of "the Sixties."

Here the story divides into two versions. A less politicized version sees journalists as hostile to authority in general, not motivated by any particular ideology, but rather part of a culture of aggression and mindless negativism. In this view, aggression has become an abstract form, a favourite form of American entertainment. Journalists act aggressively not to accomplish something, "but simply in order to be seen to be aggressive."[3] After all, aggression sells.

A more politicized version posits a systematic political ideology on the part of journalists. In some cases this goes so far as seeing newsrooms as the sites of extensive, planned communist or left-liberal infiltration (the counterpart of left-wing allegations of CIA plants). A less conspiratorial view borrows from the cultural theory of Daniel Bell, portraying journalists as part of a "new class" of bureaucrats and intellectuals with a value-system at odds with the achievement-orientation of business. This "new class" has a vested interest in expanding the regulatory activity of the state, at the expense of private business, and uses the media to promote its anticapitalist and antitechnological worldview.[4] Whatever the reason, journalists, especially in the dominant national and urban media, have become much less morally and politically conservative than the rest of the population. Because of this there is a pervasive "left-liberal" and "adversarial" bias in the news.

Critics see these perceived biases as having a number of negative consequences on politics. They increase public mistrust in government, discourage good people who value their privacy from running for office, and encourage leaders to emphasize television performing skills and become better actors than managers. They turn political campaigns into contests of images rather than issues. They erode the position of political parties, "presidentializing" the Canadian system of government by focusing on party leaders rather than on Parliament or parties. In short, they transform politics into an endless media management campaign.[5]

The right-wing commentators propose a variety of solutions to fix these problems. News media should hire more right-wing journalists and producers to restore balance and objectivity to the media system. One critic has even suggested that, as a last resort, government officials should be stationed at each of the major television networks to vet news stories for "fairness and accuracy."[6] It has also been proposed that journalists simply devote more resources to covering Main Street and fewer to the corridors of power – in the expectation that this direction would yield a more conservative sensibility.

Refuting the Right's Attack

To be sure, resentment against the media from established and conservative groups is genuine, as a recent survey of Canadian interest group perceptions of the news media shows.[7] How journalists perceive their role is often very different from the expectations and wishes of business and institutional leaders. The commercial imperatives of media companies are sometimes at odds with the economic interests of other kinds of companies. Journalists may well be more secular or morally liberal than the rest of the population; they do scorn colleagues seen as too sycophantic to authority; and they often lead with the negative in news stories or simplify, personalize, and trivialize political issues.

But as an explanation of news output, the conservative attacks on left-liberal bias and adversarial journalism are dangerously partial and misleading. For one thing, the critiques are less politically innocent than they may appear. Part of what accounts for charges of left-liberal and antibusiness media bias has been a staple of corporate and right-wing "ideological mobilization" to undo the political and cultural impact of the 1960s protest movements and to restore the unchallenged legitimacy of corporate capitalism.[8] In the United States, this conservative mobilization is spearheaded by institutes ranging from the rabid Accuracy in Media (whose director

Reed Irvine "tolerates double standards that would make a Stalinist blush") to the more reputable Center for Media and Public Affairs.[9] In Canada the cudgels have been taken up by the Fraser Institute and its National Media Archive, as well as by ongoing and ad hoc interventions from the business community.

The conservative critique also focuses on journalists as individuals and avoids considering the role of media institutions as a whole. In the face of other evidence about the career incentives and organizational pressures facing journalists, conservative attacks dubiously assume that journalists have enduring political commitments, that they exert significant control over news content, and that they are willing to use that control to inject political values into the news. They overlook the institutional or economic pressures that lead to the avoidance of news that audiences might perceive as lacking in objectivity. They also overlook the extent of management control of news content.[10]

Conservative critics offer relatively little evidence that journalists' presumably liberal attitudes directly lead to a systematic left-liberalism in actual news content.[11] A "liberal" sensibility is most evident in coverage of issues such as abortion or religious broadcasting (money-grabbing televangelists sometimes seem to be the paradigmatic religion story). But this sensibility is far less evident on issues involving the core interests of the corporate elite – for example, deficit-reduction or the legitimacy of private ownership and market relations.

As well, the conservative critique exaggerates the extent and radicalism of media attacks on authority. When the media do engage in "attack journalism," the effort tends to be negative rather than critical, and as such that negativity isn't motivated by left-liberalism. Rather, it is divorced from *any* coherent political perspective that might make sense of the political world for audiences. The necessity of objectivity and impartiality means that journalists are not allowed to advance their judgements about right and wrong or explicitly express an opinion about a subject.[12] Media reports critical of authority are rare by comparison with the routine flood of news generated by official sources. Critical reports tend to be personalized, "directed at personal flaws and failings rather than enduring, 'normal' institutional arrangements." Moreover, they are ritualized, occurring at measured intervals "as if motivated more by the desire to appear critical than out of consistent concern about whether the government is advancing public well-being."[13] Finally, by the time the story runs its course the reports usually return the situation to normal – a cabinet minister or premier may resign, a government is defeated, but the system works. Critical media reports may bring down individual politicians who do not play the game well, but they seldom question the rules of the game itself. Watergate led to a critical re-evaluation of President Richard Nixon, but not to a wholesale reassessment of the U.S. political system.

Conservative attacks of critical journalism overlook, or take for granted, the political and ideological pressures, subtle and pervasive as well as direct and obvious, that business and the state exert on the media. They focus narrowly on particular aspects of perceived "bias" in news content, taking for granted (and excluding from analysis) many ideologically significant aspects of news discourse that reinforce established power. For example, Preston Manning, the leader of Canada's right-wing Reform Party, has argued that the news media are biased in favour of the status quo, of officialdom, and of a Parliament Hill optic on the world. Conservatives bitterly denounce coverage of "the activities of socially and politically deviant actors such as strikers, protest groups, or splinter parties" as evidence of media adversarialism.[14] What they ignore is that however extensive it may be, such coverage, as U.S. political scientist Lance Bennett notes, almost always falls into one of three categories: "Reports of lawbreaking, violence, or distasteful behavior that tend to discredit the actors involved.... Reports that balance a deviant perspective with an official reaction in opposition. Reports on the positive activities of a group that quickly fade from the news, implying that the group and its goals were of little consequence."[15]

Conservative critiques overlook the selectivity of media adversarialism. What passes for investigative journalism in the 1990s more often than not points fingers of blame at the bottom of the social totem pole, not the top. Typical of this genre are exposés of refugee smuggling, welfare fraud, and murderers out on parole – frequent staples in the news, but quite the exception in social reality. When people in power are castigated, it is frequently for being insufficiently vigilant in policing the social order against threats from below or outside. White-collar and corporate crime is vastly underreported relative to its economic and social costs and compared to the amount of coverage of street crime.[16]

The liberal notion that power resides in the visible institutions of government results in a narrow journalistic notion of the media's "watchdog" role. This view, combined with a fear of the retribution that might result from offending corporate interests – for example, litigation or withdrawal of advertising – means that journalistic adversarialism is more likely to be applied to government than to private-sector institutions.[17] Adversarialism may also be directed against some brands of government more than others, amounting to a double-standard related to class, party, and specific policies. For example, the B.C. media denounced the NDP government when it attempted to impose what the press called a "wealth tax." But when the same government cut welfare recipients off, the media led the cheering squad with a crusade against welfare fraud.

The conservative denunciation of television news can sometimes tend towards a simplistic technological determinism. Such criticisms often take for granted that TV is a medium dominated by trivialization and entertainment values. They neglect to ask how far this is the consequence not of television itself, but of the commercial logic that has so powerfully shaped the medium's development in North America. These arguments overlook the rather different model of public broadcasting, which barely exists in the United States. Implicit in this kind of critique may also be an elitist suspicion of television as a mass medium and an underlying belief that issues of governance are best removed from the view of the vulgar public and discretely conducted by elite circles.

The Conservatizing Consequences of Objectivity

The conservative critique of journalism is vulnerable on a number of fronts, but the problem is not only that the argument is flawed. In many respects it completely inverts the political implications of the regime of objectivity. Far from being intrinsically radical or dissident, the regime of journalistic objectivity typically (if unwittingly) tends to reinforce dominant social relations, hegemonic worldviews, and/or established powerholders.

The press, for instance, may *appear* to take an autonomous and critical stance towards politicians, parties, governments, and other powerful institutions. It could hardly do otherwise if it is to maintain its credibility with audiences. However, if the media were fully adversarial towards politicians and established institutions, they would undermine the credibility of their own efficient newsgathering net, which is anchored upon these very institutions.[18] To conduct their everyday routines, journalists usually depend on enjoying at least a qualified welcome within governmental and corporate circles. Indeed, the journalists who get hired or promoted or assigned important stories tend to be those who get on best within these institutions. As a result they are not likely to endorse fundamental critiques of the institutions, or publicize and analyse the systemic flaws. Instead, the press adopts an adversarial posture towards politicians that is ritualistic, superficial, and personalized. News focuses on individual transgressions against the dominant values (constitutional democracy, patriotism, national security, and so on), which are themselves taken for granted.

The objectivity regime calls on journalists to seek out and use "appropriate sources," depending for its credibility on the appearance of "facts" reported as being straightforward, indisputably concrete, and value-free translations of the real. Although, as we have seen (chapter 5), the meaning of facts is not self-evident, but emerges from the context of a larger framework of concepts, or discourse, journalism most readily accepts and circulates as valid those accounts of reality – the facts – that have been produced and provided by *authoritative* sources and/or that are consistent with commonsense understandings of the social world. It just so happens that the sources who are most "appropriate" – available, articulate, convenient, and apparently authoritative – are usually spokespersons or decision-makers in powerful institutions.

The news media also typically rely on bureaucratic organizations for the very definition of "events." Through what are called "bureaucratic phase structures," institutions transform complex happenings into procedurally defined "cases," which provide the criteria of relevance, the conceptual categories, and the mechanisms of time-demarcation that define "events" for the media.[19]

Crime, for instance, is covered as a set of individual cases structured by the police and judicial bureaucracies. The stories begin with a reported crime and (sometimes following later) an arrest, and end with a trial verdict. The treatment of prisoners in their cells or the patterns of social violence and deprivation that generate crime are customarily excluded, because they are seen as "non-events" under the institutional organization of event detection. News discourse therefore typically perpetuates a status quo "law and order" storyline focusing on individual deviance rather than on structural and institutional problems. Media coverage of the O.J. Simpson trial concentrated on the trial; news reports of the Paul Bernardo trial sensationalized the details of the gruesome sex crime. Important issues, such as problems of violence against women and the performance of the police, which have broad implications and may lead to critical scrutiny of dominant and often repressive institutions, became at best side topics that attracted far less attention.

This "event orientation" is reinforced by the use of "documentary reporting practices" and the standardized story format for packaging information. Both encourage news organizations to cover occurrences that have been staged precisely in order to be reported – occurrences that the U.S. sociologist Daniel Boorstin labelled "pseudo-events."[20] Only when the performance is flawed or too blatantly self-serving, or when it is staged by actors fundamentally hostile to the ideological underpinnings of news, do the media emphasize that the event was staged for publicity purposes.

As a consequence, institutions with the resources and ability to manufacture newsworthy pseudo-events have an advantage in attracting media attention. It is easier, and more consistent with media production schedules, to report individual events (pseudo or otherwise) than to explore important, long-term, but less visible processes (such as the arms race). The exploration of structural connections *between* events and issues (such as, say, global corporate mobility and environmental degradation) also suffers from the media's event-orientation.

Further, the story format increases journalism's receptivity to stereotypical themes and plots, around which narratives can more easily be woven. Such dominant news values as drama, timeliness, negativity, conflict, and elites favour (for instance) single events over long-term processes, electoral politics over extraparliamentary alternatives, and photogenic destruction over substantive significance.

Similarly, while standards of decency and good taste may seem designed to keep journalism focused on important issues, they also serve ideologically to restrict the scope of public awareness and debate in favour of "mainstream, status quo values."[21] For example, a major consequence of the application of what is considered good taste in war and peace news may well be the muting of war's brutality and the sanitizing of its victims' suffering. The coverage of domestic issues such as poverty and homelessness may be softened by a reluctance to disturb viewers (and, more importantly, advertisers) with too stark a portrayal of the realities of dispossession and social inequality.

Underpinning all these conservatizing tendencies is the foundational practice of objective journalism – the declared separation of fact and opinion. As a culturally important form of storytelling, news implicitly addresses or positions its readers, viewers, or listeners in certain ways. The historical practices of objectivity, impartiality, and narrative realism help in this work of positioning. For example, objective news fosters the impression that the newspaper reader or television viewer is "above" the disputes narrated in the news, affected by them, perhaps, but not participating in them.[22] In this way the regime of news objectivity cultivates "a conception of passive readers, who are suited only to take in the news each new day so as to better forget the news of yesterday."[23] Audience members are situated as political spectators, rather than as participants. They become people who are "done to" by politicians and special-interest groups. Of course, audiences do not necessarily fully assume this ascribed identity. But to the extent that they do, their positioning is at odds with the kind of active global citizenship necessary to carry humanity beyond its current economic and ecological dilemmas.

Political mobilization is further inhibited by the rhetoric and practices of news "balance" and impartiality, which implicitly devalue strong political commitment (as well as engaged journalism). If the journalist truly balances between contending views (the argument goes), the news consumer may have no rational way to decide between them – and thus balance ends up promoting political cynicism, scepticism, and apathy. Other critics suggest that the (apparently) equal, balanced presentation of "both sides" of an issue has other conservatizing effects: it favours familiar, conventional views over those that are less familiar to audiences; it often reduces complex issues to a simplistic for/against format; and it allows elite voices (for example, government and opposition party leaders) to define the limits of debate.

The faith in objectivity also disguises the action of *other* conservative forces on news reporting. Common sense holds that news values are reflections of universal human needs: the news simply meets transcultural demands – curiosity, the desire for titillation, entertainment, reassurance, and social connectedness. But news values are not so simple or transparent. What journalists consider to be newsworthy is a complex by-product of many factors, including media technology and the relationships between news sources, news organizations, and their audiences – people who themselves experience their lives, and acquire their needs, in broad social and cultural formations. The criteria of what counts as news, and what does not, are profoundly, if indirectly, connected to relations of power.

The journalistic claim to objectivity systematically hides these power relations. If audiences are persuaded to perceive news reporting as simply "objective," they will probably not be critically aware of the many social influences that contribute to its production. Salient among these obscured influences is the power of market forces in shaping what counts as news. Mass-market journalism invites its audiences to think of themselves as consumers. This invitation is most evident in the advertisements and the pseudo-editorial material designed to service advertisers (such as the travel, auto, or real estate sections of a typical Canadian daily), but also appears in assumptions embedded in news stories – for example, that the most newsworthy aspect of industrial disputes is the disruption of consumer goods and services. The members of the news audience are thus addressed as consumers in a dual sense: as consumers of the specific goods and services advertised and reported in the newspaper and as consumers of the news itself.[24]

Here again, news achieves this ideological positioning not by violating the norms of objectivity, but precisely through them – presenting itself as a neutral, impartial observer, and/or an interlocutor of the powerful on behalf of the people. Such positioning of media audiences is also conservatizing because it displaces alternative ways of thinking about ourselves (as workers, as political beings) – ways that could facilitate popular political mobilization.

To be sure, it is far too simplistic to see media only as tools of business or government. We need a nuanced understanding of the institutional imperatives of media organizations. We need to recognize that they sometimes contradict, and sometimes harmonize with, the views and positions of political and corporate elites. But in general arguments about the media's anti-establishment biases overlook the conservative implications of the journalistic regime of objectivity. Indeed, mainstream journalism, despite its assertions of objectivity and independence, is fully implicated in legitimizing the established relations of power within liberal-democratic capitalism.

News Objectivity and Liberal-Democratic Ideology

As the Victorian-era people's journals developed into today's corporate media, the tenets of the liberal-democratic discourse came to provide the unquestioned frame for anglo-Canadian journalism. The democratic discourse became *the* ideological framework through which political events were defined and interpreted in liberal democracies, at least within mainstream journalism and the parliamentary parties. It provided the dominant mode of speaking and thinking about people, society, and politics, a mode that gradually and imperceptibly became natural, obvious, and unreflectingly accepted.

At its core, "classical" liberalism celebrates the organization of social life through the marketplace, which in turn implies a number of ideas and principles. First, there was the idea of individual rights, including equal and fair treatment under the law, freedom of expression and association, the right to enter into contracts, and the right to pursue, acquire, and enjoy property. Second, liberalism assumes that the competitive pursuit of self-interest in the marketplace will lead to the welfare of the whole society. This idea applies not only to material life, the cohesion of which is achieved through the "invisible hand" of the market, but also to cultural life. It is believed, for example, that truth will emerge through the competitive interplay of both true and false statements in the "marketplace of ideas." Third, classical liberalism espouses the notion of the state as a representative democracy, with its composition determined through competitive elections. In this view, the state is able to act as a neutral referee in enforcing the rules of the marketplace, arbitrating disputes, and preserving social order against criminals from within and enemies from without.

As the dominant ideology in liberal-capitalist societies, liberalism has different articulations in different countries, and at different times. In Canada, for example, there is a Tory residue of greater deference to authority and a greater acceptance of limits to the competitive pursuit of individualism than in the United States, and there is also more willingness to use the state to promote economic and social development – although these aspects of Canadian liberalism have been changing over the last two decades because of a shift to the right in the political climate.[25]

Notwithstanding such geographical and historical differences, a central moral and epistemological underpinning of liberalism is the notion of "the individual" as the basic unit of social life: a homogeneous, unified subject, possessed of rationality as well as hierarchically well-ordered but potentially unlimited wants and preferences. As a unified subject, this individual has natural rights that can be exercised so long as they do not interfere with the equal rights of others. Moreover, the individual is capable of freely entering into contractual relationships with others in the marketplace and is the author of his or her own destiny. Many thinkers have noted the resonance between this liberal notion of rational, autonomous individuality and the positivist philosophical positions that provide the intellectual basis for the regime of objectivity.

Like the regime of objectivity, liberal democracy today is an ideology under siege. In addition to challenges from both the right and the left, there is widespread cynicism in the news about the actual functioning of liberal-democratic institutions. For example, notwithstanding the principle of representative democracy, "everybody knows" that politicians are all crooks.

Nevertheless, the liberal-democratic framework continues to act as the dominant "media frame" according to which events are selected and reported in the news. It underlies the selection, interpretation, and presentation of news stories. It also influences, if not governs, the extent to which the rituals of objectivity are applied in different kinds of news. In other words, the regime of objectivity is not free-floating. It operates *within* the cultural maps constructed by the core values of liberal-democratic political ideology. The practices of objectivity do not override the media's dominant ideological frame. To the contrary, the applicability of these practices themselves is influenced by news frames.

The basic principles of liberalism help journalists implicitly to organize news stories into three categories, which Daniel Hallin identifies as the spheres of deviance, legitimate controversy, and consensus.[26] Each of these spheres is governed by different journalistic standards. Conventions of objectivity assume different degrees of relevance to events located in different spheres on the news media's ideological map. These spheres can be imagined in spatial terms as a set of concentric circles.

The sphere of consensus lies at the centre and encompasses those social objects regarded by the journalists and most of the society as non-controversial. Within this domain journalists do not feel the imperative either to present opposing views or to remain disinterested observers. News reports of such events as wheelchair athlete Rick Hansen's round-the-world fundraising odyssey for spinal cord research (1985-87) and Terry Fox's cross-Canada fundraising run fit into this category. They resonated with values that are deeply held in Canada's liberal political culture: the triumph of the individual over adversity and the notion of Canada as a caring society, one that tempers its individualism with a concern for the less fortunate.

Most of the standard objectivity strategies were not apparent in the news coverage of these events. Reporters felt free to describe the scene in their own words, without relying primarily on attributed quotes. The individuals involved became the centre of stories that evoked pathos and human interest. The narrative construction of the stories allowed embellishments, and the stories frequently offered subjective readings of the minds of the news-makers and their spectators. Rather than maintaining a sense of neutrality, the news encouraged potential spectators to join the events through the publication of dates and maps of their routes. News stories were almost never structured around balance between contending views. Editors as well as writers apparently assumed that the ideals that these individuals embodied and the meanings the events conveyed were consensual and non-political. The stories transcended all the boundaries between people – class, gender, age, race – and were therefore understood as being stories that the news did not have to be "objective" about. This consensual celebration is perhaps best illustrated in the lead of an August 26, 1986, *Globe and Mail* story describing the Hansen tour: "Politicians spoke words of praise. Corporate executives pledged money. Fiddlers fiddled. And someone dressed in a beaver costume danced a jig as balloons were sent skyward."

Outside the sphere of consensus lies the sphere of legitimate controversy: the region of electoral contests and legislative debates, of issues recognized as "issues" by the major established actors in the society. Here news is supposed to be factual, detached, straightforward, "balanced."[27] Eyewitness reports, paraphrases, and attributed quotes are the main building blocks of the news narrative. Most typical of this display of objectivity is the "first government said and then the opposition said" approach in news reporting of parliamentary politics.[28] When two or more sides of an event are identified and access to one party is impossible, a news text characteristically contains an "unavailable for comment" clause, an implicit rhetorical claim that the news organization has at least attempted to achieve "balance."

Beyond the sphere of legitimate controversy is the sphere of deviance: the realm of those political actors and views that journalists and the political mainstream of the society reject as unworthy of being heard. In this sphere the neutrality of objective journalism falls away and, according to John Hartley, journalism plays the role of "exposing, condemning, or excluding from the public agenda those who violate or challenge the political consensus. It marks out and defends the limits of acceptable political conflict."[29] Here again journalists do not feel compelled to follow conventions of objectivity; nor are they expected by mainstream society to do so.

A British government-sponsored report on broadcasting, for example, explicitly stated that broadcasters must share the assumptions of parliamentary democracy; but they "should not be expected to give equal weight or show an impartiality which cannot be due to those who seek to destroy it by violent, unparliamentary or illegal means."[30] Because those who are marked out as deviants are unworthy of being heard, there is no perceived need to seek their side of the story. In such a case an "unavailable for comment" clause becomes unnecessary. Similarly, rules of objectivity are often suspended in reporting on politics in foreign countries, especially if that country has a government that operates outside the liberal-democratic ideological framework. Indeed, a veteran foreign correspondent suggested that it is less important to maintain balance in foreign news.[31]

Of course, not all events fit unambiguously into these three spheres. Moreover, the borderlines between the spheres are politically and ideologically charged and contested; and they are established by those with the greatest power to make their definitions of political and social reality stick.

It makes a great deal of difference, for example, whether Paul Watson's "direct-action" environmentalism is narrated as a form of "terrorism" (the sphere of deviance) or as a legitimate form of protest.[32]

In general, the institutions of liberal democracy and the principles of the marketplace are assumed to be consensual values, so that opponents of these values are cast into the realm of deviance. Through that process news tends to equate liberal democracy and capitalism and to "naturalize" both, representing them as above and beyond history, the natural state of affairs to which all rational people would conform if they had the choice.

In anglo-Canadian journalism this orientation manifests itself in a tendency to equate politics with parliamentary politics. For two centuries Parliament has been journalism's most important topic. Indeed, politics in the news is virtually defined as parliamentary politics and electoral competition. This definition is consistent both with the dominant news values of conflict, personalities, elites, and drama and with the classical liberal assumption that power resides in the state's formal institutions of political representation – institutions that are separated from the economy and domestic life.

This liberal equation of power, democracy, and representative electoral politics has critical ideological consequences. Groups that may exert power but that do not make news disappear, by definition, from view. With them disappears the visibility of power itself. Prominent among the absentees are corporate owners and executives.[33] News is about parliamentary politics – not about social processes or the social consequences of the pursuit of economic self-interest by private capital. In this sense, the regime of objectivity helps to maintain the existing capitalist social order by making it difficult to perceive how economics shapes politics.

The conflation of democracy with electoral politics also implies that the non-electoral forms of politics undertaken by oppositional social movements are merely theatrical, irrelevant, or even irrational and illegitimate.[34] The activities of peace marchers, green movements, antipoverty organizations, or labour unions that take place on the streets and not in the hallowed halls of Parliament tend to be exiled from the realm of legitimate controversy, and exiled to the sphere of deviance.

Sometimes, to be sure, the operations of news values and objective journalism embarrass or even help overthrow individual politicians, discomfit particular business corporations, and lead to hostile coverage of particular government policies. However – and this is crucial – news values, like the practices of objectivity, typically assume and amplify a presumed consensus around basic social values of liberal capitalism. While journalism can topple powerful individuals who do not communicate well their adherence to the norms of liberal democracy, it is predisposed towards maintaining certain types of social power – technological expertise, patriarchy, private capital – and the liberal state. Oppositional social actors who want to publicly challenge the nature of this consensus will find themselves marginalized and denigrated – unless they moderate their stance, abandon radical, systemic critiques, and package their grievances in the form of minor reforms that can be managed by the existing political and economic system.

Naturalizing the Shift Right: Objective News and Market Liberalism

Journalistic objectivity has not only supported liberal-democratic capitalism in general, but has also greased the wheels for a major shift that has taken place within this order since about 1980 – a shift towards what we call "market liberalism."

In the late nineteenth and early twentieth centuries, popular movements involving, for instance, labour and women, as well as an elite response to crises such as the Depression, forced progressive changes in the theory and practices of liberalism. The responsibility of the state, for example, was enlarged to enact reforms on behalf of the whole society. A social welfare net was established to accommodate the failures of the marketplace, and rather than allow blind operations of the marketplace the state actively intervened in the economy through such means as public ownership, regulation, and fiscal policy. There were also attempts to expand the notion of individual rights to include not only political but also economic and social rights.

This version of contemporary liberalism provided the dominant ideological framework for the news from World War II to the 1970s. Over that period it defined the boundaries of news objectivity. Conventions of objectivity allowed the news media to cover radical challenges to this consensus while at the same time helping to contain and domesticate them.

Since the 1980s a powerful right-wing version of liberalism has attempted to undo these changes. This right-wing ideological movement has challenged the postwar liberal-democratic consensus and effectively shifted the goalposts of political debates towards the right. In Canada the establishment of pro-business think-tank and lobby groups such as the Fraser Institute (1974) and the Business Council on National Issues (1978), the electoral victories of Brian Mulroney (1984 and 1988), the creation of REAL Women (1983), the rise of the Reform Party and its electoral success, which turned "the Liberals into the Conservatives and the Conservatives into tapioca," are just some of the landmarks.[35]

There are different strands within this right-wing ideology, which is labelled variously and confusingly as neoliberal, neoconservative, or the new right.[36] But at its core is an economic agenda that attacks the welfare state and the social safety net. It advocates minimum government, deregulation, privatization of public services, and more economic freedoms for the private sector. It espouses an extreme version of individualism. It displays hostility towards unions, collective bargaining, and progressive social movements that struggle for economic and social rights for various disadvantaged groups. Because faith in market mechanisms is so central to this right-wing movement, we use the term "market liberalism" to describe it.

While some sentiments associated with this right-wing movement, such as hostility towards greater equality for women and ethnic and sexual minorities, have gone beyond the framework of enlightened liberalism, for the most part this right-wing counterattack shares many of the basic tenets of classical liberalism, such as a faith in the free market, an emphasis on individual responsibility, and a belief in the role of the state as a mere referee for market relations. The real target of market liberalism is the progressive side of contemporary liberalism, not liberalism as such.

The economic doctrine of market liberalism has been advanced in the name of the ordinary people. In the rhetoric of such champions as Preston Manning, Ralph Klein, and Mike Harris in Canada and Newt Gingrich in the United States, it is presented as a commonsense revolution or popular revolt. At root it is basically a revolt of the rich – a challenge from above, combining an appeal to popular frustration and widespread discontent at economic and social insecurity among the middle class in an era of globalization and rapid technological change. The underlying message is that liberalism has drifted too far left, that democracy has given too much power to bureaucratic and cultural elites, and that the state has intervened too much in promoting social and economic equality and protecting the poor and the weak at the expense of the upper middle class. As the well-known economist John Kenneth Galbraith points out, the definition of "the people" in these conservative revolutions covers only those in the upper-income brackets – the affluent and the rich. Individuals such as Gingrich are leading a crusade against the poor without admitting it.[37] In a sense, market liberalism has achieved a form of ideological hegemony that combines elite interests with selective channelling of middle-class sensibilities of frustration and insecurity in the economic and social sphere.

The news media have been part and parcel of this drift towards the ideological right. Conventions of objectivity have not only failed to offer an independent and detached treatment of the ideological right, but also contributed to the naturalization of right-wing ideological frames.

There have also been significant changes in the ownership and management of the elite news media. The 1980s saw the rise of right-wing news magazines, the launch of the pro-business *Financial Post*, and the expansion of the politically right-wing populist *Toronto Sun* chain. *Saturday Night*, Canada's most influential political magazine, passed into the hands of Conrad Black in 1987, and in 1994 it came under the editorship of Kenneth Whyte, a neoconservative who cut his teeth with *Alberta Report*. Paralleling the controversial makeover of *The Globe and Mail* after William Thorsell became editor in June 1989, Whyte turned *Saturday Night* "into a mouthpiece for the new right."[38] Journalist Linda McQuaig notes how under Eric Malling CTV's high-profile current affairs program, *W5*, was transformed from a program focusing on social issues and acting as "a voice for people who didn't have a voice" into a mouthpiece for the economic elites and "a showcase for the issues that concern the truly powerful."[39] Even *The Globe and Mail*'s Jeffrey Simpson, whose views tend to be moderately conservative, admits, "More commentators than ever are ideologues of the right."[40]

The conservative attack on the media's so-called left-liberal biases has had an impact. The CBC came up with the program *Venture* in 1979 after corporate complaints about antibusiness programming. Brian Mulroney appointed John Crispo in 1991 as a member of the CBC board of directors immediately after Crispo had publicly castigated the CBC for "deliberate, continuing and repeated intellectual dishonesty in virtually all its news and public affairs programming."[41] Fears of being perceived as left-liberal, along with the constant threat of slashed budgets, appeared to be behind CBC management's retreat from investigative journalism and point-of-view documentaries during the 1980s.[42]

The political and economic interests of media owners and managers help to account for the media's receptivity to the right-wing economic agenda. To deny such ownership influence is "equivalent to assuming that, should the entire media be owned by, say, labour unions, women's groups or social workers, this would have no impact on the editorial content."[43]

At the same time, though, journalism's regime of objectivity has played its own part in this shift towards market liberalism. Objectivity as it is practised leaves the news open to manipulation by those social forces with the greatest cultural and political capital – forces that are today clearly aligned with the move to the right. The routines of objectivity and the news media's reliance on the political and business elites as news sources make the news receptive to the right-wing political and economic agenda. Cutting taxes, controlling inflation, and reducing deficit/debt are the policy priorities of the business and financial elites. They are the ones who can finance their favourite political candidates and subsidize researchers to come up with charts and statistics. They have the resources to erect a deficit clock, organize conferences, and deliver speeches in well-publicized events that get media attention. The people at the bottom of the society, who depend more on the social safety net and worry more about unemployment, are less well-organized and have fewer resources for capturing attention. What's more, to give conservative critiques of the media's anti-authority bias due credit, the pervasive "stand aloof" negativity and cynicism characteristic of postmodern news objectivity, together with right-wing attacks on big government, undermine governments' capacity to act as defenders of public goods, public services, public rights – in short, citizenship – in an era of increasingly centralized and unaccountable private wealth and power.

Objectivism makes the shift in values and priorities associated with this rightward move appear to be both universal and inevitable. Market-liberalism has moved from the borderlines of deviance through the sphere of legitimate politics and now attempts to present itself as a consensus position. The conventions of objectivity help to "naturalize" this transformation. Unlike progressive social movements in the 1960s and early 1970s, whose battles were fought largely on the streets in the form of demonstrations, rallies, and marches, the current conservative revolution has been advanced through less dramatic but more effective backstage venues such as backroom lobbies and boardroom meetings. It has not had to resort to spectacular actions in which ideas often get lost. Rather, the concepts of market-liberalism have often been faithfully, and therefore "objectively," transmitted and amplified through the news media in the more authoritative forms of the speeches of political and business elites, news releases of dominant political and business institutions, interviews with experts from the academy and right-wing think-tanks, as well as editorials and endless commentaries by conservative pundits. Rather than being contained and marginalized, the new right has been able to set the news agenda and shift the goalposts of public debate.

The consequences are perhaps most visible in the news media's treatment of the deficit/debt issue. Compared with other issues, such as equal rights for minorities, this issue is at the centre of the right-wing economic agenda because it lies in the most crucial area of the distribution of wealth in society. While government deficit/debt is undoubtedly an important public policy concern, as many commentators have pointed out, the business elite have inflated the issue to the status of a new religion. Michelle Weinroth notes:

> The language of debt, of seemingly neutral but authoritative digits, has drowned out the dissonance of the country's clamouring nationalisms, securing a consensus untrammelled by political division. "Deficitism" has formed the *tabula rasa* of Canadian identity, a slate clear of the age-old wrangles that the average citizen dismisses as tiresome. As a rhetoric of numbers, this ideology has become a *supranationalism*, exalted as refreshingly different, modern and above the fray; it has made corporate profit its emblem of glory and global competitiveness its new morality.[44]

Deficit reduction has become a kind of holy grail, a "religious exercise" used extensively as a weapon by the new right to advance its conservative political and economic agenda of undermining the welfare state and cutting social services.[45]

Following the cue of the business elite, the news media wage a "deficit battle" and in an apparently "objective" fashion are constantly setting forth the announcements and the most current verbal weapons of deficit warriors to the public.[46] For example, when Grant Hill, a Reform Party MP, declared that "Debt and deficit is killing social programs; health care is being choked by debt and deficit" in southern Ontario, it was news in *The Vancouver Sun*, without qualification and balance.[47] Similarly, when the governor of the Bank of Canada made a speech urging governments to "continue fighting their deficits and debt" and create "ideal circumstances" for investors, it was again news without qualification and the need to balance.[48] These kinds of messages, repeated again and again, eventually become what McQuaig calls the "clatter in people's heads." Through sheer repetition, a media message eventually "lodges in our heads, becoming a dull background noise, a kind of invisible yet inescapable fact of life."[49]

There is no single cause for the deficit/debt. There are different assessments of the severity of the problem. Nor is there a single solution. Different economic interests have different policy priorities and different solutions for dealing with deficit/debt. But the dominant storyline for this complex issue is simple: Canada has this huge debt, which brings it to the verge of financial crisis and demands to be treated as the number-one public policy issue. The cause is the welfare state, huge public-sector spending, and overly generous social programs beyond the financial means of the country. The solution therefore lies in cuts to the public sector and the dismantling of the social programs.

Through sheer repetition and association this particular news frame, which favours the affluent and condemns the poor and underprivileged, has been advanced at the expense of other possible frames. It has become the accepted version of reality, the "objective" storyline. The frames include the pure "crisis"-mongering of business and financial elites (with various alarmist metaphors: deficit war, deficit battle, debt wall, deficit as cancer or virus, of Canada on the edge of a cliff, as the New Zealand and Mexico of the North, an honorary member of the Third World). They sometimes follow the absurd mathematical projections of right-wing think-tanks or track human-interest stories, such as how a small boy contributed his pennies to reduce the national debt. The storyline of deficit-as-primary-problem and social program cuts as the only solution becomes further entrenched through associated stories woven around the themes of government inefficiency in the management of social programs, welfare fraud, unemployment insurance abuses, crimes committed by welfare recipients, and middle-class tax revolts. As McQuaig writes:

> We are told, "The debt problem has become so extreme that we have no choice but to cut social spending." This sort of statement is presented as an objective assessment of our situation and often appears in apparently neutral news stories. Now, imagine if a media commentator made the following assertion: "The debt problem has become so extreme that we have no choice but to raise taxes on the rich." Such a statement would clearly, and correctly, be seen as the expression of an opinion, and would not be acceptable in a neutral news story. And yet, both statements express opinions – opinions about how the resources in our society should be divided up. What is remarkable is how, in the first case, the opinion expressed has become so widely endorsed and often repeated that its bias has become all but invisible.[50]

Indeed, the argument that "we cannot afford any more" is presented as being beyond partisan politics. *The Globe and Mail,* for example, proclaimed in a May 21, 1996, editorial that "the belief in balanced budgets has transcended ideology." Yet, upon close scrutiny, this statement of belief is itself highly ideological.

Like other ideological arguments, this dominant news frame of deficit/ debt and the resulting need for huge cutbacks on social spending presents the interests of certain groups as universal interests. It constructs an all-inclusive category "we" and glosses over fundamental class divisions related to the implications of this solution and inequality in the distribution of wealth in society. Its highly reified and moralized language effectively eliminates agency, the existence of conflicting interest groups and political choices. Consider again the following sentences from the May 21, 1996, *Globe and Mail* editorial: "Debt is the *natural predator* of social programs ... *rising debts ensure that more and more programs will be sacrificed to feed the voracious interest bill* ... governments have realized that regardless of how much they tax or spend, *ethical leadership* demands that the two balance so that society *knows* it has paid for what it's getting" (emphasis added).

It is impossible, of course, to negotiate with a "natural predator" that demands nothing but sacrifices. Indeed, McQuaig recounts how, as a re-porter for *The Globe and Mail*, she was called into the managing editor's office one day to hear a complaint about her use of words like "rich" in her stories about tax policies. She was instructed not to "make it sound like there is a class struggle going on."[51]

The dominant news frame also presumes the supremacy of market logic, importing it into the domain of political and social policy. It transforms political democracy into a shopping mall and turns citizens into consum-ers. In effect, the news frame invites readers to abandon certain basic social values. It is ironic that while news stories constantly remind the people about the dangers of a national debt and the unsustainability of social pro-grams, advertising continues to seduce people into personal debt in order to buy a new car or sofa. As the ads say, "No cash? No problem!"

The media's sheer attention and selective treatment of the causes and solutions of the deficit/debt have created a self-fulfilling prophecy. A na-tional consensus has been manufactured, and the deficit/debt story has reached its logical conclusion. Just a few years ago the deficit/debt was not the preoccupation of Canadians.[52] But now, after years of media attention, the views of the business elite have finally become the views of "Canadians." Thus, a February 2, 1996, *Vancouver Sun* story is able to juxtapose the Canadian Chamber of Commerce's call for further deficit reduction with the views of "ordinary Canadians," under the headline "Canadians call for elimination of debt," accompanied by an Angus Reid/Southam News poll indicating that "a lot of Canadians are prepared to accept further deficit reduction measures."

While the media's treatment of the deficit/debt issue provides a good example of the naturalization of the right-wing economic agenda in the news, the media's use of the Fraser Institute as a news source also illustrates the news media's "mainstreaming" of market-liberalism's perspective. Aimed explicitly at challenging the postwar progressive liberal-democratic consensus, the founding of this institute marked the beginning of the new-right counterattack in Canada. For many years the media portrayed the Fraser Institute as being on the extreme right, with not-so subtle labels and disclaimers, but this is no longer the case. The Institute has moved from the fringe to the centre. As one political scientist notes:

> Over the past 10 years or so, the Fraser Institute's image shifted from a comic example of ultra-right hyperbole to the representation of reason, responsibility and authority on economic and social issue. No longer is its almost daily reference in the media prefaced with "right-wing think-tank." The right has become the norm and the FI is now as respectable as the Conference Board and the C.D. Howe Institute.[53]

Indeed, the Fraser Institute and its studies are frequently featured in the front page of *The Vancouver Sun*'s business section. The Fraser Institute's many media stunts include its annual announcement of "Tax Freedom Day." The report of this date, which varies in different provinces and in different years, has become a regular media routine. "Alberta Taxhaters celebrate a week earlier this year" – "Finally you can stop working for Tax Collectors" – "Heavy burden until Monday, all you earn this year goes to pay tax" – "Tax freedom starts Sunday": these headlines appeared in the nation's major newspapers for June 16, 1995, reporting the Fraser Institute's eighteenth annual "tax survey."[54] By contrast, the media virtually ignored the Canadian Labour Congress's annual "Corporate-Tax Freedom Day."

In "objectively" reporting the Fraser Institute's view and its media stunt, the news uncritically transmits the Institute's dubious assumptions, categorizations, and polemical language: the mythic categories of "ordinary Canadians" and the "average family with two or more individuals" which has an "average" income of $60,806; the false dichotomy between "working for government" and "working for [the average family] itself"; the problematic lump of all kinds of "taxes" – sales taxes, "sin" taxes, income taxes, auto, fuel, and motor vehicle licence taxes, property taxes, import duties, social security, pension, medical and hospital taxes, natural resources levies, and corporation taxes – into one big pile and the dubious assumption that all these "taxes" somehow have the same implications for different individuals; and the emotionally charged terms about family income being "eaten" by government and residents "toiling for taxes." The reports do not consider the possibility that taxes, well-spent on public services, might actually save the average family money.

James Winter reports that one study of economic stories over the Canadian Press wire service found that during a one-year period the Fraser Institute was quoted in 140 stories, while the left-wing Canadian Centre for Policy Alternatives was quoted in 16.[55] This statistic would seem to indicate a long-term lack of the much-sought "balance." Still, the news continues to take the requirement of balance seriously – although in practice the technique has many dimensions and the relative weight of an argument can depend on context.

The Vancouver Sun's June 16, 1995, story about the Fraser Institute's "Tax Freedom Day," for example, states (as one out of sixteen paragraphs in the entire text): "Ken Georgetti, chair of the B.C. Federation of Labor, described Tax Freedom Day as reliable as Groundhog Day and criticized the media for reporting Fraser Institute research at face value." This seems to be a perfect exercise of balance: balancing the views of a business think-tank with feedback from labour. But the statement was simply thrown in without any explanation. The labour leader was not given an opportunity to elaborate any further on this point, whereas the news text begins with Fraser Institute economist Michael Walker's highly positive evaluation of the contributions of the "Tax Freedom Day" and ends with his explanation of how the "figures are scrutinized each year by 11 governments" and his claim that its calculations are "as close to truth as you can get." In short, the two sides in the story in no way square off with each other in a delicate exercise of balance.

The "achievement of balance" also involves questions of who should be balanced with whom, and how far is a news story willing to go in getting an opposing view? For example, in October 1995 The Vancouver Sun reported another Fraser Institute story. The Institute had come up with a set of astonishing statistics about the national debt – $3.1 trillion, or $105,000 for each Canadian. To get this figure it added together the gross debt of all levels of government as well as the "unfunded liabilities" of Canada's social security system: medicare, old age security, Canada pension plan, and Quebec pension plan. The Institute saw these items as "public policy time bombs that are waiting to explode." As usual, the paper made the study its top story on the front page of its "Business/Sport" section on October 6,

1995, including a coloured pie chart about the distribution of debts and an inserted sidebar with a list of recommendations on "how to decrease debt" through measures such as "stop loan guarantees, privatize Crown corporations, pass balanced budget and debt elimination laws, and reduce government spending." Unlike the pie chart, which was attributed to the Fraser Institute, these measures of debt reduction were not even attributed to the source.

The story does raise the question of methodology, but it is quickly dismissed by Robin Richardson, the author of the Institute's study. The report follows the requirement of validation, a necessary procedure of objective news, in a ritualistic fashion: "Other economists were unable to critique Richardson's methodology because the study's statistical annex is not available and none of those contacted by *Vancouver Sun* had seen the study." The *Sun* had, in other words, followed the proper procedure of objective news reporting and done the necessary legwork. But if the study was not available to others for critique, why did it garner so much attention, at least at that time? Why didn't the *Sun* make a brief report on the study's publication and hold off a more lengthy report until other assessments were available?

The *Sun* did manage to "balance" the study with quotes from two other economists from financial institutions. One of them agreed with most of the Fraser Institute recommendations, "but questioned the institute's lack of a time frame for cutting spending." The other questioned whether including unfunded liabilities "may be inflating the outstanding debt unfairly" – which was as critical as the story went in terms of "balancing" the Fraser Institute's right-wing perspective.

Another part of the "achievement of balance" in newspapers involves the occasional presentation of alternative arguments in the opinion pages and letters columns. Some columnists, such as *The Globe and Mail*'s Rick Salutin, write columns that criticize the media's role in deficit-mongering.[56] Shortly after *The Globe and Mail*'s editorial proclaiming that the belief in a balanced budget had transcended ideology, the paper printed a letter (May 27, 1996) pointing out that while this may be so, "the process of deficit-cutting is entirely ideologically driven." But for these efforts, the frequency, placement, and discursive position of being labelled as personal opinion in no way balances the dominant institutional voice and the implicit news framework.

In such cases the framing devices used, including the addition of a title, the placement, and the contextualization, can compromise the alternative message. For example, *The Vancouver Sun*'s January 19, 1996, opinion page carried an excerpt of a document jointly produced by the Canadian Centre for Policy Alternatives (CCPA) and Cho!ces, two left-wing groups that were presenting their views on the deficit and proposing an "Alternative Federal Budget." The paper published the text under the headline: "To solve our deficit problem, spend." But the text itself indicated a substantially different argument. The article identified unemployment, high real interest rates, and an unfair tax system as the "real causes of the large public debt" and proposed an alternative budget that "stimulates the creation of jobs through an easier monetary policy, a lower interest rate and a lower exchange rate." It argues that these measures would help "improve the budget by reducing government spending – both on debt-servicing and on UI and social assistance."

The two groups also made the unconventional point that government restraint would only increase the debt/deficit problems. A more appropriate headline would have been "Cutbacks make debt/deficit problem worse" or "To solve our deficit problem, reduce interest rate to create jobs" or "A budget that meets the basic needs of Canadians." But the paper's choice of headline framed the content of the article under the term "spend" – a term that matches right-wing stereotypes of left economic thinking. On the following day, however, a speech by Gordon Thiessen, the governor of the Bank of Canada, was headlined, "My way to a better life for all by the governor of the central bank."[57]

While the paper treated the Fraser Institute's deficit study of October 1995 (a study by an individual economist, and not available for critique by fellow economists in the Vancouver area) as hard news and carried it as a report on the front page of its business section, it did not treat the CCPA/Cho!ces public policy study as news – even though, according to the *Sun*, the document was "circulating among 'a wide range of labor, social and community organizations [and] academics and activists.'" Instead, the paper chose to reprint an excerpt on its opinion page, under a misleading headline. Incidentally, while the paper did not identify the Fraser Institute as a business-funded think-tank in its news story, it did clearly identify the CCPA as "an Ottawa think-tank funded mostly by trade unions" and Cho!ces as "a Winnipeg-based coalition for social justice," complete with quotation marks, indicating the *Sun*'s critical detachment regarding such an identification.

While the news media amplify the right-wing economic agenda and marginalize alternative voices on the left, they also help to marginalize the extreme right on social issues that do not threaten the fundamental interests of capital (an example is the media's persistent attention to extremist views on race and homosexuality in the Reform Party in Canada). On economic issues the news media help to contain elements within the right that threaten to challenge fundamental business interests (for example, Pat Buchanan's critique of free trade and corporate greed, and, for that matter, the Christian right's critique of market relations in general). In this way, the news media help to sustain the credibility (however partial) of the right-wing attack on their own left-liberal bias.

The Aura of Objectivity

Those critics who present contemporary journalism as inherently dissident or adversarial are profoundly deceived, not to say deceptive. On the contrary, the regime of journalistic objectivity provides a legitimation for established ideological optics and power relations. It systematically produces partial representations of the world, skewed towards dominant institutions and values, while at the same time it disguises that ideological role from its audiences. It thereby wins consent for "preferred readings" that are unavoidably embedded in the news. In contemporary North American society, these preferred readings ratify and reproduce the ideological framework of liberal-democratic capitalism. More specifically, over the last two decades or so, objective journalism has been complicit in naturalizing a move towards a right-wing market-liberalism. In this sense, the regime of objectivity is profoundly conservative.

Indeed, rather than simply serving as conduit for the views of market-liberalism, the news media have played an active role in securing right-wing ideological hegemony. Without the aura of objectivity, the shift to the right would lack credibility. The argument here is not about the abandonment of conventions of objectivity. Rather, it is about the redefinition of the guidelines of objectivity and the narrowing of the goalposts of political debates. The rules are still being followed, political labels such as "left" and "right" are still being used, and attempts are still being made to "balance" respective claims. Now, however, a different set of players and a different field have been established, and the terms have come to mean different things. But, paradoxically, while the regime of objectivity has helped produce this shift in political terrain, it may itself be undermined by the resulting tremors.

7

Regimes in Crisis: Liberal Democracy and Objective Journalism in Question

Although the regime of objectivity has long been sustained by a constellation of interests, it has now reached a point of crisis. A journalism that claims to speak to and for everybody, through the language of objective reporting and balanced commentary on public affairs, is now faced with intellectual, economic, social, and technological threats to its very conditions of existence.

The intellectual challenges to objectivity have not led to an overthrowing of the regime, but they have helped to undermine journalists' and audiences' faith in the possibility and even desirability of objectivity. Another marker of journalism's current crisis is the steady erosion of public confidence in news media, evident in polls since 1973. In 1988, 55 per cent of Americans surveyed said they had confidence in TV news reports; just five years later that number had plunged to 25 per cent.[1] Journalism's public image is less negative in Canada, but a 1994 poll found that only 17 per cent of Canadians ranked newspaper reporters (and 22 per cent, TV reporters) high in honesty, just ahead of lawyers, federal politicians, and car salesmen and far behind pharmacists, clergy, dentists, doctors, and college teachers.[2]

Declining status is also evident in journalists' portrayal in Hollywood films. The commercialism of those movies makes them barometers of (as well as influences upon) the dominant stereotypes in popular culture, and in them not so long ago journalists were torpedoes-be-damned seekers of truth and exposers of corruption, like the intrepid Watergate-breaking reporters Woodward and Bernstein in *All the President's Men* (1976); or Jane

Fonda in *The China Syndrome* (1979), defying a sinister corporation to expose a nuclear nightmare. Now most news workers on the big screen are airheads or scumbags: bending or ignoring ethical principles, revelling in glitz and sensationalism, or even committing murder (in *Natural Born Killers* and *To Die For*), in their pursuit of career advancement or psychological thrills.[3] Even in a romantic comedy like *Broadcast News*, career success goes to the photogenic rather than the intelligent or the ethical.

Journalists' slide in cultural status is no doubt related to public perceptions that they are degenerating into sleaze, trickery, and sensationalism. Such perceptions unfortunately often fail to distinguish between working journalists and the commercial strategies of the news organizations that employ them; but elite national correspondents have done much to bring public discredit on their own heads. From their handsome lecture fees to their socializing with the political elite, Washington's celebrity journalists have themselves fuelled the perception that they have become part of the very Establishment they were meant to scrutinize.[4]

Journalists' credibility haemorrhage, however disquieting it may be, is just one symptom of broader contradictions and challenges within the media system, and indeed in the political regime of liberal democracy.

The Crisis of Liberal Democracy

In 1990, as the Berlin Wall crumbled, post-Marxist scholar Paul Hirst wrote, "Western representative democracy is now secure in a way it has never been for the better part of this century."[5] That is true, insofar as there is no powerful external threat or credible alternative, and no internal conflict so severe as to threaten political revolution. Capitalism and its dominant twentieth-century form, representative liberal democracy, have survived the Russian Revolution of 1917, the Great Depression of the 1930s, the fascist aggression of World War II, the subsequent Cold War with the Soviet Union, and the new left protests and Third World national liberation struggles of the 1960s.

To be sure, other assaults on liberal-democratic capitalism, most of them quite ugly, have reared their heads in the 1990s. Within Western Europe and North America, in forms ranging from neo-fascist political parties and right-wing demagogues to white supremacist militias, racism is vomiting itself into mainstream politics. The unspeakable is being spoken, demonstrating that the Enlightenment's conception of universal rights and reason is far from secured in Western culture. Far from being a temporary aberration, fascism may be a permanent temptation.

Even more powerful direct revolts against liberal democracy, if not capitalism, are erupting outside the West. Ethnic nationalism has showed its hand most bloodily in the former Yugoslavia and elsewhere in the former Soviet bloc, and it now lurks ominously within India, the world's most populous liberal democracy. Like fascism, with which it overlaps, ethnic nationalism rejects the democratic discourse of the Enlightenment and radically denies the rights of citizenship to those who do not have the "right" ethnic or linguistic pedigree. In the form of religious fundamentalism, similarly exclusivist and repressive tendencies are evident in the Islamic world and in North America, where the Christian right seeks to roll back civil liberties in pursuit of its own vision of theocracy.

These antiliberal-democratic backlashes can be seen in part as efforts to reassert traditional or monolithic identities. In a world of collapsing communism and globalizing capitalism, with its attendant crises of meaning, identity, and community, some people may find a sense of place and control, however illusory, in authoritarian fundamentalism.

This threat is real and needs to be faced, above all by building international movements for more humane alternatives. But we do not want to exaggerate these threats; fascist and religious authoritarianism may be too out of tune with contemporary economic and cultural currents and too inherently unstable to constitute the wave of the future. In some cases, such as Iran, theocratic rule may even prove to be a vehicle of political "modernization" in disguise.[6]

In the 1990s, unlike 1917 or the 1930s, liberal democracy faces no imminent threat to its very survival. But there is a paradox: as formally representative democracy spreads around the globe, people feel more powerless than ever before.[7] Certainly there is a widespread sense of malaise, even crisis, in Western liberal democracies. There may be less agreement on just what comprises that crisis. There is, after all, a great deal at stake in defining any socio-political change as a "crisis."[8] To do so is also to define what is normal and desirable and what constitutes a threat – and to demand urgent attention and remedial action. Definitions of crisis depend upon perspective: for supporters of Quebec independence, the 1995 referendum was an opportunity; for the rest of the country, it was a crisis.

Still, the late Christopher Lasch, U.S. historian and cultural critic, was surely correct in saying that many Americans are "much less sanguine about the future than they used to be" and are even asking whether democracy *has* a future – "and with good reason."[9] Lasch points to decaying cities, disappearing industrial jobs, the shrinking middle class, the growing number of the poor, the rising crime rate, the flourishing drug trade. In a 1992 BBC production, *Legacy,* a British historian and filmmaker paints an even broader picture:

> Throughout the countries of the rich West there is a growing and pro-found disquiet: a feeling that the Western way of life itself is no longer supportable, morally or practically, because of pollution, environmen-tal destruction, and the continuing exploitation of the mass of human-ity.... Are the values of the West alone enough to guarantee the continu-ing health of the planet?... Perhaps at the moment of its triumph, the West has reached that point which comes to all civilizations when, to avoid disaster, it must transform itself by learning from others.[10]

Liberal-democratic capitalism is faced with a multifaceted crisis – one emerging not from some "external" threat but from within, from its own operating logics. The system's legitimation (material abundance, indi-vidual fulfilment, responsive government) is increasingly at odds with the lived reality of millions of people. Long-standing tensions between democ-racy and capitalism are becoming more pronounced. While liberalism, de-mocracy, and capitalism have become ideologically and historically fused, there is no inevitable articulation between them. They have different log-ics. The logic of democracy is majority rule; liberalism's core principle is individual rights (both human/civil rights and property rights, which are often in contradiction); capitalism's core logic resides in market relations and capital accumulation. Nineteenth-century North American capitalism was liberal – individual (male) citizens enjoyed formal legal equality, but gender, racial, and property restrictions on the right to vote made it pro-foundly undemocratic by today's standards.

The long-term, global, incomplete, and sometimes interrupted histori-cal fusion of capitalism and liberal democracy has modified the logic of each. Through gaining the democratic franchise the bulk of the population was able to smooth the rough edges of capitalism, forcing the state to in-troduce tax-funded social programs in Western Europe, Canada, and to a lesser extent the United States. Capitalism, though, generates not only wealth, but also economic, social, and political inequalities that, combined with its imperatives of profit-making and private ownership, place con-crete political boundaries on public policy. When elected governments with a democratic mandate have (very infrequently) challenged those core principles of capitalism, the result can be an antidemocratic backlash from the privileged elites. The most dramatic example was the bloody military coup that, with U.S. connivance, overthrew Chile's elected Marxist president Salvador Allende in 1973. The new military regime unleashed a reign of terror that saw thousands of Chileans arrested, tortured, murdered, and/ or exiled. Political parties were banned, the press was censored, and freedoms of speech and assembly were restricted. The junta pursued decidedly "free-enterprise" economic policies, but it took sixteen years for some semblance of liberal democracy to be restored.[11]

During times of relative prosperity and social consensus, such tensions within liberal-democratic capitalism are minimized. In the past two decades, however, two processes are rekindling them. First, the political triumph of market liberalism, dating back to the elections of Margaret Thatcher in Britain and Ronald Reagan in the United States, has further entrenched the dominance of market relations at the expense of alternative social and economic logics throughout the world.[12] Second, globalization, the process of integrating the world economy in the interests of capital accumulation, has brought with it profound economic dislocation, unemployment, and insecurity.

With Western social-democratic parties in electoral and ideological retreat and the Soviet Union's ugly experiment with socialism in ruins, visible and attractive alternatives to marketism are absent – not because they are impossible, but because the current hegemony of market-liberalism makes them difficult to imagine and to discuss. That absence is very much part of the democratic malaise. The contemporary Russian democratic-socialist Boris Kagarlitsky states:

> The lack of alternatives is leading to the erosion of all forms of representative democracy. But in this case the crisis of democracy, unlike the case in Europe in the 1920s or in Latin America during the 1970s, is not leading to the rapid collapse of democratic institutions. Instead, these institutions are slowly degenerating and dying out. They are increasingly by-passed not only by economic decision-making, but even by the political process itself.[13]

Market-liberalism and globalization are potentially undermining liberal democracy's *sustainability*, in two senses of that word. The first is in the sense of sustainable economies and ecologies. The capitalist economy is predicated upon the limitless expansion of human wants and of the production and acquisition of property and consumer goods, and market-liberalism is its ideological grease. Yet our planet faces a crisis of over-consumption and the degradation of global resources and environment. This crisis emerges from the very logic of capitalism, technological progress, and dominant models of development. To be sure, countertrends within the system do exist: the computer revolution and the growing proportion of commodities comprising information and images may reduce the strain on non-renewable resources.[14] But whether these countertrends are sufficient to offset capitalism's expansionist dynamics is highly doubtful, especially with the emergence of new industrialized economies in Asia.

In its political, social, and cultural consequences, market-liberalism threatens democratic sustainability in a second sense as well: in the capacity of the culture and institutions of democratic self-government to reproduce themselves over time and to achieve their potential for maximizing human well-being. Market-liberalism not only encourages acquisitive, aggressive individualism, but also makes greed and selfishness seem normal, natural, and even beneficial, if not downright sexy. It thus undermines the sense of belonging to the same community, the common culture needed to sustain reciprocal respect, and the willingness to accept democratic political decisions that run counter to one's own preferences. If the hegemony of the marketplace undermines the more traditional human values of family, community, place, ethics, and mutual obligation outside the framework of financial gain, this is a matter of indifference to market-liberals. Moreover, market-liberalism's insistence on individual decisions and contracts in the marketplace as the only legitimate way of allocating resources and determining social priorities devalues the public sphere: the consumer comes to eclipse the citizen.

The market-liberal attack on social programs and affirmative action is not gender-neutral: women disproportionately bear the brunt. For many decades after the triumph of liberal democracy, women were excluded from the body politic through denial of suffrage and full legal rights. Even with formal legal equality, neither the notion of elected, representative institutions as the embodiment of the public sphere nor the definitions of individual rights in the private sphere address the political economy of the domestic household and the exploitation of women's labour. As a means of encouraging and rewarding socially valued activity, the market has enormous limitations and biases. Vast energies are expended, particularly by women, in such tasks as housework and child-rearing, which are essential to social and cultural reproduction; but economically these jobs are poorly rewarded. Indeed, they typically do not even register as marketplace transactions.

In addition to widening the gender gap, market-liberal economic policies — the incremental dismantling of the welfare state, the upwards redistribution of income, deregulation to facilitate the mobility and accumulation of capital — reinforce growing class polarization, evident in the distribution not just of material wealth, but also of cultural capital. Class inequality engenders disparities of political and communicative power that render increasingly hollow liberal democracy's principles of formal legal and political equality. The formal right to vote is unquestionably important, but its significance is reduced if the growing cost of effective televised political campaigns and insufficient restrictions on campaign spending translate into a disproportionate agenda-setting power for the wealthy. The prerequisites for effective citizenship include access to basic communicative as well as material resources. Those who have the money, time, and skills can access a wealth of information without historical precedent; but the counterpart, in an era of commodified and privatized information and the relative decline of public institutions, is an emergent "information underclass."[15]

When widespread class inequality overlaps substantially with racial and ethnic divisions, the social order sits on a powder keg, which a single incident can sometimes ignite. It took only the acquittal of the white police officers who had been videotaped beating Rodney King to plunge parts of Los Angeles into near-civil war. While economic apartheid may be more entrenched in the United States, a classic study found correlations between economic inequality and ethnicity in Canada too.[16] Most strikingly, under conditions of internal colonialism and cultural breakdown, Aboriginal peoples experience rates of poverty, unemployment, death, illness, accidents, and incarceration far higher than the national average.

As a political ideology and a system of government, liberal democracy has not yet come to terms with the decline of the state. Along with most other modernist political ideologies, liberalism is state-centred: It assumes the state as the container of political life, the embodiment of popular will, the repository and guarantor of such "universalist" values as justice, security, and equality.[17] Yet states are losing their functions and authority and are becoming less able to protect, or repress, people as citizens.

In part the national state's authority is being eroded from above through the process of globalization and the rise of transnational corporate empires. The external imposition of austere monetarist policies by the IMF has long been familiar to Third World countries; now in the West, too, state sovereignty is being siphoned off to international financial institutions and trading arrangements. The European Union is at least evolving international democratic institutions (pan-European parties, elections, and a parliament), but NAFTA has no such mechanisms of popular accountability. Indeed, NAFTA has been described as a "new economic constitution" for North America, one that effectively alienates power from elected governments to private capital.[18]

As part of this process of globalization, civic culture in North America is being undermined by a "revolt of the elites": economic and political leaders roam the globe in wide-bodied jets and transfer vast "virtual" resources through global computer networks, increasingly detached from a sense of civic obligation to any particular national community. In the United States, moreso than in Canada, even the moderately affluent increasingly huddle in gated communities with their own medical, security, and recreational services, while city cores are plunging to Third World status.

The crisis of public finance in Western states is further reducing public expectations about what can be expected from governments. Market liberals have worked hard and long to naturalize a particular explanation of the public debt (inefficient government, wasteful social spending), at the expense of alternative diagnoses: high real interest rates, declining corporate taxation, a long-term downturn in the global capitalist economy. Market-liberal policies have yielded a greater tax burden for the middle class, cutbacks in social programs and public services, and a spiralling cycle of privatization. As the state's ability to inspire citizens' psychic investment in public life declines, so too do its perceived legitimacy and its ability to contain social conflict. It is difficult to believe that the current crisis of the Canadian federation is unrelated to the erosion of national social programs: for many people, there is simply less and less reason for the country to exist.

It is thus quite possible that market-liberalism fuels the rise of regional nationalisms. These do not necessarily take the form of violent ethnic cleansing; Scottish and Québécois nationalisms, for example, are peaceful, democratic, and socially liberal. Nevertheless, they pose a fundamental challenge to the flexibility and tolerance of existing liberal-democratic polities. The decline of the state can be further seen in the millions of people who are effectively stateless: refugees, illegal immigrants, and "guest workers." From the viewpoint of states, these people are virtually nonpersons, denied the right of citizenship and thus greatly at risk of economic exploitation or worse.

More dramatically, states are losing their monopolies over the means of legitimate violence. Warlords and private militias are no longer just a phenomenon of the Third World or ex-Soviet bloc, as shown by the recent cases of right-wing militias and terrorist actions within the United States. Witness the no-go zones in U.S. cities, where the police dare not set foot outside armoured personnel carriers. Fuelled by post-Cold War dumping, a flourishing international small arms trade adds to the threat of chaos.[19] Indeed, the concept of the state itself is an invention of Western modernism – until the twentieth century the concept applied only to countries comprising 3 per cent of the world's land area.[20] In growing parts of that geographic/cultural space often called the Third World, pressures of scarcity, crime, overpopulation, tribalism, and disease have already unravelled anything resembling state authority and have come to threaten the very fabric of social life.

Such apocalyptic scenarios suggest that not only democracy but also the very governability of human society is at stake. It would be quite easy to fall prey to the temptation of authoritarianism, to conclude that democracy is unrealizable and must be contained or even sacrificed to avoid utter chaos. This is not a new idea, even within liberal democracies' own political elites. The dominant model of democracy after World War II, competitive elitism, has held that minimal public participation is good for stability – even though it means in practice minimizing the popular education in democratic skills that can emerge from widespread and prolonged participation in the public sphere.[21] Instead of such participation, citizens have been expected to do no more than choose every few years among competing teams of political leaders, who, free of pressure from mainly deferential citizens, are supposedly able to broker intergroup political compromises between, for instance, French-speaking and English-speaking Canadians. According to this theory, elite accommodation promotes political stability in a culturally diverse society, and political elites are held sufficiently accountable through periodic elections, interparty competition, and rivalry for resources and influence with elites in other social spheres – business, labour, religion, the media, and elsewhere.

That comfortable arrangement, even assuming that it was ever anything more than a legitimizing myth, appears to be imploding, partly due to a media system that relentlessly if selectively emphasizes government scandals and failures, and partly because of the blunders of the political and other institutional elites themselves, from the U.S. intervention in Vietnam to Canada's seemingly endless and usually fruitless constitutional negotiations between provincial and federal leaders. In response, North America has seen a modestly encouraging trend to reinvigorate representative democracy within the framework of the nation-state. In the view of writer Peter C. Newman, Canadians have moved in the past decade from a culture of deference to one of defiance, demanding more directly accountable government and more effective avenues of direct participation, such as referenda.[22]

Such political alienation can unleash energy into the political system, and it is being harnessed in the 1990s mainly by the populist right: the Reform Party in Canada, and the quixotic presidential campaign of the multimillionaire Ross Perot in the United States. This trend is unfortunate, because right-wing populism can corrode sustainable democracy. It wants to democratize government only to have it do very little, apart from perhaps ensuring that the prisons are filled to capacity and enforcing the inequalities inherent in a corporate-dominated market economy. The public voice of right-wing populism is shrill, prone to self-righteousness, authoritarianism, and even racism and homophobia, but muted in expressing the civic virtues of tolerance and readiness to accommodate differing viewpoints and interests.

Still, the populist revolt has provided a much-needed wake-up call to previously complacent political elites, and it may be that some of the alienation it expresses can be turned in more progressive and positive directions. Although they cannot compete with the media access afforded the likes of Rush Limbaugh, popular movements of the left have certainly not disappeared in North America.[23] In anglo-Canada, for instance, the 60,000-member coalition assembled by the Council of Canadians has taken the lead in struggles to protect social programs and challenge corporate political power.

While populism is one expression of political disaffection, millions of North Americans have simply opted out of official politics. In the United States, voter abstention is an international joke, reaching half the potential electorate in the 1988 and 1996 presidential races, and even higher in off-year congressional elections. Voting rates are significantly higher in Canada, where meaningful political choices (and not coincidentally, election spending limits) are much better entrenched. Nevertheless, millions of people on both sides of the border have in principle effectively rejected the possibility of improving human life through collective or political means. Instead, they seek the individual Shangri-las of religious salvation or, against all the odds of social structure, personal material wealth. The amount of participation in trade unions and political parties may be inversely related to the purchase of lottery tickets and mutual funds.

In sum, public life in Canada and the United States is in decline. More and more people are economically and politically marginalized. In coping with growing inequality and strains upon limited resources, global capitalism could well become increasingly authoritarian. The uncoupling of liberalism, democracy, and capitalism is not inconceivable. The dynamic economic "dragons" of Eastern Asia have paternalistic governments that are minimally liberal or democratic, and Russia and China could evolve into authoritarian market societies.

In North America it is easy, in a culture of consumerism and market-liberal "common sense revolutions," to forget that popular progressive movements were the major forces that turned nineteenth-century undemocratic liberalism into twentieth-century liberal democracy. The cultural and political weight of the left forced elites to concede political rights and material benefits to the rest of the population. The current political weakness of the left makes it easier to roll back social rights in the name of economic freedom – a freedom that in practice benefits the few. Remarkably, even enlightened capitalists are starting to sound the alarm. For instance, billionaire George Soros suggested in a 1997 *Atlantic Monthly* article that laissez-faire capitalism, with its rampant inequality and "survival of the fittest" philosophy, has supplanted communism as the "arch enemy" of open and democratic societies.[24]

The Crisis of Objective Journalism

In however minor a way, journalism is implicated in the seeming crisis of democracy. Far from being detached observers, the transnational media conglomerates within which most news is produced are integral to the driving logics of global capitalism. If capitalism and democracy are coming to be at odds, the media are arguably serving the former better than the latter. Corporations based in the media and information sectors have helped to spearhead transnational arrangements like NAFTA, which are the heart of globalization. The senior executives and owners of leading media companies move in the same privileged and relatively closed social world as other business and political leaders. Paul Desmarais, owner of dozens of newspapers and broadcasting stations as well as large financial companies, illustrates the close connections between economic, political, and media power in Canada. He is the father-in-law of Prime Minister Jean Chrétien's daughter, former employer of finance minister Paul Martin Jr., and current employer of former prime minister Brian Mulroney.[25]

More generally, and quite in addition to the political interests of media ownership, news discourse itself is inherently political, in the sense of constructing or amplifying social power and knowledge. Even though it is generally non-partisan, independent from the state, and mainly produced within private, profit-oriented corporations, journalism sets agendas, defines reality, and constitutes much of the landscape for electoral politics. For instance, significant political and cultural consequences flow from the commercial media's role in aggressively promoting consumerism, not only through multibillion-dollar advertising revenues, but also more subtly through the points of view embedded in entertainment and information fare.

Even when it has met its own highest standards, as embodied by icons such as Walter Cronkite, Knowlton Nash, or Woodward and Bernstein, news has offered little space for the critical self-examination of the core principles of liberal-democratic capitalism. Indeed, objectivity has provided the rationale for media practices that more and more critics feel are undermining democratic public life. In the view of two eminent media scholars, journalism's presentation of politics as a horse race and a spectacle is directly related to the objectivity ethos:

> The very move of the media to the centre of the political process entails a degree of *de*politicization. This is because in Western democracies the press (and especially television) base their claims to legitimacy and credibility with the public on their non-political status and on their disavowals of explicitly political, particularly partisan, motives. Such a stance underlies in turn their preoccupations with personalities and the flow of events rather than with policies. That shift in the portrayal of the political process is then transmitted to audience members as an appropriate perspective on politics.[26]

It is not surprising, then, that politics has become debased in the popular imagination. No longer is it seen as the authoritative allocation of social values, or the collective process of setting rules and sharing costs, let alone the pursuit of excellence and justice in civic life. Instead, it appears as an institutionalized scam industry that taxpayers are forced to support at the expense of their much cherished private consumption. Such an assumption lubricates the transfer of social power from elected governments, which are at least nominally accountable, into the hands of unelected private bureaucracies, accountable only to a handful of dominant shareholders.

Another connection is less often noted: namely, the historical and structural links between objective journalism and the competitive elitist model of democracy. These links are clearest in the work of the legendary U.S. newspaper essayist Walter Lippmann, who argued that questions of substance should be decided by knowledgeable administrators. In his view, the public was incompetent and unwilling to govern itself but would accept government by experts so long as they followed the rules of fair play and government policies delivered material abundance. With expert rule necessary and inevitable in complex industrial society, direct democracy and knowledgeable citizenship were now impossible. Lippmann was highly suspicious of public opinion and debate: he saw them as being vulnerable to emotion, simplification, and stereotypes, and thus antithetical to disinterested scientific enquiry. In this rather positivist view, the role of journalism was not to stimulate debate, but to circulate objective information that would be useful to experts in reaching the best decision.[27] As Vancouver Co-op Radio pointed out in its debate with the CRTC over balance, the regime of objectivity generates journalists as "professional" communicators who speak to and for the public, or even supplant the public entirely.

So, on the one hand we have profound global crises, and on the other we have the necessity for public awareness and a critical re-examination of dominant institutions as a basis for profound social and cultural change. Such a change would obviously entail a clarification of values and options, a re-examination of basic assumptions, an active search for a new consensus – in short, a rich process of social communication that is not likely to emerge from a media system clinging to problematic notions of objectivity and driven by commercial imperatives.

If objective journalism has helped to naturalize market-liberalism and in some important ways contributed to the decline of public life, reciprocally, the globalized hegemony of market-liberalism has had significant repercussions for journalism and its potential as an independent public sphere. Recent shifts in the political and economic context of news media are eroding some of the very underpinnings of the regime of objectivity. In the first instance, increasing class polarization poses a challenge to the middle-market mass media that have historically been the mainstay of objectivity – namely, public broadcasting, the network television news divisions, and the omnibus metropolitan dailies. The urban middle class and skilled working class, the social basis of the omnibus daily, are proportionately shrinking as the gap between rich and poor widens. That gap is evident in terms not only of sheer income, but also of cultural orientations and access to information. The information-rich will have unprecedented access to symbolic resources and data that enable them to intervene effectively in political and economic life, and perhaps to dominate it. But the emerging "information underclass" will lose out as politically relevant information becomes increasingly privatized and commodified and as even tax-subsidized government information becomes accessible only after the payment of stiff user fees.[28]

Such class polarization has yielded a growing split in North American journalism since the 1970s – a split long characteristic of the British press system. For the affluent and conservative segment of the population, objectivity of the type now found in *The Wall Street Journal* or *The Globe and Mail* will remain important: accuracy in details, but within a relatively narrow and conservative range of viewpoints. "Quality" journalism within an increasingly conservative and business-oriented newsroom culture will continue to seek "the truth" – but the truth as it is defined and accepted within the walls of the palace, not among the peasantry outside.[29]

People without modems or fat wallets will have to make do with an advertising-based news media system in which deregulation, channel multiplication, and competitive pressures produce not real diversity, but rivals in conformity – a steady diet of crime and disasters, sensationalism and infotainment. Such tabloid journalism adheres to one particular aspect of the objectivity regime: it claims, however spuriously, to speak to and for the common people. But its focus on infotainment, celebrities, and scandals and its tendency to polarize issues and search for scapegoats, usually at the bottom of the social ladder, hardly make it a model of public discourse for sustainable democracy. If this claim sounds too cynical, watch an evening of local commercial TV news in the United States and ask yourself who is being addressed, what threats are identified, and what mobilizing information – information "that enables audience members to act" – is being offered.[30]

If class polarization divides the public to and for which objective news tries to speak, developments within the media's own political economy are further eroding the influence of the established news media. Although the 500-channel universe has not materialized, the TV networks' once massive audiences are fragmenting as specialty cable channels abound. Young people and mobile suburbanites, less attached to their communities than were previous generations, are losing the newspaper-reading habit. As a source of entertainment, dialogue, and information, personal computers are siphoning audiences away from the mass media. Even within those media, news is losing the authority and functions it once had as a genre. The "new news" of rock videos and talk radio expresses the sensibilities of many people in ways that "objective" journalism does not. Their fingers to the wind, politicians are starting to bypass the gatekeepers of High Journalism in favour of the "new news." Bill Clinton plays saxophone on a late-night TV talk show, the eccentric on-again off-again politician Ross Perot uses Larry King's CNN phone-in show as his campaign springboard, and Jay Leno and David Letterman become the arbiters of political images and boundaries.

Class polarization and audience fragmentation make it more difficult for news media to adopt the universalizing voice of objectivity. Partly for that reason, we are seeing a partial comeback of the partisanship and sectarianism of the nineteenth-century press, embellished with the televisual and interactive formats of the twentieth. The U.S. broadcast media have not entirely succumbed to antipolitical consumerism. Whole programs and channels are devoted to single-minded advocacy. While there is much to be said in principle for interpretation and advocacy in media, a deregulated commercial media system will tend to privilege stridency over deliberation and well-funded interest groups over others. The right-wing tilt of advocacy programs in U.S. broadcasting is no coincidence. Furthermore, audience fragmentation combined with social and political polarization carries the risk of splintering the public sphere into a cluster of smaller and mutually antagonistic constituencies.

As the main alternative to commercial broadcasting, public broadcasting in both the United States and Canada is under financial and political siege. Conservative media institutes and politicians attack public broadcasting for what they regard as its left-liberal bias.[31] Canada's federal Liberal government betrays its promise to provide the CBC with stable financing, treating it instead as an easy target for spending cuts. At risk of losing more and more of its staff and programs, CBC (like PBS) is forced to seek more commercial revenue, notwithstanding the programming biases that go with it. Vis-à-vis the regime of objectivity, such pressures have several consequences. They weaken precisely that sector of the broadcasting system with the strongest regulatory mandate for balance and objectivity, a sector that has sometimes excelled at offering the best qualities of "objective" broadcast journalism – depth, civility, diversity, thoughtfulness, and relative independence. Political and fiscal uncertainties, however, may induce public broadcasters to define objectivity more conservatively, to avoid treading too often on powerful toes in their public affairs programming, or even to avoid public affairs altogether in favour of less controversial fare – fish, fur, and feathers, as some PBS critics have put it.

The free marketeers have further undermined the regime of objectivity through the deregulation of commercial broadcasting. In the United States, the Reagan administration abolished the Fairness Doctrine during the 1980s. Balance, as a key component of objectivity, is in effect no longer a licensing requirement imposed on radio and TV. Such deregulation enabled the airwaves to be hijacked by the grossly simplistic and the simply gross, the Rush Limbaughs and the Howard Sterns, covering the political range from the centre-right to the extreme right. Perhaps the most egregious bigot in the corporate media was Bob Grant, a talk-radio host on ABC's flagship New York station. Freed from fear of on-air rebuttal, Grant's hate-mongering included a friendly chat with the well-known neo-Nazi Tom Metzger, a plug for the white supremacist organization American Renaissance, and repeated racial slurs against black Americans ("If they didn't observe Martin Luther King Day, there would be trouble from the savages").[32] Under public pressure, and doubtless concerned about its speciously apolitical "family" image, ABC's new owner (Disney) fired Grant in 1996.[33] In general, though, as mass-mediated political life becomes more commercialized, trivialized, spectacularized, and commodified, rational and deliberative ways of discussing substantive public issues are marginalized.

Free marketeers promote deregulation as freedom from oppressive government, but they ignore the biggest threat to the capacity of news media to function as an independent public forum – the deregulated media corporations themselves, with their feeding frenzy of mergers, alliances, and takeovers. Rather than slowing media concentration, public policy has facilitated it. Under the Orwellian guise of introducing more competition in lieu of regulation, the U.S. Congress passed legislation in 1995-96 that virtually gutted limitations on national concentration and on cross-media ownership and further eroded the avenues of public accountability.[34] Possibly the biggest surrender to private commercial interests in telecommunications history, the new law has huge implications for the future architecture of the U.S. and hence global media system. The major media, which stood to benefit from the Act, provided minimal coverage of it.[35]

Other related developments further potentially threaten the diversity, quality, and/or independence of journalism. News organizations are facing intensified economic pressures. These include competition for advertising revenue, the rise of certain costs (notably newsprint), the strategic allocation of capital to new media technology and to mergers and takeovers, and the priorities of a new breed of owners: by contrast with the family firms of yesteryear, today's conglomerate shareholders value high levels of short-term profit more than the long-term journalistic reputation of their media investments.[36]

These pressures have multiple consequences. Many of the traditional news media are laying off staff and trimming newsroom budgets in the name of rationalization. Take the case of Canada's dominant newspaper company, Conrad Black's Hollinger. One or two of its potential "flagship" papers have modestly expanded their reporting staff, but far more typical was Hollinger's rapid mass firing of employees at the two main Saskatchewan dailies after the 1996 acquisition. Newsroom cutbacks, the heightened focus on the bottom line, and a more conservative political climate have all contributed to the decline of potentially costly and risky investigative reporting since the 1970s. More and more of what passes for news is, in effect, commercial and institutional propaganda – produced by the burgeoning public relations industry servicing those interests, mostly governments and corporations, which can afford its image-management services. An estimated 40 to 80 per cent of the news originates with PR professionals, who now outnumber journalists by about 165,000 to 140,000 in North America.[37]

Moreover, news organizations' once-hallowed walls between editorial and commercial decision-making are crumbling. Since the 1980s the prestige, autonomy, and resources of network television news departments have been slipping. In the press the managerial philosophy of "total newspapering" has come to the fore: an approach in which "editorial, advertising, circulation, research and promotion functions are all coordinated around marketing concerns."[38] According to Doug Underwood, daily newspaper editors have begun "to behave more and more like the managers of any other corporate entity" and "to treat their readership as a market and the news as a product to appeal to that market." One of the consequences is a rising tide of infotainment – the "cult of colorful tidbits."[39]

Taken together, these recent trends in the political economy of news media contribute to the decline of public esteem for journalism. The credibility of journalism suffers to the extent that news becomes more nakedly influenced by the marketing or political interests of a handful of media corporations. To maintain their credibility with audiences, media corporations often seek to disguise their own power and self-interest – although the public profile of an owner as opinionated and interventionist as Conrad Black makes such a stance more difficult. A donation by Black's partner David Radler to the right-wing Liberal Party during British Columbia's 1996 provincial election undoubtedly caused much cringing in the region's Hollinger-owned dailies.

Still, it may be that the news media giants are now so powerful, and have so little to fear from mainly right-wing governments, that they have less need of objectivity as a legitimizing ideology. In the absence of countervailing public policy, political will, or marketplace competition, the dominant media may be tempted to indulge in blatant partisanship or self-serving media campaigns – especially when their own immediate corporate interests are at stake. A prime example is the strange case of Rupert Murdoch's relationship with the once-radical British Labour Party. Murdoch's Australian-based News Corporation, with annual revenues of some U.S.$8 billion, is "the widest-reaching media empire in the world."[40] It controls over one-third of Britain's newspaper circulation (including London's prestigious *Times*), and the United Kingdom's entire satellite broadcasting system. Murdoch has long used such unprecedented power to make and break British politicians. Even by the overtly partisan standards of the British press, his papers gave glowing coverage to Margaret Thatcher, Conservative prime minister from 1979 to 1990, and correspondingly hostile headlines to the peace movement, trade unions, progressive social programs, and the Labour opposition. Polling research suggests that the Murdoch tabloid *Sun* swayed enough voters to win the close 1992 general election for John Major's Conservatives.[41] More recently, though, in an attempt to pressure the government to kill a bill that would limit cross-media ownership, Murdoch turned against Major and began to court Labour Party leader Tony Blair. After Murdoch and Blair, the most conservative Labour leader in decades, talked things over at an Australian island resort in July 1995, Blair began writing opinion pieces for Murdoch's papers.[42] Labour's once-unthinkable adoption of a Murdoch-friendly policy stance indicates that parties and governments go cap in hand to the media giants, not vice versa.

The recent expansion of media commercialism will surely have an impact on the culture of journalism. Commercial television journalism would seem to be increasingly defining professionalism in terms of entertainment values, audience ratings, celebrity status, and presentational performance rather than objectivity and investigation. In the emerging online "cyberspace" newsrooms, such as MSNBC, a partnership of Microsoft and NBC, it is still too early to evaluate the changes. Although created mainly as extensions of existing major news media, these outlets seem to be emphasizing immediacy and the repackaging of information into different formats, generating a "new breed" of journalist who, according to veteran investigative reporter Steve Weinberg, concentrates on "how to create attractive graphics and mount databases without knowing about information-gathering and interpretation."[43] Even journalists in the daily press are finding it difficult to cling to the self-image of objective and independent truth-seekers. News workers are becoming uncomfortably aware of how marketing imperatives and their employer's ever-expanding corporate interests are impinging on their work, overriding or redefining the "professional" norms.

Although it was market logic that engendered the regime of objectivity nearly a century ago, the two may now be parting ways. The challenge of nineteenth-century journalism, which created an opening for objectivity, was to deal with a shortage of reliable information and an excess of partisan opinion in an era of the economic and political emergence of "the masses." The challenge for journalism (and democracy) in the 1990s is a glut of information, and a shortage of time and perspective to sift through and make sense of it all, in an era when the "public," its sense of attachment to community, and its commitment to political participation are in decline. The market incentive for the early commercial dailies was to appeal to the broadest possible number of middle-market or affluent readers of different partisan persuasions, by offering accessible and impartial but politically significant information. A century later profit-driven information providers are dealing with fragmented audiences that have increasingly given up on public life.

The malaise of democratic public life and the crumbling bases of the objectivity regime raise with fresh urgency the need to rethink the public philosophy of journalism. The first step is a critical reconsideration of some of the liberal justifications of the media often associated with the idea of objectivity.

An Ideology Exhausted:
Liberal Justifications of the Media

Traditional liberal conceptions of the appropriate role of the press do not adequately address the current crises of journalism and democracy. The first line of defence, for instance, is an assertion of the importance of a *press free from government censorship or interference*, as guaranteed in the U.S. constitution's First Amendment or in Canada's Charter of Rights.

We certainly do not endorse authoritarian control of the news: an independent and pluralistic media system is of fundamental importance. But as a normative guideline the libertarian concept of press freedom has several major limitations. As law professor Harry Glasbeck predicted after Canada's Charter of Rights came into effect in 1982, the courts interpret the free press guarantee conservatively.[44] That is, the courts regard press freedom as in effect a property right of media owners, and the Charter could well be used to protect the owners of media conglomerates from government policies intended to diversify the control or content of the press.

The Canadian and U.S. courts have not given a similarly strong endorsement to what can be seen as more democratic definitions of press freedom: the right of citizens to inform themselves (part of the Kent Commission's vision of press freedom); the right of journalists to express themselves without editorial intervention from corporate management; a right of reply for individuals or groups attacked in the media; or a right of access to the media for those whose voices are currently excluded. Media owners – and often journalists as well – defend the conservative version of the free press concept – a version that has little to say about press accountability to the public or about the constraints imposed on free and diverse expression by commercial imperatives or by media corporations themselves. In common with traditional liberalism, this approach focuses narrowly on government as the main threat to human freedom and does not offer journalists a positive public philosophy about how to act on their legally protected independence.

A second liberal rationale, *the press as a public watchdog against governmental abuses of power*, suggests a journalistic role that at its best can serve democratic purposes well. This watchdog tradition still has considerable life, as coverage of several recent stories shows:
- the Chrétien government's decision to renew cruise missile testing;
- details of the millions of dollars in contracts that the Canadian government strikes annually with tobacco companies, while it spends millions on anti-smoking campaigns;
- plans by Canada's secret electronic spy agency, the Communications Security Establishment (CSE), to develop the ability to identify individual human voices as it scans the skies for "intelligence";
- revelations by a former CSE analyst that the agency spied on Canada's allies and Canadian citizens;
- serious structural and potentially catastrophic flaws with Canadian Candu nuclear reactors in Pakistan and India;
- the exchange of information by Canada's spy agency, the Canadian Security Intelligence Service, with countries with woeful human rights records;
- millions of dollars of waste and mismanagement at the Department of External Affairs and the Canadian International Development Agency;

- secret intergovernmental negotiations for the sale of Canadian CF-5 fighters to Turkey, where they could have potentially been used against Kurdish civilians. This story and the reaction to it apparently killed the deal.[45]

Despite occasional stories like these, political journalism in the major media more typically exposes scandals and conflicts of interest involving individual politicians and fails to challenge state power on issues of major accountability: the big questions of economic and foreign policy, for instance. Given its implicit liberal assumptions about what is public and what is private, watchdog journalism pays even less systematic critical attention to powerful private-sector corporations than it does to government.

The watchdog ethic also ignores the media's own immense power. There is, it seems, no watchdog on the watchdog. On the really big issues, as journalists of integrity have themselves noted, the press acts more often like a lapdog than a watchdog.[46]

In 1995, according to Project Censored, the U.S. press underplayed or ignored these stories, among others:
- the massive deregulation of telecommunications;
- $167 billion in annual subsidies to business, whose elimination could enable the U.S. government to balance its budget without slashing social programs;
- lax enforcement of U.S. child labour laws, resulting in thousands of injuries and even deaths of children in the workplace;
- a multibillion-dollar project to enhance the explosive power of nuclear warheads;
- $100 billion or more lost annually in medical fraud;
- ABC's cancellation of a hard-hitting documentary on the tobacco industry at the same time as a tobacco company filed a $10 billion libel suit against Capital Cities/ABC;
- the U.S. chemical industry's fight to prevent the banning of methyl bromide, a toxic ozone-killing pesticide;
- the death through error or negligence of up to 180,000 patients in U.S. hospitals each year.[47]

Perhaps because Canada is too small to sustain infamy on such a scale, perhaps because its media system and political culture are more pluralistic, Project Censored Canada's lists of underreported stories pale next to the U.S. ones. Still, similar media blind spots are evident north of the border too, including tax breaks for the wealthy, Canada's cosy trade-and-aid relationship with regimes, such as Indonesia, that violate human rights, and

Canada's substantial participation in the international arms trade, contrary to its self-image as a peacekeeper.[48]

Although the watchdog ideal is a worthy one – if the United States had more journalists following in the footsteps of Upton Sinclair, George Seldes, or I.F. Stone, and if Canada had more programs like CBC's *the fifth estate*, perhaps power would be exercised more justly and accountably – the watchdog role is too limited to provide anything like a comprehensive public philosophy for journalism. At its best it can bring serious wrongdoers to account or call attention to the need for specific reforms. In practice, it is at least equally likely that media organizations use the watchdog ethic selectively, to justify a stance of general hostility to government or to launch vendettas or crusades that serve their own commercial or political interests (against welfare recipients or sex offenders, for example, people who make much safer targets than corporate law-breakers).[49]

Even at its best, the watchdog tradition is unlikely to improve greatly the conditions of public debate and democratic decision-making. It is rooted in an outdated classical liberal view of government as the primary potential threat to individual freedom, a view that precludes not only the social-democratic philosophy of government as potentially an instrument of common purpose, but also a recognition of the immense but unaccountable power wielded by private-sector institutions. Moreover, the watchdog tradition draws implicitly upon a faith in the availability of public energy and political will to enact reforms, an energy much less evident now than it was a century ago during the golden age of the muckrakers. Finally, watchdog journalism does not easily permit a critical re-examination of liberal democracy itself, because it essentially consists of morality tales about *violations* of liberal-democratic norms that are themselves taken for granted. Watchdogs may be good at barking at intruders; they are less good at analysing whose house they are defending and how they know what to bark at.

A third shopworn liberal conception posits the press as *an information smorgasbord*, enabling representative government by providing people with the diverse viewpoints and information they need to make rational, individual choices in the political marketplace. Diversity is indeed an important criterion for a democratic media system. Yet the "information smorgasbord" implies a naive notion of "information" as something neutral, non-ideological, and apolitical – in short, objective. But as James Curran points out, information takes on meaning within discourses, which are political and ideological: "Ideas and systems of representation are part of the ideological arsenal which competing groups use to advance their interests....

The media's informational role is never purely informational; it is also a way of arbitrating between the rhetorical claims of rival interests."[50]

At stake in such information-presentation, no matter how neutral it may seem, are the allocation of material and cultural resources and the hegemony of particular interests and values. Journalism cannot hide behind claims that it simply provides information; it must pay attention to who is accorded access, and to what perspectives are being used to frame stories.

The ideal of press as information smorgasbord overemphasizes the individual as a unit of analysis, ignoring modern political structures such as parties and interest groups, which help to advance individual interests within collectively organized society. Traditional liberal theory, Curran says, "has nothing to say" about how media should relate to these interests and "enhance their performance."[51]

Moreover, by prescribing that citizens need to absorb extensive information on all relevant issues from the news media before making meaningful political choices, the smorgasbord ideal imposes too great a burden on both press and public. As Walter Lippmann wrote in 1922, if we expect the press to translate "the whole public life of mankind, so that every adult can arrive at an opinion on every moot topic," then the press is bound to fail, if only because this expectation presupposes "an appetite for uninteresting truths which is not discovered by any honest analysis of our own tastes."[52] The smorgasbord model overemphasizes the rationality of political psychology and public discourse. The twentieth century has shown us that human rationality, to say the least, cannot be taken for granted. If a reason-based public sphere is anything more than a rationalist fiction, it has conditions of existence well beyond simply the availability of adequate information – and journalism may well have a role in helping to create or sustain those conditions of existence.

The excessive rationalism of the smorgasbord model is also evident in its apparent privileging of "information" about "serious" high politics in the print media. It has little to say about the entertainment or visual media, which have an important if often unrecognized role in making relations of power meaningful in popular culture. Such "low-information" media nevertheless may resonate with lived experience, and they constitute important sites of political and cultural struggle.

Finally, although Lippmann debunked the ideal of the fully informed citizen, the smorgasbord concept does fit all too neatly with his competitive elitist model of democracy in at least one sense. The concept of a marketplace of ideas and political options reduces citizens to the role of consumers of information provided for them by professional communicators, and to choosing between the options provided for them by political parties. The excluded alternative is active popular participation in the production of political meanings and options.

A fourth liberal conception calls for the press to act as a first-hand observer of history in the making, an *eyewitness on behalf of the public.* This was the view expressed by CBC correspondent Ann Medina at a 1991 Ottawa conference on the media and international conflict.[53] In the wake of the Gulf War, which saw reporters grouped into pools, largely excluded from combat zones, and reduced to dependence on Pentagon handouts, Medina was expressing an honourable aspiration. The notion of witnessing is rightly a valued one in journalism's lexicon, and many TV programs particularly have tried to claim this tradition as their own – from CBC Newsworld's *Witness* to the innumerable *Eyewitness News* of U.S. local TV stations.

Yet this, too, is too narrow and problematic as a comprehensive public philosophy for journalism. Many journalism tasks (interpretation, analysis, opinion) cannot be reduced to witnessing and recording events. More crucially, as critics of the objectivity ethos point out, vexing questions remain: who decides what is worth witnessing, and can even the most professional and detached of observers record the essential truth or meaning of an event? It is possible but not easy to transcend the filters of culture, class, and gender. Notwithstanding postmodernism's faddish excesses, we do need to recognize that the very concept of an "essential truth or meaning" has been problematized beyond repair.

The very effort to remain detached and appear objective can itself be deceptive, biased, intrusive, or otherwise self-defeating. Rita Shelton Deverell, a producer at Vision TV, tells of a young, white male journalist who pursued, too aggressively and insensitively, the role of detached observer and recorder and thus lost a potential video story on a healing circle, part of traditional Aboriginal medicine; while another reporter's personal search for his own roots shaped a powerful documentary on India's tiny anglo-Indian community. In Deverell's view the central challenge of reporting is not "being objective, standing above reality as if we were not involved in it," but rather "accurately revealing and assessing our subjectivity and the subjectivity of others, knowing where 'we' stand in relation to 'them.'"[54]

The Myth of Consumer Sovereignty

In these market-liberal times one other conception of the press is especially prominent: the ideal of *consumer sovereignty.* According to this view, the media best serve society when market mechanisms are unleashed from regulatory constraints, so that the media's programming reflects the tastes and preferences of their audiences.

But as either a legitimizing explanation of the media's current performance or a normative ideal for media reform, consumer sovereignty falls seriously short as a model for democratic communication. The model assumes that media audiences have conscious and well-ordered preferences that shape their media consumption. But media consumption is just as often the product of habit and habituation, of choices made between the most readily available alternatives that media corporations find profitable and convenient to offer. Along these lines, cultural theorist Raymond Williams argued that popular tastes in television are partly generated by program planners and producers themselves, responding to commercial imperatives.[55]

Even if media consumers do have autonomous preferences, their power is greatly reduced by the economic characteristics of the major media industries (see chapter 3). The prime-time hours on Canada's commercial TV networks are full of U.S. fare, but not because audiences prefer U.S. programs to homegrown shows of equal production values. Rather, Canadian broadcasters find that it is simply far cheaper to import programs that have already recovered their production costs in the huge U.S. market than it is to finance the production of similar Canadian shows. Similarly, the frequent violence in Hollywood films is driven not by blood-lust on the part of moviegoers but by the ease with which good-versus-evil action dramas can be exported to different national markets without losing much in translation.[56] The proliferation of talk shows on commercial radio and TV is accounted for not by consumers' appetite for more screaming matches and exposés of everyday grotesqueries, and still less by democratic motives on the part of broadcasters, but by the economic reality that these programs are relatively cheap ways to fill airtime and still reach acceptably large audiences.

Foremost among the economic factors that influence content in the traditional commercial news media is advertising. Those who defend advertising as the basis of the media argue that commercialism reduces the direct cost of media fare to consumers and ensures responsiveness to audience tastes, because advertising rates are related to the size of the audience.[57] They also argue that it ensures financial independence from the government and hence makes possible freedom of the press. While freedom from government coercion (except where untrammelled expression would

infringe on other rights, such as an accused's right to a fair trial) is fundamental in a democracy, what is less widely recognized is that market relations, just as easily as the state, can inhibit popular democratic communication.

Historically the systematic pressure to produce profitable audiences can
be understood to have constituted a powerful form of de facto censorship
– if we adopt a definition of censorship that is broader and more applicable
to contemporary realities than the traditional liberal conception of government suppression of publication. Project Censored Canada defines censorship as the exclusion or marginalization of significant information that
should be in the public domain, is attributable at least in part to inequalities of power resources, and is backed through fear, threat, or imposition of
penalties, whether formal or informal, explicit or implicit.[58] Media commercialism has generated censorship in this sense, insofar as it tailors content to appeal to the consumers (especially the affluent) that advertisers
want to reach, rather than to other segments of the population.[59] In determining what kind of media survive in a commercial system, the logic is one
dollar, one vote, rather than one person, one vote.

Similar biases are introduced by the way information and entertainment
programming – which we are accustomed to regard as media content –
work as a "free lunch" to entice an audience for the most important content
– the advertisements.[60] That logic helps to explain why the commercial
media privilege the pleasures of privatized consumption over the values of
democratic citizenship – over participation in the public process of setting
rules that apply collectively.

It is difficult to see how a market-oriented media system can overcome
these structural biases. Niche marketing, audience fragmentation, and subscription or user-pay specialty broadcasting services may reduce the pressure towards broadest-common-denominator homogenization, but they
are likely to maintain or intensify the relative influence of advertisers and/
or affluent consumers. Desk-top publishing and computer-mediated communication may have reduced the costs of reaching small audiences, but
the truly agenda-setting media are now in the hands of global giants tower-
ing above any foreseeable new competitors.

The economic biases make media markets something less than democratic forums equally available and responsive to all citizens. They are by-
products not of malevolence or manipulation, but of rational business decisions. At the same time, media owners and companies may have political
as well as commercial interests and ambitions. Their political interests may

sometimes favour greater openness and glasnost in society, as when news organizations pressure the government for better access to information legislation. But at least as often, in the globalized 1990s, the political power of media corporations favours de facto censorship. Rupert Murdoch's muscle-flexing is an example of this tendency. In 1995, to take another example, the Fox network cancelled the highly entertaining quasi-newsmagazine *TV Nation*, notwithstanding its audience of up to fifteen million people, when Fox executives finally realized that producer/director Michael Moore was not just a goofy-looking yukmeister. He was a goofy-looking left-wing political satirist – and on U.S. network television, apparently, that is beyond the pale.[61]

For all these reasons commercial media do not simply "give people what they want." They give some of the people part of what they think they want – programming that media corporations find economical and convenient to offer, that is generally compatible with a consumerist stance, and that affluent and/or mass consumers (who lack ready access to the full range of potential alternatives) are prepared to accept as a reward for joining the audience. The commercial media satisfy primarily the needs compatible with the marketing of commodities. The needs that no one can make money from or that threaten our consumerist culture are left unattended. These include the need, in a democracy, for a space for civil public discourse. In Canada the discrepancy between market logic and the preconditions of a democratic polity has long been evident, not just to left-wingers. After all, a Conservative government created non-commercial public broadcasting in the 1930s as a condition of Canada's very existence as a meaningful national entity.

In the end, though, even if the media system could be made to be more responsive to consumer demand, it would not necessarily produce the kind of public, communal conversation that would sustain the somewhat different and more egalitarian logic of democracy. For democracy to work, people need to think of themselves as citizens, not simply as consumers pursuing their individual interests in the shopping mall.

8

Straws in the Wind: Alternatives to the Regime?

Some people argue that because of the inherently democratizing nature of new media technology, we do not need to worry unduly about the crisis of democracy or the global concentration of media power. In their view, journalism and other social practices are being transformed by the rapid expansion of telecommunications delivery systems, including satellite communication, fibre optics, and digital broadcasting – which will greatly increase the number of available channels – combined with the exponential evolution of personal computers and other digital/microchip-based devices for capturing, storing, combining, retrieving, analysing, and editing data, text, sound, and images. Previously separate technological systems – computers, newspapers, cable TV, telephones, broadcasting – are converging.

Following the lead of Vancouver science-fiction writer William Gibson, some people call the new kind of media/experience generated by these technologies "cyberspace," a conceptual realm in which "words, human relationships, data, wealth, and power are manifested by people using CMC [computer-mediated communication] technology."[1] The hot buzz now is the Internet, the "loosely interconnected computer networks that use CMC technology to link people around the world into public discussions."[2] Its most popular corner, the World Wide Web, enables potentially millions of users to "publish" their own multimedia documents.

After two decades of false starts and wild predictions, these technologies now appear to have reached an irreversible takeoff point, promising to transform how journalism is "produced, processed, transmitted, and consumed."[3] In the near future, according to a distinguished Harvard specialist, "Networked computers in the workplace and the home will compete on an equal footing with the existing news media as a routine source of news for over half the public in the industrialized world."[4]

Cyberspace and Other New Media: Democratic Saviour or Digital Dystopia?

Beyond its undoubted continuation and a potentially profound impact on human culture, the future trajectory of the information revolution is unclear. Even the most informed front-line specialists and online participants readily admit to a sense of their own uncertainty, and so do we. In this new wave of technology and communications, two kinds of visions seem to be competing for attention: an optimistic view of technotopia, highlighting the potential economic, cultural and political benefits of the new technology to humankind; and a more critical view, darker but unfortunately more realistic, stressing the absence of a powerful movement to democratize communication and the implementation of technology. Both views foresee profound changes for journalism.

The technotopian view rests on several key interpretations of emerging technology, especially cyberspace. First, the Internet was deliberately structured in a decentralized manner so a U.S. government communication network could survive nuclear attack. Such a system rests on distinct "nodes," which are independent yet simultaneously linked with each other and the larger and ever-expanding "web."[5] Thus the Internet can be seen as a more "grassroots" system, inherently resistant to centralized control and censorship. More importantly, the Internet allows users to both send and receive information, allowing for previously unknown interactivity and control over the media environment.

Even more broadly, in the view of technotopians the new media are unleashing creativity, flattening hierarchies, reinvigorating democracy, and creating new kinds of communities. Old limitations of time, space, medium, and place seem to collapse magically, as the Internet and related technologies bring an unprecedented combination of immediacy, interactivity, and depth. (Here, time and place seem to be regarded consistently as constraints, rather than fundamental dimensions of human existence endowing it with meaning, continuity, and a necessary sense of limitation.) Technotopians talk of replacing the broadcast model (from the few to the many) of conventional mass media with a network model (from many to many).[6]

The ultimate technotopian vision is a global electronic public sphere: a world in which everybody has a cheap communication device that enables them to receive and transmit, from nearly anywhere, visual, textual, or voice messages to or from other individuals, groups, or organizations. A decades-old metaphor from Canadian communication visionary Marshall McLuhan has been appropriated to describe the Internet of the 1990s: "As people all over the world begin to produce and then share information within McLuhan's prophetic 'global village,' they naturally depend less and less on the information ... from more traditional sources."[7] Those traditional sources include the newspapers and broadcasting media at the heartland of the regime of objectivity.

In terms of packaging and presenting news, the Net and the Web mean that newsholes and newscasts "no longer have bounds."[8] For a given news story, consumers can reference precedents and parallels or summon background with the touch of a key, or ignore it altogether. Increasingly, print, audio, and video modules can be combined into a multimedia fare far richer than anything available through the conventional media.

Technophiles hail the Net as a significant shift of discursive power to people who had previously been passive consumers of one-way news.[9] Not only can Net users tailor their news consumption to their own interests – for example, by using software that will conduct automated customized searches – but they can also become reporters, storytellers, and witnesses. Community groups and non-governmental organizations (NGOs) will be able to mobilize themselves far more effectively and "become more active players in the information marketplace, especially for complicated policy issues that most mainstream media organizations treat superficially, if at all."[10] The Net may also increase the capacity of NGOs to intervene in political crises: its use by the Zapatistas and their sympathizers throughout the world may have moderated the Mexican government's response to the 1994 Chiapas rebellion. So the range of public conversation is extended, ending the monopoly of professional journalists and supposedly even reversing traditional hierarchies. As Chris Lapham points out, "Unlike the one-to-many model where information came from the top, news on the Internet bubbles up from the bottom and meanders its way upward."[11]

Technotopians believe that the new media are undermining the model of "objective" news delivered from the few (professional journalists) to the many (passive, anonymous audiences). Many technotopians welcome the ways that new media blur the boundaries between journalists, sources, and audiences. News can be constructed far more interactively and dialogically, perhaps reducing distance and tension in journalists' relationships with their audience or potentially bypassing journalists altogether, "making some of the new news an unmediated collaboration between the sources and the audience," according to Ellen Hume's report for the Annenberg Washington Program on the future of news.[12] News subjects are less likely to have their voices muffled or distorted, and stories are less likely to be frozen into rigid frames.

In breathless cyberprose, one young online reporter describes her hopes for connecting with her audience:

> People worldwide making intimate, direct use of my work is more than I had hoped for. How better to keep me honest, when I get that deific high of a news touchdown, than to know that the people reading that story care about what I'm saying.... Channelling the word, the image, the information in bundles unthought of before, comprehensive beyond belief, putting the resources of world-wide ingenuity into the hands of the populace.... Maybe the online, organic news connection can [give] us a channel for pure news delivery, through a vehicle of incredible flexibility and power. We will be heard by a willing audience.[13]

Conventional news organizations have been experimenting for several years with audience feedback through e-mail. One of the first experiments by a senior U.S. journalist was in June 1994, when *Time*'s managing editor went online to "make himself accountable to the public" for his magazine's infamous cover photo touch-up of O.J. Simpson.[14] Meanwhile, at *Newsweek*, the editor responsible for the magazine's "chat forums" and "newsgroup" describes his hopes that the participants will develop into "a new kind of reporting team, producing stories that are seen less as edicts and more as conversations" among readers.[15]

By enabling audiences to become more active communicators, new technology opens the gates for more subjective interpretations and experiences – a welcome new era of personal journalism, in the view of its advocates. For example:

1) Prodigy, a commercial online service launched by IBM and Sears, covered the 1996 U.S. election using non-professional "stringers" from across the country on its news bulletin board. One stringer said the reports would be different from those produced by the professional media, because personal biases would be explicitly exposed. The reports would be "honest," the stringer said. "What the real people are thinking."[16]

2) The new forthcoming "portable newsroom" offers a similar potential for "anybody-as-journalist." A lone journalist in the field will be able to produce every stage of a report, from downloading background text and video

clips from news services, to editing the piece digitally in the field, to transmitting the report directly via satellite to a video distribution system.[17] The
one-person crew – a combination correspondent, camera operator, sound
recordist, and editor – saves costs and minimizes the teamwork now
needed for video news.

3) Likewise, the lightweight camcorder engenders personalized, grassroots
stories not previously possible on television. Its ability to bypass professional journalists and to embarrass official sources was most strikingly revealed by the famous home videorecording of white Los Angeles policemen
beating up Rodney King, a black man.

There are, however, grounds for considerable scepticism about these developments – the blurring of boundaries between reporter and audience, the
more interactive nature of news, and the flowering of personal journalism.
They do not necessarily mean that journalism is about to leave behind the
regime of objectivity and its elitist model of democracy and enter an era of
democratic, horizontal communication from the many to the many; nor
that the new model will serve as a viable alternative to the old regime of objectivity and provide an adequate forum for democratic communication in
the twenty-first century.

While new digital technologies, especially the Net, hold enormous potential for revitalizing journalism and democratic communication, the
technotopian vision of cyberspace as democratic saviour is staggeringly
blind to the historical, economic, and power realities of a market society.
Technologies have distinct logics and capabilities, but there is nothing inevitable about how or even whether they are developed. That development
is conditioned by economic and political forces. Since 1994 in the United
States, the Internet has been commercialized "at an exponential rate," according to Wisconsin professor Robert McChesney, and the Telecommunications Act of 1996 ensures that the market, not public policy, will direct
the evolution of the Internet and the information highway.[18] If the technology's antimonopoly biases are strong enough to foil the profit-seeking
ambitions of the corporate giants, the Internet will simply languish on the
margins of media culture; the huge investment needed to upgrade it and to
make it popularly accessible and affordable will not be forthcoming.[19] But
if it proves to be profitable, new "nodes" on the Net will be owned and operated by private interests operating on a profit motive. Either case minimizes the potential of cyberspace to counterbalance a communication system dominated by the corporate pursuit of profit.

The same scenario has unfolded before. When radio appeared in the 1920s, its democratic and educational potential was also hailed – until commercial interests defeated a movement for non-profit public broadcasting and transformed the U.S. airwaves into a conduit for capturing audiences and selling their attention to advertisers. In Canada a stronger public policy ensured the creation of a public broadcaster before advertiser-based radio was sufficiently entrenched to overwhelm it.[20] Although under fiscal and political attack in the 1990s, CBC continues to offer a dignified and inclusive tone in stark contrast to the shrill soap-selling and hate-mongering of commercial U.S. radio.

To be sure, as a network – rather than broadcast – model medium, the Internet has much greater capacity than radio for diversity and interactivity. Many online activists are working hard to enhance its accessibility and use as a public service, through community-based Freenets, for example. But the logic of a market-driven model in which any further development of the Internet will come from the profit-oriented private sector is working against public accessibility and interactivity. Previously the generation of profit through the Internet had been thwarted because content had traditionally been free on the Net and surfing the Net (the user clicking from one information site to another) was not ideally suited to advertising. Commercial forces, though, are proving quite adept at overcoming these blockages to profit.

Since advertising dollars seek mass (or at least niche) audiences, new content is being developed under such a commercial rubric. An example is Women's Wire, an online site geared towards female cyberconsumers. Information and resources are offered for "free" but underwritten by organizations such as Levi-Strauss.[21] Commercial media sites such as the PointCast Network are also flourishing; its Canadian rights are held by *The Globe and Mail*. Users are given "free" access to some mainstream news, weather, entertainment, and sports, as well as up-to-the-minute stock quotations, but this "free" information must be viewed in relative captivity. Revolving, clickable advertisements grace the corners of the screen, and upon leaving the network you are delivered to the Web site of the last sponsor.

Another ploy has been the dumbing-down of Internet technology to more easily serve commercial imperatives. Sony has introduced Web TV, which is capable of receiving information but has limited or non-existent facilities for sending information. Sega and Nintendo have also made their new game platforms Net friendly. Such technologies convert a potentially liberating medium into a point-and-click information exploration game.

Under this kind of commercial logic it is questionable whether content will serve any purpose other than attracting the desired audience for advertisers. (Indeed, online advertising has invaded the World Wide Web at an astonishing rate, increasing by 83 per cent in the first to second quarter of 1996 alone; for the first half of 1996, ad revenues reached U.S.$64 million.[22])

In this commercialized environment, community bulletin boards, alternative newsgroups, and the like may well survive at the margins, and specialty and niche services in broadcasting and cyberspace are multiplying. Although market-liberals hail this multiplication as a cornucopia of diversity and choice, the diversity is constrained by what "content providers" find convenient and profitable to produce. Most users will probably be seduced by consumer-friendly, high-production-value, prepackaged multimedia entertainment offered by global media conglomerates with deep pockets and economies of scale – with interactivity largely reduced to choices from preset menus or online commodity purchases. The software colossus Microsoft has already retooled its online provider Microsoft Network (MSN) to provide "a television like line-up of six channels and 20 shows that are structured to deliver new materials to consumers, rather than wait for them to explore on their own."[23] Thus, oligopolistic access providers may well have the power to restrict subscribers' access to other computer users, or to censor messages in their own interests, just as the commercial Prodigy system already does.[24]

Electronic libertarians focus on the potential nightmare of government censorship and surveillance through the Net.[25] But the far likelier threat to democratic communication is the marginalization of information that is not profitable to produce and sell or that too directly challenges the interests of the media conglomerates. As Howard Rheingold, one of the most vocal but thoughtful Net enthusiasts, admitted in 1994:

The transition from a government sponsored, taxpayer-supported, relatively unrestricted public forum to a privately owned and provided medium has accelerated recently, and this transition might render moot many of the fantasies of today's true believers in electronic democracy and global online culture. When the telecommunications networks becomes [sic] powerful enough to transmit high-fidelity sound and video as well as text, the nature of the Net – and the industry that controls it – might change dramatically ...[to become] a hybrid of cable company conduits, telephone company money, and entertainment company content.[26]

195

In short, unless there is strong public policy to nurture it, a horizontal, participatory model of communication will most likely not result from the new technology alone. Notwithstanding the individualistic "electronic frontier" mythology of the Internet, the new media could well be dominated, like other media, by a handful of behemoths (the "gorillas"), with a multitude of "small, nimble players who find and grab niche audiences" (the "guerrillas") in the margins.[27] Already, the gorillas, such as Time Warner, are jockeying for position and making unprecedented strategic alliances. One example is the partnership between Microsoft and NBC to produce MSNBC, a twenty-four-hour news service that began to be distributed on cable television and the Internet in July 1996.

While on the supply side the new media and their content could be dominated by the gorillas, the configuration on the receiving end could increase the gap between the information-rich and the information-poor (terms that to a great extent are euphemisms for the rich and the poor). While more people do have more ready access to more information than ever before, the new media have also made possible the multiplication of market niches that disproportionately benefit the institutions and the affluent consumers who can afford the "Cadillac" information services. Universal access and computer literacy are far from guaranteed in an increasingly market-dominated economy. Schools and libraries – public institutions that could promote access and competence – are facing cutbacks. Personal computers are still not affordable for many of the 60 or 70 per cent of North American households that do not have one. The cyberspace audience in 1996 was an estimated 15 per cent of North Americans.[28] Manufacturers concentrate on the business-driven top end of the PC market, and planned obsolescence is almost legendary. Without public resources to offset market imperatives, the PC may well become "a tool that further increases economic and educational disparities in our society."[29] The information gap makes any celebration of electronic democracy premature.

Although the new media have the potential for expanding horizontal dialogue throughout society, that very capacity could also generate an infoswamp, drowning important public information in a sea of "corporate posturing, glossy infomercials, electronic debates, special-interest-group pitches" and other information of dubious validity.[30] A related possibility is the "balkanization" of public discourse, in which "most people's consumption choices simply reinforced their own prejudices and platitudes, or even worse."[31] Cyberspace cannot on its own produce a new participatory political culture. "Having mass, interactive bulletin boards is a truly magnificent advance," argues McChesney, "but what if nobody knows what they are talking about?"[32] That judgement may be a trifle harsh: the Internet does create communication openings for informed activists (but also for racists and fascists) marginalized by the conventional news media; and it may be that participants in virtual communities do, incrementally, become more civically competent.

Nevertheless, even if it were possible, it is not necessarily desirable that journalism's society-wide agenda-setting function be entirely drowned by horizontal, mass-participant communication, or sliced and diced by a fragmenting media system whose apparent diversity is constrained by its underlying structural biases. While the regime of objectivity often functions as a conservative ideology, it also has an important democratic kernel. It is difficult to imagine that democratic public life can flourish without some form of independent, analytical, and investigative journalism, oriented to the public interest, addressed to broad audiences, and facilitated by skilled and specialized researchers and communicators. Certainly, in an age of infoglut many news consumers themselves will be desperate for reliable filters and sense-makers who can select, edit, verify, prioritize, emphasize, synthesize, and interpret.

This expressed need on the part of audiences (and citizens) gives leaders of the conventional news media hope for their own position in the new digital environment. As *The New York Times'* publisher put it: "The future victims of an information data dump will be greedy as never before for a trustworthy guide through this maze. In other words, our role as newspapers, regardless of the method of distribution, will become more valuable, not less, in the days ahead."[33] For example, a *Philadelphia Inquirer* reporter covering county politics found himself forced to pay attention to an online bulletin board devoted to lively debates and information on local government. At first he worried that users were pulling the information they needed offline for free and thus encroaching on his job. As time passed, he concluded that "people still count on the paper to sort and present vital information in an unbiased manner."[34] The *Ottawa Citizen*'s media columnist expresses the hope that the electronic newspapers and the Internet could make journalism "a growth industry and journalists a much sought-after commodity."[35] And some journalists and other observers have not only made their peace with the new technology but actively embraced it, trumpeting the dawn of a new "golden age of real Journalism."[36]

Such optimism needs to be tempered, though, by considering how the commercial appropriation of digital technology poses a challenge not only for its interactive communicative potential, but also for independent, public-interest journalism. The corporate giants of the converging new media will most likely have even less commitment to the best traditions of independent journalism than the U.S. networks that have been succumbing to the competitive pressures of "tabloid TV" since the 1980s. The emerging commercial imperatives of the information highway may result in a structural bias against controversial or challenging political content. Michael Eisner, CEO of the Walt Disney Company, has said that his firm's projected growth is based on globally distributing a "non-political" product, one that most governments would not find threatening.[37] Chillingly, Eisner is now also the ultimate boss of ABC News, one of the world's largest news organizations.

The use of the camcorder in television production is also illustrative. In the commercial networks, camcorder journalism has mainly been confined to the silliness of *America's Funniest Home Videos*, or the choreographed realism of law-and-order morality tales like *Cops*. By contrast it is public broadcasting that has most used the camcorder to open up the airwaves to new voices. PBS has already aired several grassroots point-of-view camcorder documentaries – such as *The Ride*, a cross-country van odyssey by six teenagers of different ethnic backgrounds who encountered dope, racism, and death, as well as other young people.[38]

Digitalization in a profit-driven context may also undermine journalists' ability to pursue independent journalism. Computerization has long been a saviour to the corporate bottom line but a bane to workers. When linked with institutional and economic imperatives, it can exert a highly undemocratic and prescriptive influence. The use of computerized command-and-control systems has radically deskilled industrial work and created "electronic sweatshops" in which labour is constantly metered and monitored.[39]

Journalists are not immune to such negative technological-economic logic. To be sure, many journalists find computer-mediated communications a useful tool, and the new technology can increase "a journalist's capacity to do big, important stories," says Nancy Hicks Maynard.[40] Through computers journalists have unprecedented access to storehouses of information, and they can produce analyses of trends or situations never before possible. As early as 1986 a computer-assisted feature on racial bias in public housing won a Pulitzer Prize for the *Dallas Morning News*.[41] At the same time, though, many journalists rightly suspect that behind corporate buzzwords like "empowerment," management uses the technology to trim costs, cut jobs, and intensify work, resulting in electronic sweatshops like the highly successful Bloomberg Business News. At this much-touted computerized financial information service, young news workers toil long and continuous hours hunched over terminals, lunching chez computer on company-supplied snacks, crunching numbers, punching in "real-time" financial news, and bunching bandages on their wrists to ward off repetitive stress syndrome.[42]

The economic incentive in the current wave of technological innovation lies in "secondary and derivative rights of information: repackage, compile, make into something new" – in other words, reformatting and recycling old information, rather than researching and generating new information.[43] Typically, rather than being able to use the technology to generate original stories of Pulitzer Prize quality, journalists might increasingly find themselves working in organizational environments that emphasize the efficient re-processing of information generated by self-serving sources.

Most crucially, the digital communication revolution also throws into question the financial basis of public affairs journalism. For most of the twentieth century, even with the advent of broadcast media, the daily press was the most important generator of news stories in the media system. But new services in the new media are likely to hive off some of the most profitable newspaper components (such as classified and real estate advertising, and commodity information), which currently pay for public affairs journalism in the press. In the words of the president of the San Francisco-based Institute for Alternative Journalism: "Strip away some of the more profitable or popular items under this current umbrella, and you could strip away the means of paying for serious reporting aimed at mass audiences. One very important thing to understand about the new media world is just how easy such unbundling becomes."[44] Journalists themselves seem uncertain about their prospects in the new information age. At a 1996 conference on Media & Democracy, a panel of front-line experts expressed sombre warnings on the theme "New roles for journalists: Models for surviving and thriving in the information age."[45] Nancy Hicks Maynard, one of the foremost newspaper industry analysts in the United States, worried that journalism in the new landscape was in danger of losing the power to influence public discussion. "We will not be successful in navigating the gap between where we were, and where we're going," she said, because the very existence of a market basis for independent public affairs journalism cannot be taken for granted. In the absence of public policy to offset market logic, she may well be right.

The technotopian vision of electronic democracy, then, is based on far too uncritical a celebration of technologies that were originally driven by military priorities and have now been taken over by business. Considering the enormous impact of these technologies, their structure, purpose, and development have never been democratically and sufficiently debated. However unintended they may be, the dystopian consequences – the isolation and marginalization of people, the erosion of autonomous leisure time, increasing knowledge gaps within society – are at least as plausible as technotopian results.[46] While the new technologies promise to decentralize and disperse media power, their subordination to market development would seem to indicate more problematic outcomes. Class polarization, audience fragmentation, and other aspects of market logic threaten mass-disseminated public affairs journalism with decline, or transformation into something else. It appears that more democratic forms of public communication are not likely to emerge from technology and market forces operating blindly. Maintaining the democratic potential of the Net will require appropriate public policy, and that is something well worth struggling for, but we also need to consider other kinds of efforts to democratize the media. Encouragingly, one particular reform movement is emerging within the mainstream media themselves.

Reforming from Within: Public Journalism and Its Limits

Although in the past the regime of objectivity has either incorporated or marginalized various challenges to its supremacy, it may be more difficult for the objectivity regime to fend off this latest challenger. In the 1990s hundreds of U.S. newsrooms are experimenting with a new approach called civic or public journalism. As a serious effort to rethink the public philosophy of the craft, public journalism is evidence of a certain capacity for vitality and renewal within media institutions. It has much to commend it. It also has serious blind spots and limitations.

The "gurus" of public journalism, as it is evolving in the United States, are Jay Rosen, an academic at New York University, and "Buzz" Merritt, editor of the *Wichita Eagle*. As expressed in their writings, public journalism begins with a recognition that both journalism and democracy are in crisis.[47] Newspaper circulation, public confidence in the media and other civic institutions, public participation in the political system, and the very existence of any entity that could meaningfully be called a "public" are all in decline. Conversely, Rosen and Merritt point to growing demoralization among journalists, public cynicism about politics, and a sense of disconnection between public concerns and "official" political debate.

Rosen and Merritt argue that in conjunction with broader cultural forces, journalism has contributed to the decline of public life. Journalism has generated cynicism and alienation through its "gotcha" coverage in which the archetypal story is the political scandal, its polarized presentation of political issues, its obsession with electoral horse races and personalities, insiders, and experts, its pseudo-adversarial (as distinct from healthily sceptical) style – all at the expense of the voices and concerns of ordinary voters.[48]

These problems cannot be addressed by more rigorously adhering to prevailing practices of objectivity. Those very practices (such as balance between two sides, and the preoccupation with personalities rather than policies as a means of maintaining the appearance of non-partisanship) have contributed to the problems. Thus, while they do not use the term, Rosen and Merritt are indirectly critiquing the regime of objectivity in their analysis of the crisis of public communication.

For Rosen and Merritt, journalism can and should help to resolve that crisis, both because journalism has contributed to it in the first place and because the existence of a public is a precondition for journalism as a meaningful cultural activity. Accordingly, journalists need to redefine their roles and responsibilities, to facilitate the rise of a rational, critical public. Journalists should seek to find out what issues the public is concerned with and pursue them, providing avenues for their discussion and potential resolution. This implies that journalists should stop thinking of the public as passive spectators of politics, or as a market for information. Instead, journalists should ensure, and if necessary initiate, public discussion about the values and policies of their particular communities. Journalists should not only raise public consciousness about issues, but also aid the public to "work through" community problems by helping to identify the root causes of those problems, the implications, and the "core values" at stake.[49] Ideally, such public deliberation should culminate in "public judgement," a resolution of the issue based upon widespread participation, informed debate, and, as far as possible, consensus.[50]

Public journalists, in short, should actively help to make public life work, and in so doing strengthen the bonds between journalism and the community to which it is addressed.

What do public journalists do in practice? There is no single model; public journalism defines itself more as an attitude than a technique. It has inspired a range of initiatives. In some cases news media have devised and sponsored mechanisms (ranging from feedback sections in the newspaper to public forums, focus groups, neighbourhood roundtables, and mock legislatures and juries) for public participation in defining the political agenda, and they have reported on the results of such public discussion. In other experiments newspapers have been asking readers to help decide what the newspaper covers and how, to become more of an active player and less of a passive observer in raising issues of community concern. In some cases newspapers have lobbied in the news pages, not just the editorials, for particular public policy changes when these are considered to reflect a community consensus. Public journalism may involve intermedia cooperation, typically between newspapers and a broadcasting station, co-producing a particular project. In covering politics, public journalism de-emphasizes the horse-race theme of party strategies and opinion polls and moves away from the conventional expert and elite sources to include a broader range of citizens' voices.

Public journalism is far more a U.S. than Canadian phenomenon, triggered in particular by the manifest irrelevance of political journalism and election campaigns to millions of citizens.[51] The perceived crisis of public life is less severe north of the border. Nevertheless, Canadian media too have been uneasy about their standing with audiences. While they appear to reject the most radical participatory experiments of U.S. public journalism (a label not much adopted in Canada), Canadian journalists have recently experimented in reconnecting with their audiences. One notable wake-up call was the failed 1992 Charlottetown constitutional amendment, when public rejection overwhelmed a virtual consensus within the economic elite, the three major federal parties – and the national media. In response, CBC news began televising "town hall" meetings in which selected "ordinary citizens" were invited to discuss issues of the day. In another experiment, normally rival news organizations in Calgary and Edmonton co-produced a week-long series, *Eyes on Alberta*. Incorporating polls and public forums, the series generated hours of radio and television programming and hundreds of inches of newspaper copy, focusing on changes to Alberta society wrought by the spending cutbacks of the Ralph Klein government.[52]

In important ways, public journalism challenges the regime of objectivity. It asks journalism to abandon a stance of detachment in order to actively reinvigorate public politics – "self-government through the deliberation of a rational-critical public."[53] Making public life work, rather than simply providing a balanced and "objective" flow of information, becomes journalism's primary legitimation. Public journalism challenges the "mirror of the world" model, calling attention to the unavoidable value-laden qualities and political role of journalism as a form of storytelling. Instead, it asks that journalists be more self-reflective about their own practices and assumptions, how stories are framed, how the audience is positioned, and what master narrative is being used.

At the same time, public journalism is a return neither to the partisanship of the nineteenth century nor to the advocacy journalism of today's alternative media. Public journalism does not ask news workers to stop checking the accuracy of facts and the reliability of sources, or to abandon neutrality on which particular party or policy to support. Public journalism maintains the ethic of objectivity with respect to coverage of "legitimate controversies" in which no community consensus exists. But it does advocate press activism in two situations. First, journalists should not pretend to be neutral on the issue of whether there has been active public participation and debate, or whether the community is addressing its problems. Journalists have never claimed to be neutral about certain values essential to their own occupation, such as free speech. Public journalism can be seen as an extension of that position.

Second, public journalists can actively advocate policy solutions once there is a community consensus. For most of its critics, and some of its supporters, this is a grey area for public journalism. What counts as a genuine consensus? What is to stop the press from using an apparent consensus it has helped to orchestrate in order to pursue its own agenda?

The public journalism movement shares some of the features of a crusade for earthly salvation. It has aroused passionate debate in newsrooms. In part, this is because public journalism to some extent challenges the regime of objectivity. It may be no coincidence that public journalism has taken the strongest hold in newspapers in small- to medium-sized cities, with geographically contained and relatively homogeneous readerships, and that the strongest opposition comes from journalists at *The New York Times*, the *Washington Post*, and *Newsday*. These are operations with horizons wider than a local community and whose legitimacy and reputation owe much to the regime of objectivity.

Some of the defenders of the objectivity regime see public journalism simply as an unwelcome turn to activist journalism, "extending the traditional role of the journalist beyond mere reporter to participant: one who contributes to building a better community instead of merely holding up a mirror to that society." It is "the logical extension for the objectivity-doesn't-exist school," rife with potential conflicts of interest as news media cover events that they may have actively promoted.[54] Media risk their credibility when they become active players rather than observers and chroniclers. In the words of Marvin Kalb, former White House press secretary: "When the journalist literally organizes the change and then covers it, I'm uncertain about such traditional qualities as detachment, objectivity, toughness.... The whole point of American journalism has always been detachment from authority so that critical analysis is possible."[55]

If Kalb were correct about the "whole point" of U.S. journalism – how detached from authority has it really been? – perhaps neither it nor representative democracy would be in a state of malaise. More to the point, even the most "objective" of media have been active shapers of political life, even if only by amplifying the voices of the powerful or by swamping them in a search for wrongdoing. This critique of public journalism rests upon an untenable image of "traditional" journalism as passive and mirror-like.

A more telling critique is made by upholders of the watchdog tradition. Some of them worry that public journalism extravaganzas may detract further from the already dwindling resources devoted to hard-newsgathering and investigative journalism. Others see public journalism as a market-driven gimmick to boost circulation, opening the doors to pandering, puffery, and boosterism. In this view public journalism overvalues community consensus and evades the responsibility to give people not just what they want to hear, but what they need to know – even when that knowledge offends them. "Two decades ago, outspoken newspaper editors in the South who denounced Jim Crow and endorsed civil rights were hated in their communities," says one critic. "Speaking out against racism was a noble but dangerous tactic, yet the progressive writings of these editors eventually helped bring about change. If those editors had established their news agenda by survey research, however, they certainly would have found that citizens wanted something else."[56]

Such a criticism may be too sweeping. Public journalism means different things to different people, and certainly Rosen and Merritt have warned their would-be followers of this potential pitfall. Even so, the charge of boosterism is sometimes uncomfortably close to the mark. The Knight-Ridder chain has supported experiments in public journalism at its papers, doubtless because it sees them as potential ways to stop sliding circulations, and because market research tells the company that people who feel more connected to their communities are more likely to read the local paper. Such corporate self-interest makes public journalism more viable within existing media, but it also places real tensions and limits on the process. The civic goal of actively addressing controversial and divisive issues may not be compatible with the commercial goal of improving circulation.

Another pitfall of public journalism is the possible use of controlled public participation to disguise and legitimize the media's own political agendas. Some conservatives saw the *Eyes on Alberta* series as being too heavily focused on the negative impact of fiscal restraint. On the other side of the coin, during the 1996 provincial election in British Columbia, *The Vancouver Sun* conducted a clip-in survey of readers' views of the issues, which in theory helped to organize the paper's subsequent features on various issues. In practice the survey was framed by introductory statements that emphasized the financial costs of government programs. The paper's subsequent coverage focused on government deficits far more than was warranted by public opinion as measured in more representative polls.[57]

The most fundamental and telling critiques of public journalism have emerged from outside the regime of objectivity. One such critique suggests that public journalism overestimates the possibility and desirability of community consensus, because it overlooks the extent of conflicting interests and standpoints. It may be no coincidence that the strongest public journalism experiments have been around issues that involve a broad consensus. Most people would agree that local crime, youth violence, or childhood poverty are bad things, and that jobs and community economic development are desirable. Issues with more fundamental conflicts of values (abortion policy at local hospitals, for instance) and interests (such as inequalities of class, gender, and race) are far less amenable to consensus-building. Nor is an apparent consensus inherently desirable, if it means ratifying an unjust status quo or precluding further debate.

Even more seriously, public journalism underestimates the breadth of the crisis of democracy and journalism. Its U.S. proponents critique the alienating impact of political journalism, but not the structural inequalities that reduce the opportunities for democratic participation. They are also disturbingly silent on the question of monopolization, concentration, and layoffs in media industries. Rosen rather cavalierly dismisses the question of whether "corporate culture" and "public culture" can co-exist. He overestimates the collective autonomy of newsrooms and journalists from the commercial and political interests of media corporations, and far too readily dismisses questions of power relations in news media structures. For instance, replacing elite sources with popular voices may be a worthwhile aim, but public journalism has not taken into account the imperatives of bureaucratic efficiency, which make it very difficult for news organizations to move in this direction. At the same time as they lead the charge for civic journalism, Knight-Ridder and another large newspaper chain, Gannett, are engaged in a bitter labour dispute in Detroit, demanding concessions from their news workers at the same time as they make record profits and purchase major new properties. Whatever public journalism may mean to these companies, it does not necessarily entail democratizing the newsroom or spending more on editorial quality.[58]

Public journalism may well succeed in complementing or even replacing the fraying ethos of objectivity, but with its blind spots it too could become a legitimizing ideology. Under conditions of commercial news production, it is likely to provide certain kinds of audience participation in public conversation and could even shift the news agenda – but only so long as it is consistent with building commercially viable audiences for the corporate media without bringing the wrath of powerful elites on their heads.

Despite its limitations, though, public journalism has raised a crucial question: what should journalism's public philosophy be? Nobody argues that news media should have a self-serving or hidden political agenda. Rather, public journalism rightly recognizes that news media are unavoidably implicated in the political order, that both democracy and journalism have conditions of existence, and that far from being neutral regarding its own preconditions (the existence of a public as well as free speech and much else), journalism should reinforce them. Whether public journalism offers the most appropriate approach to sustaining democracy and the independent public affairs journalism that a democracy needs is more debatable.

Nibbling at the Margins: Alternative Media

Potentially positive alternatives to the regime of objectivity are especially likely to be found outside the dominant media, among the so-called "alternative" media. Their very existence implicitly challenges the dominant news media's claims to speak to and for everybody. Sometimes alternative journalists make that critique of mainstream objectivity quite explicit. While many contemporary alternative periodicals have their immediate origins in the Vietnam War protest and counterculture of the 1960s and 1970s, they have precursors in journals of political dissent and labour radicalism dating back to the nineteenth century.[59] The muckraking populist journalism of the early twentieth century has been another source of inspiration for alternative media, especially *Mother Jones*, a U.S. periodical that emphasizes investigative stories.

The boundaries of the very category of "alternative media" are unclear. A wide range of production practices, presentational styles, editorial groups, and media types – staid monthly magazines, entertainment-oriented urban weeklies, street sheets for the homeless, upstart desktop-published fan zines, community radio and cable TV channels, news groups on the Internet, and others – have all been described as alternative media. They also vary in terms of how they are funded (foundation grants, subscription revenue, entertainment, and classified advertising), how commercialized or profit-oriented they are, how explicitly political they are, and the constituencies they are addressed to.

They have great diversity. Even within the alternative weekly tabloids, for instance, there is now a notable generation gap. As a phenomenon dating back to the 1960s, established alternative weeklies now speckle the continent, from Vancouver's *Georgia Straight*, Victoria's *Monday Magazine*, the *Seattle Weekly*, the *San Francisco Bay Guardian*, and the *L.A. Weekly* in the west, to New York's *The Village Voice*, Toronto's *NOW*, and the *Montreal Mirror* in the east. With a revenue basis in entertainment advertising, these grey-haired weeklies typically offer editorials and solid, serious, lengthy news features in the left-leaning, idealistic, gadfly tradition of investigative journalism. Increasingly, these baby-boomer-attuned weeklies are facing competition from upstart Generation-X tabloids, like Vancouver's *Terminal City*, Dallas's *The Met*, or Seattle's *The Stranger*, papers with a style that has been called "hip vacuousness." These newer efforts shun not only the "objective" journalism of the dominant news media, but also the moralistic investigative journalism of the baby-boomer weeklies. They disdain not only the electoral politics of the established parties and press, but also the progressive you-can-fight-city-hall populism of the older alternatives. Instead they favour the politics of identity and sexuality, music and arts coverage, social and cultural commentary, in-your-face humour and satire, often written in the decidedly non-objective first person.[60]

Clearly, the category of "alternative media" is problematic, a residual category defined by what it is alternative *to* – the dominant commercial media. Such a negative definition unfortunately implies that the "alternatives" are confined to permanently marginal status. Moreover, the concept needs to be narrowed before it can be useful for analysis. Does it include all volunteer or non-profit media, or specialized commercial media (say, a magazine for opera buffs) that try to win market niches ignored by the major commercial or state media? Does it include white supremacist computer bulletin boards or other explicitly racist media, simply because they see themselves as radical opponents of mainstream politics?

In addition to the category's internal heterogeneity, even its demarcation from dominant media is not clear. What does "alternative" mean when beer and tobacco companies market "alternatives" to their own major brand-name products? Newspapers have followed suit. To protect its advertising revenues from an urban weekly founded by political radicals, *The Toronto Star* launched its own entertainment weekly with some of the bark if not always the bite of its competitor. For similarly market-driven reasons, companies owning mainstream dailies in Fort Lauderdale, Milwaukee, and San Jose have also started weeklies that have become dubbed "McAlternatives."[61]

In Canada, with greater state involvement in cultural production, the boundaries are even less clear. Notwithstanding the constraints of political pressure and partial dependence on commercial revenue, the CBC nevertheless still provides a service distinct from commercial radio and television, and the federally funded National Film Board has produced films that shine in festivals of alternative cinema.

The growing age and affluence of its baby-boomer audiences, and its own very success, have provoked an identity crisis for survivors of the sixties-era alternative press. Indeed, a veteran editor at the *Utne Reader* (a *Reader's Digest* of the alternative press) has asked, "Do we still need the alternative press?" Jay Walljasper argues that the alternative press flourished during the Reagan-Bush era of the 1980s, when the mainstream media sank to new depths of political timidity, failing to break the Iran-Contra arms deal or the savings and loans crisis until it was too late. Meanwhile, the newly emerging baby-boomer market, with its taste for hip products and lifestyles, spawned or revitalized alternative urban weeklies throughout the land. While some of them "simply brought a sassy style to arts and lifestyle reporting," others "became an important source of progressive opinion and investigative reporting in their communities."[62]

Faced with eroding audiences and revenues, mainstream publications have struck back in the 1990s. They have started to ape the alternative press, to poach its talent, and to encroach on its style and topics, paying more attention, for example, to "women, African-Americans, gays, young people, pop culture, and environmental issues."[63] Some commercial dailies have been trying to de-emphasize official politics and elite sources in favour of voices from Main Street. They have also been experimenting with more "featurish" writing styles – even if these retain an ambivalent and subordinate status vis-à-vis the "objective" reportage of hard news.[64]

The alternative/mainstream distinction should be regarded as a continuum rather than a sharp dichotomy. There is probably no "pure" alternative medium. Nevertheless, to varying degrees, the alternative media *tend* to have distinctive characteristics – of ownership, funding, internal organization, political orientation, relations to their audiences, philosophy of journalism – that distinguish them from the hegemonic commercial media. In significant ways these characteristics provide examples of democratic communication and challenge the institutions, ideals, and practices of the objectivity regime.[65]

However young and hip reporters for mainstream media may be, for instance, they are not in a position to challenge the social order's fundamental assumptions about efficiency, technology, progress, or economic growth. As Walljasper puts it:

> When writing about pollution, youth angst, poverty, education, crime, politics, urban affairs, or even the closing of a beloved neighborhood store, they usually stop short of asking deep questions about the underlying causes of these problems. That's because the answer often points to abuses of corporate power and stark inequality in the distribution of wealth – two subjects that are still off-limits in most mainstream media.[66]

For some analysts, the alternative media can be defined on just this basis, as "politically dissident media that offer radical alternatives to mainstream debate" and that have a progressive orientation, broadly defined as the political and cultural project of sharing wealth, power, and status more equitably.[67] Far from claiming to be objective, alternative media "avowedly reject or challenge established and institutionalized politics, in the sense that they all advocate change in society, or at least a critical reassessment of traditional values," and "they frequently represent groups who feel that their viewpoints and concerns are not sufficiently represented within existing local and national media."[68] Furthermore, media that advocate intensifying rather than combating the most repressive aspects of the existing political culture are not "alternative," as we use the term here. We exclude white supremacist publications that are extensions of "the mainstream cultural reality of White racism ... even if their love of violence seems to set them apart."[69] And we exclude journals promoting the inequalities of the free market (like Canada's *Next City*, a new glossy magazine apparently intended to win urban baby-boomers and environmentalists to a market-liberal agenda, and generously funded by the right-wing U.S. Donner Foundation) or religious fundamentalism (like the newsmagazine *B.C. Report*), even though they may present themselves as an alternative to the commercial press.

Moreover, by contrast with the mainstream's hierarchical division of labour, alternative media to varying degrees have experimented with co-operative and democratic ways both of governing themselves and of producing programs and editorial matter. With its elected board, its volunteer programmers, and its membership-based funding, Vancouver's Co-op Radio embodies these principles. Its operations contrast sharply with those of media organizations owned by chains, conglomerates, or the state, which are oriented towards profit-making and derive their revenues mainly from advertising or state subsidies.

To the extent that they engage in journalism, alternative media also tend to challenge the mainstream's definition of who or what counts as newsworthy. For instance, alternative media access a range of voices – activists, minorities, ordinary people affected by governmental and corporate policies – usually marginalized in the major media. They give less weight to the voices privileged in the dominant press by virtue of their presumed objective expertise or representative status – officials, politicians, accredited experts. Moreover, whereas conventional news often consists of events that threaten or disrupt established institutions and values, alternative media are more inclined to represent such values and institutions as being themselves a potential threat to the well-being and rights of ordinary people. Such an approach is likely to seem unprofessional or biased – to those who fail to notice the biases of the mainstream's own "objectivity."

Many alternative media see themselves as promoting horizontal communication with and among their audiences, as distinct from the vertical top-down communication patterns typical of conventional news media.[70] In such a project of audience empowerment, the distinction between the receivers and the producers of media texts is less rigid than in the professionalized model of commercial media. Audiences may be regarded as participants in a common struggle, rather than as a commodity whose attention must be captured and sold. While usually organizationally independent, some alternative media orient themselves towards the politics of movements for social change, drawing ideas and activists from those communities into their own production processes. Some alternative media have experimented with participatory journalism, giving voice to volunteer reporters in the community – by contrast with the model of "objective" professionalism.

Alternative media are often explicitly sceptical of the criteria of balance and objectivity. In their mode of address, their presentational style, alternative media often adhere to advocacy or subjective models of journalism.

As Walljasper argues, by contrast with the mainstream's practice of objective reporting – "amassing cold facts and delivering them in a detached manner" with "no place for emotion or personal experience" – alternative journalists "pride themselves on ditching the constraints of objectivity in order to tell the real story."

> They provide details and background – what the inside of someone's home looks like or the feel of walking through a particular neighborhood – that frequently reveal as much about a topic as what sources say in interviews. They freely offer their own opinions and feelings, rather than slyly slipping them in between the lines. They are allowed to speak in their own voices, rather than chasing around to find sources who they can then quote ... saying what the reporters themselves really want to say.[71]

The alternative media, so defined, constitute a long-standing challenge to the dominant media and their regime of objectivity. Partly for that reason, they face significant limits to their effectiveness. Within a commercialized media system, alternative media are almost bound to be marginalized. They face structural bottlenecks in trying to expand beyond an audience ghetto of the committed. They do not reach audiences whose demographics are sufficiently attractive to advertisers; and their editorial content is non-complementary, or even antagonistic, to the consumerism of the advertising messages. Not only advertisers but periodical distributors discriminate against magazines without high production values and mass appeal. Without adequate funding, few alternative periodicals can pay writers to invest the time needed to research and write groundbreaking stories. To be sure, some U.S. periodicals (*Mother Jones*, the *Progressive*, or *The Nation*, for example) have been able to generate compelling, well-researched, and important journalism. Canada too has good alternative periodicals that have survived for decades, such as *Canadian Forum*, *This Magazine*, and *Canadian Dimension*. But with smaller markets and much less foundation funding than their U.S. counterparts, Canadian periodicals find it more difficult to consistently generate eye-opening investigative, timely, agenda-setting journalism. "Alternative" Canadian writers are more likely to save their best work for books published by small independent publishers, which struggle against the odds in a continentalized market dominated by multimedia conglomerates to access an oligopolistic distribution system, or even to survive economically.[72]

Nor should the alternative media simply be romanticized as white-hatted Davids taking on Goliath. They can easily fall prey to a mentality and style of permanent opposition and can attract angry, alienated people who will reproduce their own marginalization. They may become blatantly propagandistic, apologists for a particular cause, or just plain kooky. Partly because of their democratic ambitions, they are prone to factionalism and internal disputes. Moreover, there is an uncomfortable tradeoff between providing unmediated access for the voiceless and producing the kind of quality journalism that could appeal to broader audiences. The Vancouver-based *Allies* newspaper demonstrates the dilemmas of this approach. It usefully provides a political communication vehicle, with a free distribution of 35,000, for the advocacy groups that produce its individual pages and sections. But because of this approach its content lacks quality control, and it is not generally regarded as a credible journalistic medium. Alternative papers also sometimes succumb to the temptation to become less oppositional, less distinct, more profitable, and more up-market. They may attract people who see the organ simply as a stepping stone to a career in "real" journalism.

Nevertheless, the importance of the alternative media cannot be reduced to their current size. They have proven themselves able to influence the style and content of the dominant media. At least as important, for all their limitations, they provide living models for doing journalism outside the regime of objectivity. Indeed, even if this is not their main objective, the alternative media can be seen as engaging in a twofold project of democratization: insofar as they provide access for voices that are marginalized in the mainstream press, alternative media are promoting the democratization *of* the media system itself, by making it more pluralistic; and they are part of a process of democratization *through* the media.[73] They can, at their best, facilitate the work of critical social movements pursuing broader democratic goals, such as making authority more accountable, redistributing wealth and power more equally, or empowering previously marginalized or exploited social groups.

In their political communication strategies, social movements do not rely upon the independent alternative media alone. Indeed, the alternative press has a role-ambivalence towards movements: should it act as a conduit, an advocate, a neutral observer, or even a watchdog and critic, of social movements? Movements could hardly survive without having some communication channels of their own, no matter how small in scale — telephone trees, newsletters, direct mail, Internet mail lists, and Web sites.

At the same time, few movements can ignore the mass media, which significantly influence social movements at each stage of their political trajectories – their emergence, organizational consolidation and self-maintenance, and ultimate success or disintegration.[74] Accordingly, social movements do try to influence the agenda and framing of issues in the dominant media. Through their practices of objectivity, through the blind contingencies of newsworthy events (such as the 1989 Exxon Valdez oil tanker disaster), and through other "cracks in the monolith," dominant media do provide openings for movements to raise new issues or to challenge the terms of debate.[75] At various times in recent history, movements for civil rights, peace, ecology, abortion rights, or gender equality have received welcome boosts from news coverage. Although the approach seems to have become counterproductive in recent years, Greenpeace built itself into the world's largest environmental organization partly through its skilful staging of media spectacles. Even so, the media on the whole play a "conservatizing" role, delegitimizing and marginalizing radical protest, or inducing it to adopt bureaucratic structures and more moderate stands and tactics.[76]

In light of such a persistently conservatizing role, it is encouraging that in the 1990s there are signs of more direct challenges to the structure, priority, and interests of the dominant media themselves.

The Liberating Alternative: A Movement in Formation?

What do culture jamming, news monitoring, and media policy advocacy have in common? When these activities, scattered and diverse though they be, are informed by the democratic values of pluralism, equality, participation, and inclusion, they all tend towards *democratization of the media*. While it can hardly yet be called a full-fledged movement, media democratization shows encouraging signs of coalescing into a coherent project during the 1990s.

Impetus for such a project has several sources in contemporary society. Since the 1960s political parties have declined as vehicles of communication and mobilization, relative to both professionalized political marketers and to single-issue advocacy groups that campaign through the media. The dominance of television as a mass source of political news has increasingly turned political campaigns into expensive contests of televisual leadership images. The ensuing trivialization of political debate, as well as the relative exclusion of parties and candidates who cannot afford the high costs of effective political marketing and television advertising, has generated a backlash against the media-driven commercialization of political life.

Other impetuses for media democratization derive from the frustration of some activists at how the media systemically hinder progressive social change and how, by contrast, the media seem to impose unwanted social or cultural change. Long-standing concerns about the impact of mass media on social mores, order, and solidarity continue to find expression in current debates. One of many examples is the work of Canadians Concerned About Violence in Entertainment (C-CAVE). Founded by Rose Dyson in Toronto, it focuses on the perceived impact of commercially driven television violence on the socialization of children.

Another kind of impetus comes from those with the most direct material stake in the survival of independent journalism, including journalists defending their craft against the increasingly direct intrusion of commercial logic. For journalists and other media workers, not only their (limited) professional autonomy but even their very jobs are under threat from the processes of ownership concentration, economic rationalization, and the emphasis on "total newspapering" – which integrates everything from circulation and sales to editorial work in the interests of "marketing news-information."[77] Historically, North American media unions outside of Quebec have been reluctant to venture beyond short-term bread-and-butter issues to tackle questions of editorial control, media ownership, or government policy on communication. More and more, however, media workers are concluding that defending their economic interests means forging new alliances and speaking the language of broader democratic principles, such as freedom and diversity of expression.

Overdetermining these specific sources of progressive media activism is the evolution of a so-called "information society," in which much of the workforce produces and distributes data and images, and in which the cultural terrain is saturated with mediated symbols. It is hardly surprising that media institutions and representations are emerging as central sites of political contestation.

To be sure, apart from media workers and their unions, activism on media issues is usually a secondary concern, and when it happens it tends to be motivated by the media's connection to achieving some other primary goal. An example is MediaWatch, now based in Toronto, which monitors images of women in the media. MediaWatch was an outgrowth of the feminist movement, whose primary goal is gender equality. It would be difficult to imagine a movement concerned with media democratization in the abstract, given the multiple meanings of the concept of democracy and the radically contradictory interests with a stake in the media. The Fraser

Institute and Vancouver Co-op Radio both put forth critiques of the mainstream media, but ideologically they are not on the same wave length. In calling for "an expanded debate" but in rejecting pluralism for its own sake, the Women's Desk co-ordinator of the media monitoring group Fairness and Accuracy In Reporting (FAIR) makes clear that the social and political consequences of media coverage, not abstract ideals, are a driving force behind media activism.

> FAIR isn't interested in preventing the airing of viewpoints we disagree with; we're working for the inclusion of more. *A more pluralistic media would be nice ... but that's not the point* either. The slighting of public interest and minority viewpoints is dangerous.... The sort of coverage that followed the Oklahoma City bombing showed the price we pay for racism, homophobia and sexism in mainstream media.... The price of homophobia in the press is ignorance – and ignorance and hate can cost us all our lives.[78]

We should not exaggerate the strength, unity, or single-mindedness of advocacy for media democratization. Its secondary or derivative nature is in part a weakness. Advocacy groups may find it hard to justify spending scarce resources on a goal that seems too difficult, too broad, or too indirectly related to their primary interests. Many groups remain resigned to scrambling for access in the existing media system. They seem grateful for any coverage that could bring their work to the attention of potential funders and members.[79] Still, the reality that such a broad range of progressive values and causes is trivialized or denigrated in a commercialized media system creates real scope for a powerful common front.

Hundreds of initiatives for media democratization complement and overlap with the alternative media throughout North America. They include the following main types.

Culture jamming lies at the hip end of the media activist spectrum. Imagine: in the pre-dawn darkness, a handful of people stalking the streets of Vancouver, inserting coins in *Vancouver Sun* news boxes and opening them up – not to take a copy of the paper, but to wrap hundreds of copies in four-page spoof editions, called the *Vancouver Stump*. With a banner headline announcing a merger of the provincial government and a major forest company, the *Stump* satirized B.C.'s forestry practices as well as the *Sun*'s arguably pro-industry coverage of environmental issues. Welcome to the world of Guerrilla Media, where the goal is low-intensity semiotic warfare, direct-action media critiques using satirical mimicry to invert the messages of mainstream media.

In a similar vein, the Vancouver-based *Adbusters* magazine produces television counterads and glossy satires of magazine ads, intended to highlight the connection between consumerism and social ills such as alcoholism, anorexia, and environmental degradation. Elsewhere, groups like Artfux, the Guerrilla Girls, and San Francisco's Billboard Liberation Front exercise their creativity by illicitly "editing" outdoor billboards.

Media hoaxing is another variant of culture jamming. Joey Skaggs stages fake events or disguises himself as an expert to attract media attention and then publicly exposes the prank to reveal the extent to which television journalism, with its short memory span, its pursuit of trivia, and its avoidance of independent research, can be manipulated. Skaggs once circulated a fake letter, supposedly from a Korean company seeking U.S. dogs to turn into food. He used the ensuing media-fuelled outrage to illustrate the media's ready acceptance of negative ethnic stereotypes.

In many cases, the political intent of such culture jamming may be animated by nothing more than a postmodernist penchant for playful rebellion. At its best, though, culture jamming can denaturalize the dominant media's practices and assumptions that audiences had come to take for granted, and it can foreground some of the excluded alternatives.

Media monitoring and analysis offer a more rationalist and "serious" approach to media democratization, or at least accountability. Independent journals of professional self-critique, such as the Canadian Association of Journalists' *Media* magazine, CBC Radio's *And Now the Details*, the *Ryerson Review of Journalism*, or the well-respected *Columbia Journalism Review* fall within this category. Sometimes fundamental critiques of journalism's structures or working philosophies appear in these professionally oriented forums, but more typically they serve as barometers of what is considered acceptable within journalism's dominant paradigms.

Various institutes, often less bound to journalism's own occupational norms, also undertake regular media monitoring. Typically these are content analyses distributed through newsletters to subscribers and media organizations. This kind of work usually takes one of two forms. It may examine news coverage of a variety of issues from a single political perspective, as did the now defunct periodical *Lies of Our Times*, a leftist critique of *The New York Times*' news coverage. Alternatively, like New York University's Center for War, Peace and the News Media, it may examine news treatment of a single issue-field from a variety of perspectives.

The labour-intensive nature of this kind of work, as well as the costs of distribution, make it expensive. Not surprisingly, the field is dominated by corporate-funded conservative think-tanks, such as the Fraser Institute or the Washington D.C.-based Accuracy in Media, established in 1971 by Reed Irvine to combat what he sees as liberal bias in the national news media. But progressive counterparts have arisen, notably the U.S. national media monitor FAIR, which publishes the monthly newsletter *Extra!*. Other examples include Paper Tiger Television, which produces brief low-budget media commentaries by public figures for distribution on cable TV; Project Censored, founded in California in 1976 by Carl Jensen to publicize significant stories overlooked by the major media; and its counterpart in Canada, which now researches systemic blind spots in the news agenda.

Teachers and ethicists are in the vanguard of the emerging *media literacy* or *media education* movement, which is intended to promote critical awareness, through both public school and adult education, of the values, conventions, and impact of media. In some jurisdictions, such as Ontario, media education has been institutionalized in the public school curriculum.

A number of groups specialize in *advocacy on media policy issues*. In Canada, Friends of Canadian Broadcasting promotes the principles of public broadcasting and lobbies the government against the continuing cutbacks to the CBC's budget. In the left-leaning federal New Democratic Party, author Herschel Hardin founded an ad hoc caucus on culture and communication to try to make concentration and commercialization of the media a central issue in the party's platform. In the United States the Center for Media Education, the Women's Institute for Freedom of the Press, and many other progressive groups undertake research, education, and policy development on media censorship, commercialized television violence, the public interest in the information highway, the representation of women and minorities in media, and other issues.

All of these initiatives are encouraging. On their own, though, they are inadequate for challenging the media system. Such a monumental political project would require a broad-based movement equivalent to the civil rights and women's equality protests of the 1960s and 1970s. This movement would first place media democratization at the centre of its own agenda and then attempt to influence the terms of national political debate through alliances with other popular movements that find themselves disadvantaged by the current media system.

Fortunately, two singular events, occurring two weeks apart in early 1996, offered hopeful signs that just such a movement is emerging.

At the end of February, 650 independent and alternative media journalists, producers, activists, and analysts gathered in San Francisco for the first Media & Democracy Congress. Hosted by the Institute for Alternative Journalism, with thirty-two other co-sponsors from a broad range of North America's alternative publications and political left organizations, the Congress focused on the urgency of confronting the "right-wing juggernaut" of conservative-dominated, corporate media. As the IAJ's president put it, the Congress was intended to "begin building a collaborative media infrastructure that can promote public-interest journalism and combat the social fragmentation and erosion of democratic values encouraged by the concentration of media power."[80] Beyond sharing lessons and developing better links, the Congress consciously sought to begin the process of making "the world of independent and alternative media greater than the sum of its many parts."[81]

With participants from thirty-two U.S. states, as well as Canada and several other countries, the Congress was sufficiently large and unprecedented to attract the attention of even the national elite dailies – which predictably trashed it as "a who's who of what's left of the Left ... stewing in their own irrelevance," and "trapped in the time warp of the old fratricidal left ... alternative press navel-gazing."[82] Some of the more cynical alternative journalists present had similar judgements. "Although a smattering of young people was on hand, this was primarily a reunion of veterans from the 1960s and earlier, buffeted by several decades' worth of defeats," sniffed the *Boston Phoenix*, which not surprisingly concluded that the conference was focused less on "solutions than it was on whining and complaining about the power and influence of the right and the abject helplessness of the left."[83]

Our own (and no more "objective") personal impression of the Congress differs. Although grey hair and pessimism were not absent, the conference was an exhilarating collective experience of networking, launching practical and collaborative projects, and searching for common ground while respecting differences. Workshops brought together communities of interest, from editors of alternative newsweeklies to cyberjournalists and youth media. The panel and plenary discussions balanced theory and practice on a range of urgent questions. How do the corporate media represent class, race, and gender? Can public journalism and electronic publishing help save journalism from extinction? How can independent media voices be funded?

As well, the Congress endorsed an "Information Bill of Rights," which emphasized the principles of diversity, accountability of information providers, quality media culture, access to publicly significant information, basic and media literacy, right of expression without discrimination, privacy, and fair use of intellectual property. Perhaps the key commitment was to the right of citizens "to a full diversity of social and political information," including that offered by "independent, local, and noncommercial modes of media production and distribution," which are "necessary to the health of our democracy and must be protected by public policies."[84]

A fortnight later, the Cultural Environment Movement held its founding convention in St. Louis, attended by over 260 invited media activists, scholars, and representatives of the dozens of affiliated organizations. Founded in 1991 by the internationally respected communication scholar George Gerbner, CEM has goals compatible with those of the Media & Democracy Congress; indeed, Gerbner was a scheduled speaker at the latter. The emphases and core constituencies differ somewhat. The Congress was rooted in the world of North American independent journalism and alternative media practitioners. CEM probably draws a larger proportion of its supporters from academia, policy-makers, and religious, environmental, and children's rights groups. Its goals extend beyond journalism to mass-mediated entertainment culture; its energies lean towards research, education, and policy action more than media production; and its orientation is more international. (Its supporters and its 150 affiliated organizations span sixty-three countries on six continents.)

In St. Louis the conference's fifteen working groups recommended an action program on a range of concerns. As summarized on the CEM's Web site, these included media monopoly, independent media production, media education, health promotion, religion, technology and ecology, labour, cultural diversity and integrity, children and family, aging, gender, racial and ethnic issues, media violence, non-commercial storytelling alternatives, and problems of media reform and advocacy. The delegates also approved an organizational structure and debated and endorsed two important documents – documents remarkable for their contrast with the usual framing of communication issues in the corporate news media and market-liberal politics. A *Viewer's Declaration of Independence* offered the basic rationale for CEM's existence: the need to alter a cultural environment that had become destructive of people's humanity and potential and of children's development of "responsibility, trust and community rather than force, fear, and violence." No longer are the myths and stories of our culture told by families, schools, or churches; rather, they are "the products of a complex mass-production and marketing process" dominated by "a small group of global conglomerates that have something to sell." The declaration denounced consolidation of ownership, homogenization of media content, privatization of the airwaves with virtually no public debate, and "taxation without representation" through consumer advertising that fostered "an invisible, unelected, unaccountable, private Ministry of Culture making, behind closed doors, decisions that shape public policy." The consequences of such consolidated private power include brutalizing media violence, the promotion of unhealthy practices, marginalizing stereotypes for women and minorities, global cultural homogenization, growing gaps between the information rich and the information poor, and distortions of the democratic process that divert attention from basic problems – such as the drift towards "ecological suicide," growing economic inequality, and the "silent crumbling" of infrastructure, education, and arts: all of this with no constitutional or legislative relief in sight to help "loosen the noose of market censorship." The document concluded: "We, therefore, declare our independence from a system that has drifted out of democratic reach. Our CEM offers the liberating alternative: an independent citizen voice in cultural policy-making, working for the creation of a free, fair, diverse, and responsible cultural environment for us and our children."

As if signalling its international orientation, the CEM approved as a statement of principles a draft of *The People's Communication Charter*, initiated by the Third World Network (Malaysia), the Centre for Communication and Human Rights (Amsterdam), and the World Association of Community Radio Broadcasters. The People's Charter overlapped with the Media & Democracy Congress's Information Bill of Rights on a number of points: support for accountability, access, literacy, privacy, respect and non-discrimination, diversity, and independent media. In important respects, though, the Charter was broader and more internationalist in scope and arguably more radical in its proposals for media reform. It endorsed people's right to protect their cultural identity and to free expression in their own language. It called for international law to protect journalists, for people's right of reply and redress from media misinformation, for popular participation in cultural policy-making, for universal access and freedom of expression in cyberspace, for media products that nurture rather than harm children, and for fair media coverage of trials.

In language reminiscent of the New World Information Order debates of the 1970s, the People's Charter also called on media to "actively counter incitement to hate, prejudice, violence, and war" and to avoid glorifying violence and using degrading stereotypes. Perhaps anticipating accusations of censorship, the Charter did not address this clause directly to the media; rather, it prefaced the statement by saying that "People have the right to demand" such behaviour from the media. The Charter was less ambiguous in making another proposal with truly radical implications for a culture and media system saturated with commercialism: "Media should avoid and, if necessary, expose promotion disguised as news and entertainment ... and the creation of wasteful, unnecessary, harmful or ecologically damaging needs, wants, products and activities." It concluded with a pledge to work for national and international mechanisms to publicize, implement, and monitor these principles.

Canadians are involved in CEM through its advisory board and affiliated organizations, and by 1996 a similar non-partisan movement for media reform appeared to be in formation in Canada. The Council of Canadians, the largest progressive umbrella group in anglo-Canada, was spearheading a campaign against the country's extreme concentration of press ownership in the wake of Hollinger's takeover of the Southam chain. With support from individual journalists, academics, civil libertarians, and (importantly) media unions, this common front has the potential for a long-term, broadly based campaign for media diversity. Such a project could draw from the experience of the Campaign for Press and Broadcasting Freedom in Britain. Formed in 1979 to help develop media policy for the Labour Party, the CPBF has since broadened its activities and alliances and is arguably the most advanced project of its kind in Europe.

The kind of media activism represented by CEM and the Media & Democracy Congress constitutes a new kind of progressive politics, focused centrally on democratizing the media system in the sense of expanding the range of accessed voices, topics, experience, and perspectives, and on challenging the monolithic logic of corporate commercialism. In the words of its founder, CEM "calls for a radical shift from traditional arenas of the struggle for equity, justice, and the fulfillment of the democratic promise, to the cultural arena."[85]

In key respects the media democratization movement also constitutes a challenge to the regime of objectivity. Clearly it rejects the regime's assumption that the dominant journalistic practices and institutional arrangements of the news system generate value-free or objective accounts of the world. It is less clear as to whether the movement rejects the very ideal of objectivity as (epistemologically) impossible or as (normatively) undesirable. Unresolved and perhaps partly unrecognized differences of epistemology exist within the movement. For one thing, a tendency towards relativism is perhaps most evident in the politics of identity and in some versions of feminist theory. This view holds that different social and cultural locations generate different criteria and perceptions of truth, that there is no abstract truth apart from the interests and standpoint which generate it. This is a view that clearly has merit, but also limitations (see chapter 5).

In another apparent tendency, many activists offer critiques of the media that are, essentially, based on a realist epistemology. Edward S. Herman and Noam Chomsky's analyses of double standards in the news media clearly imply that there is an objectively knowable social and political world, which the corporate media have distorted.[86] Such a position is also implied in Gerbner's work on "cultural indicators" – the ways that television constructs pictures of the world, and associated emotional reactions, which are at odds with (for example) actual crime rates. A further example of this realist epistemology is evident in a criticism, made by the executive director of the Institute for Alternative Journalism, of "the growing tabloid mentality" which "distorts citizens' perceptions of reality." He calls instead for "truth-seeking journalism" to "provide for a lively, active, and informed citizenry."[87]

Not surprisingly, a parallel ambivalence concerns objectivity as a normative ideal. Some activists, particularly in community and participatory media, would reject it as an ideology of professional privilege, one that justifies the denial of direct citizens' access to the media. More common, though, is a call to reinforce independent journalism in the public interest, against the intrusions of infotainment and corporate censorship. While activists debunk the corporate media's claims of objectivity, they tend to be unwilling to themselves radically reject the language of objectivity, to call for open and naked partisanship or subjectivity. Instead, one activist for FAIR, for instance, argues that FAIR is not asking the media for any favours – simply for "good reporting – better reporting."[88]

In many respects the language of objectivity, independence, and public interest continues to provide the terms of media critique, even on the left.[88] This is an acceptance and usage, though, that has more in common with the progressive and universalizing idealism of the nineteenth-century labour press than with the regime institutionalized by the twentieth-century corporate media.

9

Conclusion: Towards Public Communication for Sustainable Democracy

If ours is a time of crisis, it is not a time for detailed blueprints for reform. In the public communication system, technological, economic, and political transformations would soon render any such blueprints rapidly obsolete. Instead, we should start by re-examining conceptual categories and normative commitments, even if only ultimately to reaffirm them. In doing this we can begin by taking a cue from the public journalism movement. It has its limitations, but it has usefully raised crucial questions about the substance and role of journalism's public philosophy in a democracy.

Two essential points emerge from the public journalism movement and other critiques of the objectivity regime. First, journalism is unavoidably selective, influenced by the subjectivities of the individuals and especially the organizations that produce it. It cannot divorce itself from choices and values. Even the most "objective" forms of journalism have systematic consequences and allegiances, in favour of commercialism, liberal democracy, and much else. Journalism cannot choose to have no philosophy. It can only choose whether its philosophy is openly acknowledged or not. The key problem with North American journalism, we believe, is that its self-proclaimed philosophy of objectivity is not the actual master it serves in practice.

Second, no human institution can take its own reproduction for granted. Any institution has conditions of existence that, if removed, would lead by definition to its demise, or to its transformation into something else. Because journalism and democracy are interconnected, because both are vulnerable, journalists have a legitimate interest in protecting both activities or spheres. A stance of neutrality with respect to a revitalized democratic public sphere would be either self-defeating or spurious. After all, journalists do not pretend to be indifferent to the values, such as freedom of speech and press, on which their very craft is premised. Those commitments are evident even in the (objective?) process of news selection, when government "gag laws" and other perceived threats to free speech are highlighted.

These same explicit value commitments can legitimately and appropriately be extended to the requirements of democratic self-government. We propose that journalism be evaluated as a form of *public communication for sustainable democracy*.

Public Communication? Sustainable Democracy?

The idea of *public communication* positions journalism as part of a broader media system. It evokes not simply the passive role of reportage, as important as that is, but the more active role of promoting communal dialogue about matters of shared concern. Our current media and political systems have shown a notably limited ability for – or even interest in – helping to create civic conversation, or democratic publics, and for providing for equitable participation in reasoned dialogue about fundamental options and values. A market-driven media system is unlikely to overcome its own biases in favour of affluent consumers, consumerist lifestyles, and seemingly apolitical but sometimes socially corrosive entertainment. Moreover, in a highly regionalized and culturally and economically colonized country such as Canada, with strong economic ties to its southern neighbour, a commercialized media system is even less likely to sustain an arena for public discourse that parallels its national political institutions. Market-liberals are quite content to allow public communication, such as it is, to be shaped by the logic of profit maximization in an economic climate dominated by a handful of media giants.

The idea of nurturing *sustainable democracy* relates, in one sense, to the environmental concept of restricting and managing growth in the interests of ecological survival, as a precondition for any humanly livable social order. Our current media system consciously promotes excessive and wasteful consumption, primarily in the interests of advertising revenues. While we would not expect the media to go as far as advocating environmentalism, a huge step forward would be an attempt to achieve a balance or neutrality between consumerism and ecology.

In another sense, sustainability also refers to the ability of democratic institutions to maintain and reproduce themselves over time. Democracy has no historical guarantees. The events of the 1930s and 1940s intimated the very real possibility of its extinction. The reproduction of democracy involves unavoidable paradoxes. Certain kinds of policies may need to be precluded in advance, even when they are decided by majority vote. Is it legitimate for a people to democratically elect a dictatorship, or to decide by majority vote to wage aggressive war against a neighbour? There are many troubling historical examples, from France's plebiscitary dictatorship of Louis-Napoléon in the 1850s, to the electoral triumph of Nazism in the 1930s, to the current referendum-legitimized dictatorships in former Soviet republics like Belarus.

The advocacy of ethnic hatred and genocide presents a similar kind of dilemma. Surely it must be unacceptable for a democracy to permit its freedoms to be used to destroy the very basis of human rights – a dilemma highlighted by Yugoslavia's bloody civil war, a war preceded by mass-mediated hate campaigns.[1] Before that war began, political theorist John Keane explained why democratically accountable legislatures may need to order "the arrest and punishment of individuals who cry fire, for fun, in crowded theatres," or groups that worship "the divine right of the gun." According to Keane, "An open and tolerant civil society can degenerate into a battlefield, in which, thanks to the existence of certain civil liberties such as 'liberty of the press,' lions can roar and foxes can come to enjoy the freedom to hunt down chickens. Under extreme conditions, a quarrelling civil society can even bludgeon itself to death."[2]

Paradoxically, then, majorities must sometimes consent to placing permanent restraints upon future majority decisions. Protecting democratic order from the excesses of democracy itself is a key purpose of written constitutions and the judicial review of laws.

Yet the sustainability of democracy not only is a question of maintaining order and legitimacy through formal documents and procedures, such as laws and elections, but also hinges upon the development of democratic subjectivity, the fostering of civic competence and democratic values on the part of ordinary citizens in the microworlds of everyday life.[3] Public journalism, the alternative media, and the media democratization movement all usefully remind us that, potentially, journalism can help to nurture democratic subjectivity. The kinds of subjectivity fostered by the media through their mode of address form an integral part of the shaping of political culture. The commercial media's tendency to position their audiences as consumers has adverse consequences not only for environmental sustainability, but for democratic citizenship. As Peter Dahlgren argues:

The semiotic environment envelopes the globe in images of consumerist redemption, while huge populations are excluded from participating and many other groups and individuals challenge and reject such images of fulfilment. One of the major negative features of consumerism as an ideological force is that it mitigates against collective identities and actions: solutions are always individualistic. *Thus, the tension between consumer and citizen as identities is fundamental.* Their incompatibility and conflictual character become increasingly visible in the context of the crisis of the welfare state and the political promotion of market forces as the ideological bedrock for societal relations. Any gains in the identity of citizenship will, to a large extent, have to be won at the expense of consumerist identities.[4]

If Dahlgren is correct, and if journalism's raison d'être is the democratic public sphere, as public journalism argues, then it is appropriate for journalism to be reorganized in a way that will free it from the commercial imperative of addressing audiences as consumers.

Such a proposal is highly political and contentious, as is the whole question of which cultural and institutional conditions should be seen as the prerequisites for democracy – which is itself, as we've seen, a highly contested concept. Any public philosophy of journalism will endorse (at least implicitly) a particular model of democracy.

As we've also seen, the objectivity regime, with its "professional" communicators speaking to and on behalf of broad publics, seems to suit a competitive elitist model of democracy, in which mass political participation is mainly limited to voting. But with that version of democracy facing a crisis of legitimacy, other, more thoroughgoing models are seeking to apply democratic principles not only in the formal political system, but also in civil society. These alternative models critique competitive elitism, precisely on the basis of democratic values such as participation, equality, representation, efficacy, and choice.[5]

Participatory democracy calls for the right of people affected by decisions in their neighbourhoods or workplaces to participate in making those decisions. It would imply a "democratic-participant" model to enable horizontal communication within geographical and interest-based communities, as exemplified by Vancouver Co-op Radio and other community-based media.[6] Socialist or social democracy sees approximate *equality* of economic resources, not just individual legal rights, as a precondition of effective citizenship; and it calls for democratic decision-making in industry as well as politics. It implies a media system that consciously acts as agents for communicative *equity*. In this model, media would be organized in a way that offsets the inequalities in political and communicative resources created by market relations and a culture of promotion.

Representation implies the ability of a diverse range of social interests, not just those who can afford professional image-makers, to find voice within the media and political systems. More diversity is not *always* necessarily better democracy; providing greater access for racist skinheads to the airwaves might somewhat increase broadcasting's diversity, but it would not help to sustain democratic values. Still, it is important to counterpose the general value of representative diversity to the homogenizing biases of a commercialized media system and to concretize it through the struggles of specific marginalized communities or subordinate social groups – even those that constitute a majority, like women and working people – for access.

Efficacy refers to our collective belief in our ability to participate in public reasoning and to achieve useful results through public policy. We need to consider whether the current media cultivate such a sense of agency vis-à-vis political life, or whether they promote cynicism, incomprehension, and withdrawal.

A significant *choice* implies moving beyond the pseudo-choices offered within consumer culture (Coke versus Pepsi) towards the availability and clarification of fundamental alternatives, within civil society as well as political life. In the political system it means providing access, and critical scrutiny, to a wider range of political alternatives, especially in the United States, where the excessive influence of wealth on the electoral process has narrowed voters' options. Backed by their megamillions, publisher Steve Forbes and businessman Ross Perot were able to muscle their way onto the political/media agenda. Without comparable wealth, candidates like consumer advocate Ralph Nader are left in the political wilderness, however deserving of a public hearing their programs may be. Canada's political system embodies greater diversity, but it too could do better at providing respectful though not undue access to minor parties.[7]

Choice also means challenging the hidebound liberal distinctions between private and public, in order to raise as public issues those "private" choices that have a cumulative impact on the entire society. Examples could include the introduction of technology in the workplace, patterns of urban development premised on continuing growth and the unsustainable dependence on automobiles, the distribution of income and jobs in a society increasingly polarized between the underemployed and the overworked, and the gendered division of labour that disproportionately burdens women with unpaid or underpaid work. These and other forces that affect the quality of our lives are too rarely raised as public issues within the news media.

The values of participation, equality, representative diversity, efficacy, and choice are dimensions of a sustainable and thoroughgoing democratic culture; but they differ from, and are sometimes at odds with, the market-liberal emphasis on privatized, individual consumer choice in the market-place. And they have not always been well-served by a media system that clings to traditional liberal justifications – and to objectivity, the god who won't die.

Objectivity or Not?

If journalism were indeed a form of public communication for sustainable democracy, would that imply that journalism should abandon the ethic of telling publicly pertinent truths? Should journalism leave objectivity in the dustbin and simply embrace its long-standing opposites – open partisanship or unabashed subjectivity?

The answer to these questions does not come easily. Few people would want journalism to be guided by hidden and improper motives, to publicize false news, to stifle relevant voices, or to suppress important information in order to protect privilege or prejudice. Certain elements of the objectivity regime are clearly worth preserving or revitalizing. After all, the original version of objectivity, in the nineteenth-century labour press, held an emancipatory promise of democratizing information, of telling stories about the world in a way that could lead to improvements. That version of objectivity did not claim to be value-free; it was born of a time when the distinction between facts and values, between news and opinion, was much less pronounced. It was an era when journalism's political commitments were not so much stronger as more open.

We cannot, of course, simply return to the naive universalism of the nineteenth-century democratic discourse. The twentieth century has taught us bitterly how Reason can fool us, how utopian abstractions can be wedded to nightmarish totalitarian politics, and how even apparently innocent or laudable universal categories can be the agent of particular interests, a vehicle for hierarchy and exclusion. (One thinks of the backlash against Aboriginal rights and multiculturalism among citizens' groups whose battle cry is "equality for all.")[8] Enlightenment concepts of truth, progress, and the public interest are contested and problematic. The postmodernist critique of the Enlightenment, which at its best can be seen as "the Enlightenment's reflexive encounter with itself," serves as a healthy warning that no single regime, whether in politics or journalism, ought to be applied universally.[9] Pluralism, experimentation, and openness are now the order of the day.

Nevertheless, we do need to revitalize the emancipatory spirit of the democratic discourse of the Enlightenment, and of the labour press's version of objectivity. The Enlightenment ideals of equality and emancipation continue to inspire projects of progressive political and social change – progressive not in the sense of a vanguard leading us to some blue-printed utopia, but as a never-completed project of working for the more egalitarian distribution of wealth and power.[10] We need this approach more than ever in the era of globalization, when capitalism is seriously constraining, if not divorcing itself from, liberalism and democracy. Market logic must be subordinated to democratic criteria if we are to preserve the best of liberalism – not only formal, legal individual rights, but also the dignity and fulfilment of the human personality – and democracy – not only representative government and periodic elections, but also meaningful citizen participation and democratic procedures in broader domains of social life.

Although the muckrakers of a century ago might remind us of a deep-rooted progressive impulse in the culture of North American journalism, we are certainly not arguing that the society's central media should become merely adjuncts of political movements. Such a merger would both undermine the credibility of journalism and threaten to impose a monolithic model that would be inherently undesirable in a pluralistic society. The former Soviet press system illustrated the authoritarian monstrosity that can result from the suppression of media diversity and autonomy in the interests of a historical mission defined by the state and a political party. Globally, independent journalism continues to be threatened by political authoritarianism as much as by unrestrained commercialism. When the two forces are combined, the hybrid can be truly grotesque, as China's contemporary press system suggests.[11] A democratic communication system could well include specific media directly controlled by groups and institutions addressing their constituencies.[12] But in general there would have to be a necessary distance between governments, parties, and movements, on the one hand, and journalism, on the other.

At this time and place – North America at the end of the twentieth century – there is a coincidence of interest between independent journalism and a "progressive" political stance – one that challenges the inequalities and imperatives generated by market-liberalism. Such a coincidence results from how current market forces are undermining the very institutional basis for journalism as an independent public sphere. Conglomerate ownership of the news media and new strategies of profitability are eroding the relative autonomy of editorial from marketing functions.[13] New technology not only creates the uncertain promise of horizontal interactivity, but may also fragment the economic basis for popular-oriented public affairs journalism. Meanwhile, as newsroom budgets are squeezed and the public relations industry grows in size and sophistication, the prospects for independent investigative journalism in mainstream newsrooms are in decline.

Journalism has a right to be concerned with the preconditions of its own existence. That means reigning in the forces of commercialism as they apply to media industries – which perforce means challenging the hegemony of market-liberalism throughout social and political life. At the least this in turn means preserving within the core of journalism's occupational culture, and its institutional supports, a sense of public interest and purpose broader than that of individual consumption. That does *not* mean simply endorsing and resuscitating the elitist and unreflexive notions of professionalism characteristic of the regime of objectivity. As Daniel Hallin puts it, echoing the public journalism movement: "The 'high modernist' conception of professionalism is clearly no longer viable, and needs to be rethought in important ways." Hallin points out that "journalists will probably have to shift from conceiving of themselves as, in effect, a representative or stand-in for a unitary but inactive public, toward a role of facilitating and publicizing public dialogue."[14]

Nevertheless, an important and inescapable democratic function remains in place for a specialized occupational group, guided by an ethic of truth-telling in the public interest. The tasks of this group include sifting, presenting, and making sense of information regarding democratic citizenship. In the workaday world of news production, the criteria of objectivity cannot simply be dismissed as inherently irrelevant, conservative, deceptive, or manipulative. It is often a good thing that journalists attempt to put aside or reserve personal judgements in an effort to produce honest reportage. It is indeed appropriate that audience-citizens have access to contending interpretations and positions on controversial issues.

The objectivity criteria also have positive uses in public discourse about news. At a time of globalized concentration and conglomerization of media power, it is more important than ever to identify and critique specific instances – and general patterns – in which news reportage violates journalism's own best professional standards. Are Conrad Black's newspapers really as independent from his own political ambitions as he likes to claim? Does *The Globe and Mail* really deserve its reputation for authoritative objectivity, or does it typically amplify the worldview of Bay Street stockbrokers and bankers? As we have argued, and as Dahlgren reminds us, we can engage in such debates without uncritically endorsing either the practices or the epistemology of the regime of objectivity:

> We can ... speak of the informational, factual dimensions of ... journalism ... without at the same time having to buy into an exclusively rational, information model of communication. Some accounts are simply more valid and have more practical implications than others. Information can still be evaluated according to criteria of importance, relevance, comprehensiveness, accuracy and so on without one having to accede to the dominant journalistic conceptions of objectivity and impartiality, and the empiricist epistemology from which they derive.[15]

While the objectivity regime does, then, provide useful openings and resources for democratizing communication, its associated epistemology, practices, and institutions do need to be rethought, and in some respects replaced.

We should not, for instance, equate the very idea of objectivity with the specific journalistic practices that the concept has been used to legitimate – practices that, for example, may result in amplifying official definitions of reality or, conversely, that confuse critical independence with mindless cynicism. It is possible to critique these practices on the basis of more rigorous standards of objectivity – disciplined observation, better research, greater real independence from, and awareness of, the previously unacknowledged interests and assumptions that may influence the production of news.

In other words, it is possible to critique the current practices of journalistic objectivity precisely on the basis of the ideal of *better* objectivity, as it is understood in science or academia, for example. This kind of critique can usefully expose superficiality and sheer inaccuracy in the news, as well as how news is complicit with power. At the same time, it seems pointless to denounce the news for failing to meet the standards of social-scientific rigour and observation. Journalism, after all, is better suited for providing acquaintance with events of the moment than knowledge of the social world over time.

Moreover, we should not forget how feminist and postmodernist critiques, especially, have challenged the very idea of objectivity.[16] All critics have their own standpoints; no knowledge is produced in an entirely disinterested and value-free fashion.

That consideration opens the door to another kind of critique of objective journalism: not that it is insufficiently objective, but that it illegitimately disguises its own textuality. The stance of detachment, the claim of neutral observation, is no longer tenable. Critics and educators should repeatedly call attention to how the rhetoric of news constructs its authority as accounts of the Real at the expense of other possible accounts. For its part, journalism should be more self-reflexive, more aware of its own frames and master narratives, and more pluralistic in its usage of them. Epistemologically, such a proposal does not mean embracing relativism or nihilism but calls for a stance of open, pluralistic, and critical realism.

The objectivity regime defines journalism as a cognitive and rational phenomenon, and this is a definition that privileges the literary over the oral, the middle class over the working class, high politics over the everyday, and information over storytelling. This kind of hierarchy, with its cultural and social exclusions, implies a hasty dismissal of popular or tabloid journalism, which at its best can evoke and connect private meanings and emotions with public issues. Objectivity offers few strategies for reconciling the personal and emotional with the political and the rational, which may be one of the reasons for its current crisis. There is an extremely important democratic role for a popular journalism that can tell interesting and personalized stories without losing the link with the public good and citizenship. The problem with most tabloid journalism within a commercialized media system is not its reliance on human interest and emotion, but its shrillness and its tendency to seek scapegoats and reinforce popular prejudice – characteristics not unrelated to the commercial imperative of finding the fastest way to the largest possible audience. There is a world of difference between the jagged-edged, commercially driven, authoritarian populism of *The Toronto Sun* and the public-oriented, human interest, and humane coffee-mug conversation of Peter Gzowski's *Morningside* on CBC Radio.

Yes, But What Is to Be Done?

Often in media interviews we are asked what our research implies for how journalists should do their job. This is a question that can only be addressed with extreme caution, especially given the high probability of any detailed blueprint being quickly rendered obsolete. We would also not be willing to argue that objectivity-as-usual be replaced by a single, monolithic model. We need different types of journalism for different purposes and constituencies; and we have neither the desire nor the standing to issue prescriptions to working people employed in a demanding occupation that is not our own. We are more interested in positing ideas and questions for collective debate.

Media reform is too often and too quickly reduced to questions surrounding the behaviour of individual journalists and the ethics of particular situations. Did a radio reporter step over the line that separates politics from journalism when he filed a conflict-of-interest complaint against British Columbia's premier? Does a particular story find the right balance between individual privacy and the public's right to know? Should reporters be compelled to reveal their sources in certain court cases? Questions like these are important in the everyday world of journalism, but they often serve to deflect attention from the broader philosophies, structural interests, and institutional contexts that shape the contours of that everyday world.[17]

Still, we believe strongly that there are potential sites and directions of struggle at a moment when both journalism and democracy are at a crossroads. To begin with, it is important not to mechanistically "read off" the functioning of journalism from the structure of news media. Despite their inbuilt tendencies, commercial news organizations are the site of conflicting pressures that allow a certain space for dissent and change.[18] The public journalism movement indicates the possibility, within limits, of renewing – and experimenting with – journalism practices within the dominant news institutions.

The media could, for instance, institutionalize self-reflexivity (if that is not a contradiction in terms). Journalists and their audiences need to analyse the fundamental biases and impacts of news discourse, to clarify and discuss the frames and master narratives in play, and to consider how the audience is being addressed. We need more media commentary from outside the objectivity paradigm, and a more open acknowledgement of journalism's intrinsic values and interests. Such self-reflexivity would help open up debate about alternative values and interests that journalism should serve.

As public journalism suggests, the media could actively facilitate civic conversation and substantive political debate and participation, at the relative expense of the traditional but somewhat spurious stance of detachment.

Such a facilitating role would imply replacing the cynical and horse-race mode of political journalism with an approach that clarifies options, values, and alternatives. It might also mean giving greater prominence to the positive possibilities of human agency. We refer here not to "happy news" and shaggy-dog stories, or to individual success stories, which are plentiful, but to legitimately newsworthy yet undercovered stories of people working together to make a difference. One example is the remarkable progress made by governments as well as non-governmental organizations in 1995-96 towards global nuclear disarmament.[19] Another example is the growth of, and linkages between, protest movements, from India to France to Mexico to Ontario, struggling to provide alternatives to capital-driven globalization.

Journalism for sustainable democracy would try to minimize the impact of the structural inequalities of market society on democratic participation in the public sphere. It would consciously search for intellectually, politically, and culturally significant voices that do not necessarily have their own PR firms or think-tanks, for standpoints that challenge conventional wisdom, and for significant events that occur outside the well-beaten paths of conventional news beats.

For instance, during a time when the public authority of the nation-state is in decline, the "watchdog" role that journalism has traditionally (and very insufficiently) adopted towards government could be extended to other potential problems for democratic civil co-existence. One of the most important, obviously, is the issue of environmental degradation. If as many media resources were devoted to covering the environment as party politics or celebrity murder trials, it would probably be higher on the public agenda. Journalism's biases towards free speech and economic prosperity should be expanded to include ecological survival and the peaceful resolution of political disputes. On a shrinking planet, the media's promotion of consumption-oriented "lifestyles" must be abandoned, even reversed.

Another potential "watchdog" beat concerns the relatively unexamined, unaccountable, multinational institutions that wield vast economic and political power, including global conglomerates and politico-financial arrangements such as NAFTA, the World Trade Organization, the World Bank, and the International Monetary Fund. People evaluating news about such private-sector quasi-governments might look not only at the amount of coverage, but also at its intended purposes and audiences. Michael Schudson states:

Executives of large corporations who may often have more influence on the daily lives of citizens than government officials are invariably less visible in general news. Their names may be found on the business pages – but there the way they are covered is radically different. On the front page, journalists write in anticipation of readers who ask, "What is happening in the world today that I should know about *as a citizen* of my community, nation, and world?" On the business page, journalists presume readers who ask, "What is happening in the world today that I should know about *as an investor* to protect or advance my financial interests?"[20]

Democratic journalism surely includes news *about* business *for* citizens – something that is undertaken by a handful of research and advocacy groups throughout North America but is all too rare in the mainstream press.

These and other fundamental changes to journalism's practices and ethos are unlikely to be achieved without intense and continuing pressure from outside and below, comparable to the paradigm shift in the nineteenth century that replaced the elite partisan press. As Michael Clow says: "It was public pressure which created the accommodation of 'objective' journalism almost a century ago. It will take the same energy to change our current form of journalism."[21] Most of these changes are, we admit, not likely to take place within the current system. They will more likely require new institutional forms for journalism, as well as public policy to reduce the dominance of commercial logic and corporate power within the media system.

Democratic alternatives to both corporate and state control do exist, including restrictions on further takeovers by oligopolistic media conglomerates and the adoption of a regulatory framework to protect the autonomy of journalism from other media functions such as advertising, circulation, and ownership's political interests. A revitalized public broadcasting system, which would include the often overlooked provincial educational networks as well as CBC, could help counterbalance the blind spots of the commercialized news media. This revitalization is not simply a matter of reversing funding cutbacks, but of exploring new mandates for public broadcasting and new relations with its audiences. Public broadcasting could be financed in part by a tax on advertising. Because advertising promotes both wasteful consumption and homogenization in the media system, such a tax is eminently reasonable from a democratic standpoint. Public policy also needs to ensure improved access to oligopolistic distribution systems for non-commercial, non-state, community, and alternative media.

To be sure, such reforms will encounter massive resistance from the elites with the most to lose. Media owners greeted much more modest proposals by Canada's 1980-81 Royal Commission on Newspapers with hysterical outrage. Moreover, although it is an essential component, media reform alone cannot bring about a sharing of economic security and political power. Media democratization can only be initiated and sustained by other social and political changes, including how we organize our daily lives. Democratized and self-reflexive journalism needs the support of audiences who insist on their right and need to participate in public life.

For all those reasons, media democratization only makes sense as part of a broader (and mutually constitutive) project of social transformation. The local level is a good place to begin. Some professional associations and trade unions have already achieved paid work-time to discuss issues relating to their workplace and occupation. If expanded into a widespread form of workplace-based adult education and discussion connected with public issues, this social practice could contribute hugely to a more participatory culture. Media will probably change fundamentally only when audiences change their orientation to the news, seeking to get useful information from it rather than entertaining spectacles. In turn audiences will demand new kinds of news when they need it in order to participate meaningfully in making decisions whose consequences they must live with.[22]

Specific proposals for reform are less important than the process of thoroughgoing democratization. Changes of this scale are most likely to emerge from the margins and, at least initially, from a sense of desperation. Journalists, whose own economic security is increasingly tenuous, have a common interest with labour, the alternative media, non-governmental organizations, and critical social movements in revitalizing a culture of publicness (as distinct from publicity), in placing the issue of media structure on the political agenda, in supporting public policy that would counterbalance the negative impacts of unimpeded market logic on communication (centralized agenda-setting power, commercial promotionalism, the information gap), and, above all, in developing new institutional bases for journalism oriented towards the public interest. The struggle for democratized media will not be mobilized by abstract ideals, but by thousands of ordinary people recognizing that a commercial media system that still trumpets its objectivity, however hollowly, places at risk the values essential to the quality of their lives: ecological sustainability, the fair distribution of wealth and power, and the negotiation of national and cultural identities.

In the project of democratizing the media a great deal is at stake – not only quality and equality in public life, but also in some ways the very definition of what it means to be fully human. The paradox of such a project, according to Cultural Environment Movement founder George Gerbner, is that it is "impossible" – and yet, it must be done.

Notes

Introduction: In Search of a Metaphor

1. Peter Dahlgren, *Television and the Public Sphere: Citizenship, Democracy and the Media* (London: Sage, 1995), p.7.
2. Canada, *Royal Commission on Newspapers* (Hull, Que.: Minister of Supply and Services Canada, 1981), p.34.
3. C.B. Macpherson, *The Real World of Democracy* (Toronto: Canadian Broadcasting Corporation, 1965).
4. C.B. Macpherson, *The Life and Times of Liberal Democracy* (Oxford: Oxford University Press, 1977). See also David Held, *Models of Democracy* (Stanford, Cal.: Stanford University Press, 1987).
5. Held, *Models of Democracy*, ch.5.
6. These criteria are loosely adapted from Denis McQuail, "Mass Media in the Public Interest: Towards a Framework of Norms for Media Performance," in *Mass Media and Society*, 2nd ed., ed. James Curran and Michael Gurevitch (London: Arnold, 1996), pp.66-80. For a fuller treatment, see Denis McQuail, *Media Performance: Mass Communication and the Public Interest* (London: Sage Publications, 1992).
7. The literature along these lines is voluminous. For recent Canadian examples of each kind of critique, see Barry Cooper, *Sins of Omission: Shaping the News at CBC TV* (Toronto: University of Toronto Press, 1994); and James Winter, *Democracy's Oxygen: How Corporations Control the News* (Montreal: Black Rose Books, 1996).
8. Ben H. Bagdikian, *The Media Monopoly*, 4th ed. (Boston: Beacon Press, 1992), pp.3-4; Mark Crispin Miller, "Demonopolize Them!" *Extra!* (November/December 1995), p.9; see also "The National Entertainment State," *The Nation*, vol.262, no.22 (June 3, 1996), pp.23-6, for a chart summarizing the holdings of the four corporate conglomerates.
9. Robert W. McChesney, "The Global Struggle for Democratic Communication," *Monthly Review*, vol.48, no.3 (July-August 1996), p.2.
10. See ibid.
11. Herbert Schiller, "On That Chart," *The Nation*, June 3, 1996, p.16.
12. See Foucault's essay "Truth/Power," in *The Foucault Reader*, ed. Paul Rabinow (New York: Pantheon Books, 1984), pp.54-5.
13. Scott Lash, *Sociology of Postmodernism* (London and New York: Routledge, 1990),

pp.4-5; Dahlgren, *Television and the Public Sphere*, pp.83-7. Lash had in turn adapted this notion from the political economists of the "Regulation School" and their concept of "regime of accumulation." On that, see David Harvey, *The Condition of Postmodernity* (Oxford: Blackwell, 1989), pp.121-4.

14. To Foucault and Lash, we should add a more recent usage that is remarkably similar to ours: Mark Pedelty's concept of "disciplinary apparatuses," a hybrid notion that blends Foucault's concept of discipline with the French structural Marxist Louis Althusser's notion of "ideological state apparatuses." Pedelty means to combine, as do we, Foucault's concept of power as productive and enabling, not simply repressive, with the Marxian concern with political economy and its "hierarchical regimes of production and distribution." See Mark Pedelty, *War Stories: The Culture of Foreign Correspondents* (New York and London: Routledge, 1995), pp.5-6.

15. Robert A. Hackett, "An Exaggerated Death: Prefatory Comments on 'Objectivity' in Journalism," in *Deadlines and Diversity: Journalism Ethics in a Changing World*, ed. Valerie Alia, Brian Brennan, and Barry Hoffmaster (Halifax: Fernwood Publishing, 1996), pp.40-3.

16. Loren Lind, "The Death of Objectivity," *The Globe and Mail*, March 3, 1990, p.C3.

17. Shari Graydon, "Freedom of Speech Lessons from Russia," *The Vancouver Sun*, June 19, 1996, p.A11.

18. Quoted by Doug Smith, "Offensive Lines," *Canadian Dimension*, vol.30, no.4 (July/August 1996), p.48.

19. Robert Hackett, "Decline of a Paradigm? Bias and Objectivity in News Media Studies," *Critical Studies in Mass Communication*, vol.1, no.3 (September 1984), pp.229-59.

20. Yuezhi Zhao, *Media and Democracy in China: Between the Party Line and the Bottom Line* (Urbana: University of Illinois Press, forthcoming).

21. Armande Saint-Jean, "The Evolution of Journalistic Ethics in Quebec," in *Deadlines and Diversity*, ed. Alia, Brennan, and Hoffmaster, pp.21-9.

22. Our thanks to Nick Dyer-Witheford for some of these formulations.

1. Democratic Discourse and the Origins of News Objectivity

1. See Peter Desbarats, *Guide to Canadian News Media*, 2nd ed. (Toronto: Harcourt Brace Canada, 1996), p.7, for a brief description of the case.

2. "The dark ages of partisan journalism" phrase is from Frank Luther Mott, *The News in America* (Cambridge, Mass.: Harvard University Press, 1962), p.167.

3. Norman Penner, *The Canadian Left: A Critical Analysis* (Scarborough, Ont.: Prentice-Hall Canada, 1977), pp.8, 15.

4. Although they may have ideological elements such as populism in common, the nineteenth-century Reform movement should not be confused with the current party of that name led by Preston Manning. Organizationally at least, the current federal Liberals have greater claim to descending from the Victorian-era Reformers.

5. Penner, *Canadian Left*, p.17.

6. Douglas Fetherling, *The Rise of the Canadian Newspaper* (Toronto: Oxford University Press Canada, 1990), p.79.

7. The federal Conservatives, for example, were spending $100,000 per year in the 1860s to buy favourable newspaper treatment. See Fetherling, *Rise of the Canadian Newspaper*, p.79.

8. Fetherling, *Rise of the Canadian Newspaper*, p.78. Fetherling (pp.100-1) notes important regional differences in the Canadian partisan press. For example, while papers in Central Canada were generally polarized along Liberal/Conservative party lines, papers in the three Prairie provinces were generally less beholden to political parties because of the newness of the cities and towns there and the relative weakness of party organizations. The British notion of the press baron, the proprietor who was a politician or statesman *ex officio*, took particular hold in British Columbia.

9. J.M.S. Careless, "Mid-Victorian Liberalism in Central Canadian Newspapers, 1850-67," *Canadian Historical Review*, 3 (1950) pp.226-7.

10. Before the end of the nineteenth century, socialist ideas began to make inroads in labour circles. Socialism replaced the democratic assumption of a one-class society with the idea of two social classes in conflict and posed the need to achieve a classless society through a revolutionary transformation.

11. Ed Finn, "Foreword," in Ron Verzuh, *Radical Rag: The Pioneer Labour Press in Canada* (Ottawa: Steel Rail, 1988), p.vii.

12. A statement in the Knights of Labor organ *The Palladium of Labor* (Dec. 15, 1883), published in Hamilton, Ont., illustrates how notions of natural rights were being extended to criticize the economic as well as political systems – but in terms that fell well short of the Marxist position that class exploitation was inherent to capitalism:

> We are thorough believers in Democracy – for without a free expression of the opinion of the people in the enactment of laws but little advance can be made. But ... mere Democracy – if carried no further – will never in itself redress social injustice or remedy the evils of the industrial system.... Our political system is bad enough, it abounds in abuses. But they are not the worst or most flagrant abuses or those that press most hardly on people. It is wrongs which flow from the deprivation of natural opportunities – from the crushing, paralysing effect of unchecked competition – from the power which capital has obtained to dictate the terms upon which the toilers shall continue to exist – from the huge monopolies which count men but as machines, and ignore all consideration of justice in their insensate greed for grain – it is this class of abuses rather than those purely political in their nature which cry aloud for speedy redress.

13. Dan Schiller, *Objectivity and the News* (Philadelphia: University of Pennsylvania Press, 1981), p.30.

14. Ibid.

15. Eric Foner, *Tom Paine and Revolutionary America* (New York: Oxford University Press, 1976), p.88, quoted in Schiller, *Objectivity and the News*, p.31.

16. Verzuh, *Radical Rag*, p.30.

17. Ibid., pp.52-3.

18. *Wage-Worker*, March 8, 1883, in Verzuh, *Radical Rag*, p.50.

19. Iorworth J. Prothero, *Artisans and Politics in Early Nineteenth-Century London* (Folkestone, Eng.: Wm. Dawson & Son, 1979), p.315.

20. Quoted in Verzuh, *Radical Rag*, p.30.

21. Quoted in ibid., pp.70-1; emphasis added.

22. Quoted in Schiller, *Objectivity and the News*, p.45; emphasis added.

23. Michael Schudson, *Discovering the News: A Social History of American Newspapers* (New York: Basic Books, 1978), p.5.

24. Verzuh, *Radical Rag*, pp.41, 87-8.

25. Ron Verzuh, "The Labour Press," *content*, May/June 1985, p.12.

26. William Lyon Mackenzie's *Colonial Advocate*, founded in 1824 in Ontario, was in all likelihood the first Canadian popular newspaper that came close to resembling, in its combination of radical commentary and "sensational" news stories, both the British Sunday papers and the U.S. penny press. But the *Colonial Advocate* was different from both. It was a political paper that fought for a cause, rather than a commercial paper whose main purpose was profit. Mackenzie was a political leader rather than a business entrepreneur – by contrast with many of the publishers of U.S. penny dailies and British Sunday papers. The *Colonial Advocate* ceased publication in 1837 with the defeat of the rebellion he led. Other papers that attempted to imitate the U.S. penny paper before the 1870s only survived either "by becoming the purveyors of news and views, ads and entertainment for the bourgeois family" or by succumbing to "the excitement of party warfare." See Paul Rutherford, *A Victorian Authority: The Daily Press in Late Nineteenth Century Canada* (Toronto: University of Toronto Press, 1982), p.51.

27. Rutherford, *Victorian Authority*, p.51.

28. James Curran, "The Press as an Agency of Social Control: An Historical Perspective," in *Newspaper History: From the 17th Century to the Present Day*, ed. George Boyce, James Curran, and Pauline Wingate (London: Constable, 1978), p.55.

29. Ibid., pp.54-5.

30. Schiller, *Objectivity and the News*, pp.74-5.

31. Verzuh, *Radical Rag*, p.68.

32. Ibid., p.58.

33. Quoted in ibid., p.79.

34. Roger Bird, "Sketchy Portrait," *content*, May/June 1989, pp.35-7, esp. p.36; also Verzuh, *Radical Rag*, p.79.

35. Verzuh, *Radical Rag*, p.68.

36. Schiller, *Objectivity and the News*, p.46.

37. Rutherford, *Victorian Authority*, p.51.

38. Verzuh, *Radical Rag*, p.67.

39. Rutherford, quoted in Verzuh, *Radical Rag*, p.68.

40. Quoted in Rutherford, *Victorian Authority*, p.51.

41. Independent journalism did not take hold at once. The partisan press lasted long after the emergence of the popular commercial dailies. In the United States, as Michael McGerr argues in *The Decline of Popular Politics* (New York: Oxford University Press, 1986), although the penny press emerged in the 1830s and signalled the possibility of successful independent journalism, independent journalism did

not come into full force until the 1870s and 1880s. In Canada, different types of newspapers – the partisan press, the labour press, the sectarian press of different ethnic or religious groups, and the independent commercial press – co-existed until well into the late nineteenth century, a period sometimes called the golden age of Canadian print journalism.

42. Schiller, *Objectivity and the News*, p.75.
43. Rutherford, *Victorian Authority*, pp.71-2; see also Schudson, *Discovering the News*, pp.22-6.
44. McGerr, *Decline of Popular Politics*, pp.107-37.
45. Schudson, *Discovering the News*, p.87; see also p.6.
46. Brian Beaven, "Journalism," *The Canadian Encyclopedia* (Edmonton: Hurtig, 1985), p.923.
47. McGerr, *Decline of Popular Politics*, p.118.
48. For a detailed case study of the democratic storyline in action, see Satu Repo, "Journalistic Objectivity, the Discourse on Democracy, and the Birth of the Popular Press" Ph.D. dissertation, Department of Education, University of Toronto, 1986, pp.129-48.
49. Rutherford, *Victorian Authority*, pp. 161, 162.
50. Schudson, *Discovering the News*, p.22.
51. *The New York Herald*, May 6, 1835, quoted in Schiller, *Objectivity and the News*, p.87; see also p.181.
52. For an account of these developments in the British context, see Anthony Smith, "The Long Road to Objectivity and Back Again: The Kinds of Truth We Get in Journalism," in *Newspaper History*, ed. Boyce, Curran, and Wingate, pp.153-71.
53. Beaven, "Journalism," p.923.
54. Virginia Berridge, "Popular Sunday Papers and Mid-Victorian Society," in *Newspaper History*, ed. Boyce, Curran, and Wingate, p.259.
55. Schiller, *Objectivity and the News*, p.197.

2. From Positivism to Negative News: The Evolution of Objectivity

1. Schudson, *Discovering the News*, pp.71-7.
2. For our usage of the unconventional term "facticity" to connote the status of factuality as an occupational ideology, linguistic purists can blame Gaye Tuchman, *Making News: A Study in the Construction of Reality* (New York: The Free Press, 1978), pp.82ff.
3. Julius Chambers, *News Hunting on Three Continents* (New York: Mitchell, Kennerly, 1921), p.7; quoted in Schudson, *Discovering the News*, p.77.
4. Lincoln Steffens, *The Autobiography of Lincoln Steffens* (New York: Harcourt, Brace, 1931), p.179; quoted in Schudson, *Discovering the News*, p.77.
5. Mitchell Stephens, *A History of News: From the Drum to the Satellite* (New York: Penguin Books, 1988), p.253.
6. Krishan Kumar, "Holding the Middle Ground: The BBC, the Public and the Professional Broadcaster," in *Mass Communication and Society*, ed. James Curran,

Michael Gurevitch, and Janet Woollacott (Beverly Hills, Cal.: Sage Publications, 1979), pp.236, 238.

7. The following summary of McArthur's concept of objectivity is summarized from Robert Albota, "Dan McArthur's Concept of Objectivity for the CBC News Service," in *Beyond the Printed Word: The Evolution of Canada's Broadcast News Heritage*, ed. Richard Lochead (Kingston, Ont.: Quarry Press, 1991), pp.223-30.

8. Frank W. Peers, *The Politics of Canadian Broadcasting 1920-1952* (Toronto: University of Toronto Press, 1969), p.345.

9. Albota, "Dan McArthur's Concept," p.225.

10. Ibid.

11. Ibid., p.226.

12. Don Macdonald, in *Beyond the Printed Word*, ed. Lochead, p.234.

13. Romeo Leblanc, quoted in David Taras, *The Newsmakers: The Media's Influence on Canadian Politics* (Scarborough, Ont.: Nelson Canada, 1990), p.53.

14. George Bain, *Gotcha! How the Media Distort the News* (Toronto: Key Porter Books, 1994), pp.vii-viii.

15. Taras, *Newsmakers*, pp.53-4.

16. Schudson, *Discovering the News*, pp.122ff.

17. Quoted in ibid., p.153.

18. Ibid., p.138; see also Stephens, *History of News*, pp. 260-1.

19. For a more detailed analysis of this transformation, see Schudson, *Discovering the News*, ch.4.

20. Ibid., p.122. For "organizational mechanisms," see Herbert J. Gans, *Deciding What's News* (New York: Vintage Books, 1980), p.185. For "strategic rituals," see Gaye Tuchman, "Objectivity as Strategic Ritual: An Examination of Newsmen's Notions of Objectivity," *American Journal of Sociology*, 77 (1972), pp.660-79.

21. Schudson, *Discovering the News*; and W. Lance Bennett, *News: The Politics of Illusion*, 2nd ed. (White Plains, N.Y.: Longman, 1988), p.120.

22. Quoted in Schiller, *Objectivity and the News*, p.195.

23. Of course, in important respects all reporting is unavoidably interpretive. Here we adopt the more restricted and conventional meaning of "interpretive reporting."

24. Cf. Schudson, *Discovering the News*, pp.148-9.

25. Curtis D. MacDougall, *Interpretive Reporting* (New York: The Macmillan Company, 1968), p.17.

26. Commission on Freedom of the Press (Hutchins Commission), *A Free and Responsible Press* (Chicago: University of Chicago Press, 1947).

27. Schudson, *Discovering the News*, p.150.

28. Albota, "Dan McArthur's Concept of Objectivity," pp.229-30.

29. David Levy, comment made at a symposium on broadcasting news sponsored by the National Archives of Canada, Oct. 20-22, 1988, published in *Beyond the Printed Word*, ed. Lochead, p.233.

30. Andrew M. Osler, *News: The Evolution of Journalism in Canada* (Toronto: Copp Clark Pitman, 1993), p.174.

31. Quoted in Yuezhi Zhao, "Objectivity and Commercial News," M.A. thesis, Department of Communication, Simon Fraser University, Burnaby, B.C., 1989.

32. Both quotations are from Mott, *News in America*, pp.79, 80; emphasis added in the Cooper quote.

33. Albota, "Dan McArthur's Concept of Objectivity," p.230.

34. Gene Gilmore and Robert Boot, "Ethics for Newsmen," in *Ethics and the Press: Readings in Mass Media Morality*, ed. John C. Merrill and Ralph D. Barney (New York: Hastings House, 1975), p.28.

35. Canada, *Royal Commission on Newspapers*, p.218; emphasis added.

36. Bernard Roshco, *Newsmaking* (Chicago and London: University of Chicago Press), p.53.

37. Richard V. Ericson, Patricia M. Baranek, and Janet B.L. Chan, *Visualizing Deviance: A Study of News Organization* (Toronto: University of Toronto Press, 1987), p.261.

38. Schudson, *Discovering the News*, p.192.

39. Harvey Molotch and Marilyn Lester, "Accidental News: The Great Oil Spill," *American Journal of Sociology*, 81 (1975), pp.235-60; cited in Tuchman, *Making News*, p.83.

40. Mark Hertsgaard, *On Bended Knee: The Press and the Reagan Presidency* (New York: Schocken Books, 1988); see, for example, pp.62-71, 145, 334.

41. The phrase is from Ron Verzuh, *Underground Times: Canada's Flower-Child Revolutionaries* (Toronto: Deneau, 1989), p.xii. The book is a useful guide to Canada's alternative press of the 1960s.

42. For Canadian examples of this kind of critique, see Anthony Westell, "The Press: Adversary or Channel of Communication?" in *Parliament, Policy and Representation*, ed. H.D. Clarke, C. Campbell, F.Q. Quo, and A. Goddard (Toronto: Methuen, 1980), pp.25-34; Taras, *Newsmakers*, pp.53-65; and Bain, *Gotcha!*, pp.6-7.

43. Taras, *Newsmakers*, pp.95-112.

44. Paul H. Weaver, "Is Television News Biased?" *The Public Interest*, 26 (Winter 1972), p.68.

45. Chris Dornan, "Logical Positivism under the Electronic Gun: The Naturalistic Fallacy in Television News," paper presented to the Canadian Communications Association conference, Dalhousie University, Halifax, 1981.

46. Richard Gruneau and Robert A. Hackett, "The Production of T.V. News," in *Questioning the Media: A Critical Introduction*, ed. John Downing, Ali Mohammadi, and Annabelle Sreberny-Mohammadi (Newbury Park, N.J., London, New Delhi: Sage Publications, 1990), pp.281-95.

47. Taras, *Newsmakers*, pp.59, 60.

48. Arthur Siegel, *Politics and the Media in Canada* (Toronto: McGraw-Hill Ryerson, 1983), pp.207-33, analyses the contrast between French-language and English-language coverage of the October Crisis.

49. Taras, *Newsmakers*, pp.54-5.

50. Bain, *Gotcha!*, p.60.

51. Ibid.

52. Schudson, *Discovering the News*, pp.187-8.

53. J. Herbert Altschull, *From Milton to McLuhan: The Ideas behind American Journalism* (New York: Longman, 1990), p.317.

54. Taras, *Newsmakers*, p.57.

55. David Hayes, *Power and Influence: The Globe and Mail and the News Revolution* (Toronto: Key Porter Books, 1992), p.176.

56. McQuail, *Media Performance*, p.191.

57. Private correspondence to the authors.

58. A project that researches blind spots in Canada's news agenda found an article by Neil Brooks and Linda McQuaig on tax breaks for the wealthy to be the second-most underreported story of 1993. See *Project Censored Canada 1994 Yearbook* (Burnaby, B.C.: PCC, Simon Fraser University, 1994). Black's comment, made in an interview on CBC Radio's *Morningside*, was reported by James Winter and Amir Hassanpour, "Building Babel," *The Canadian Forum*, January/February 1994, p.10.

59. Altschull, *From Milton to McLuhan*, p.317.

60. Ibid., p.318.

61. Ibid.

62. Schudson, *Discovering the News*, pp.187-8.

63. Jack Newfield, "Is There a 'New' Journalism?" *Columbia Journalism Review*, vol.10, no.2 (July/August 1972), p.45.

64. Schudson, *Discovering the News*, p.193.

65. Journalist Douglass Cater, for example, criticized the "captive press" and the "strait-jacketed reporter" who passed McCarthy's lies and accusations as hard news of public record and without commenting on whether or not his charges were true. See Douglass Cater, "The Captive Press," *The Reporter*, 2 (June 6, 1950), p.18. To be sure, as media sociologist Michael Schudson suggested (interview with Robert Hackett, February 1992), journalists may be overemphasizing the failure of a specific newsgathering method rather than offering more profound political and ideological reasons for the U.S. media's complicity in Cold War McCarthyist hysteria.

66. See, for example, Robert Entman, *Democracy without Citizens: Media and the Decay of American Politics* (New York: Oxford University Press, 1989), p.37; Leon V. Sigal, "Sources Make the News," in *Reading the News*, ed. Robert Karl Manoff and Michael Schudson (New York: Pantheon Books, 1986), p.30.

67. William A. Dorman and Mansour Farhang, *The U.S. Press and Iran: Foreign Policy and the Journalism of Deference* (Berkeley: University of California Press, 1987), p.215.

68. Andrew MacFarlane and Robert Martin, quoted by Vernon Epp, "Professional Values Win," *content,* July/August 1986, p.9.

69. *The Toronto Star*, for instance, requires its reporters to sign a contract prohibiting them from engaging in political activities and endorsing any political candidates or cause. The paper argues that journalists are obliged to "ensure that our reputations as objective fact-finders are not compromised by an open display of political or partisan views on public issues." See Epp, "Professional Values Win," pp.9-10.

70. For example, in the 1960s CBC-TV newscaster Stanley Burke was fired for openly espousing the Biafran cause in Nigeria's civil war; see Ericson, Baranek, and Chan,

Visualizing Deviance, p.105. Similarly, when his union took a stand against the 1988 U.S.-Canada free trade deal, Dale Goldhawk (now with CTV National News) had to choose between his position as a union officer and his bread and butter as a CBC Radio host; see Knowlton Nash, *Prime Time at Ten: Behind-the-Camera Battles of Canadian TV Journalism* (Toronto: McClelland and Stewart, 1987), pp.23-4.

71. E. Barbara Phillips, "Approaches to Objectivity: Journalistic versus Social Science Perspectives," in *Strategies for Communication Research*, ed. Paul M. Hirsch, Peter V. Miller, and F. Gerald Kline (Beverly Hills, Cal.: Sage Publications, 1977), pp.63-77.

72. Rilla Dean Mills, "Newspaper Journalists' Perceptions of Ethical Decisions," paper presented to the Association for Education in Journalism, Athens, Ohio, 1982; cited in Robert J. Griffin, D. Molen, C. Schoenfeld, and J. Scotton, *Interpreting Public Issues* (Ames: Iowa State University Press, 1991), p.87.

73. Robert Miraldi, *Muckraking and Objectivity: Journalism's Colliding Traditions* (New York: Greenwood Press, 1990), p.14.

74. Griffin et al., *Interpreting Public Issues*, p.88, excerpt the code.

75. Ericson, Baranek, and Chang, *Visualizing Deviance*, p.104. See also the same authors' *Negotiating Control: A Study of News Sources* (Toronto: University of Toronto Press, 1989).

76. Graham Knight, "News and Ideology," *Canadian Journal of Communication*, vol.8, no.4 (September 1982), p.23.

77. Walter Lippmann, "The American Press," in *The Yale Review*, vol.30 (1930-31), p.440-1.

78. John Pauly, "Rupert Murdoch and the Demonology of Professional Journalism," in *Media, Myths and Narratives: Television and the Press*, ed. James Carey (Beverly Hills, Cal.: Sage Publications, 1988).

79. On cynicism in journalism, for instance, see Walter Stewart, "The Only Side of the Street," in *The Journalists*, ed. Robert Fulford et al., vol.2, Research Studies for the Royal Commission on Newspapers (Ottawa: Minister of Supply and Services Canada, 1981), p.81.

80. See Pauly, "Rupert Murdoch," for an analysis of the U.S. journalism establishment's reaction against Murdoch's "invasion" of the U.S. media market.

81. See, for example, Walter Stewart, "Fulfilling a Prophesy," *content*, March/April, 1989, pp.21-2; Murray Goldblatt, "Integrating Business and News," and other articles in the same issue of *content*; and Lorne Slotnick, "Purging the *Globe and Mail*," *Canadian Dimension* (June 1989), p.47.

82. Hayes, *Power and Influence*, p.181.

83. Stewart, "Fulfilling a Prophesy," p.21.

84. Desbarats, *Guide to Canadian News Media*, p.136.

85. Ibid., p.137.

86. Joseph N. Gelmon, *The Gazette Style* (Montreal: The Gazette, 1991), pp.vi-vii.

87. Desbarats, *Guide to Canadian News Media*, pp.136, 141.

88. Walter Truett Anderson, *Reality Isn't What It Used to Be* (San Francisco: Harper & Row, 1990).

89. For the media sociologist, see Herbert J. Gans, *Deciding What's News* (New York: Vintage Books, 1990), p.184; for the reviewer, see Lind, "Death of Objectivity."

90. Walter Stewart, "No, Virginia, There Is No Lou Grant," in *Canadian Newspapers: The Inside Story*, ed. Walter Stewart (Edmonton: Hurtig, 1980), p.15; Knowlton Nash, "This Imperfect Necessity," *content* (January/February 1988), p.10; Canada, *Royal Commission on Newspapers*, p.24.

91. Desbarats, *Guide to Canadian News Media*, p.140.

92. Bennett, *News*, pp.118-20.

3. Institutional Logics: Why It Still Pays to Be Objective

1. Desbarats, *Guide to Canadian News Media*, p.62.

2. Ibid., pp.45-6.

3. As noted in the Introduction, the process of concentration is international; the worldwide market is dominated by a handful of global, vertically integrated multimedia companies – Disney, Time Warner, Viacom, Tele-Communications Inc. (TCI), and Rupert Murdoch's News Corp. See McChesney, "Global Struggle for Democratic Communication," p.2. Even within Canada it is almost impossible to keep up to date with the breathtaking speed of media mergers. Winter's *Democracy's Oxygen* (1996) contains the most recently published summary of press ownership in Canada, but some of its data were already outdated by the time it reached readers.

4. For some of these points, see Peter J.S. Dunnett, *The World Newspaper Industry* (London: Croom Helm, 1988), esp. pp.42-51, 188-200.

5. Fetherling, *Rise of Canadian Newspapers*, p.112, 102; see also Tim Creery, "Newspapers," *Canadian Encyclopedia* (1985), vol.2, p.1255.

6. See, for example, Rohan Samarajiwa, "The Canadian Newspaper Industry and the Kent Commission: 'Rationalization' and Response," *Studies in Political Economy*, 12 (Fall 1983), pp.125-34.

7. Paul Audley, *Canada's Cultural Industries* (Toronto: James Lorimer, 1983), p.36.

8. Winter, *Democracy's Oxygen*, pp.21-41. It is worth noting that the Hollinger newspaper empire does include some "quality" right-wing flagship papers, notably London's *Daily Telegraph*.

9. Frederick J. Fletcher, *The Newspaper and Public Affairs*, vol.7, Research Studies for Royal Commission on Newspapers (Ottawa: Minister of Supply and Services Canada, 1981), pp.6-7.

10. Bagdikian, *Media Monopoly*, p.132.

11. *The New York Times*, March 22, 1860, quoted in Schiller, *Objectivity and the News*, p.87.

12. Dallas W. Smythe, *Dependency Road: Communications, Capitalism, Consciousness and Canada* (Norwood, N.J.: Ablex, 1981), pp.37-8.

13. James Curran and Jean Seaton, *Power without Responsibility* (London and New York: Methuen, 1985), p.41.

14. Bagdikian, *Media Monopoly*, pp.129-30.

15. Lysiane Gagnon, "Journalism and Ideologies in Quebec," in *Journalists*, ed. Fulford, p.25.

16. Canada, *Royal Commission on Newspapers*, p.15.
17. Stephens, *History of News*, p.259.
18. See Fred Siebert, Theodore Peterson, and Wilbur Shramm, *Four Theories of the Press* (Urbana: University of Illinois Press, 1963), p.60; and James Carey, "Communication Revolution and the Professional Communicator," *The Sociological Review Monograph*, no.13 (1969), pp.23-38. Another U.S. media scholar, Donald L. Shaw, attempted to demonstrate quantitatively the role of the wire service in the advancement of the objectivity concept in news. He sampled Wisconsin daily papers during the 1852-1910 period and found a decline in partisan reporting as the use of the telegraph became more common. However, Shaw failed to establish a convincing *causal* relationship between the decline of news bias and the use of wire services. See Donald Shaw, "News Bias and the Telegraph: A Study of Historical Change," *Journalism Quarterly*, 44 (Spring 1967), pp.3-12.
19. Schiller, *Objectivity and the News*, p.4.
20. Ibid.
21. Margaret Morse, "The Television News Personality and Credibility: Reflections on the News in Transition," in *Studies in Entertainment: Critical Approaches to Mass Culture*, ed. Tonia Modleski (Bloomington and Indianapolis: Indiana University Press, 1986), p.57.
22. John Meisel, "The Decline of Party in Canada," in *Party Politics in Canada*, 4th ed., ed. Hugh G. Thorburn (Scarborough, Ont.: Prentice-Hall, 1979), pp.125-6.
23. Jay G. Blumler and Michael Gurevitch, "The Political Effects of Mass Communication," in *Culture, Society and the Media*, ed. Michael Gurevitch, Tony Bennett, James Curran, and Janet Woollacott (London: Methuen, 1982), p.248.
24. Peers, *Politics of Canadian Broadcasting*, p.12.
25. Robert W. McChesney, "The Battle for the U.S. Airwaves, 1928-1935," *Journal of Communication*, vol.40, no.4 (Autumn 1990), p.34.
26. Anthony Podesta, "The Necessity of the Fairness Doctrine Given the Religious Right Televangelists," *Journal of Broadcasting*, vol.28, no.3 (Summer 1984), pp.271-2.
27. Edward Jay Epstein, *News from Nowhere* (New York: Vintage Books, 1974), p.64.
28. For a detailed discussion of the concept of balance in Canadian broadcasting regulation, see Peter G. Cook and Myles A. Ruggles, "Balance and Freedom of Speech: Challenge for Canadian Broadcasting," *Canadian Journal of Communication*, vol.17, no.1 (Winter 1992), pp.37-60.
29. David Ellis, *Evolution of the Canadian Broadcasting System: Objectives and Realities, 1928-1968* (Hull, Que.: Canada, Department of Communications, 1979), p.83.
30. Walter I. Romanow and Walter C. Soderlund, *Media Canada: An Introductory Analysis* (Toronto: Copp Clark Pitman, 1992), pp.147, 335.
31. Ibid., p.55.
32. Robert E. Babe, *Canadian Television Broadcasting: Structure, Performance and Regulation* (Ottawa: Economic Council of Canada, 1979), pp.229-30.
33. Kimberly A. Neuendorf, "The Public Trust versus the Almighty Dollar," in *Religious Television: Controversies and Conclusions*, ed. Robert Abelman and Stuart M. Hoover (Norwood, N.J.: Ablex, 1990), pp.71-84.

34. Peers, *Politics of Canadian Broadcasting*, pp.44-8.
35. Canada, Broadcasting Act of 1991, quoted in *Media Canada*, ed. Romanow and Soderlund, p.337.
36. Canadian Broadcasting Corporation, *Journalistic Policy* (Ottawa: CBC, 1982), p.7.
37. Peter Stursberg, *Mister Broadcasting: The Ernie Bushnell Story* (Toronto: Peter Martin Associates, 1971), p.169.
38. Blumler and Gurevitch, "Political Effects," p.248.
39. For a summary of laws affecting freedom of the press in Canada prior to the Charter, see Walter Tarnopolsky, "Freedom of the Press," in *Newspapers and the Law*, ed. Walter Tarnopolsky, C. Wright, G-A. Beaudoin, and E. Cody-Rice, vol.3, Research Studies for the Royal Commission on Newspapers (Ottawa: Minister of Supply and Services Canada, 1981), pp.1-48.
40. Daniel C. Hallin, *The "Uncensored War": The Media and Vietnam* (Berkeley: University of California Press, 1989), pp.68-70.
41. Tuchman, *Making News.*
42. Mark Fishman, *Manufacturing the News* (London and Austin: University of Texas Press, 1980), p.92.
43. W. Lance Bennett, *News: The Politics of Illusion* (New York and London: Longman, 1983), p.131.
44. Creery, "Newspapers," p.1254.
45. "Personal Ads Have NOW in Court," *Marketing*, vol.95, no.38 (Sept. 17, 1990), p.6; Stan Sutter, "Crown Withdraws Charges," *Marketing*, vol.95, no.43 (Oct. 20, 1990), p.11.
46. Canadian Dimension staff, "War Declared on Quebec," *Canadian Dimension* (December 1970), p.9; Dan Daniels, *Quebec/Canada and the October Crisis* (Montreal: Black Rose Books, 1973); Denis Smith, "October Crisis," in *Canadian Encyclopedia* (1985), vol.2, p.1311.
47. H.J. Glasbeek, "Comment: Entrenchment of Freedom of Speech for the Press – Fettering of Freedom of Speech of the People," in *The Media, The Courts and the Charter*, ed. Philip Anisman and Allen M. Linden (Toronto: Carswell, 1986), pp.100-3.
48. Myles A. Ruggles, "CFRO Balance Workshop: Discussion Paper," unpublished manuscript, 1988, p.3.
49. Historically, objectivity has not carried the same weight in the journalism of Quebec's "distinct society," although, as noted in the Introduction, that difference may be dissolving.

4. The God Who Won't Die: News Objectivity as a Regime

1. Anderson, *Reality Isn't What It Used to Be.*
2. On the CBC and free trade, see Hackett, "Exaggerated Death"; on "defence of objectivity," see articles by Doug Herrington and Chris Szuskiewicz, "Podium: In Defence of Objectivity," *content,* September/October 1991, pp.20-1; Gilles Gauthier, "In Defence of a Supposedly Outdated Notion: The Range of Application of Journalistic Objectivity," *Canadian Journal of Communication*, vol.18, no.4 (Autumn 1993), pp.497-506; and Judith Lichtenberg, "In Defence of Objectivity

Revisited," in *Mass Media and Society*, 2nd ed., ed. Curran and Gurevitch, pp.225-42.

3. Wolfgang Donsbach and Bettina Klett, "Subjective Objectivity: How Journalists in Four Countries Define a Key Term of Their Profession," *Gazette*, vol.51, no.1 (1993), pp.53-83.

4. McQuail, *Media Performance*, p.197.

5. This breakdown draws upon McQuail, *Media Performance*, pp.196-204; summarized in McQuail, "Mass Media in the Public Interest," pp.74-5; and Jorgen Westerstahl, "Objective News Reporting," *Communication Research*, vol.10, no.3 (July 1983), pp.403-24.

6. McQuail, "Mass Media in the Public Interest," p.70.

7. Ibid., p.74.

8. Indeed, one interpretation of insurgent terrorism sees it as an extreme form of communication that results partly from "the effective denial of the right to communicate through normal channels." See Alex P. Schmid and Janny de Graaf, *Violence as Communication: Insurgent Terrorism and the Western News Media* (London and Beverly Hills: Sage Publications, 1982). The quote above is from Denis McQuail's Foreword to *Violence as Communication*, p.iii.

9. McQuail, *Media Performance*, pp.202-3.

10. Peter Golding and Philip Elliott, *Making the News* (London: Longman, 1979), p.207.

11. Ericson, Baranek, and Chan, *Visualizing Deviance*, p.105.

12. Frances Bula, "No News Here: The Feature Genre, Newspapers' 'Other' Storytelling Form," unpublished M.A. thesis, School of Communication, Simon Fraser University, Burnaby, B.C., 1996, p.105.

13. Bennett, *News*, p.120.

14. Ericson, Baranek, and Chan, *Negotiating Control*, p.15.

15. Bennett, *News*, p.120.

16. Bula, "No News Here," p.106.

17. McQuail, *Media Performance*, p.183.

18. Donsbach and Klett, "Subjective Objectivity," pp.66, 78.

19. Bula, "No News Here," pp.106-7.

20. Robert Fulford, "CRTC's Lack of Respect Indicates Grim Future for CBC," *The Globe and Mail*, March 19, 1997.

21. Gina Bailey, "Body Politics and Missing Themes of Women in American News," *Media Development*, 1 (1995), p.31.

22. Bailey, "Body Politics," p.32; see also Kay Mills, *A Place in the News* (New York: Columbia University Press, 1990); and John Hartley, *Understanding News* (London and New York: Routledge, 1982), pp.23, 80-1, 146-7.

23. Canadian Broadcasting Corporation, *Journalistic Policy* (Ottawa: CBC, 1982), pp.6-7.

24. Mark Lowes et al., *Project Censored Canada 1996 Yearbook: Blindspots in the News Agenda?* (Burnaby, B.C.: Project Censored Canada, 1996), pp.65-6; the research was conducted by Angela Austman. See also Colleen Fuller, "Our Pale Male Media," *Canadian Forum*, vol.71, no.809 (May 1992), pp.5-7.

25. Interview with Robert Hackett, October 1991.

26. Randy Boswell, "Duel over CBC 'Bias,'" *content,* May/June 1991, p.11. A more recent example dismisses content analysis as a "strange science" by which left-wing and right-wing critics offer spurious proof of their own offsetting preconceptions of the news. See Doug Saunders, "Manufacturing Media Bias," *The Globe and Mail,* March 22, 1997, p.D2.

27. Michael Karlberg and Robert A. Hackett, "Cancelling Each Other Out? Interest Group Perceptions of the News Media," *Canadian Journal of Communication,* vol.21, no.4 (1996), pp.461-72.

28. The term "bias calls" is used in Richard Pinet, "Bias and the Bias Call," unpublished M.A. thesis, School of Communication, Simon Fraser University, Burnaby, B.C., 1987, esp. ch.5.

29. Murray Edelman, *Political Language: Words That Succeed and Policies That Fail* (New York: Academic Press, 1977), p.152.

30. Robert A. Hackett, *News and Dissent: The Press and the Politics of Peace in Canada* (Norwood, N.J.: Ablex, 1991), ch.10.

31. Ericson, Baranek, and Chan, *Negotiating Control,* pp.346-9.

32. Canada, *Royal Commission on Newspapers,* p.149. On the record of press councils, see also Desbarats, *Guide to Canadian News Media,* ch.7.

33. Desbarats, *Guide to Canadian News Media,* pp.194, 196, 197.

34. Dominique Clift, "Press Councils and Ombudsman," in *The Journalists,* ed. Fulford et. al., p.139.

35. Stan Persky, "Free Is Just Another Word," *The Vancouver Sun,* May 16, 1992, p.D2; Chris Cobb, "Ombudsman Fired for L.A. Riot Column," *The Vancouver Sun,* May 6, 1992, p.A4.

36. The facts of the *Winnipeg Free Press* case are in dispute. See Don Sellar, "Another One Bites the Dust," *The Toronto Star,* Feb. 24, 1996; and "Press Ombudsmen: Are They Fair, Accurate Reporters?" a letter to the editor from Maurice H. Switzer, Ex-Publisher, Winnipeg Free Press, *The Toronto Star,* March 2, 1996, p.B2.

37. Created in 1987, the Canadian Broadcast Standards Council (CBSC) offers voluntary membership to commercial broadcasters. (Public broadcasters, such as the CBC, and specialty networks are not included.) Funded by but autonomous from the Canadian Association of Broadcasters (CAB), the Council administers a CRTC-instigated but industry-designed code on violence in programming. Viewer complaints about violence, balance, or other matters are usually addressed and resolved by individual broadcasters; those not resolved are passed on to one of the Council's five regional councils, each comprising three members of the industry and three public representatives (often lawyers or civil servants). The regional council bases its decisions on standards drafted by the CAB, and if found in violation the licensee must broadcast the decision on air. If it fails to do so the broadcasters can be expelled from the Council, with probable negative repercussions at the licensee's next CRTC licence renewal hearing.

   See Steve McLaren, "Broadcasters Set up Own 'Press Council,'" *content,* July/August, 1989, pp.14-15; Greg Quill, "Power Rangers: The Watchdog behind the Fuss," *The Toronto Star,* Nov. 3, 1994, p.E6; Michael McHugh, "Advertisers Back Violence Code," *Financial Post,* Nov. 4, 1993, p.16.

38. David Waters, "The U.S. Press of Quebec," *content*, January/February 1986, pp.2-6, esp. p.3.

39. Cook and Ruggles, "Balance and Freedom of Speech," p.42.

40. Ibid., p.47

41. "Behind the Mike," policy statement, Vancouver Co-op Radio.

42. Philip Savage, "Doing Community Radio," unpublished M.A. thesis, Department of Communication, Simon Fraser University, Burnaby, B.C., 1989, p.143.

43. Canadian Radio-television and Telecommunications Commission (CRTC), *Decision CRTC, 88-694: Vancouver Co-operative Radio, Vancouver, British Columbia – 873250500*, Ottawa, Sept. 29, 1988.

44. Ibid. See also Peter Royce, "CRTC Forces Co-op Radio into a Balancing Act," *New Directions*, January/February 1989, pp.33-5.

45. The chair of the CJC's community relations committee, Michael Eltermen, defined the case as "not about free speech," but "about balanced reporting." But the CJC did not accept an invitation from CFRO to produce its own program to balance *Voice of Palestine*. The CJC's publications indirectly indicate that the actual agenda behind the balance rhetoric was the program's cancellation. See "Jews Question 'Balance' on Local Radio Program," *The Vancouver Sun*, Feb. 25, 1988.

46. CRTC, *Public Notice CRTC 1988-61: Balance in Programming in Community Access Media*, Ottawa, Sept. 29, 1988, p.11.

47. Interview with Peter Royce by Yuezhi Zhao, July 18, 1989.

48. Vancouver Co-op Radio, "Response to Decision CRTC 88-649," Vancouver, 1988.

49. Cook and Ruggles, "Balance and Freedom of Speech," p.49.

50. Ibid., p.52.

51. Ibid., p.53.

52. Ibid.

53. Ibid., p.55.

54. Quoted in ibid., p.43.

55. Canada, Standing Committee on Communications and Culture, *Proceedings*, Issue no.36, sec. 4.2.5., Ottawa, May 4, 1987, p.38.

56. The following critique of the NMA and *On Balance* largely derives from Robert Hackett, William O. Gilsdorf, and Philip Savage, "News Balance Rhetoric: The Fraser Institute's Political Appropriation of Content Analysis," *Canadian Journal of Communication*, vol.17, no.1 (Winter 1992), pp.15-36.

57. *On Balance*, October 1988.

58. Hackett, Gilsdorf, and Savage, "News Balance Rhetoric."

59. For a critique of such research, see Hackett, "Decline of a Paradigm?" pp.229-59.

60. William C. Adams, "Network News Research in Perspective: A Bibliographic Essay," in *Television Network News: Issues in Content Research*, ed. W.C. Adams and F. Schreibman (Washington, D.C.: Washington School of Public and International Affairs, George Washington University), p.18.

61. Andrew Coyne, *Financial Post*, Aug. 9, 1989, p.11.

62. *On Balance*, vol.9, no.7 (July 1996).

63. Bob Hackett, "The B.C. Media's Election Priorities," *The Vancouver Sun*, May 30, 1996, p.A17.

64. Hackett, Gilsdorf, and Savage, "News Balance Rhetoric," pp.18, 34.

65. On the concept of information subsidies as a major influence on the news agenda, see Oscar Gandy, *Beyond Agenda-Setting: Information Subsidies and Public Policy* (Norwood, N.J.: Ablex, 1982).

66. Marc Raboy, "Balance Is in the Eye of the Beholder," *Canadian Journal of Communication*, vol.17, no.1 (Winter 1992), p.117.

5. Epistemologies in Contention:
Journalistic Objectivity as (Un)workable Philosophy

1. See Ross Eaman, *The Media Society: Basic Issues and Controversies* (Toronto: Butterworths, 1987), ch.2; G. Stuart Adam, "The Journalistic Imagination," in *Journalism, Communication and the Law,* ed. G. Stuart Adam (Scarborough, Ont.: Prentice-Hall of Canada, 1976), pp.3-22; and, for the classic statement of the acquaintance with/knowledge of distinction in journalism, Robert E. Park, "News as a Form of Knowledge: A Chapter in the Sociology of Knowledge," *American Journal of Sociology*, vol.45 (March 1950), pp.669-86.

2. D.C. Anderson and W.W. Sharrock, "Biasing the News: Technical Issues in 'Media Studies,'" *Sociology*, vol.13 (1979), pp.367-85.

3. Eamon, *Media Society*, ch.2.

4. McQuail, *Media Performance*, p.187.

5. Epstein, *News from Nowhere*, p.67.

6. Some accounts classify "positivism" as a type of "empiricism"; others subsume "empiricism" within "positivism." While we remain agnostic on this question, our discussion has been influenced by Terry Lovell, *Pictures of Reality: Aesthetics, Politics and Pleasure* (London: British Film Institute, 1980), p.10.

7. Thomas McCoy, *Voices of Difference: Studies in Critical Philosophy and Mass Communication* (Cresskill, N.J.: Hampton Press, 1993), p.21.

8. McCoy, *Voices of Difference*, p.73.

9. Canada, Special Senate Committee on Mass Media, *The Uncertain Mirror: Report,* vol.1 (Ottawa: Information Canada, 1970).

10. For example, defending his network from charges of biased reporting of the failed Meech Lake constitutional accord, CBC's Ottawa bureau chief Elly Alboim, in *content*, May/June 1991, countered that "media can only reflect the reality that Canadians are accepting and dealing with." He added that he had "no responsibility for social change" and had "never allowed personal opinion to interfere with professional responsibilities." Even when issues of profound cultural bias are raised, the conventional standards of professional disinterest (the separation of observer from observed), objectivity, and straight factuality are often the preferred defences. The adequacy of these standards for conveying understanding of an event with deep historical and cultural roots was brought into question by the 1990 standoff at Oka, pitting Mohawks against Quebec police and the federal army. Yet in their postmortems on the news coverage, journalists tended to reinforce rather than challenge the objective narrative form that "demands a clear separation between story-teller and subject, between the writer and the cause depicted." In response to charges of bias, journalists challenged critics to identify

(merely) factual errors in the news, according to writer Randy Boswell, and "scrambled to protect their professional credibility at the expense of more meaningful appraisals of native coverage." See Randy Boswell, "Oka: Crisis in Journalism," *content*, January/February 1991, pp.116-17.

11. Sandra Harding, *The Science Question in Feminism* (Ithaca, N.Y.: Cornell University Press, 1986), cited in Suzanne Strutt and Lynne Hissey, "Feminisms and Balance," *Canadian Journal of Communication*, vol.17, no.1 (Winter 1992), pp.61-74.

12. One example is the controversy over Canadian media coverage of the 1988 "free trade" election campaign. *The Toronto Star*, one of the few dailies to take an editorial position against free trade, was denounced by politicians and pundits for allowing its own editorial philosophy to override the objective presentation of news. Presumably such critics saw the rest of the media coverage as the balanced and objective norm against which the *Star's* reportage could be trashed. As we have noted, journalists find the resources to respond to such claims in the language of objectivity.

This view of "bad objectivity" is often shared by those who make more far-reaching critiques of media structures, addressing the institutional or organizational constraints on journalism. For example, the federal government's 1980 Kent Commission, while taking for granted the private ownership and advertising basis of newspapers, was critical of the ownership of newspapers by conglomerates. This critique was framed in terms of threats to the objectivity of newspapers as "the medium of record providing, by disinterested selection, investigation and interpretation, the information that is significant to the lives of Canadians in as comprehensive, balanced, fair, and understandable a way as is humanly possible. The adequate performance of that task is essential to the free democratic system of government.... We cannot allow it to be tainted or subverted by commercial, any more than by political, interests and ambitions." Canada, *Royal Commission on Newspapers*, p.234.

13. Schudson, *Discovering the News*, pp.134-44.

14. Ibid., p.122.

15. McCoy, *Voices of Difference*, p.72.

16. Eleanor MacLean, *Between the Lines* (Montreal: Black Rose Books, 1981), p.56.

17. Denis McQuail, *The Analysis of Newspaper Content: Study for the Royal Commission on the Press* (London: HMSO, 1977), p.107.

18. H.D. Doll and B.E. Bradley, "A Study of the Objectivity of Television News Reporting of the 1972 Presidential Campaign," *Central States Speech Journal*, vol.25 (1974), pp.254-63.

19. William O. Gilsdorf, "Getting the Message Across: Media Strategies and Political Campaigns," in *Communication Studies in Canada*, ed. Liora Salter (Toronto: Butterworths, 1981), p.64.

20. Hackett, "Decline of a Paradigm?" p.233.

21. Lovell, *Pictures of Reality*, pp.14-17.

22. Thomas Kuhn, *The Structure of Scientific Revolutions* (Chicago: University of Chicago Press, 1970).

23. Harvey Siegel, "Relativism," in *A Companion to Epistemology*, ed. Jonathan Dancy

and Ernest Sosa (Cambridge, Mass., and Oxford: Blackwell Publishers, 1992), pp.428-30.

24. David Morley, "Industrial Conflict and the Mass Media," *Sociological Review*, vol.24 (1976), pp.246-7.

25. Stuart Hall, C. Critcher, T. Jefferson, J. Clarke, and B. Roberts, *Policing the Crisis: Mugging, the State, and Law and Order* (London: Macmillan, 1978), p.19.

26. Todd Gitlin, *The Whole World Is Watching: Mass Media in the Making and Unmaking of the New Left* (Berkeley: University of California Press, 1980), p.7. There is now a substantial literature analysing the use of frames in the news. In addition to Gitlin, see also Tuchman, *Making News*, for early examples. R. Hackett and Y. Zhao, "Challenging a Master Narrative: Peace Protest and Opinion/Editorial Discourse in the U.S. Press during the Gulf War," *Discourse and Society*, vol.5, no.4 (October 1994), pp.509-41, combines discourse and frame analysis.

27. This simple and useful formulation is adapted from George Gerbner and Nancy Signorielli, "The World of Television News," in *Television Network News: Issues in Content Research*, ed. William Adams and Fay Schreibman (Washington, D.C.: School of Public and International Affairs, George Washington University, 1978), p.192.

28. For an excellent analysis of these different focuses and evaluative criteria, see Gertrude J. Robinson and Armande Saint-Jean, "From Flora to Kim: Thirty Years of Representation of Canadian Women Politicians," in *Seeing Ourselves: Media Power and Policy in Canada*, ed. Helen Holmes and David Taras, 2nd ed. (Toronto: Harcourt and Brace, 1996), pp.23-36.

29. Golding and Elliott, *Making the News*, p.207; McQuail, *Media Performance*, p.197.

30. David L. Altheide and R.P. Snow, *Media Logic* (Beverly Hills, Cal.: Sage Publications, 1979), pp.10, 12, 15, 146.

31. Daniel J. Boorstin, *The Image: A Guide to Pseudo-Events in America* (New York: Atheneum, 1980), p.11.

32. A complex example derives from the work of Stuart Hall and his colleagues. They saw an interaction between (a) reports of "mugging" in the British press; (b) increased sensitivity to this apparently new crime by police, judiciary, and public; (c) the upsurge of "mugging" incidents in police crime statistics; and (d) the emergence of a "moral panic" over the issue in British society. In this process the media were an active participant, not a neutral and detached observer. See Hall et al., *Policing the Crisis*.

From a different direction, Harvey Molotch and Marilyn Lester, "News as Purposive Behavior: On the Strategic Use of Routine Events, Accidents, and Scandals," *American Sociological Review*, vol.39 (1974), p.105, also attack the notion that "the media stand as reporter-reflector-indicators of an objective reality 'out there,' consisting of knowably 'important' events of the world." They radically problematize the concept of "event." What counts as an "event" is socially determined: events are what we are accustomed to pay attention to. An event, in their definition, is an occurrence (any cognized happening) that is used creatively for time-demarcating purposes. Occurrences become events according to their usefulness to an individual or organization trying to order experience. Different people or institutions may have different, even conflicting, "event needs" and hence will attempt to order or define reality in different ways. In such a case, an "issue" has arisen. However, with the exception of accidents or scandals (which are leaked by non-official informers), most press stories are "routine events" that are promoted by political and bureaucratic powerholders: their event needs are complementary with those of journalists.

33. Hartley, *Understanding News*, p.12.
34. For the clearest available application of a structuralist approach to the study of news, see Hartley, *Understanding News*.
35. See entries for Semiotics, Structuralism, etc., in Tim O'Sullivan, John Hartley, Danny Saunders, Martin Montgomery, and John Fiske, *Key Concepts in Communication and Cultural Studies*, 2nd ed. (London: Routledge, 1994), for a very clear introductory elaboration of some of these concepts.
36. Terry Eagleton, *Literary Theory: An Introduction* (Oxford: Basil Blackwell, 1983), p.128.
37. Judith Lichtenberg, "In Defense of Objectivity," in *Mass Media and Society*, ed. James Curran and Michael Gurevitch (London: Edward Arnold, 1991), p.217.
38. O'Sullivan et al., *Key Concepts*, p.259.
39. Jean Baudrillard, *Simulations* (New York: Semiotext(e), 1983), p.2.
40. Stuart Allan, "News, Truth and Postmodernity: Unravelling the Will to Facticity," in *Theorizing Culture: An Interdisciplinary Critique after Postmodernism*, ed. Barbara Adam and Stuart Allan (London: University College London Press, 1995), pp.129-44; Neville Wakefield, *Postmodernism: The Twilight of the Real* (London: Pluto Press, 1990), p.36.
41. For a broader analysis of the contributions of "posts" to media studies, see Yuezhi Zhao, "The 'End of Ideology' Again? The Concept of Ideology in the Era of Postmodern Theory," *Canadian Journal of Sociology*, Winter 1992, pp.70-85.
42. John Hartley, "News in a Post-Truth Society," paper presented to International Communication Association (ICA), Sydney, Australia, July 1994.
43. An off-the-record comment at the International Communication Association conference (ICA), Sydney, Australia, July 1994; Hartley, "News in a Post-Truth Society."
44. Jean Baudrillard, *The Gulf War Did Not Take Place* (Bloomington: Indiana University Press, 1995) p.25. This book contains the *Libération* articles.
45. Ibid.
46. Ibid., pp.66-7.
47. Christopher Norris, *Uncritical Theory: Postmodernism, Intellectuals and the Gulf War* (London: Lawrence and Wishart, 1992), p.59.
48. Norris, *Uncritical Theory*, pp.59-60.
49. Perry Anderson, *In the Tracks of Historical Materialism* (London: Verso, 1983), p.11.
50. Lichtenberg, "In Defense of Objectivity," p.221.
51. Jurgen Habermas, "Modernity versus Postmodernity," *New German Critique*, 22 (1981), pp.3-14.
52. Linda Alcoff, "Continental Epistemology," in *A Companion to Epistemology*, ed.

Jonathan Dancy and Edward Sosa (Cambridge, Mass., and Oxford: Basil Blackwell Publishers, 1992), pp.79-80.

53. Harvey, *Condition of Postmodernity*.

54. For an excellent polemic against the political roots and implications of postmodernism, see Terry Eagleton, "Where Do Postmodernists Come From?" *Monthly Review*, July/August 1995, pp.59-70.

55. For an interesting discussion of this point, see Wolfgang Natter, Theodor R. Schatzki, John Paul Jones III, "Contexts of Objectivity," in *Objectivity and Its Others*, ed. Wolfgang Natter, Theodore R. Schatzki, and John Paul Jones III (New York: Guilford Press, 1995), pp.1-17.

56. See Roy Bhaskar, *Reclaiming Reality: A Critical Introduction to Contemporary Philosophy* (London: Verso, 1989); and William Outhwaite, *New Philosophies of Social Science* (London: Macmillan, 1987).

57. Lovell, *Pictures of Reality*, p.17.

58. Ibid., p.22.

59. Vincent Mosco, *The Political Economy of Communication* (New York: Sage Publications, 1996), p.2.

60. Ibid.

61. Bhaskar, *Reclaiming Reality*, pp.23-4.

62. Outhwaite, *New Philosophies of Social Science*, pp.33-4.

63. Lovell, *Pictures of Reality*, p.22.

64. Hilary Wainwright, *Arguments for a New Left: Answering the Free Market Right* (Oxford: Blackwell, 1994), p.104.

65. Bhaskar, *Reclaiming Reality*, pp.23-4.

66. Christopher Norris, *What's Wrong with Postmodernism: Critical Theory and the Ends of Philosophy* (New York: Harvester, 1990), p.102.

67. Wainwright, *Arguments for a New Left*, p.107.

68. Ibid., pp.107-8.

69. Dahlgren, *Television and the Public Sphere*, pp.148-9.

6. The Politics of Objective Journalism

1. Ralph Klein, "On the Media (2): How to Make Governments, and Newspapers, Relevant Again," *The Globe and Mail*, May 8, 1995.

2. Westell, "The Press," pp.25-34; Rick Ouston, "Watergate It Wasn't," *Equity*, December 1995.

3. Adam Gopnik, "Read All about It," *The New Yorker*, December 12, 1994, p.92.

4. S.R. Lichter, S. Rothman, and L.S. Lichter, *The Media Elite* (Bethesda, Md.: Adler and Adler, 1986); Edith Efron, "The Media and the Omniscient Class," in *Business and the Media*, ed. Craig E. Aronoff (Santa Monica, Cal.: Goodyear, 1979), pp.3-32; Irving Kristol, "Business and the 'New Class,'" *The Wall Street Journal*, May 19, 1975, p.8. Our discussion here draws from Hackett, *News and Dissent*, pp.53-4.

5. Taras, *Newsmakers*, pp.233-8.

6. Walter Schneir and Miriam Schneir, "The Right's Attack on the Press," *The Nation*, March 30, 1985, p.361, citing James L. Tyson, *Target America: The Influence of Communist Propaganda on U.S. Media*.

7. Karlberg and Hackett, "Cancelling Each Other Out?"

8. Peter Dreier, "Capitalists vs. the Media: An Analysis of an Ideological Mobilization among Business Leaders," *Media, Culture and Society*, vol.4 (1982), pp.111-32.

9. Alan Wolfe, "The Real Aim Is Ideological," *The Nation*, September 13, 1986, pp.215-19.

10. Epstein, *News from Nowhere*, p.45; Winter, *Democracy's Oxygen*, provides numerous examples of management control of news.

11. Herbert J. Gans, "Are U.S. Journalists Dangerously Liberal?" *Columbia Journalism Review*, November/December 1985, pp.29-33.

12. Gopnik, "Read All about It," p.92.

13. Bennett, *News*, pp.53-4.

14. Ibid., p.52.

15. Ibid., pp.52-3.

16. Katherine Manson, Robert Hackett, Jim Winter, Donald Gutstein, and Richard Gruneau, eds., *Blindspots in the News? Project Censored Canada 1995 Yearbook* (Burnaby, B.C.: PCC, Simon Fraser University, 1995).

17. Rick Ouston, "Watergate It Wasn't," pp.34-8.

18. Bennett, *News*, p.124; Tuchman, *Making News*, p.87.

19. Fishman, *Manufacturing the News*, ch.2, 3.

20. Boorstin, *The Image*.

21. Bennett, *News*, pp.127-8.

22. Skirrow, "Education and Television," pp.30-1; Ian Connell, "Television News and the Social Contract," in *Culture, Media, Language*, ed. Stuart Hall, Dorothy Hobson, Andrew Lowe, and Paul Willis (London: Hutchinson, 1980), pp.139-56.

23. Revolutionary Left Movement (MIR), "On Journalism and Objectivity," in *Communication and Class Struggle*, vol. 1, *Capitalism and Imperialism*, ed. Armand Mattelart and Seth Siegelaub (New York: International General, 1979), p.131.

24. For instance, the content of commercial media disproportionately massages the relatively conservative sensibilities of affluent consumers, because these are the people advertisers are most keen to reach. Such class bias helps explain, for instance, why upper-middle-income "tax revolts" get much more media play than the hardship of the genuinely poor. In major media, such bias may also be reinforced by the social milieu of journalists themselves. When the Vancouver press crusaded against (and helped reverse) a 1993 attempt by B.C.'s NDP government to increase property taxes on the tiny minority of houses worth over $400,000, a study by journalism students revealed that many of *The Vancouver Sun*'s top managers and columnists themselves owned such homes. Anne Roberts, "All the News We Can Manage," *New Directions*, October 1993, p.30.

25. On the willingness to use the state in economic and social development, see Gad Horowitz, "Conservatism, Liberalism and Socialism in Canada: An Interpretation," in *The Canadian Political Process*, ed. Orest Kruhlak, Richard Schultz, and Sidney Pobihushchy (Toronto: Holt, Rinehart and Winston of Canada, 1970), pp.47-74.

26. Hallin, *"Uncensored War,"* pp.116-17.

27. Ibid., p.116.

28. Hartley, *Understanding News*, p.51.

29. Ibid., p.117.

30. *Report of the Committee on the Future of Broadcasting* (Annan Report), London, 1977, quoted in Hartley, *Understanding News*, p.51.

31. Interview with Yuezhi Zhao, Aug. 21, 1992.

32. Watson, a participant in the Greenpeace anti-whaling and anti-sealing campaigns of the 1970s, later became head of the Sea Shepherd Conservation Society. See Stephen Dale, *McLuhan's Children: The Greenpeace Message and the Media* (Toronto: Between the Lines, 1996), pp.88, 148-9.

33. Golding and Elliott, *Making the News*, p.210.

34. Philip Schlesinger, *Putting 'Reality' Together: BBC News* (London: Constable, 1978), p.168.

35. Clive Thompson, "Whyte," *This Magazine*, vol.29, no.1 (July 1995), p.22.

36. For example, while neoliberal free marketeers, as represented by the Fraser Institute, take the free-market ideology as religion, the social conservatism of the Christian right, as represented by Pat Buchanan in the United States, whose bidding for the U.S. Republican presidential nomination caused great uneasiness in the U.S. political mainstream, attacks corporate greed and such free-market doctrines as free trade.

37. John Kenneth Galbraith, interview with Alison Smith, *The Lead*, CBC Newsworld, Jan. 23, 1996.

38. Thompson, "Whyte," p.21.

39. Linda McQuaig, *Shooting the Hippo: Death by Deficit and Other Canadian Myths* (Toronto: Viking, 1995), pp.16-17.

40. *The Globe and Mail*, April 1996, quoted in Winter, *Democracy's Oxygen*, p.71.

41. Philip Savage, Bill Gilsdorf, and Robert Hackett, "Guest Editors' Introduction," *Canadian Journal of Communication*, vol.17, no.1 (Winter 1992), pp.7-8.

42. Lorraine Griffin, "Strictly by the Book," *Ryerson Review of Journalism*, Spring 1989, pp.43-6.

43. McQuaig, *Shooting the Hippo*, p.12; see also Winter, *Democracy's Oxygen*, ch.4.

44. Michelle Weinroth, "The Drama of the Deficit," *Canadian Forum*, October 1995, p.9.

45. Galbraith, interview with Alison Smith.

46. See, for example, *The Vancouver Sun*, Feb. 1, 1995, p.A1. The topic "deficit battle" is accorded the same discursive status on the front page with such topics as "television," "internet," and "Kelowna."

47. "Health-Care Cuts Vital, Reform Agrees," *The Vancouver Sun*, Feb. 8, 1995, p.A7.

48. "Lower Interest 'Hinges on Cuts,'" *The Vancouver Sun*, Jan. 20, 1996.

49. McQuaig, *Shooting the Hippo*, p.13. For example, on the front page of its business section, *The Vancouver Sun*, Jan. 17, 1995, faithfully reported a statement made by the chairman of the Bank of Montreal in an annual meeting. On the same day the same message was delivered by yet another member of the elite, this time by Auditor General Denis Desautels in a speech to the Canadian Club. The *Sun* first paraphrased his argument and then used a direct quote in the typical narrative style of objective journalism: "People disagree on where cuts should be made and

how quickly, he said, but there is now a national consensus that the deficit must be lowered and the economy placed on firmer ground. 'That consensus, as far as I'm concerned, was not there just three years ago.'" Yet again, on the same day, in the front page of the business section, a headline announced: "Don't raise taxes, business tells feds."

50. McQuaig, *Shooting the Hippo*, pp.10-11.

51. Cited in Winter, *Democracy's Oxygen*, p.102.

52. McQuaig, *Shooting the Hippo*, pp.35-6.

53. Marjorie Cohen, "Neo-Cons on Campus: How the Fraser Institute Captured the Hearts and Minds of Students While the Left Stood by and Did Nothing," *This Magazine*, July 1995, p.30.

54. *The Vancouver Sun*, which shares the same home base as the Fraser Institute, ran more than a short news story on this day. Instead, this eighteenth annual routine was the top story of the *Sun*'s front page of its Business/Sports section. Its headline "Survey Deters Deficit, Economist Says" ran nearly across the entire page. A self-congratulatory statement by institute director Michael Walker, the authoritative economist mentioned in the headline, was extracted outside the main text and highlighted, as if it were a quote from the gospel: "It is very promising that provincial elections are now being fought and won on commitments to reduce the tax burden." Just as Cohen notes, the prefix "right-wing" is nowhere to be seen before references to either the institute itself or its director. In one case, the prefix "Vancouver-based" is used. In another case, the institute is referred to as "the free-market institute."

55. Winter, *Democracy's Oxygen*, p.81.

56. See, for example, Rick Salutin, "Church of the Deficit Holy Rollers," *The Globe and Mail*, Oct. 1, 1993, p.C1.

57. *The Vancouver Sun*, Jan. 20, 1996, p.A19.

7. Regimes in Crisis:
Liberal Democracy and Objective Journalism in Question

1. Chris Cobb, "How Bad a Shape Is Journalism In? Pretty Bad!" *Media*, Fall 1995.

2. Alex Strachan, "When It Comes to Reporting, Real News Doesn't Always Rate," *The Vancouver Sun*, April 20, 1996, p.H4; citing the October 1994 *Gallup Poll Monthly*.

3. Christopher Hanson, "Where Have All the Heroes Gone?" *Columbia Journalism Review*, March/April 1996, pp.45-8. Hanson notes that in the Hollywood movie *Just Cause* the hero's occupation was changed from journalist (in the original novel) to law professor, now presumably the icon of integrity. As academics, blushing with pride we are not. As universities become extensions of corporate R&D while academics obliviously and endlessly debate "academic freedom" and "political correctness," we too will have our turn in the doghouse.

4. James Fallows, "Why Americans Hate the Media," *The Atlantic Monthly*, February 1996, pp.45-64.

5. Paul Q. Hirst, *Representative Democracy and Its Limits* (Oxford: Polity Press, 1990), p.1.

6. Gwyn Dyer, *Ideas*, CBC Radio, May 1995.

7. Robert W. McChesney, "The Internet and U.S. Communication Policy-Making in Historical and Critical Perspective," *Journal of Communication*, vol.46, no.1 (Winter 1996).

8. Marc Raboy and Bernard Dagenais, eds., *Media, Crisis and Democracy: Mass Communication and the Disruption of Social Order* (Newbury Park, Cal.: Sage Publications, 1992), p.3.

9. Christopher Lasch, *The Revolt of the Elites and the Betrayal of Democracy* (New York: W.W. Norton, 1995), p.3.

10. Michael Wood, *Legacy: A Search for the Origins of Civilization* (London: Network Books [BBC Books], 1992), pp.207, 209.

11. For a brief description and bibliography, see David R. Kohut, "The Overthrow of Salvador Allende's Leftist Government in Chile," in *Read More About It: An Encyclopedia of Information Sources on Historical Figures and Events*, vol. 3 (Ann Arbor, Mich.: The Pierian Press, 1989), pp.21-3.

12. By "market liberalism," we mean the ideology of individual choice, deregulation, market competition, and privatization as the overriding principles of social and economic life. We owe our use of this term, which avoids the more confusing labels of "neoliberalism" and "neoconservatism," to John Keane, *The Media and Democracy* (Cambridge: Polity Press, 1991), pp.x-xi and passim.

13. Boris Kagarlitsky, "The Agony of Neo-Liberalism or the End of Civilization?" *Monthly Review*, vol.48, no.2 (June 1996), p.38.

14. We are indebted to John Keane for this point; interview with Hackett, November 1995.

15. Peter Calamai, "The Emerging Information Underclass," *Media*, vol.1, no.1 (April 1994).

16. John Porter, *The Vertical Mosaic: An Analysis of Social Class and Power in Canada* (Toronto: University of Toronto Press, 1965).

17. R.B.J. Walker, "Culture, Discourse, Insecurity," in *Towards a Just World Peace*, ed. S.H. Mendlovitz and R.B.J. Walker (London: Butterworths), pp.171-90.

18. Richard Gwyn, "NAFTA: A Charter for Marketplace Rules," *The Vancouver Sun*, Nov. 22, 1993; Frances Russell, "Is Free Trade Really a New Economic Constitution?" *Winnipeg Free Press*, Nov. 27, 1993.

19. Carl Jensen and Project Censored, *Censored: The News that Didn't Make the News – and Why: The 1996 Project Censored Yearbook* (New York: Seven Stories Press, 1996), pp.92-5.

20. Robert D. Kaplan, "The Coming Anarchy," *The Atlantic Monthly*, February 1994, pp.44-76.

21. We take the term "competitive elitism" from Held, *Models of Democracy*.

22. Peter C. Newman, *The Canadian Revolution, 1985-1995: From Deference to Defiance* (Toronto: Viking, 1995).

23. Consider the case of Jim Hightower, a former politician and progressive populist from Texas. Notwithstanding his decent ratings and entertainingly humorous and humane persona, Hightower was fired from his ABC radio program after remarking, in the wake of the Disney takeover of ABC, that now his boss really was

Mickey Mouse. (Hightower told his story in a keynote speech to the Congress on Media & Democracy, San Francisco, Feb. 29-March 4, 1996.) Rush Limbaugh can pontificate with much greater impunity, presumably because his vitriol is directed against those with the least rather than the most economic and political power.

24. David Usborne, "Currency Overlord Proclaims Dangers of Capitalism," *The Vancouver Sun*, Jan. 17, 1997, p.D1.

25. Winter and Hassanpour, "Building Babel," pp.10-17.

26. Jay G. Blumler and Michael Gurevitch, *The Crisis of Public Communication* (London and New York: Routledge, 1995), p.213.

27. Lasch, *Revolt of the Elites*, pp.167-71. Lippmann's faith in social science, objective information, and "social organization based on a system of analysis and record" is evident in his essays on the press and the public. See Clinton Rossiter and James Lare, eds., *The Essential Lippmann: A Political Philosophy for Liberal Democracy* (New York: Random House, 1963), pp.398-417.

28. Calamai, "Emerging Information Underclass."

29. This metaphor was used in "Why America Hates the Press," a documentary broadcast on *Frontline*, PBS, Oct. 22, 1996.

30. The quote is from James B. Lemert, *Criticizing the Media: Empirical Approaches* (Newbury Park, Cal.: Sage Publications, 1989), p.48.

31. We have already discussed the Fraser Institute's critiques of the CBC. On the conservative critique of PBS, see William Hoynes, *Public Television for Sale: Media, the Market and the Public Sphere* (Boulder, Col., San Francisco, Oxford: Westview Press, 1994), esp. pp.6-11.

32. Jack Newfield, "Bob Grant Poisons the Airwaves Again," *New York Post*, March 8, 1996.

33. We should certainly not infer any liberal political motives from this firing, given Disney's axing of Jim Hightower. See note 23 above.

34. For different perspectives on this legislation, see Neil Hickey, "Revolution in Cyberia," *Columbia Journalism Review*, July/August 1995, pp.40-7.

35. Jensen and Project Censored, *Censored*, pp.50-3.

36. On these trends and their implications, see Daniel C. Hallin, "Commercialism and Professionalism in the American News Media," in *Mass Media and Society*, 2nd ed., ed. Curran and Gurevitch; James D. Squires, "Plundering the Newsroom," *Washington Journalism Review*, December 1992, pp.18-24; Doug Underwood, *When MBAs Rule the Newsroom: How the Marketers and Managers Are Reshaping Today's Media* (New York: Columbia University Press, 1995).

37. Bruce Livesey, "PR Wars: How the PR Industry Flacks for Big Business," *Canadian Dimension*, November-December 1996, p.10. See also Joyce Nelson, *Sultans of Sleaze: Public Relations and the Media* (Toronto: Between the Lines, 1989).

38. Underwood, *When MBAs Rule the Newsroom*, p.16.

39. Ibid., pp.15, 95.

40. Sasha Abramsky, "Citizen Murdoch: The Shape of Things to Come?" *Extra!*, November/December 1995, pp.16-17.

41. "Wot Won It?" *The Economist*, Nov. 4, 1995, p.58.

42. Abramsky, "Citizen Murdoch."

43. Steve Weinberg, "The New Media: Can 'Content Providers' Be Investigative Reporters?" *Columbia Journalism Review*, November/December 1996, p.38.

44. Glasbeek, "Comment," pp.100-18.

45. These stories were unearthed in recent years by a specialized investigative reporter for CTV National News. Andrew Mitrovica, from correspondence to Project Censored Canada, April 1996.

46. See, for example, Mark Hertsgaard, *On Bended Knee: The Press and the Reagan Presidency* (New York: Schocken, 1989); Lewis H. Lapham, "Trained Seals and Sitting Ducks," in *The Media and the Gulf War*, ed. Hedrick Smith (Washington, D.C.: Seven Locks Press, 1992), pp.256-63.

47. Jensen and Project Censored, *Censored*, pp.50-113.

48. Manson et al., *Blindspots in the News?*

49. Aaron Freeman and Craig Forcese, "Get Tough on Corporate Crime," *The Toronto Star*, Nov. 17, 1994; Doug Fischer, "Investigator Fears Fraud Cases Ignored," *Calgary Herald*, July 9, 1994; Manson et al., *Blindspots in the News?*, pp.30-1.

50. James Curran, "Mass Media and Democracy Revisited," in *Mass Media and Society*, 2nd ed., ed. Curran and Gurevitch, p.101.

51. Ibid.

52. Walter Lippmann, *Public Opinion* (New York: The Free Press, 1965 [1922]), p.228.

53. The conference was sponsored by the now dissolved Canadian Institute for International Peace and Security.

54. Rita Shelton Deverell, "On Subjectivity: What You Can See Depends on Where You Stand and How 'Short' You Are," in *Deadlines and Diversity*, ed. Alia, Brennan, and Hoffmaster, pp.60-2.

55. Raymond Williams, *Communications* (London: Penguin Books, 1976 [1962]), pp.108-9.

56. George Gerbner, Michael Morgan, Nancy Signorielli, *Television Violence Profile No. 16: The Turning Point: From Research to Action*, January 1994.

57. The concluding paragraphs of this chapter derive from Robert Hackett, Richard Pinet, and Myles Ruggles, "News for Whom? Hegemony and Monopoly versus Democracy in Canadian Media," in *Seeing Ourselves*, ed. Holmes and Taras, p.265.

58. Manson et al., *Blindspots in the News?*, p.15.

59. See, for example, James Curran, "Capitalism and Control of the Press, 1800-1975," in *Mass Communication and Society*, ed. Curran, Gurevitch, and Woollacott, pp.195-230.

60. Smythe, *Dependency Road*, pp.37-8.

61. Guerrilla Media, "Network Execs Got the Joke, but the Punchline Was Cancellation," *Pacific Current*, February/March 1996, pp.34-5.

8. Straws in the Wind: Alternatives to the Regime?

1. Howard Rheingold, *The Virtual Community: Homesteading on the Electronic Frontier* (New York: HarperPerennial, 1994), p.5.

2. On the Internet, see Rheingold, *Virtual Community*, p.5.

3. Desbarats, *Guide to Canadian News Media*, p.261.

4. W. Russell Neuman, quoted in Katherine Fulton, "A Tour of Our Uncertain Future," *Columbia Journalism Review*, March/April 1996, p.20.

5. Our discussion of recent developments regarding the Internet draws in part from Michael Jones, "The Commercial Colonization of Cyberspace: Internet Advertising and Democratic Communication," unpublished paper, School of Communication, Simon Fraser University, Burnaby, B.C., 1996.

6. Rheingold, *Virtual Community*, p.244.

7. Chris Lapham, "The Evolution of the Newspaper of the Future," *Computer-Mediated Communication Magazine*, July 1, 1995, p.7.

8. Fulton, "Tour of Our Uncertain Future," p.22.

9. Lapham, "Evolution of the Newspaper."

10. Fulton, "Tour of Our Uncertain Future," p.21.

11. Lapham, "Evolution of the Newspaper."

12. Ellen Hume, "Tabloids, Talk Radio, and the Future of News," quoted in Frank Houston, "The Virtual Trail," *Columbia Journalism Review*, January/February 1996, p.27.

13. Anne Bilodeau, "Into the Net: A Reporter's Transformation," *Computer-Mediated Communication Magazine*, vol.1, no.3 (July 1, 1994), p.8.

14. Jennifer Wolff, "Opening Up Online," *Columbia Journalism Review*, November/December 1994, p.62.

15. Todd Oppenheimer, "Virtual Reality Check," *Columbia Journalism Review*, March/April 1996, p.29.

16. Houston, "Virtual Trail," pp.26-7.

17. Stephen D. Isaacs, "Have Newsroom, Will Travel," *Columbia Journalism Review*, September/October 1995, p.51.

18. McChesney, "Internet and U.S. Communication Policy-Making," p.104.

19. Ibid., p.105.

20. Ibid., pp.101-2.

21. J. Hodges in *Advertising Age*, October 1996, cited in Jones, "Commercial Colonization of Cyberspace."

22. D. Williamson in *Advertising Age*, September 1996, cited in Jones, "Commercial Colonization of Cyberspace."

23. *The Wall Street Journal*, Oct. 31, 1996, p.B4, cited in Jones, "Commercial Colonization of Cyberspace."

24. Rheingold, *Virtual Community*, pp.277-8.

25. For a user-friendly summary of this "panoptic" potential of the Internet, see Rheingold, *Virtual Community*, pp.289-97.

26. Rheingold, *Virtual Community*, pp.273-75.

27. Nancy Hicks Maynard, "Where Is Page One in Cyberspace?" *The Deeper News*, vol.6, no.2 (Emeryville, Cal.: Global Business Network, June 1996), p.6.

28. Chris Cobb, "Jobs. Jobs. Jobs. Gone. Gone. Gone," *Media*, vol.3, no.1 (Spring 1996).

29. Nicholas Baran, "Computers and Capitalism: A Tragic Misuse of Technology," *Monthly Review*, vol.47, no.4 (September 1995), pp.40-6.

30. Diane C. Mermigas, "Can Legitimate News Coverage Survive Convergence and

Commercialism in the New Media Age?" in *News in the Next Century: Dollars and Demographics: The Evolving Market for News* (Washington, D.C.: Radio and Television News Directors Foundation, 1996), p.36.

31. Cass R. Sunstein, "The First Amendment in Cyberspace," in *News in the Next Century*, p.69.

32. McChesney, "Internet and U.S. Communication Policy-Making," p.114.

33. Arthur Ochs Sulzberger Jr., excerpted by Joan Konner, "It's the Content, Stupid," *Columbia Journalism Review*, November/December 1994, p.4.

34. Jere Downs, "A Window at the County Seat," *Columbia Journalism Review*, May/June 1995, p.64.

35. Cobb, "Jobs. Jobs. Jobs," p.6.

36. Stephen D. Isaacs, "The Golden Age, Maybe?" *Columbia Journalism Review*, November/December 1994, p.64.

37. K. Auletta, "Awesome," *The New Yorker*, May 14, 1995, cited in McChesney, "Internet and U.S. Communication Policy-Making," p.115.

38. Pat Aufderheide, "Vernacular Video," *Columbia Journalism Review*, January/February 1995, p.46.

39. See P. Atwell, *Computerization and Controversy: Value Conflicts and Social Choices* (Boston: Academic Press, 1991); and Harry Braverman, *The Social Shaping of Technology* (Milton Keynes, Eng.: Open University Press, 1993).

40. Maynard, "Where Is Page One?" p.15.

41. Desbarats, *Guide to Canadian News Media*, pp.247-8.

42. Joe Holley, "What's a Bloomberg?" *Columbia Journalism Review*, May/June 1995, pp.46-50. The bad rhymes are ours.

43. Maynard, "Where Is Page One?" p.6.

44. Fulton, "Tour of Our Uncertain Future," p.21.

45. This panel at the 1996 Media & Democracy Congress in San Francisco, sponsored by the Institute for Alternative Journalism, was attended by Robert Hackett. Moderated by Katherine Fulton, the panel included consultant Nancy Hicks Maynard, Newspaper Guild president Linda Foley, *The Nation* publisher Victor Navasky, and KQED-FM news director Raul Ramirez. See also Richard Byrne's report on the panel, at http://www.alternet.org/an/congress/newrole.html.

46. McChesney, "Internet and U.S. Communication Policy-Making," pp.114-17.

47. See, for example, Davis Merritt Jr., "Public Journalism: What It Means, How It Works," and Jay Rosen, "Public Journalism: First Principles," in *Public Journalism: Theory and Practice* (Dayton, Ohio: The Kettering Foundation, 1994); Davis Merritt Jr., *Public Journalism and Public Life: Why Telling the News Is Not Enough* (Hillsdale, N.J.: Lawrence Erlbaum, 1995); Jay Rosen, "Making Journalism More Public," *Communication*, vol.12 (1991), pp.267-84.

 Our discussion here owes a good deal to James Compton, "Communicative Politics and Public Journalism," unpublished M.A. thesis, Simon Fraser University, Burnaby, B.C., 1996.

48. Other scholars not connected with the public journalism movement offer complementary analyses. For Jay Blumler and Michael Gurevitch, the "crisis of communication for citizenship" has five components:

• the depoliticization of media portrayals of politics, as personalities and events are favoured over policies due precisely to the media's investment in its perceived non-partisanship;

• an excess of political communication that generates cynicism;

• a lack of political communication that serves the citizen role;

• the exclusion of voters from having "any say or significant stake in public communication";

• the media's adoption of the role of surrogate opposition, overemphasizing criticism and exposure.

See *Crisis of Public Communication*, pp.203-21.

49. Merritt, "Public Journalism: What It Means," cited in Compton, "Communicative Politics," p.19.

50. The term "public judgement" was popularized by Daniel Yankelovich, *Coming to Public Judgment: Making Democracy Work in a Complex World* (Syracuse, N.Y.: Syracuse University Press, 1991).

51. Some observers see a precursor of public journalism in the "social animation" experiments of Canada's National Film Board, in the 1960s and 1970s. Peter Desbarats, personal communication.

52. *And Now the Details*, CBC Radio, May 19, 1996.

53. Compton, "Communicative Politics," p.46.

54. Nick Russell, "Public Journalism: An Old Game with a New Name?" *Media*, March 1995, pp.16-17.

55. Quoted in Alicia C. Shepard, "The Gospel of Public Journalism," *American Journalism Review*, September 1994, pp.33-4.

56. John Bare, quoted in Shepard, "Gospel of Public Journalism," p.34.

57. Hackett, "B.C. Media's Election Priorities."

58. Compton, "Communicative Politics."

59. Verzuh, *Underground Times*, pp.11-15.

60. Jeff Gremillion, "Showdown at Generation Gap: Here Come the Young Guns of the Alternative Press," *Columbia Journalism Review*, July/August 1995, pp.34-8.

61. Jay Walljasper, "Do We Still Need the Alternative Press?" in *Media and Democracy*, ed. Hazen and Smith, p.143.

62. Ibid., p.142.

63. Ibid., p.144.

64. Bula, *No News Here*.

65. John Nerone suggests that a model of the alternative media would serve a useful normative purpose. It would help to highlight "things that should be avoided and, consequently, things that should be goals." See John Nerone, ed., *Last Rights: Revisiting Four Theories of the Press* (Urbana: University of Illinois Press, 1996), p.149.

66. Walljasper, "Do We Still Need the Alternative Press?" p.144.

67. John Downing, "Alternative Media and the Boston Tea Party," in *Questioning the Media*, ed. Downing, Mohammadi, and Sreberny-Mohammadi, p.181.

68. O'Sullivan et al., *Key Concepts in Communication and Cultural Studies*, p.10.

69. Downing, "Alternative Media," p.191.

70. Ibid., p.182.

71. Walljasper, "Do We Still Need the Alternative Press?" p.143.

72. For some good recent Canadian books of this type, see Mark Lowes et al., *Project Censored Canada 1996 Yearbook*, Appendix A.

73. Janet Wasko, "Introduction: Go Tell It to the Spartans," in *Democratic Communications in the Information Age*, ed. Janet Wasko and Vincent Mosco (Toronto: Garamond Press, 1992), p.7.

74. R.B. Kielbowicz and C. Scherer, "The Role of the Press in the Dynamics of Social Movements," *Research in Social Movements, Conflict and Change*, vol.9 (1986), pp.71-96.

75. See Hackett, *News and Dissent*, esp. pp.20-23, 169-81.

76. Hackett, *News and Dissent*. On Greenpeace and the media, see Dale, *McLuhan's Children*.

77. Hallin, "Commercialism and Professionalism," p.246; Underwood, *When MBAs Rule the Newsroom*, p.16.

78. Laura Flanders, "Media, Culture and Communication," in *Media and Democracy*, ed. Hazen and Smith, p.73; emphasis added.

79. Don Hazen, "Seeking Vision: Ten Steps toward Fighting Media Monopoly," in *Media and Democracy*, ed. Hazen and Smith, p.162.

80. Don Hazen, "World of Infotainment," *The San Francisco Bay Guardian*, Feb. 21, 1996.

81. Z Staff, "Media and Democracy Congress," *Z Magazine*, April 1996, reprinted in *Report from the Media & Democracy Congress* (San Francisco: Institute for Alternative Journalism, 1996).

82. Holman W. Jenkins, Jr., "All These Progressives, and Nary an Idea," *The Wall Street Journal*, March 12, 1996, p.A19, reprinted in *Report from the Media & Democracy Congress*; Frank Rich, "Mixed Media Message," *The New York Times*, March 6, 1996, reprinted in *Report from the Media & Democracy Congress*.

83. Dan Kennedy, "Don't Quote Me: Fine Whine," *The Boston Phoenix*, March 8, 1996, reprinted in *Report from the Media & Democracy Congress*.

84. "Information Bill of Rights," in *Report from the Media & Democracy Congress*.

85. George Gerbner, "Cultural Wars and the Liberating Alternative," in *Media and Democracy*, ed. Hazen and Smith, p.91.

86. See, for instance, Edward S. Herman and Noam Chomsky, *Manufacturing Consent: The Political Economy of the Mass Media* (New York: Pantheon Books, 1988).

87. Hazen, "World of Infotainment."

88. Flanders, "Media, Culture and Communication," p.73.

89. Interestingly, in a survey of about one hundred U.S. media-watching organizations, the most explicit rejection of objectivity comes from *Spotlight*, an anti-semitic far-right organ that backed the presidential campaign of ex-Nazi activist David Duke. In its own words:

    You can trust *The Spotlight* to give you "the other side of the news" – to report on events which are vital to your welfare but which would otherwise be hushed up or distorted by the controlled press. So don't expect us to be "objective" or "unbiased." We are biased toward the best interests of the majority of the consumers, taxpayers and voters: the hardworking, misled, exploited and brainwashed American producer ... who pays the bills for the super rich and the very poor. We make no attempt to give you "both sides." We'll leave the Establishment side to your daily newspaper, TV and radio.

See John S. Detweiler, "Media Watcher Directory," paper presented to AEJMC conference, Montreal, August 1992.

9. Conclusion:
Towards Public Communication for Sustainable Democracy

1. See Mark Thompson, *Forging War: The Media in Serbia, Croatia and Bosnia-Hercegovina* (London: Article 19, May 1994).
2. Keane, *Media and Democracy*, pp.149-50.
3. Dahlgren, *Television and the Public Sphere.*
4. Ibid., p.148; emphasis added.
5. We owe some of these ideas to Kathy Cross and Gina Bailey.
6. The term "democratic-participant" is Denis McQuail's, in *Mass Communication Theory*, pp.131-2.
7. Robert A. Hackett with James Mackintosh, David Robinson, and Arlene Shwetz, "Smaller Voices: Minor Parties, Campaign Communication and the News Media," in *Reporting the Campaign: Election Coverage in Canada*, ed. Frederick J. Fletcher, vol. 22, Research Studies for Royal Commission on Electoral Reform and Party Financing (Toronto and Oxford: Dundurn Press, 1991), pp.189-271.
8. Rudy Platiel, "Vast Changes Sought to Aid Natives," *The Globe and Mail*, Nov. 22, 1996, p.A8.
9. The quote is from Dahlgren, *Television and the Public Sphere*, p.73.
10. We adapt this definition from Dahlgren, *Television and the Public Sphere.*
11. Zhao, *Media and Democracy in China.*
12. James Curran calls for such "civic media" as one of five components of a more democratic media system. See his "Mass Media and Democracy Revisited."
13. For a similar analysis of what he calls the period of "high modernism" in U.S. journalism, see Hallin, "Commercialism and Professionalism," pp.243-62.
14. Hallin, "Commercialism and Professionalism," p.259.
15. Dahlgren, *Television and the Public Sphere*, p.149.
16. See, for example, Natter, Schatzki, and Jones III, eds., *Objectivity and Its Other.*
17. However, for more detailed discussions of structural reforms from a perspective similar to ours, see Curran, "Democracy and the Media Revisited"; and Douglas Kellner, *Television and the Crisis of Democracy* (Boulder, Col., San Francisco, and Oxford: Westview Press, 1990), ch.5. Kellner focuses on public access television.
18. Hackett, *News and Dissent*, ch.12.
19. Douglas Roche, "Canada and Nuclear Abolition: Finishing the Job," *The Ploughshares Monitor*, September 1996, pp.9-14.
20. Michael Schudson, *The Power of News* (Cambridge, Mass., and London: Harvard University Press, 1995), p.14.
21. Michael Clow with Susan Machum, *Stifling Debate: Canadian Newspapers and Nuclear Power* (Halifax: Fernwood Publishing, 1993), p.98.
22. Herbert J. Gans, *Deciding What's News*, p.290.

Index

ABC 4, 177, 198

Aboriginal peoples 75, 168, 185, 228

accuracy, made possible by telegraph 32; tied to objectivity 32, 41, 44, 83, 84; in code of ethics 54; factor in credibility 59; in CBC policy manual 88; as an ethical obligation 111; in objectivist epistemology 112-13, 114-15; movement away from 124; in "quality" journalism 175; in public journalism 203

Accuracy in Media 138-9, 217

activist journalism 203-4. *See also* alternative media

Adbusters 216

adversarial journalism. *See* critical journalism

advertising, effect on early press 28; and "news hole" 65; homogenizing effect 66-7; press-control effect 68-9; as an institutionalizing factor 86; in relation to press councils 92; and the right of reply 98; in commercial broadcasting 100; mystifying reality 123; role in power relations 144-5; and personal debt 156; as influence on content 186, 187; on World Wide Web 195; tax on 235; and audiences 259n24

advocacy groups. *See* social movements

advocacy journalism 41, 49, 50, 52, 176, 217. *See also* alternative media

AIDS 103

Air of Death (CBC, 1967) 43

Alberta Report 152

Alboim, Elly 254n10

Allende, Salvador 166

Allies (Vancouver) 212

alternative media 206-13, 225; and objectivity benchmark 8; in U.S. 12, 52; book publishers 50; marginalized 65, 68-9; and media concentration 70-1; urban weeklies 79; effect of Charter of Rights 80; seen as representing special interests 99; public broadcasting 176; and public journalism 203; influence on mainstream media 208; magazines 211; and social movements 212; and public policy 235-6. *See also* Vancouver Co-op Radio

Altschull, J. Herbert 51-2

American Newspaper Guild 41

Anderson, Perry 126

And Now the Details (CBC) 216

attack journalism. *See* critical journalism

attribution technique 44-5

audience, expectations regarding objectivity 58; assumptions about 68; expectations of news 86; as passive 143-4; as consumers 144-5; erosion of confidence 162; fragmentation of 175-6, 200; cyberspace 196; media reconnecting with 202; and alternative media 210. *See also* consumerism/consumers; consumer sovereignty

authoritarianism 164, 170, 172, 229, 232

Bain, George 39, 48-9

balance, as a standard 5; instead of objectivity 8; as part of naturalization process 12-13; of interpretations 45; as journalists' goal 58-9; in TV news 73; use of term 90; ideological function of 95; as Vancouver Co-op Radio issue 95-9; as seen by Fraser Institute 102-3; as rhetorical term 103; as tool to avoid bias 114-15; effects of notion of 116; conservatizing effects of 144; of controversial items 148; and Fraser Institute case study 158-9; alternative media's view of 210-11. *See also* bias; fairness.

Baranek, Patricia 45, 85, 91

Barthes, Roland 123-4, 125

Baudrillard, Jean 123, 125-6

B.C. Report 51, 209

BCTV News (Vancouver) 82

Belarus 225

Bell, Daniel 137

Bennett, James Gordon 36

Bennett, R.B. 76

Bernardo (Paul) trial 142

Bhaskar, Roy 128, 131

bias, accusations of 3, 78, 176, 217; in partisan press 20, 23, 67; and news ethos 38, 41; CRTC report (1970) 43; as unavoidable 44, 59; technological 47; journalistic 57-8, 70, 233-4; as a freedom 80; as a matter of vantage point 89-91; and press councils 91-2, 94; selective attention to calls of 94; and CRTC policy 98; and religious broadcasting 100; from the NMA perspective 102-3, 105; as departure from objectivity-as-usual 112; concept critiqued 113-14; and journalists' ideology 137-8; exposing personal 192; racial 198; of objectivity 210; economic/consumerism 187, 224. *See also* balance; fairness

Black, Conrad 56, 62, 64, 65-6, 231; newspaper acquisitions 4; as product of a system 8; dismissal of journalists 11; and Linda McQuaig 50; and Fraser Institute 101; and *Saturday Night* 152. *See also* Hollinger Inc.

"Black Tuesday" 63, 70

Blair, Tony 179

Bloomberg Business News 198-9

Boorstin, Daniel 143

Boswell, Tom 89

British Broadcasting Corporation (BBC) 38

British Columbia, 1995 NDP budget 49; and social movements 95; Fraser Institute founding in 101; 1996 election 104, 178, 205; "wealth tax" 141; environmental issues 215; complaint against premier of 233

British United Press 39

Broadcasting acts (1968, 1991) 75, 100-1

broadcasting industry 61; concentration of ownership 63-4; trend to homogenization 67; implications of emergence 72-3; and state regulation 73-6; and issue of access 100-1; as a system converging 189; digital 189. *See also* private broadcasting; public broadcasting; radio; religious broadcasting; television

broadcast model 190

Buchanan, Pat 161

Burke, Stanley 246n70

Business Council of British Columbia 105

Business Council on National Issues 150

business news 68, 152-3, 157, 160, 235

Cable News Network (CNN) 64

cable television 64, religious programming on 75; CRTC licences 99; specialty channels 175; as a system converging 189, 195; as alternative medium 207, 217

Calgary Herald 192

Campbell, Gordon 49

Campbell, Kim 120

camcorder 193, 198

Campaign for Press and Broadcasting Freedom 221

Canadian Association of Broadcasters (CAB) 252n37

Canadian Broadcasting Corporation (CBC), cutbacks 4; Radio news 38, 61; standard for newswriting 38-9; and objectivity 42-3; and interpretive reporting 43, 44; replaces Canadian Radio Broadcasting Commission 60; relation to government 61; commercial pressures on 64; as public service 75-6; as institution 86; reflects social hierarchies 88; and free trade issue 102, 105; funding cuts and objectivity 176; "townhall meetings" 202; as alternative service 208

Canadian Broadcast Standards Council (CBSC) 252n37

Canadian Centre for Policy Alternatives 160

Canadian Dimension 49, 211

Canadian Forum 211

Canadian International Development Agency (CIDA) 181

Canadian Jewish Congress (CJC) 96, 98, 253n45

Canadian Labour Reformer 21, 23-4

Canadian Press (CP) 39, 61, 66

Canadian Radio Broadcasting Commission 60

Canadian Radio-television and Telecommunications Commission (CRTC) 64, 87; inquiry into bias 43; issue of balance 96-9; and regulation of broadcasters 75; as content regulator 93, 94-5; approach to "special-interest" broadcasters 99-100; and religious broadcasting 99-100; concept of balance 100; and Vancouver Co-op Radio 174

Canadians Concerned About Violence in Entertainment (C-CAVE) 214

Canadian Security Intelligence Service 181

Capital Cities/ABC 4

CBC Newsworld 87

CBS 4

celebrity journalism 51-2

censorship 180, 187, 188

Center for Communication and Human Rights (Amsterdam) 220

Center for Media and Public Affairs 103, 139

Center for Media Education 217

Center for War, Peace and the News Media 217

Chan, Janet 45, 85, 91

Charlottetown accord (1992) 202

Charter of Rights and Freedoms 79, 180-1

chemical industry 182

child labour 182

Chile 166

China 9, 11-12, 229

Cho!ces 160

Chomsky, Noam 222

Chrétien, Jean 172, 181

Christian right 161

Christian Science Monitor 43

civic culture 169

civic journalism. *See* public journalism

class, and business press 68; and advertisers 69; effects of market-liberalism on 168; polarization 174-5, 176, 200

Clinton, Bill 176

Colonial Advocate 242n26

Columbia Journalism Review 216

columnists "invented" 42

commercial press, origins of 25-6; emergence of in U.S. and Canada 18, 27-8; early approaches to news stories 28-9; foreshadowing objectivity regime 29; political perspectives 31-2; as profit-driven 33, 65; and class issues 34; and labour movement 34; and media centralization 34-5. *See also* news media; penny papers

Committee for Justice and Liberty Foundation 100

Communications Security Establishment (CSE) 181

Communist Party of Canada 79

competitive elitism 170, 173-4, 184-5, 226

computer bulletin boards 195, 207

computer literacy 196

computer-mediated communication (CMC) technology 189-90, 198

computers, in precision journalism 51; effect on overconsumption 167; and decline of civic culture 169; eroding news media influence 175; converging with other systems 189, 194; and journalists 189-90, 198-9; in households 196; and labour 198

Comte, Auguste 109
concentration of media ownership. *See* media ownership
consensus, and public communication 2-3; and partisan press 20; in news stories 147-8, 149-50; right-wing challenge to 150; and market-liberalism 153; created on deficit/debt issue 154, 156-7; search for new 174; and public journalism 201-2, 203, 204, 205
Conservative Party 19-20, 146, 241n7
consumerism/consumers 5, 259n24; and transformation of news 35; and power 64; as a force in the commercial logic 65; as the flip side of depoliticization 68; as newspaper audience 69; as identity 144-5, 156, 184-5; eclipsing the citizen 167; political and economic consequences of 173, 225-6; as antipolitical 176; as passive 191; and alternative media 211; connection with social ills 216; and public communication 224; and significant choice 227-8. *See also* consumer journalism; consumer sovereignty; cyberconsumers
consumer journalism 60
consumer sovereignty 185-8
content regulation 88-95. *See also* Canadian Radio-television and Telecommunications Commission; state, regulation of media
conventionalism 108, 116-18, 128; compared with critical realism 129, 131. *See also* relativism
Cook, Peter 94-5, 97, 98
Cooper, Barry 103
Cooper, Kent 44
Co-op Radio. *See* Vancouver Co-op Radio
Copps, Sheila 120
corporate subsidies 182
Council of Canadians 171, 221
counterculture (1960s) 49, 52, 79, 137, 206
courts. *See* law and courts
Coyne, Andrew 103
credibility, and objectivity 1, 8; gap 47; and newscasters 51-2; as journalistic

concept 58-9; in television 73; CBC 76; challenge to 92; and press 141-2; and right-wing attack 161; haemorrhage 163; and politics 173, 226; and corporate influence 178; and public journalism 203-4; and alternative media 212
crime 142, 256n32
Crispo, John 105, 152
critical journalism 46-50, 139-41; right-wing 51; and shift away from uncritical journalism 59; as movement 51; as selective 140-1; restrained 141-2
critical realism 108, 128-34, 135, 232
Cronkite, Walter 38, 52, 173
CTV National News 52, 82
Cultural Environment Movement (CEM) 219-21
cultural indicators 222
culture jamming 213, 215-16
culture of defiance 171
Curran, James 26, 183-4
cyberconsumers 194
cyberspace 179, 189, 190-7, 200

Dahlgren, Peter 134-5, 225-6, 231
Dallas Met 207
Darwin, Charles 19
Davey, Keith 92
debt, government. *See* deficit/debt issue
deconstruction 122, 123
defence spending 182
deficit/debt issue 153-7, 158-9; reducing public expectations 169
democracy, as contested concept 2; and participation 2, 205, 226-7; declining participation 6, 180; as approached by 19th-century press 31-5; representative 170-1; direct 171, 174; and subjectivity 225-6; alternative models of 226-8; sustainable 224-5, 228, 234. *See also* liberal democracy; media democratization; liberal-democratic ideology
democratic liberalism. *See* democracy
democratization of the media. *See* media democratization
Department of External Affairs 181

depoliticization 65, 67-8, 76, 173
deregulation of media 176-7, 182
Derrida, Jacques 123
Desbarats, Peter 57-8, 92
Desmarais, Paul 62, 172
Deverell, Rita Shelton 185
deviance 147, 148
Devoir, Le 62
dialectical model of reporting 108
Dickens, Charles 36, 110
digital broadcasting 189
Disney Corporation (ABC). *See* Walt
   Disney Company
dissident media. *See* alternative media
distortion 44, 89, 112-3, 114, 222
diversity, controversies over 3, 5; in
   commercial press system 34; contribu-
   tion of chains to 66-7; in evaluation of
   media performance 83; in CRTC
   requirements 99-100; missing in recent
   systems 175; in public broadcasting
   176; further threats to 177; as criteria
   for media system 183; potential of
   Internet for 194; constrained in new
   media 195, 197; in alternative media
   207; in "Information Bill of Rights"
   219; in People's Charter 220; and
   Council of Canadians campaign 221; as
   a factor in political representation and
   choice 227; Soviet suppression of 229
"documentary reporting practices" 142-3
Donner Foundation 209
Duplessis, Maurice 79
Dyson, Rose 214

Eastern Asia 172
ecology. *See* environmentalism
editorial practices 85
efficacy value 226, 227, 228
Eisner, Michael 198
election campaigns 104, 114, 121; voter
   abstention 171; journalism sets agendas
   173; free trade 255n12
Elterman, Michael 253n45
e-mail 192
empiricism 108, 109-10, 231; naive, 30;
   belief in facts crumbling 37; emphasis

on facts 67; epistemological assumptions of 111; and critical realism 129
Enlightenment thinking, background 16-
   18; in labour press 23; as adopted by
   early commercial press 33; ideals
   revisited 229
enterprise journalism 51
entertainment values 13, 68, 71; as TV
   imperative 6, 136, 141; in TV news 73,
   119; CRTC *This Hour* decision 87; as a
   conservative force 144; political/
   cultural consequences of 173; and
   professionalism 179; as structural bias
   187; and alternative media 206-7, 208;
   and CEM 219; critiqued 221; as socially
   corrosive 224; and fundamental change
   236
environmentalism, and media licences
   100; and news labels 118; "direct-
   action" 149; and capitalist crisis 165;
   and market-liberal agenda 209; and
   Greenpeace 213; and sustainability 224;
   news coverage of 234
epistemology, as a dimension of objectivity regime 84; defined 107; in journalism 107-9, 110-13, 115-16, 121; as social
   construction 131-2; as empiricist 231;
   and proposed journalism stance 232
Epstein, Edward Jay 108
equality, as journalistic principle 83-4
equity, as ideal of public communication
   227
Ericson, Richard 45, 85, 91
ethics, code of 41, 54-5, 109, 233
ethnic nationalisms 164, 169, 225
European Union 169
events, as news 108, 109, 111; as framed
   119; and bureaucratic definitions of
   142-3; political 145; liberal-democratic
   framework of 146-7. *See also* pseudo-
   events
Extra! 217
Eyes on Alberta 202, 205
eyewitness, as press ideal 185

facticity, defined 36, 110; and journalists
   36-7; in newswriting 37-8; in public

broadcasting 39; as a business approach 67-8; as part of objectivity 83; and positivism 109, 110, 115; and separating facts/news from opinion/values 29, 32, 111, 117, 120, 143, 228; scepticism about 112-13, 129; as political weapon 113; and bias 114; and "straight facts" 114; postmodern critique of 124; "will to" 124; and objectivity regime 135, 142; and public journalism 203; and alternative journalism 211

facts, factuality. *See* facticity

fairness, journalists' stress on 8; as journalistic obligation 44, 55, 76; as shift in news practice 58-9; as fallback position 113; in Canadian policy 75; as element in objectivity 83-4; CBC position on 88; as vague concept 89; as part of market discourse 101; and Fraser Institute 102; as ethical obligation 111; in a more narrowly defined objectivity 113

Fairness and Accuracy in Reporting (FAIR) 215, 217, 222

Fairness Doctrine (U.S., 1949) 74, 75, 177

fascism 163, 164

Federal Communications Commission (FCC) 74

feminism, critique of objectivity 87-8, 232; and media licences 100; and epistemological theory, 112; critique of objectivity 135, 232; and MediaWatch 214; tendency towards relativism 222. *See also* gender bias; women

fibre optics 189

filters (in the news) 109, 116, 133-4, 197

Financial Post 152

Fisher, Doug 105

FLQ 79

Forbes, Steve 227

foreign correspondence 42-3, 148

Foucault, Michel 6, 7, 123

Fox, Terry 147

Fox TV network 188

frames (of reference) 118-20; liberal-democratic 145-8, 150, 161; right-wing 152-5; deficit/debt 155-6; and alternative messages 159-60

Fraser Institute 150, 214-15, 217; NMA research 101-5, 139; mainstreaming of image 157-60

freedom of the press/expression 2, 26, 180-1, 224; and Russia 9; and conglomerate ownership 61; and legislation 76-7; as defined by state 80; as one of society's core values 83-4; threatened by state 86; and groups seeking power 89; in classical liberalism 145; critiqued as a normative guideline 180-1; and role of advertising 186; in cyberspace 220

Freenets 194

free trade debate 82, 105

Friends of Canadian Broadcasting 217

Galbraith, J.K. 151

Galipeau, Céline 9

Gannett newspaper chain 205-6

gender bias 87-8, 91, 165, 167. *See also* feminism; women

genres (of news) 37, 42, 45, 85, 86-7

Georgetti, Ken 158

Georgia Straight 207

Gerbner, George 219, 222, 237

Gibson, William 189

Gingrich, Newt 151

Glasbeek, H.J. 80, 180-1

globalization 4, 166-7, 229, 234

Globe and Mail 63, 231; decline of investigative reporting 50; effect of Megarry's changes 56-7; and objectivity ethos 69; study of editing practices 91; and free trade issue 102; makeover under Thorsell 152; on deficit/debt issue 156, 159; and PointCast Network 194

Goldhawk, Dale 247n70

Graham, Hugh 26

Gramsci, Antonio 31

Grant, Bob 177

Great Britain 25, 26-7, 148, 175

Greene, Lorne 38

Greenpeace 213

Gulf War (1991) 89, 105, 118, 125-6, 185

Habermas, Jurgen 127
Hackett, Robert 11
Hall, Stuart 256n32
Hallin, Daniel 147, 230
Halton, David 39
Halton, Matthew 39
Hamilton Herald 26
Hansen, Rick 147-8
Hardin, Herschel 217
hard news 85, 86-7
Harris, Mike 151
Harvey, David 127
Hayes, David 50, 56-7
Herman, Edward S. 222
Hightower, Jim, 262n23, 263n33
Hill, Grant 154
Hirst, Paul 163
Hollinger Inc., Southam takeover 5, 221;
    1996 holdings 62; Saskatchewan firings
    66, 178. *See also* Black, Conrad
Holocaust, denial of 128
homelessness 143
homophobia 171
horizontal communication 193, 196-7,
    210, 226, 230
hospitals 182
Howe, C.D. 48
Howe, Joseph 15
human interest stories 67, 69
Hutchins Commission (U.S., 1947) 42

impartiality. *See* balance
independent dailies 60, 62, 66
independent journalism 5, 29, and
    corporate media/digitalization 197-8;
    under threat 214; and CEM 219; call to
    reinforce 222; and progressive politics
    229-30; history of 242n41
India 164
infoglut 197
Information Bill of Rights 219, 220
"information underclass" 168, 175
infotainment 13, 47, 175, 178. *See also*
    entertainment values
Institute for Alternative Journalism 199,
    218, 222
interest groups 88-90

international development 181
International Monetary Fund (IMF) 168,
    234
Internet 189, 190-7, 200, 207. *See also* new
    media technology
interpretive journalism 42-6, 51, 59, 82
inverted pyramid style. *See* pyramid style
investigative journalism, decline since late
    1970s 49-50; as movement 51; shift
    away from uncritical reporting 59;
    decline in CBC 152. *See also* critical
    journalism
irony, as media stance 8, 58, 82, 112
Irvine, Reed 139, 217
Irving family 62

Jefferson, Thomas 17
Jensen, Carl 217
journalism, as public knowledge 1; and
    democracy 1-2; link with power 7-8; as
    democratic public communication 11;
    in crisis 13-14, 162, 172-80; origins in
    Enlightenment thought 17-18;
    "people's" 26, 145; newswriting
    standards and conventions 38, 41, 84-5;
    culture of 39-40, 59, 175, 179, 229, 230;
    importance of professional standards
    52, 54-6, 111-12, 230-1; cost optimiza-
    tion 66; language 85; as providing
    acquaintance with 108, 231; right-wing
    attacks on 136-8; right-wing attack
    critiqued 138-41; influence of market
    forces on 144-5; and politics 136-81,
    172-3; 1990s challenge to 180; public
    philosophy of 223, 226; reform of 223,
    233-7; and democracy 223-4; progres-
    sive impulse in 229-30; facilitator role
    230, 233-4; self-reflexivity 233, 236. *See
    also* journalists; news; public commu-
    nication; truth (and truth-claims)
journalists, as truth-seeking 11, 56, 83,
    125, 162, 175, 180, 222; and objectivity
    ethos 53-6, 58-9; and detachment 83;
    importance of objectivity for 86; as
    philosophers 107; as "new class" 137;
    careers and attitudes 139; anglo-
    Canadian 145, 149; credibility in

decline 162-3; Hollywood portrayals of 162-3; and self-image 180; and broader democratic principles 214; common interests with other groups 236; and freedom of the press 224

Kagarlitsky, Boris 166
Kalb, Marvin 204
Keane, John 225
Kent, Tom 92. *See also* Kent Commission
Kent Commission (Royal Commission on Newspapers, 1981) 1, 70, 92, 181, 255n12; and interpretive newswriting 44; on fairness over objectivity 59; and commercialism 69; 236
King, Larry 176
King, Rodney 168, 193
Klein, Ralph 136, 151, 202
Knight-Ridder newspaper chain 204, 205-6
Knights of Labor 21, 23, 241n12
knowledge-production 45, 107-35; as social process 131-2, 134. *See also* conventionalism; critical realism; empiricism; epistemology; positivism; relativism
Kuhn, Thomas 116-17

labels. *See* language
labour issues 104
labour-management issues 68
labour movement, role in journalism 16; and democratic discourse 18; in 19th-century Canada 21; relations to commercial press 34; and socialism 34, 241n10; notions of natural rights 241n12
Labour Party (U.K.) 179
labour press 243n41; origins of 20-1; examples of 21-2; democratic perspective 22; and political issues 22-3; distinguishing from partisan press 23; and origins of objectivity 23-4; legacy for commercial press 24; limitations of 24-5; lack of class analysis 24; decline of 26-8; and public discourse 31; effect of commercial press on 33-4; marginalization of 34; coverage of labour-management issues 68;

precursor of alternative media 206; original version of objectivity 228, 229
language, in news 111, 114, 118-19, 120; in conventionalist theories 117-18; power of 117, 118, 122; in postmodernist theory 124; meaning confused with referent 127; constructivist view of 127. *See also* semiotics
Lasch, Christopher 164-5
Lash, Scott 6
law and courts 80-1, 181. *See also* public policy; state, regulation of media by
L.A. Weekly 207
left-wing politics, views underrepresented in media 69; and state repression 79; vanguard groups reject objectivity 89; and postmodernism 127; and deficit/debt issue 159-61; and popular movements 171, 171; and Media & Democracy Congress 219
left-liberal bias accusations 3, 90, 100, 103, 104-5, 136-9, 152
Legacy (BBC) 165
Leninism 10
Leno, Jay 176
Letterman, David 73, 176
"letters to the editor" 91
Levy, David 42-3
liberal-democratic governance 1-2
liberal-democratic ideology, as frame for news writing 31, 150-61; as frame for journalism 145-50
liberal democracy 163-72. *See also* competitive elitism; democracy; liberalism; market-liberalism
liberalism, basic tenets, 145-8, 151, 165; media conceptions 180-5. *See also* liberal-democratic governance; liberal-democratic ideology
Liberal Party (B.C.) 104
Lies of Our Times 216
Limbaugh, Rush 171, 263n23
Lippmann, Walter 40, 55, 174, 184
Los Angeles riot 168. *See also* King, Rodney
Lovell, Terry 116, 128, 129, 130

Mackenzie, William Lyon 242n26
Maclean, Eleanor 114
Macpherson, C.B. 2
magazines, as alternative media 211
Major, John 179
Malling, Eric 152
Malthus, Thomas 19
Mannheim, Karl 115
Manning, Preston 140, 151, 240n4
market-liberalism 12, 262n12; ascendence and effects of 150-1, 153, 166-7; and women's inequality 167; effects on objectivity regime 174-5; view of Internet 195; complacency regarding media structures 224; at odds with democratic values 228; challenging the hegemony of 229-30
Martin, Paul Jr. 172
Maynard, Nancy Hicks 199
McArthur, Dan 38-9, 43
McCarthy, Joseph 45, 53
McChesney, Robert 193, 196-7
McCoy, Thomas 110, 111, 113
McLaughlin, Audrey 120
McLuhan, Marshall 191
McQuaig, Linda 50, 152, 154, 155, 156
McQuail, Denis 2, 114
Media (Canadian Association of Journalists) 216
media activism. *See* media democratization
media corporations. *See* broadcasting industry; media ownership; news media
Media & Democracy Congress (1996) 199, 218-19, 220, 221
media democratization 213-22, 225, 232-7; movements in U.S. 12
media education movement. *See* media literacy movement
media frames. *See* frames (of reference)
media hoaxing 216
media industries, impact of specialization in 86-7; political interests 187-8; expanded commercialization 179-80
media literacy movement 217
"media logic" 120

media monitoring 213, 216-17
media ownership, concentration of 3-4, 62-4, 214; effects of 56; effects of chains 65-6; changes in 1980s 152; serving political interests 172-3; and editorial/ marketing 230, global and national concentration 248n3. *See also* broadcasting industry; newspaper industry
media performance evaluation 83-4
media policy advocacy 213
media reform. *See* media democratization
media unions 205-6, 214, 221
MediaWatch 214
medical fraud 182
Medina, Ann 185
Meech Lake accord 89, 254n10
Megarry, Roy 56-7
Merritt, Davis "Buzz" Jr. 200-1, 204
Merz, Charles 40
Mexico 191
Microsoft 179, 195, 196
Microsoft Network (MSN) 195
Middle East conflict 96, 97
Monday Magazine (Victoria) 207
Montreal Daily Advertiser 69
Montreal Gazette 58
Montreal Mirror 207
Montreal Star 29, 30
Moore, Michael 188
Mosco, Vincent 129-30
Mother Jones 206, 211
MSNBC 179, 196
muckraking journalism 50, 206, 229
Mullin, Barry 93
Mulroney, Brian 150, 152, 172
Murdoch, Rupert 56, 64, 179, 188

Nader, Ralph 227
naive realism. *See* empiricism
Nash, Knowlton 59, 173
Nation, 211
National Film Board (NFB) 208
nationalism. *See* ethnic nationalisms; regional nationalisms
National Media Archive (NMA). *See* Fraser Institute
National Public Radio 75-6

nature, as Enlightenment concept 19
NBC 179, 196
neo-fascism 128, 163
neoliberalism. *See* market-liberalism
network model 190
neutrality 44; as journalistic standard 45,
    55, 83; sense of, bolstered by TV news
    47; in investigative reporting 50;
    compared to a "camera" 57; mainte-
    nance of, in public 58; "hypocritical"
    59; political 68; in broadcasting 76,
    100; as self- and public image 77; as
    epistemological position 84, 111;
    signalled in passive voice 85; possibility
    of, denied by journalists 113; claim of,
    no longer tenable 135, 232; and sphere
    of deviance 148; in public journalism
    203, 206; in democratic public sphere
    223-4
New Democratic Party (NDP), B.C.
    budget issue 49; in British Columbia
    95; and Fraser Institute founding 101;
    in 1996 B.C. election 104; and
    McLaughlin's leadership 120; de-
    nounced and cheered as B.C. govern-
    ment 141; caucus on culture and
    communication 217
Newfield, Jack 52
New Journalism 49, 52, 124
Newman, Peter C. 171
new media technology, and journalism
    191-4, 197-200; effects of 195-7, 230
new right 128, 151, 153-4
news, as information 71, 73, 78; and
    reality judgement 119, 120; as narrative
    119-20, 124; underreported stories
    182-3. *See also* entertainment values;
    facticity; frames (of reference); news
    media
news agencies 37, 72, 249n18
News Corporation 179
news hole 65
news media, public attitudes towards 1, 6;
    institutional criteria 2-3; controversies
    over independence 3; marginalization
    of alternatives 65, 68-9; commercial
    imperatives 65-70; relation to state/

politicians 77-81; institutional
    constraints 134; event orientation 142-
    3; dominant values 143; economic
    pressures 177-8; and politics 178-9; as
    information smorgasbord 183-5; as
    eyewitness 185; network and broadcast
    models 190; compared to alternative
    208; conflicting interests 233. *See also*
    commercial press; media ownership;
    journalism
news monitoring. *See* media monitoring
newspaper industry, history of 60;
    ownership of 61-3; specialized
    audiences 67; division of labour 69-70;
    objectivity as political legitimation 70-
    1; and state regulation 76-7; as a system
    converging 189. *See also* media
    ownership
news values 144, 149-50
Newsweek 192
New World Information Order 221
New York Herald 36
New York Mechanic 24
New York Times 40, 67, 69
Next City 209
Nieman Reports 43
Nixon, Richard 46, 49
Norris, Christopher 125-6, 128, 131
North American Free Trade Agreement
    (NAFTA) 4, 169, 172, 234
NOW (Toronto) 79, 207
nuclear disarmament 234
nuclear industry 181

objectivism, as epistemology 70. *See also*
    critical realism; empiricism; positivism
objectivity, ideal in early commercial
    dailies 18; 19th-century version 29-31;
    as developed in CBC news 38-9;
    becomes entrenched 39-40; ethos
    encouraged 40; transformed after WWI
    41-2; includes interpretation 43;
    manipulated by powerful 45-6, 53; and
    occupational psychology 56; as
    legitimation 65, 70-1; North American
    compared to European 71; and role of
    technology 71-3; and relations with

politicians 78; dimensions of 82-7; and Western society's core values 83-4; as ideology 87; as a form of empiricism 111; "bad" 112, 116, 255n12; critiques of 112, 116-27, 223, 231-2; -as-such 112, 113; in critical realist perspective 133-4; conventions of 147-50; eroding conditions of 174-80; and crisis of public communication 200-2; positive democratic functions 230-1; rejection of 268n89. See also balance; facticity; fairness; journalists; objectivity regime

objectivity regime, usage of term 6-9; as model for democratic journalism 13; in crisis, 13, 162-3; foreshadowed in 19th century 29; interacting forces 65; institutionalization of 85-6; conservatizing tendencies 141-5; and liberal-democratic political ideology 147; and shift towards market liberalism 152-3, 161; and market logic 180; challenged by public journalism 202-3. See especially chapter 4; objectivity

October Crisis (1970) 48, 79

Oka confrontation (1990) 254n10

ombudsman 92-3

On Balance (Fraser Institute) 102-4

Ontario Press Council 91, 94

Ontario Workman 21, 22, 23

Ottawa Citizen 63

Ottawa Journal 26

Ottawa Press Gallery 47-8

Outhwaite, William 128, 130

ownership of media. See media ownership

Padlock Act (Quebec, 1937) 79

Paine, Tom 16, 22, 33

Palladium of Labor 21, 23

Paper Tiger Television 217

paradigm 117

parliamentary politics 149

partisan press 242n41; history of 15; origins and practice 20; replaced by commercial press 30; superseded by objectivity 39-40; recent partial comeback 176; regional variations 241n8

partisanship 30

patriarchal categories (in news coverage) 87. See also gender bias; feminism; women

pay-TV 64

Pedelty, Mark 240n14

Peladeau, Pierre 62

penny papers 242n26, 242n41; development of 15-16; emergence (1830s) 25-6; as business enterprises 28-9; exploit telegraph 72;

People's Communication Charter 220-21

Perot, Ross 171, 176, 227

photo-engraving 37

photography 37

pipeline debate (1956) 48

Pocklington, Peter 101

PointCast Network 194

populism 171

pornography 3

portable newsroom 192-3

positivism 40, 108-16, 129, 131

postmodernism 6, 13, 108, 121-8, 228-9, 232

poststructuralism 122-3, 127

"post-truth society" 124, 133

poverty 143

precision journalism 51

press councils 91-2

press gallery. See Ottawa Press Gallery

press history, conventional 15-16, 26. See also commercial press; labour press; partisan press

private broadcasting, favoured treatment of 3; and radio news 61; as special interest group, 98, 100

private/public distinction 227-8, 232

Prodigy 192, 195

Progressive 211

Project Censored (U.S.) 182, 217

Project Censored Canada 182-3, 187, 217

propaganda, and new media 40-1; and "honest bias" 43; stations 74; and alternative media 99, 212; and CBC 105; wartime 113; mystifying reality 123; in Gulf War 125-6; as news 178

protest movements. See social movements

pseudo-events 120, 143

public affairs journalism 13, 199-200, 206, 230

public broadcasting, role of 3; standard for reporting 38; and factuality 39; as tradition in Canada 75-6; under attack 176; as counterbalance 235. *See also* Canadian Broadcasting Corporation; Public Broadcasting Service

Public Broadcasting Service (PBS) 61, 75, 176, 198

public communication 2, 11, 223; ideals of 224-8. *See also* efficacy; diversity; journalism

public journalism 9, 200-6, 223, 225; in 19th century 24; renewing practices 233; and civic media 269n12

public judgement 201

public policy 5, 61, 73-8, 81, 226, 235-6, 237. *See also* state, regulation of media by

public relations industry 41, 113, 178

pyramid style 37, 72

"quality" press 69, 71, 175

Quebec, and journalism in 12, 48; October crisis 79; movement for independence 164, 169; media unions 214; and idea of objectivity 250n49

Québec Press Council 94

racism 24, 163, 171, 209

radicalism, as commodity in early press 33

radical press. *See* labour press

radio 60-1, 72, 194. *See also* broadcasting industry; Vancouver Co-op Radio

Radler, David 66, 178

Reagan, Ronald 46, 74, 166

realism 36, 40, 72, 142, 198. *See also* critical realism; empiricism; positivism

REAL Women 150

Reform movement (pre-Confederation Canada) 19, 240n4

Reform Party 140, 150-1, 161, 171, 240n4

regime of objectivity. *See* objectivity regime

regional nationalisms 169

relativism 115, 117, 124, 126, 127, 128, 134

religious broadcasting 75, 99-101

religious fundamentalism 89, 164, 209

repetitive stress syndrome 199

Report on Business (*Globe and Mail*) 56

representative democracy. *See* democracy

Rheingold, Howard 195

Richardson, Robin 159

Ride, The (PBS) 198

Riefenstahl, Leni 40

right-wing ideology, rise of 150-1; and populism 171

Robertson, Lloyd 38, 52

rock videos 175

Rogers Cable 4

Rosen, Jay 200-1, 204, 205

Roshco, Bernard 44

Rousseau, Jean-Jacques 16, 19, 33

Royal Canadian Air Farce 87

Royal Canadian Mounted Police (RCMP) 50, 79

Royal Commission on Newspapers. *See* Kent Commission

Royce, Peter 97

Ruggles, Myles 94-5, 97, 98

Russia 9, 172. *See also* Soviet Union

Ryerson Review of Journalism 216

Saint-Jean, Armande 12

Salutin, Rick 159

San Francisco Bay Guardian 207

Sapir, Edward 117-18, 122

satellite communication 179, 189, 193

Saturday Night 152

Saussure, Ferdinand de 122

scepticism, epistemological 128

Schiller, Dan 22, 27, 29, 35

Schiller, Herbert 5

Schudson, Michael 40, 41, 52, 113

Scottish nationalism 169

Seattle Stranger 207

Seattle Weekly 207

seditious libel 15, 26

semiotics 122-3

Senate Committee report on the mass media (1970) 92

Simpson, Jeffrey 152
Simpson (O.J.) trial 142, 192
Skaggs, Joey 216
Smythe, Dallas 68
social constructionism, 117-18, 120-1. *See also* epistemology, as social construction
Social Credit Party (B.C.) 104
social Darwinism 19
social movements, and critical realism 128, 132; outside sphere of legitimate controversy 149-50; and democratization of the media 212; and mass media 212-13
social order 84
Sony Corporation 194
Soros, George 172
Southam Inc. 61-2, 63, 65-6, 221
Southam News Service 66
Soviet Union 9, 10, 43, 163, 164, 166, 225, 229. *See also* Russia
Spencer, Herbert 19
Stamp Duty (U.K.) 25, 26-7
Stanfield, Robert 114
state, repression of press 15, 16, 79-80; regulation of media 76-7; erosion of authority 168-70. *See also* Canadian Radio-television and Telecommunications Commission
Stewart, Walter 59
straight news. *See* hard news
structuralism 122, 124
Stursberg, Peter 76
subjectivity, in early journalism 40; recognized in journalism 42, 115; fallible 113; need to celebrate 124; intrusion of individual, 131-2; need to reveal and assess 185; democratic 225-6
Sun (U.K.) 179

tabloid journalism 13, 71, 137, 175, 232
talk radio 175
talk shows 13, 87, 186
Taras, David 39-40, 48
taxation issues 157-8, 169
technology 189; and newspaper industry 37, 60; and media biases 47; and objectivity 71-3; and global electronic

public sphere 190-1. *See also* computer-mediated technology; computers; Internet; new media technology; telecommunications; telegraph; telephone
telecommunications 189
Telecommunications Act (U.S., 1996) 4, 177, 193
telecommunications legislation 4-5
telegraph 32, 37, 71-2, 249n18
telephone industry 189, 195
television, logic of "flow" 47; programming 186
television news, empires 4; reinforces objectivity 47; and objectivity conventions 72-3; as constructed 134-5; as politically destructive 136-7
Terminal City (Vancouver) 207
terrorism 149, 251n8
Thatcher, Margaret 166, 179
Thiessen, Gordon 160
Third World 170
Third World Network (Malaysia) 220
This Hour Has Seven Days 48
This Hour Has Twenty-two Minutes 87
This Magazine 49, 211
Thompson, T.P. 28
Thomson newspaper chain 62, 63
Thorsell, William 152
Time magazine 192
Times (London) 179
Time Warner 4, 196
tobacco industry 181, 182
Toronto News 26, 29
Toronto Star 30, 62, 192, 208, 246n69, 255n12
Toronto Sun 63, 71, 152
Toronto Telegram 26, 30, 34
Toronto World 26
Torstar Corporation 62
"total newspapering" 178, 214
trade unions. *See* labour movement; media unions
Triumph of the Will (1935) 40
Trudeau, Pierre 48, 79, 114
truth (and truth-claims) 107-9, 111-17; evaluation of 123-4; Baudrillard

argument 125-6; critique of post-modern approach to 127; in critical realist perspective 130, 133; related to "marketplace of ideas" 146; in "quality" journalism 175; concept problematized beyond repair 185; relativist position on 222; as ethic 228, 230
Turner, Ted 4
TV Nation 188

"underground" journalism 49, 52, 79
unions. *See* labour movement
United Kingdom. *See* Great Britain
United States, journalism 12; emergence of commercial press 25, 27; media legislation (1995-96) 177
utilitarianism 19

Vancouver Co-op Radio (CFRO) 100, 215; style of operation 95-6; CRTC/balance debate 96-9, 174; represented marginalized 101; budget compared to NMA's 105; embodies democratic principles 210; and horizontal communication 226
Vancouver Sun, and NDP budget (1995) 49; on deficit/debt issue 156; and Fraser Institute stories 157-60; and 1996 B.C. election 205; and culture jamming 215-16
Venture (CBC) 152
Vietnam War 47, 115
Viewer's Declaration of Independence (CEM) 219
Village Voice (New York) 207
Vision TV 75, 100
Voice of Palestine. See Vancouver Co-op Radio

Wage-Worker 23
Wainwright, Hilary 128, 130, 131, 132
Walker, Michael 158
Walljasper, Jay 208, 209, 211
Walt Disney Company 4, 177, 198
War Measures Act (1970) 48, 79
war and peace 143
War of the Worlds (1938) 72

watchdog role 140-1, 181-3; critique of public journalism 204; and alternative media 212; could be extended 234
Watergate scandal 47, 49, 137
Waters, David 94
Watson, Paul 149
Web TV 194
Welles, Orson 72
Western European press 71
Westinghouse 4
W5 (CTV) 152
Whorf, Benjamin Lee 117-18, 122
Whyte, Kenneth 152
Williams, Raymond 186
Winnipeg Free Press 63, 93
Winnipeg Tribune 63
Winter, James 158
wire services. *See* news agencies
women, excluded in Enlightenment thought 17; treatment in labour press 24; equal rights in Broadcasting Act 75; and news 87-8; politicians in the news 120; as "objects of display" 130; violence against, as issue 142; right-wing hostility towards equality 151; and ownership influence 152; effects of market-liberalism on 167; and the recent mainstream press 208; and media images/representation 214, 217, 220; and public/private issues 227-8
Women's Institute for Freedom of the Press 217
women's movement 132, 150, 217
Women's Wire 194
World Association of Community Radio Broadcasters 220
World Bank 234
World Trade Organization 234
World Wide Web 189, 191, 194, 195, 212, 219

Yeltsin, Boris 9
Yugoslavia 225

Zapatistas, and Internet 191
Zhao, Yuezhi 11-12
Zundel, Ernest 79

If you have enjoyed reading this book, you will be interested in the following recently published Garamond Press titles:

Pat and Hugh Armstrong et al
MEDICAL ALERT: New Work Organizations in Health Care

Alison Beale and Annette Van den Bosch eds.
GHOSTS IN THE MACHINE: Women and Cultural Policy in Canada and Australia

William K. Carroll ed.
ORGANIZING DISSENT: Contemporary Social Movements in Theory and Practise, (second, revised edt.)

Catherine Cavanaugh and Jeremy Mouat, eds.
MAKING WESTERN CANADA: Historical Essays

Tania Das Gupta
RACISM AND PAID WORK

David Livingstone and J. Marshall Mangan
RECAST DREAMS: Class and Gender Consciousness in Steeltown

John McMurty
UNEQUAL FREEDOMS
The Global Market as an Ethical System

Sylvia O'Meara and Doug West, eds.
FROM OUR EYES: Learning from Indigenous Peoples

Chris Schenk and John Anderson, eds.
RE-SHAPING WORK: Union Responses to Technological Change

Dennis Thiessen, Nina Bascia and Ivor Goodson
MAKING A DIFFERENCE ABOUT DIFFERENCE:
The Lives and Careers of Racial Minority Immigrant Teachers

Garamond Press, 67 Mowat Ave., Suite 144, Toronto, On. M6K 3E3, Phone 416-516-2709, fax 416-516-0571, e-mail Garamond@web.net

Write, phone, fax or e-mail us at the following address for more information or if you would like to receive a catalogue. Check out our Home Page at http//www.garamond.ca/garamond